"We can change our lives. We can do, have, and be exactly what we wish."

ANTHONY ROBBINS

knows what he's talking about. Three years ago, this six foot seven inch, clean-cut twenty-six-year-old was living in a 400-square-foot bachelor apartment, where he had to wash his dishes in the bathtub. He was thirty pounds overweight and extremely unhappy, with floundering relationships and limited prospects. But by discovering the hidden powers of his mind, transforming his inhibitions into strengths, and developing strategies for excellence, Robbins has become a super success, a self-made millionaire who lives with his family in a castle by the sea and reaches tens of thousands of people each year with his *proven* programs for personal achievement. Mr. Robbins conducts his internationally recognized seminars for professional athletes, politicians, Fortune 500 executives, housewives, and even children.

UNLIMITED POWER
The national bestseller that has transformed lives.
Please turn the page to see what they're
saying about

UNLIMITED POWER

UNLIMITED POWER

Anthony Robbins

FAWCETT COLUMBINE · NEW YORK

A Fawcett Columbine Book
Published by Ballantine Books
Copyright © 1986 by Robbins Research Institute

Library of Congress Catalog Card Number: 87-91177

ISBN: 0-449-90280-3

Cover design by Barry Littmann
Text design by Holly Johnson
Manufactured in the United States of America

First Ballantine Books Edition: September 1987
10

The author wishes to express his thanks and appreciation to the following who granted permission to use the following material:

AP/Wide World Photos for permission to use photographs of Martin Luther King, Jr., Ronald Reagan, and Bruce Springsteen.

"A Boy of Unusual Vision," © 1985, the Baltimore *Sun*, printed with permission of the Baltimore *Sun*. The story was written by Alice Steinbach, Pulitzer-Prize winner for feature writing in 1985.

Artemas Cole for "Ten Salads" cartoon © 1985. Reprinted with permission of Artemas Cole. Originally appeared in *New Woman*.

Harper & Row for permission to quote from *In Search of Excellence* by Thomas J. Peters and Robert H. Waterman, Jr.

Bill Hoest for "Call the Cat, Harry" cartoon © 1981. Reprinted courtesy of Bill Hoest.

Jay Milton Hoffman, N.D., Ph.D., for permission to quote from *The Missing Link in the Medical Curriculum Which Is Food Chemistry in Its Relationship to Body Chemistry*, printed by Professional Press Publishing Company, 13115 Hunza Hill Terrace, Valley Center, CA 92082.

Hank Ketcham for DENNIS THE MENACE® used by permission of Hank Ketcham and © by News America Syndicate.

The Federal Express story, as related by William Lackey, was used with permission from Skip Lackey.

Los Angeles Times for photograph of John F. Kennedy, taken by John Malmin, published November 2, 1960. © 1960 Los Angeles Times. Photograph of Jane Fonda with Academy Award, taken by Gary Friedman, published April 9, 1982. © 1982 Los Angeles Times.

W. W. Norton for permission to quote from *Anatomy of an Illness* by Norman Cousins © 1979 by W. W. Norton & Company, Inc. Material used by permission of W. W. Norton & Company, Inc.

Playboy for photograph of Jesse Jackson © 1984 by Playboy. Photo by Ron Seymour, courtesy of *Playboy* magazine.

Simon & Schuster for permission to quote from *The Mind/Body Effect* by Herbert Benson © 1979 by Simon & Schuster.

Simon & Schuster for permission to quote from *Life-Tide* by Lyall Watson © 1979 by Lyall Watson.

United Feature Syndicate, Inc., for permission to use PEANUTS cartoon © 1960 United Feature Syndicate, Inc.

Universal Press Syndicate for permission to use ZIGGY cartoon. Copyright, 1985, Universal Press Syndicate. Reprinted with permission. All rights reserved.

Warner Bros., Inc., for permission to reprint portions of the lyric "It's Alright Ma (I'm Only Bleeding)" by Bob Dylan © 1965 Warner Bros., Inc. All rights reserved. Used by permission.

Dedicated to the greatest power within you, your power to love, and to all those who help you share its magic

Most of all for me, to Jairek, Joshua, Jolie, Tyler, Becky, and my Mom

ACKNOWLEDGMENTS

As I began to think of all the people to whom I would like to express my appreciation for their support, suggestions, and hard work in making this book possible, the list continued to grow. First, I would like to thank my wife and family for creating an environment where I could let the creative juices flow at any hour of the day or night and have my ideas received by sympathetic ears.

Then, of course, there were the combined efforts of the outstanding editing on my brainstorms by Peter Applebome and Henry Golden. At various stages of development, the suggestions of Wyatt Woodsmall and Ken Blanchard were extremely valuable. The book could never have come into being without the efforts of Jan Miller and Bob Asahina, who, along with the staff at Simon & Schuster, hung in there with me in those final hours of last-minute changes.

The teachers whose personalities, methods, and friendships have affected me most—from my early communications development with Mrs. Jane Morrison and Richard Cobb to Jim Rohn, John Grinder, and Richard Bandler—can never be forgotten.

Thanks also to the art, secretarial, and research staff who worked hard under deadline pressures: Rob Evans, Dawn Aaris, Donald Bodenbach, Kathy Woody, and, of course, Patricia Valiton.

And last but not least, special thanks to the Robbins Research corporate staff, center managers, and the hundreds of promotional staff members around the country who daily support me in getting our message out to the world.

CONTENTS

Foreword by Kenneth Blanchard, Ph.D.   xv
Introduction by Sir Jason Winters   xvii

SECTION I: The Modeling of Human Excellence
    I. The Commodity of Kings   3
    II. The Difference that Makes the Difference   22
    III. The Power of State   35
    IV. The Birth of Excellence: Belief   53
    V. The Seven Lies of Success   69
    VI. Mastering Your Mind: How to Run Your Brain   83
    VII. The Syntax of Success   112
    VIII. How to Elicit Someone's Strategy   125
    IX. Physiology: The Avenue of Excellence   149
    X. Energy: The Fuel of Excellence   166

SECTION II: The Ultimate Success Formula
XI. Limitation Disengage: What Do You Want? 197
XII. The Power of Precision 216
XIII. The Magic of Rapport 230
XIV. Distinctions of Excellence: Metaprograms 253
XV. How to Handle Resistance and Solve Problems 276
XVI. Reframing: The Power of Perspective 289
XVII. Anchoring Yourself to Success 314

SECTION III: Leadership: The Challenge of
Excellence
XVIII. Value Hierarchies: The Ultimate Judgment of
Success 343
XIX. The Five Keys to Wealth and Happiness 371
XX. Trend Creation: The Power of Persuasion 385
XXI. Living Excellence: The Human Challenge 404

Glossary 415
Robbins Research Institute 420

FOREWORD

When Tony Robbins asked me to write the foreword for *Unlimited Power*, I was very pleased for several reasons. First of all, I think Tony is an unbelievable young man. Our first meeting came in January 1985, when I was in Palm Springs to play golf in the Bob Hope Desert Classic Pro-Am Tournament. I had just left a typical golfer's happy hour at the Rancho Las Palmas Marriott, where everyone was competing for the days bragging rights. On our way to dinner, a friend of mine from Australia, Keith Punch, and I passed a sign announcing Tony Robbin's Firewalk Seminar. "Unleash the power within you," read the sign. I had heard of Tony, and my curiosity was piqued. Since Keith and I had already had a drink, and we did not want to take any chances, we decided we could not walk across the coals, but we did decide to attend the seminar.

For the next four and a half hours, I watched Tony mesmerize a large crowd made up of business executives, housewives, doctors, lawyers, and the like. When I say mesmerize, I'm not referring to any black magic. Tony had everyone on the edge of their seats with his charisma, charm, and the depth of his knowledge of human behavior. It was the most exhilarating and uplifting seminar I have ever attended in twenty years of involvement in management training. At the end, everyone but Keith and me walked across a fifteen-foot bed of hot coals that had been burning throughout the evening. And all without injury. It was a sight to see and an uplifting experience for everyone.

Tony uses the firewalk as a metaphor. He is not teaching a mystical skill, but rather a practical set of tools on how to be able to get yourself to take effective action in spite of any fear you might have, and the ability to get yourself to do whatever it takes to succeed is a very real power. So the first reason I am delighted to write this foreword is that I have tremendous respect and admiration for Tony Robbins.

The second reason I am excited about writing this foreword is that Tony's book, *Unlimited Power*, will show everyone the depth and breadth of his thinking. He is more than a motivational speaker. At age twenty-five, he is already one of the leading thinkers in the psychology of motivation and achievement. I think this book has the capacity to be the definitive text in the human potential movement. Tony's thoughts on health, stress, goal setting, visualization, and the like are the cutting edge and a must for anyone committed to personal excellence.

My hope is that you will get as much out of this book as I have. While it is longer than *The One Minute Manager*, I hope you are willing to hang in and finish the entire book so you can use Tony's thinking to unleash the magic within you.

Kenneth Blanchard, Ph.D.
Coauthor, *The One Minute Manager*

INTRODUCTION

All of my life I've had difficulty with public speaking, even while acting in movies. Just before my scenes, I would get physically ill. So with my relentless fear of public speaking one can imagine the excitement I felt when I heard that Anthony Robbins, the man who puts fear into power, could cure me.

Even though I was excited when I accepted the invitation to meet with Tony Robbins, I couldn't help feeling doubtful. I had heard of NLP and the other methods at which Tony is an acclaimed expert, but still, in all, I had spent countless hours, and thousands of dollars, seeking professional help.

The early professionals had told me that because my fear had developed over the years, I could hardly expect to gain a rapid cure. They scheduled me for weekly return visits to work on my problem endlessly.

When I met Tony I was surprised that he was so big. It's

very seldom that I meet anyone taller than me. He must have been six feet six inches tall and 238 pounds. So young, so pleasant. We sat down and I found myself extremely nervous when he started asking me about my problem.

Then he asked what I wanted and how I wanted to change. It seemed that my phobia rose up to defend itself, to prevent what was happening from happening. But with Tony's soothing voice, I started listening to what he was saying.

I began to relive my panicky feelings about public speaking. Suddenly I replaced them with the new feelings made up of strength and confidence. Tony had me go back in my mind to a time I was on stage giving a successful speech. While I mentally spoke, Tony gave me anchors. Anchors are things I can call on to reinforce my nerve and confidence while speaking. You'll read all about them in this book.

I had my eyes closed during the interview, for about forty-five minutes, while listening to Tony. Periodically he would touch my knees and hands, providing me with physical anchors. When it was over, I stood up. I had never felt so relaxed, calm, and peaceful. I had no feelings of weakness. Now I felt quite confident to do the Luxembourg television show with a potential audience of 450 million people.

If Tony's methods work as well on others as they have on me, then people all over the world will benefit. We have people lying in bed with their minds dwelling on death. Their doctors have told them that they have cancer, and they are so upset that their bodies are full of stress. Now, if my lifetime phobia can be eliminated in one hour, Tony's methods should also be made available to all of those who are suffering any kind of illness—emotional, mental, or physical. They, too, can be released from their fears, stress, and anxieties. I think it is most important that we do not delay any longer. Why should you be afraid of water, heights, public speaking, snakes, bosses, failure, or death?

I'm free now, and this book offers you the same choices. I'm sure that *Unlimited Power* will be a bestseller because it goes far beyond eliminating fears to teaching you what triggers any form of human behavior. By mastering the information in this book, you will be in complete control of your mind and body; thus, your life.

Sir Jason Winters
Author of *Killing Cancer*

SUCCESS

To laugh often and much; to win the respect of intelligent people and the affection of children; to earn the appreciation of honest critics and endure the betrayal of false friends; to appreciate beauty, to find the best in others; to leave the world a bit better, whether by a healthy child, a garden patch or a redeemed social condition; to know even one life has breathed easier because you have lived. This is to have succeeded.

—Ralph Waldo Emerson

The Modeling
of Human
Excellence

CHAPTER I

The Commodity
of Kings

"The great end of life is not knowledge but action."

—*Thomas Henry Huxley*

I had heard about him for many months. They said he was young, wealthy, healthy, happy, and successful. I had to see for myself. I watched him closely as he left the television studio, and I followed him over the next few weeks, observing as he counseled everyone from the president of a country to a phobic. I saw him debate dieticians, train executives, and work with athletes and learning-disabled kids. He seemed incredibly happy and deeply in love with his wife as they traveled together across the country and around the world. And when they were through, it was time to jet back to San Diego to spend a few days at home with their family in their castle overlooking the Pacific Ocean.

How was it that this twenty-five-year-old-kid, with only a high school education, could have accomplished so much in such a short period of time? After all, this was a guy who only three years ago had been living in a 400-square-foot bachelor apartment and washing his dishes in his bathtub. How did he go from an extremely unhappy person, thirty pounds overweight, with floundering relationships and limited prospects, to a centered, healthy, respected individual with great relationships and the opportunity for unlimited success?

It all seemed so incredible, and yet the thing that amazed me most was that I realized that he is me! "His" story is my own.

I'm certainly not saying that my life is what success is all about. Obviously, we all have different dreams and ideas of what we want to create for our lives. In addition, I'm very clear that who you know, where you go and what you own are not the true measure of personal success. To me, success is the ongoing process of striving to become more. It is the opportunity to continually grow emotionally, socially, spiritually, physiologically, intellectually, and financially while contributing in some positive way to others. The road to success is always under construction. It is a progressive course, not an end to be reached.

The point of my story is simple. By applying the principles you will learn in this book, I was able to change not only the way I felt about myself, but also the results I was producing in my life, and I was able to do so in a major and measurable way. The purpose of this book is to share with you what made the difference in changing my life for the better. It is my sincere hope that you will find the technologies, strategies, skills, and philosophies taught within these pages to be as empowering for you as they have been for me. The power to magically transform our lives into our greatest dreams lies waiting within us all. It's time to unleash it!

When I look at the pace at which I was able to turn my dreams into my present-day life, I can't help feeling an almost unbelievable sense of gratitude and awe. And yet I'm certainly far from unique. The fact is we live in an age where many people are able to achieve wondrous things almost overnight, to achieve successes that would have been unimaginable in earlier times. Look at Steve Jobs. He was a kid in blue jeans with no money who took an idea for a home computer and built a Fortune 500 company faster than anyone in history. Look at Ted Turner. He took a medium that barely existed—cable television—and created an empire. Look at people in the entertainment industry like Steven Spielberg or Bruce Springsteen, or businessmen like Lee Iacocca or Ross Perot. What do they have in common other than astounding, prodigious success? The answer, of course, is . . . power.

Power is a very emotional word. People's responses to it are varied. For some people, power has a negative connotation. Some people lust after power. Others feel tainted by it, as if it were something venal or suspect. How much power do you want? How much power do you think is right for you to obtain or develop? What does power really mean to you?

I don't think of power in terms of conquering people. I don't think of it as something to be imposed. I'm not advocating that you should, either. That kind of power seldom lasts. But you should realize that power is a constant in the world. You shape your perceptions, or someone shapes them for you. You do what you want to do, or you respond to someone else's plan for you. To me, ultimate power is the ability to produce the results you desire most and create value for others in the process. Power is the ability to change your life, to shape your perceptions, to make things work for you and not against you. Real power is shared, not imposed. It's the ability to define human needs and to fulfill them—both your needs and the needs of the people you care about. It's the ability to direct your own personal kingdom—your own thought processes, your own behavior—so you produce the precise results you desire.

Throughout history, the power to control our lives has taken many different and contradictory forms. In the earliest times, power was simply the result of physiology. He who was the strongest and the fastest had power to direct his own life as well as the lives of those around him. As civilization developed, power resulted from heritage. The king, surrounding himself with the symbols of his realm, ruled with unmistakable authority. Others could derive power by their association with him. Then, in the early days of the Industrial Age, capital was power. Those who had access to it dominated the industrial process. All those things still play a role. It's better to have capital than not to have it. It's better to have physical strength than not to. However, today, one of the largest sources of power is derived from specialized knowledge.

Most of us have heard by now that we are living in the information age. We are no longer primarily an industrial culture, but a communication one. We live in a time when new ideas and movements and concepts change the world almost daily, whether they are as profound as quantum physics or as mundane as the best-marketed hamburger. If there's anything that characterizes the modern world, it's the massive, almost unimaginable, flow of information—and therefore of change. From books and movies and boomboxes and computer chips, this new information comes at us in a blizzard of data to be seen and felt and heard. In this society, those with the information and the means to communicate it have what the king used to have—unlimited power. As John Kenneth Galbraith has written, "Money is what fueled the industrial society. But in the informational society, the fuel, the power, is knowledge. One has now come to see a new class structure divided by those who have information and those who must function out of ignorance. This new class has its power not from money, not from land, but from knowledge."

The exciting thing to note is that the key to power today is available to us all. If you weren't the king in medieval times, you might have had a great deal of difficulty becoming one. If you didn't have capital at the beginning of the industrial revolution, the odds of your amassing it seemed very slim indeed. But today, any kid in blue jeans can create a corporation that can change the world. In the modern world, information is the commodity of kings. Those with access to certain forms of specialized knowledge can transform themselves and, in many ways, our entire world.

We're left with an obvious question. Surely in the United States the kinds of specialized knowledge needed to transform the quality of our lives is available to everyone. It's in every bookstore, every video store, every library. You can get it from speeches and seminars and courses. And we all want to succeed. The bestseller list is full of prescriptions for personal excellence: *The One Minute Manager*, *In Search of Excellence*, *Megatrends*, *What They Don't Teach You at Harvard Business School*, *Bridge Across Forever* . . . The list goes on and on. The information is there. So why do some people generate fabulous results, while others just scrape by? Why aren't we all empowered, happy, wealthy, healthy, and successful?

The truth is that even in the information age, information is not enough. If all we needed were ideas and positive thinking, then we all would have had ponies when we were kids and we would all be living our "dream life" now. Action is what unites every great success. Action is what produces results. Knowledge is only potential power until it comes into the hands of someone who knows how to get himself to take effective action. In fact, the literal definition of the word "power" is "the ability to act."

What we do in life is determined by how we communicate to ourselves. In the modern world, the quality of life is the quality of communication. What we picture and say to ourselves, how we move and use the muscles of our bodies and our facial expressions will determine how much of what we know we will use.

Often we get caught in the mental trap of seeing enormously successful people and thinking they are where they are because they have some special gift. Yet a closer look shows that the greatest gift that extraordinarily successful people have over the average person is their ability to get themselves to take action. It's a "gift" that any of us can develop within ourselves. After all, other people had the same knowledge Steve Jobs did. People other than Ted Turner could have figured out that cable had enormous economic potential. But Turner and Jobs were able to take action, and by doing so, they changed the way many of us experience the world.

We all produce two forms of communication from which the experience of our lives is fashioned. First, we conduct internal communications: those things we picture, say, and feel within ourselves. Second, we experience external communications: words, tonalities, facial expressions, body postures, and physical actions to communicate with the world. Every communication we make is an action, a cause set in motion. And all communications have some kind of effect on ourselves and on others.

Communication is power. Those who have mastered its effective use can change their own experience of the world and the world's experience of them. All behavior and feelings find their original roots in some form of communication. Those who affect the thoughts, feelings, and actions of the majority of us are those who know how to use this tool of power. Think of the people who have changed our world—John F. Kennedy, Thomas Jefferson, Martin Luther King, Jr., Franklin Delano Roosevelt, Winston Churchill, Mahatma Gandhi. In a much grimmer vein, think of Hitler. What these men all had in common was that they were master communicators. They were able to take their vision, whether it was to transport people into space or to create a hate-filled Third Reich, and communicate it to others with such congruency that they influenced the way the masses thought and acted. Through their communication power, they changed the world.

In fact, isn't this also what sets a Spielberg, a Springsteen, an Iacocca, a Fonda, or a Reagan apart from others? Are they not masters of the tool of human communication, or influence? Just as these people are able to move the masses with communication, it is the tool we also use to move ourselves.

Your level of communication mastery in the external world will determine your level of success with others—personally, emotionally, socially, and financially. More important, the level of success you experience internally—the happiness, joy, ecstasy, love, or anything else you desire—is the direct result of how you communicate to yourself. How you feel is not the result of what is happening in your life—it is your *interpretation* of what is happening. Successful people's lives have shown us over and over again that the quality of our lives is determined not by what happens to us, but rather by what we do about what happens.

You are the one who decides how to feel and act based upon the ways you choose to perceive your life. Nothing has any meaning except the meaning we give it. Most of us have turned this process of interpretation on automatic, but we can take that power back and immediately change our experience of the world.

This book is about taking the kinds of massive, focused, congruent actions that lead to overwhelming results. In fact, if I were to say to you in two words what this book is about, I'd say: Producing results! Think about it. Isn't that what you're really interested in? Maybe you want to change how you feel about yourself and your world. Maybe you'd like to be a better communicator, develop a more loving relationship, learn more rapidly, become healthier, or earn more money. You can create all of these things for yourself, and much more, through the effective use of the information in this book. Before you can produce new results, however, you must first realize that you're already producing results. They just may not be the results you desire. Most of us think of our mental states and most of what goes on in our minds as things that happen outside our control. But the truth is you can control your mental activities and your behaviors to a degree you never believed possible before. If you're depressed, you created and produced that show you call depression. If you're ecstatic, you created that, too.

It's important to remember that emotions like depression do not happen to you. You don't "catch" depression. You create it, like every other result in your life, through specific mental and physical actions. In order to be depressed, you have to view your life in specific ways. You have to say certain things to yourself in just the right tones of voice. You have to adopt a specific posture and breathing pattern. For example, if you wish to be depressed, it helps tremendously if you collapse your shoulders and look down a lot. Speaking in a sad-sounding tone of voice and thinking of the worst-possible scenarios for your life also helps. If you throw your biochemistry into turmoil through poor diet or excessive alcohol or drug use, you assist

your body in creating low blood sugar and thus virtually guarantee depression.

My point here is simply that it takes effort to create depression. It's hard work, and it requires taking specific types of
actions. Some people have created this state so often, though,
that it's easy for them to produce. If fact, often they've linked
this pattern of internal communication to all kinds of external
events. Some people get so many secondary gains—attention
from others, sympathy, love, and so on—that they adopt this
style of communication as their natural state of living. Others
have lived with it so long that it actually feels comfortable. They
become identified with the state. We can, however, change our
mental and physical actions and thereby immediately change
our emotions and behaviors.

You can become ecstatic by immediately adopting the point
of view that creates that emotion. You can picture in your mind
the kinds of things that create this feeling. You can change the
tone and content of your internal dialogue with yourself. You
can adopt the specific postures and breathing patterns that create
that state in your body, and voilà! You will experience ecstasy.
If you wish to be compassionate, you must simply change your
physical and mental actions to match those the state of compassion requires. The same is true of love or any other emotion.

You might think of the process of producing emotional states
by managing your internal communication as being similar to
a director's job. To produce the precise results he wants, the
director of a movie manipulates what you see and hear. If he
wants you to be scared, he might turn up the sound and splash
some special effects on the screen at just the right moment. If
he wants you to be inspired, he'll arrange the music, the lighting,
and everything else on the screen to produce that effect. A director can produce a tragedy or a comedy out of the same event,
depending upon what he decides to put on the screen. You can
do the same things with the screen of your mind. You can direct
your mental activity, which is the underpinning of all physical
action, with the same skill and power. You can turn up the light
and sound of the positive messages in your brain, and you can

dim the pictures and sounds of the negative ones. You can run your brain as skillfully as Spielberg or Scorsese runs his set.

Some of what follows will seem hard to believe. You probably don't believe there's a way to look at a person and know his exact thoughts or to instantly summon up your most powerful resources at will. But if you had suggested one hundred years ago men would go to the moon, you would have been considered a madman, a lunatic. (Where do you think the word came from?) If you had said it was possible to travel from New York to Los Angeles in five hours, you would have seemed like a crazy dreamer. But it only took the mastery of specific technologies and laws of aerodynamics to make those things possible. In fact, today one aerospace company is working on a vehicle that they say in ten years will take people from New York to California in twelve minutes. Similarly, in this book you will learn the "laws" of *Optimum Performance Technologies®* that will give you access to resources you never realized you had.

> *"For every disciplined effort there is a multiple reward."*
> —*Jim Rohn*

People who have attained excellence follow a consistent path to success. I call it the Ultimate Success Formula. The first step to this formula is to know your outcome, that is, to define precisely what you want. The second step is to take action—otherwise your desires will always be dreams. You must take the types of actions you believe will create the greatest probability of producing the result you desire. The actions we take do not always produce the results we desire, so the third step is to develop the sensory acuity to recognize the kinds of responses and results you're getting from your actions and to note as quickly as possible if they are taking you closer to your goals or farther away. You must know what you're getting from your actions, whether it be in a conversation or from your daily habits in life. If what you're getting is not what you want, you need to note what results your actions have produced so that you learn from every human experience. And then you take the fourth step, which is to develop the flexibility to change your behavior until you get what you want. If you look at successful people, you'll find they followed these steps. They started with a target, because you can't hit one if you don't have one. They took action, because just knowing isn't enough. They had the ability to read others, to know what response they were getting. And they kept adapting, kept adjusting, kept changing their behavior until they found what worked.

Consider Steven Spielberg. At the age of thirty-six, he's become the most successful filmmaker in history. He's already responsible for four of the ten top-grossing films of all time, including *E. T., The Extra-Terrestrial*, the highest-grossing film ever. How did he reach that point at such a young age? It's a remarkable story.

From the age of twelve or thirteen, Spielberg knew he wanted to be a movie director. His life changed when he took a tour of Universal Studios one afternoon when he was seventeen years old. The tour didn't quite make it to the sound stages, where all the action was, so Spielberg, knowing his outcome, took action. He snuck off by himself to watch the filming of a real movie. He ended up meeting the head of Universal's editorial department, who talked with him for an hour and expressed an interest in Spielberg's films.

For most people that's where the story would have ended. But Spielberg wasn't like most people. He had personal power. He knew what he wanted. He learned from his first visit, so he changed his approach. The next day, he put on a suit, brought along his father's briefcase, loaded with only a sandwich and two candy bars, and returned to the lot as if he belonged there. He strode purposefully past the gate guard that day. He found an abandoned trailer and, using some plastic letters, put Steven Spielberg, Director, on the door. Then he went on to spend his summer meeting directors, writers, and editors, lingering at the edges of the world he craved, learning from every conversation, observing and developing more and more sensory acuity about what worked in moviemaking.

Finally, at age twenty, after becoming a regular on the lot,

Steven showed Universal a modest film he had put together, and he was offered a seven-year contract to direct a TV series. He'd made his dream come true.

Did Spielberg follow the Ultimate Success Formula? He sure did. He had the specialized knowledge to know what he wanted. He took action. He had the sensory acuity to know what results he was getting, whether his actions were moving him closer to or farther from his goal. And he had the flexibility to change his behavior to get what he wanted. Virtually every successful person I know of does the same thing. Those who succeed are committed to changing and being flexible until they do create the life that they desire.

Consider Dean Barbara Black of the Columbia University School of Law, who envisioned herself to be dean one day. As a young woman, she broke into a predominantly male field and successfully obtained her law degree from Columbia. She then decided to put her career goal on hold while she created another goal—developing a family. Nine years later, she decided that she was ready again to go after her first career goal, so she enrolled in a graduate program at Yale, and developed the teaching, researching, and writing skills that led her to "the job that she had always wanted." She had expanded her belief system— she had changed her approach and had combined both goals and is now the dean of one of the most prestigious law schools in America. She broke the mold and proved that success could be created on all levels simultaneously. Did she follow the Ultimate Success Formula? Of course she did. Knowing what she wanted, she tried something, and if it didn't work, she kept changing— changing until now she learned how to balance her life. In addition to heading an important law school, she's a mother and a family woman as well.

Here's another example. Ever had a piece of Kentucky Fried Chicken? Do you know how Colonel Sanders built the empire that made him a millionaire and changed the eating habits of a nation? When he started, he was nothing but a retiree with a fried-chicken recipe. That's all. No organization. No nothin'. He had owned a little restaurant that was going broke because the main highway had been routed elsewhere. When he got his first Social Security check, he decided to see if he could make some money selling his chicken recipe. His first idea was to sell the recipe to restaurant owners and have them give him a percentage of the proceeds.

Now that's not necessarily the most realistic idea for beginning a business. And, as things turned out, it didn't exactly rocket him to stardom. He drove around the country, sleeping in his car, trying to find someone who would back him. He kept changing his idea and knocking on doors. He was rejected 1,009 times, and then something miraculous happened. Someone said "Yes." The colonel was in business.

How many of you have a recipe? How many of you have the physical power and charisma of a chunky old man in a white suit? Colonel Sanders made a fortune because he had the ability to take massive, determined action. He had the personal power necessary to produce the results he desired most. He had the ability to hear the word "no" a thousand times and still communicate to himself in a way that got him to knock on the next door, totally convinced that it could be the one where someone said yes.

In one way or another everything in this book is directed toward providing your brain with the most effective signals to empower you to take successful action. Almost every week I conduct a four-day seminar called "The Mind Revolution." In this seminar, we teach people everything from how to run their brains most effectively to how to eat, breathe, and exercise in a way that maximizes personal energy. The first evening of this four-day process is called "Fear Into Power." The design of the seminar is to teach people how to take action instead of being stopped by fear. At the end of the seminar, people are given the opportunity to walk on fire—across ten to twelve feet of burning coals, and in advanced groups I've had people walking across forty feet of coals. The firewalk has fascinated the media to the point I fear its message is getting lost. The point is not to walk on fire. I think it's fair to assume there's no great economic or social benefit to be gained from a blissful stroll across a bed of hot coals. Instead, the firewalk is an experience in personal power and a metaphor for possibilities, an opportunity for people to produce results they previously had thought impossible.

People have been doing some version of firewalking for thousands of years. In some parts of the world, it's a religious test of faith. When I conduct a firewalk, it's not part of any religious experience in the conventional sense. But it is an experience in belief. It teaches people in the most visceral sense that they can change, they can grow, they can stretch themselves, they can do things they never thought possible, that their greatest fears and limitations are self-imposed.

The only difference between whether you can walk on fire or not is your ability to communicate to yourself in a way that causes you to take action, in spite of all your past fear programming about what should happen to you. The lesson is that people can do virtually anything as long as they muster the resources to believe they can and to take effective actions.

What all this leads to is a simple, inescapable fact. Success is not an accident. The difference between people who produce positive results and those who do not is not some sort of random roll of the dice. There are consistent, logical patterns of action, specific pathways to excellence, that are within the reach of us all. We can all unleash the magic within us. We simply must learn how to turn on and use our minds and bodies in the most powerful and advantageous ways.

Have you ever wondered what a Spielberg and a Springsteen might have in common? What do a John F. Kennedy and a Martin Luther King, Jr., share that caused them to affect so many people in such a deep and emotional way? What sets a Ted Turner and a Tina Turner apart from the masses? What about a Pete Rose and a Ronald Reagan? All of them have been able to get themselves to consistently take effective actions toward the accomplishment of their dreams. But what is it that gets them to continue day after day to put everything they've got into everything they do? There are, of course, many factors. However, I believe that there are seven fundamental character

traits that they have all cultivated within themselves, seven characteristics that give them the fire to do whatever it takes to
succeed. These are the seven basic triggering mechanisms that
can ensure your success as well:

Trait Number One: Passion! All of these people have discovered
a reason, a consuming, energizing, almost obsessive purpose that
drives them to do, to grow, and to be more! It gives them the
fuel that powers their success train and causes them to tap their
true potential. It's passion that causes a Pete Rose to continuously dive headfirst into second base as if he were a rookie playing his first major-league game. It's passion that sets the actions
of a Lee Iacocca apart from so many others. It's passion that
drives the computer scientists through years of dedication to
create the kind of breakthroughs that have put men and women
in outer space and brought them back. It's passion that causes
people to stay up late and get up early. It's passion that people
want in their relationships. Passion gives life power and juice
and meaning. There is no greatness without a passion to be great,
whether it's the aspiration of an athlete or an artist, a scientist,
a parent, or a businessman. We'll discover how to unleash this
inner force through the power of goals in chapter 11.

Trait Number Two: Belief! Every religious book on the planet
talks about the power and effect of faith and belief on mankind.
People who succeed on a major scale differ greatly in their beliefs
from those who fail. Our beliefs about what we are and what
we can be precisely determine what we will be. If we believe
in magic, we'll live a magical life. If we believe our life is defined
by narrow limits, we've suddenly made those limits real. What
we believe to be true, what we believe is possible, becomes
what's true, becomes what's possible. This book will provide
you with a specific, scientific way to quickly change your beliefs
so that they support you in the attainment of your most desired
goals. Many people are passionate, but because of their limiting
beliefs about who they are and what they can do, they never
take the actions that could make their dream a reality. People

who succeed know what they want and believe that they can get it. We'll learn about what beliefs are and how to use them in chapters 4 and 5.

Passion and belief help to provide the fuel, the propulsion toward excellence. But propulsion is not enough. If it were, it would be enough to fuel a rocket and send it flying blindly toward the heavens. Besides that power, we need a path, an intelligent sense of logical progression. To succeed in hitting our target, we need

Trait Number Three: Strategy! A strategy is a way of organizing resources. When Steven Spielberg decided to become a film-maker, he mapped out a course that would lead to the world he wanted to conquer. He figured out what he wanted to learn, whom he needed to know, and what he needed to do. He had passion, and he had belief, but he also had the strategy that made those things work to their greatest potential. Ronald Reagan has developed certain communication strategies that he uses on a consistent basis to produce the results he desires. Every great entertainer, politician, parent, or employer knows it's not enough to have the resources to succeed. One must use those resources in the most effective way. A strategy is a recognition that the best talents and ambitions also need to find the right avenue. You can open a door by breaking it down, or you can find the key that opens it intact. We'll learn about the strategies that produce excellence in chapters 7 and 8.

Trait Number Four: Clarity of Values! When we think of the things that made America great, we think of things like patriotism and pride, a sense of tolerance, and a love of freedom. These things are values, the fundamental, ethical, moral, and practical judgments we make about what's important, what really matters. Values are specific belief systems we have about what is right and wrong for our lives. They're the judgments we make about what makes life worth living. Many people do not have a clear idea of what is important to them. Often individuals do things that afterward they are unhappy with themselves about simply because they are not clear about what they unconsciously believe is right for them and others. When we look at great successes, they are almost always people with a clear fundamental sense about what really matters. Think of Ronald Reagan, John F. Kennedy, Martin Luther King, Jr., John Wayne, Jane Fonda. They all have had different visions, but what they have in common is a fundamental moral grounding, a sense of who they are and why they do what they do. An understanding of values is one of the most rewarding and challenging keys to achieving excellence. We will consider values in chapter 18.

As you've probably noticed, all these traits feed on and interact with one another. Is passion affected by beliefs? Of course it is. The more we believe we can accomplish something, the more we're usually willing to invest in its achievement. Is belief by itself enough to achieve excellence? It's a good start, but if you believe you're going to see a sunrise and your strategy for achieving that goal is to begin running west, you may have some difficulty. Are our strategies for success affected by our values? You bet. If your strategy for success requires you to do things that do not fit your unconscious beliefs about what is right or wrong for your life, then even the best strategy will not work. This is often seen in individuals who begin to succeed only to end up sabotaging their own success. The problem is there's an internal conflict between the individual's values and his strategy for achievement.

In the same way, all four of the things we've already considered are inseparable from

Trait Number Five: Energy! Energy can be the thundering, joyous commitment of a Bruce Springsteen or a Tina Turner. It can be the entrepreneurial dynamism of a Donald Trump or a Steve Jobs. It can be the vitality of a Ronald Reagan or a Katharine Hepburn. It is almost impossible to amble languorously toward excellence. People of excellence take opportunities and shape them. They live as if obsessed with the wondrous opportunities of each day and the recognition that the one thing no one has enough of is time. There are many people in this world who have a passion they believe in. They know the strategy that would ensure it, and their values are aligned, but they just don't have the physical vitality to take action on what they know. Great success is inseparable from the physical, intellectual, and spiritual energy that allows us to make the most of what we have. In chapters 9 and 10, we'll learn and apply the tools that can immediately increase physical vibrancy.

Trait Number Six: Bonding Power! Nearly all successful people have in common an extraordinary ability to bond with others, the ability to connect with and develop rapport with people from a variety of backgrounds and beliefs. Sure, there's the occasional mad genius who invents something that changes the world. But if the genius spends all his time in a lonely warren, he will succeed on one level but fail on many others. The great successes—the Kennedys, the Kings, the Reagans, the Gandhis—all have the ability to form bonds that unite them to millions of others. The greatest success is not on the stage of the world. It is in the deepest recesses of your own heart. Deep down, everyone needs to form lasting, lving bonds with others. Without that, any success, any excellence, is hollow indeed. We'll learn about those bonds in chapter 13.

The final key trait is something we talked about earlier.

Trait Number Seven: Mastery of Communication! This is the essence of what this book is about. The way we communicate with others and the way we communicate with ourselves ultimately determine the quality of our lives. People who succeed in life are those who have learned how to take any challenge that life gives them and communicate that experience to themselves in a way that causes them to successfully change things. People who fail take the adversities of life and accept them as limitations. The people who shape our lives and our cultures are also masters of communication to others. What they have in common is an ability to communicate a vision or a quest or a joy or a mission. Mastery of communication is what makes a great parent or a great artist or a great politician or a great teacher. Almost every chapter in this book, in one way or another, has to do with communication, with bridging gaps, with building new paths, and with sharing new visions.

The first part of this book will teach you how to take charge and run your own brain and body more effectively than ever before. We will be working with factors that affect the way you communicate with yourself. In the second section, we'll be studying how to discover what you really want out of life and how you can communicate more effectively with others as well as how to be able to anticipate the kinds of behaviors that different kinds of people will consistently create. The third section looks from a larger, more global perspective at how we behave, what motivates us, and what we can contribute on a broader, extrapersonal level. It's about taking the skills you've learned and becoming a leader.

When I wrote this book, my original goal was to provide a textbook for human development—a book that would be packed with the best and the latest in human change technology. I wanted to arm you with the skills and strategies that would enable you to change anything you wanted to change, and to do it faster than you'd ever dreamed of before. I wanted to create an opportunity for you in a very concrete way to immediately increase the quality of your life experience. I also wanted to create a work you could come back to again and again and always find something useful for your life. I knew that many of the subjects I would be writing about could be books in themselves. However, I wanted to give you information that was complete, something you could use in each area. I hope you find this book to be all these things for you.

When the manuscript was completed, the advance readings were very positive, except for one thing—several people said, "You've got two books here. Why don't you split them up, publish one now, and market the other one as a follow-up twelve months later?" My goal was to get to you, the reader, as much quality information as quickly as I could. I did not want to dole out these skills a piece at a time. However, I became concerned that many people would not even get to the parts of the book that I think are most important simply because it was explained to me that several studies have shown that less than 10 percent of the people who buy a book read past the first chapter. At first, I couldn't believe that statistic. Then I remembered that less than 3 percent of the nation is financially independent, less than 10 percent have written goals, only 35 percent of American women—and even fewer men—feel they are in good physical shape, and in many states one out of every two marriages ends up in divorce. Only a small percentage of people really live the life of their dreams. Why? It takes effort. It takes consistent action.

Bunker Hunt, the Texas oil billionaire, was asked once if he had any one piece of advice he could give people on how to succeed. He said that success is simple. First, you decide what you want specifically; and second, you decide you're willing to pay the price to make it happen—and then pay that price. If you don't take that second step, you'll never have what you want in the long term. I like to call the people who know what they want and are willing to pay the price to get it "the few who do" versus "the many who talk." I challenge you to play with this material, to read it all, to share what you learn, and to enjoy it.

In this chapter, I've stressed the primacy of taking effective action. But there are many ways to take action. Most of them depend on a large degree of trial and error. Most people who have been great successes have adjusted and readjusted countless times before they got what they wanted. Trial and error is fine, except for one thing: it uses a vast quantity of the one resource none of us will ever have enough of—time.

What if there was a way to take action that accelerated the learning process? What if I could show you how to learn the precise lessons that people of excellence have already learned? What if you could learn in minutes what someone took years to perfect? The way to do this is through *modeling*, a way to reproduce precisely the excellence of others. What do they do that sets them apart from those who only dream of success? Let's discover . . .

CHAPTER II

The Difference
that Makes
the Difference

"It's a funny thing about life; if you refuse to accept
anything but the best, you very often get it."

—*W. Somerset Maugham*

He was traveling along the highway at sixty-five miles an hour when suddenly it happened. Something along the side of the road caught his eye, and when he looked back in the direction in which he was traveling, he had only a second to respond. It was almost too late. The Mack truck in front of him had suddenly come to an unexpected stop. Instantly, in an effort to save his life, he laid his motorcycle down into a sickening skid that seemed to last forever. In agonizingly slow motion, he slid beneath the truck. The gas cap popped off his motorcycle, and the worst occurred: fuel spilled out and ignited. His next moment of consciousness is the experience of waking up in a hospital bed in searing pain, unable to move, fearing to breathe. Three-quarters of his body is covered by terrible third-degree burns. Still, he refuses to give up. He struggles back to life and resumes a business career, only to suffer another staggering blow: an airplane crash that leaves him paralyzed, from the waist down, for life.

In every man and woman's life there comes a time of ultimate challenge—a time when every resource we have is tested. A time when life seems unfair. A time when our faith, our values, our patience, our compassion, our ability to persist, are all pushed to our limits and beyond. Some people use such tests as opportunities to become better people—others allow these experiences of life to destroy them. Have you ever wondered what creates the difference in the way human beings respond to life's challenges? I certainly have. For most of my life I have been fascinated by what triggers human beings to behave the way they do. For as long as I can remember, I've been obsessed with discovering what sets certain men and women apart from their peers. What creates a leader, an achiever? How is it that there are so many people in this world who live such joyous lives in spite of almost every adversity, while others who would seem to have it all live lives of despair, anger, and depression?

Let me share another man's story with you, and let's note the differences between the two men. This man's life seems much brighter. He is a fabulously wealthy, enormously talented entertainer with a huge following. At twenty-two he was the youngest member of Chicago's famed Second City comedy troupe. Almost immediately he became the show's acknowledged star. Soon there is a major theatrical hit in New York. He becomes one of the great television successes of the seventies. Then he becomes one of the nation's hottest film stars. He branches into music and enjoys the same instant success there. He has dozens of admiring friends, a good marriage, wonderful homes in New York City and Martha's Vineyard. He seems to have everything a person could possibly ask for.

Which of these two people would you rather be? It's hard to imagine anyone choosing the first life over the second.

But let me tell you more about the two people. The first is one of the most vital, strong, and successful people I know. His name is W. Mitchell, and he's alive and well and living in Colorado. Since his terrible motorcycle accident, he's known more success and joy than most people know in a lifetime. He's developed phenomenal personal relationships with some of the most influential people in America. He's become a millionaire in business. He even ran for Congress, despite the fact that his face was grotesquely marked. His campaign slogan? "Send me to Congress, and I won't be just another pretty face." Today he has a fabulous relationship with a very special woman, and he is happily campaigning for lieutenant governor of Colorado in 1986.

The second person is someone you knew well, someone who probably brought you a great deal of pleasure and joy. His name was John Belushi. He was one of the most celebrated comedians of our time, and one of the great entertainment success stories of the seventies. Belushi was able to enrich countless lives, but not his own. When he died at the age of thirty-three of what the coroner ruled "acute toxicity from cocaine and heroin," few who knew him were surprised. The man who had everything had become a bloated, out-of-control drug abuser, old beyond his years. Externally he had everything. Internally, he'd been running on empty for years.

We see similar examples all the time. Ever hear of Pete Strudwick? Born with no hands and no feet, he has gone on to become a marathon runner who has already run 25,000 miles. Think of Helen Keller's astounding story. Or think of Candy Lightner, the founder of Mothers Against Drunk Driving. She took a terrible tragedy, the death of a daughter who was run over by a drunk driver, and she formed an organization that has probably saved hundreds—maybe thousands—of lives. At the other extreme, think of people like Marilyn Monroe or Ernest Hemingway, people who had fabulous successes and ended up destroying themselves.

So I ask you, What's the difference between the haves and the have-nots? What's the difference between the cans and the cannots? What's the difference between the dos and the do-nots? Why do some people overcome horrible, unimaginable adversity and make their lives a triumph, while others, in spite of every advantage, turn their lives into a disaster? Why do some people take any experience and make it work for them, while others take any experience and make it work against them? What's the difference between W. Mitchell and John Belushi? What's the difference that makes the difference in the quality of life?

I've been obsessed by that question for my entire life. As I grew up, I saw people who had great riches of all types—great jobs, wonderful relationships, and well-developed physiques. I had to know what caused their lives to be so different from mine and that of my friends. The difference all comes down to the way in which we communicate with ourselves and the actions we take. What do we do when we try everything we can and things still turn out wrong? People who succeed do not have fewer problems than people who fail. The only people without problems are those in cemeteries. It is not what happens to us that separates failures from successes. It is how we perceive it and what we do about what "happens" that makes the difference.

When W. Mitchell received the information from his body that three-quarters of it was covered with third-degree burns, he had a choice in how to interpret that information. The meaning of this event could have been a reason to die, to grieve, or anything else he wanted to communicate. He chose to consistently communicate to himself that this experience had occurred for a purpose. And that this would someday provide him with even greater advantages in his goal to make a difference in the world. As a result of this communication with himself, he formed sets of beliefs and values that continued to direct his life from a sense of advantage rather than tragedy—even after he became paralyzed. How was Pete Strudwick able to successfully run Pike's Peak, the most difficult marathon in the world, even though he has no hands and no feet? Simple. He mastered his communication with himself. When his body senses sent him signals that in the past he had interpreted as pain, as limitation, as exhaustion, he simply relabeled their meaning and continued to communicate to his nervous system in a way that kept him running.

"Things do not change; we change."
—*Henry David Thoreau*

What I was always curious about was specifically how people produce results. Long ago, I realized that success leaves clues, that people who produce outstanding results do specific things to create those results. I realized that it was not enough just to know that a W. Mitchell or a Pete Strudwick communicated to themselves in a way that produced results. I had to know specifically how they did it. I believed that if I precisely duplicated the actions of others, I could reproduce the same quality of results that they had. I believed that if I sowed, I would also reap. In other words, if there were someone who could be compassionate even in the most dire of circumstances, I could find out his strategy—how he looked at things, how he used his body in those situations—and I could become more compassionate. If a man and a woman had developed a successful marriage where for twenty-five years they still felt deeply in love with each other, I could find out what actions they had taken, what beliefs they had that created that result, and I could adopt those actions and beliefs and produce similar results in my own relationships. In my life, I had produced the result of being extremely overweight. I began to realize that all I needed to do was model people who were thin, find out what they ate, how they ate, what they thought, what their beliefs were, and I could produce the same result. This is how I lost my excess thirty pounds. I did the same thing in the financial area and in my personal relationships. So I began my pursuit of models of personal excellence. And in my own search for excellence, I studied every avenue I could find.

Then I came across a science known as Neuro-Linguistic Programming—or NLP for short. If you analyze it, the name comes from "neuro," referring to the brain, and "linguistic," referring to language. Programming is the installation of a plan or procedure. NLP is the study of how language, both verbal and nonverbal, affects our nervous system. Our ability to do anything in life is based upon our ability to direct our own nervous system. Those who are able to produce some outstanding result do so by producing specific communications to and through the nervous system.

NLP studies how people communicate to themselves in ways that produce optimum resourceful states and thus create the largest number of behavioral choices. The name "Neuro-Linguistic Programming," although it is an accurate term for what the science is about, may also be responsible for the fact that you may never have heard of it before. In the past, it has primarily been taught to therapists and to a small number of fortunate business executives. When I was first exposed to it, I immediately realized it was something quite different from anything I had ever experienced before. I watched a practitioner of NLP take a woman who had been in therapy for over three years for phobic responses, and in less than forty-five minutes, no more phobia. I was hooked. I had to know it all! (By the way, many times the same result can be produced in five or ten minutes.) NLP provides a systematic framework for directing our own brain. It teaches us how to direct not only our own states and behaviors, but also the states and behaviors of others. In short, it is the science of how to run your brain in an optimal way to produce the results you desire.

NLP provided exactly what I was looking for. It provided the key for unlocking the mystery of how certain people were able to consistently produce what I called optimum results. If someone else is able to wake up in the morning, quickly and easily and full of energy, that is a result they produced. The next question is, How did they produce it? Since actions are the source of all results, what specific mental or physical actions produced the neurophysiological process of waking up from sleep quickly and easily? One of the presuppositions of NLP is that we all share the same neurology, so if anyone can do anything in the world, you can, too, if you run your nervous system in exactly the same way. This process of discovering exactly and specifically what people do to produce a specific result is called modeling.

Once again, the point is if it's possible for others in the world, it's possible for you. It's not a matter of whether you can produce the results that another person produces; it's a matter of strategy—that is, how does that person produce the results? If someone is a terrific speller, there's a way to model him so you can be, too, in a matter of four or five minutes. (You'll learn this strategy in chapter 7.) If someone you know communicates perfectly with his kid, you can do the same thing. If someone finds it easy to wake up in the morning quickly, so can you. Simply model how other people direct their nervous systems. Obviously, some tasks are more complex than others and may take more time to model and then duplicate. However, if you have enough desire and the belief that will support you while continuing to adjust and change, virtually anything any human being does can be modeled. In many cases, a person may have spent years of trial and error to find the specific way to use his body or mind to produce a result. But you can step in, model the actions that took years to perfect, and produce similar results in a matter of moments, months—or at least in a lot less time than it took the person whose results you desire to duplicate.

The two men primarily responsible for NLP are John Grinder and Richard Bandler. Grinder is a linguist, one of the most prominent in the world. Bandler is a mathematician, Gestalt therapist, and computer expert. The two men decided to pool their talents for a unique task—to go out and model the people who were the very best at whatever they did. They looked for people who were most effective at creating the one thing they felt most human beings wanted—change. They looked at successful businessmen, successful therapists, and others in order to distill the lessons and patterns those people had discovered through years of trial and error.

Bandler and Grinder are best known for a number of effective behavioral-intervention patterns that they codified in the modeling of Dr. Milton Erikson, one of the greatest hypnotherapists that ever lived; Virginia Satir, an extraordinary family therapist; and Gregory Bateson, an anthropologist. The two discovered, for example, how Satir was able to consistently produce relationship resolution where other therapists had failed. They discovered what patterns of actions she produced to create results. And they taught these patterns to their students, who were then able to apply them and to produce the same quality of results, even though they did not have the noted therapist's years of experience. They sowed the same seeds, so they reaped the same rewards. Working with the fundamental patterns they modeled from these three masters, Bandler and Grinder began to create their own patterns and to teach them as well. These patterns are commonly known as Neuro-Linguistic Programming—NLP.

These two geniuses did much more than provide us with a series of powerful and effective patterns for creating change. More important, they provided us with a systematic view of how to duplicate any form of human excellence in a very short period of time.

Their success is legendary. However, even with the tools available, many people simply learned the patterns for creating emotional and behavioral change and never had the personal power to use them in an effective and congruent way. Once again, having the knowledge is not enough. Action is what produces results.

As I read more and more books about NLP, I was amazed that I found little or nothing written about the process of modeling. To me, modeling is the pathway to excellence. It means that if I see anyone in this world producing a result I desire, I can produce the same results if I'm willing to pay the price of time and effort. If you want to achieve success, all you need to do is find a way to model those who have already succeeded. That is, find out what actions they took, specifically how they used their brain and body to produce the results you desire to duplicate. If you want to be a better friend, a richer person, a better parent, a better athlete, a more successful businessman, all you need to do is find models of excellence.

The movers and shakers of the world are often professional modelers—people who have mastered the art of learning everything they can by following other people's experience rather than their own. They know how to save the one commodity none of us ever get enough of—time. In fact, if you look at the *New York Times* bestseller list, you'll find that most of the books at the top of the list contain models on how to do something more effectively. Peter Drucker's latest book in *Innovation and Entre-preneurship*. In it, Mr. Drucker outlines the specific actions one must take to be an effective entrepreneur and innovator. He makes it explicitly clear that innovation is a very special and deliberate process. There is nothing mysterious or magical about being an entrepreneur. It's not in the genetic makeup. It's a discipline that can be learned. Sound familiar? He's looked to as founder of modern business practices because of his modeling skills. *The One Minute Manager* (Kenneth Blanchard and Spencer Johnson) is a model for human communication and simple and effective management of any human relationship. It was put together by modeling some of the most effective managers in the country. *In Search of Excellence* (Thomas J. Peters and Robert H. Waterman, Jr.) is obviously a book that provides a model of successful corporations in America. *Bridge Across Forever* (Richard Bach) provides another viewpoint, a new model of how to look at relationships. The list goes on and on. This book, too, is filled with a whole series of models on how to direct your mind, your body, and your communication with others in a way that will produce outstanding results for everyone involved. However, my goal for you is to not only learn these patterns of success, but also go beyond them by creating your own models.

You can teach a dog patterns that will improve its behavior. You can do the same thing with people. But what I want you to learn is a process, a framework, a discipline that will allow you to duplicate excellence wherever you find it. I want to teach you some of the most effective patterns of NLP. However, I want you to become more than just an NLPer. I want you to become a modeler. Someone who seizes excellence and makes it your own. Someone in constant pursuit of *Optimum Perform-ance Technologies®*, so you're not stuck, committed to any one series of systems or patterns, but instead are consistently looking for new and effective ways to produce the results you desire.

To model excellence, you should become a detective, an investigator, someone who asks lots of questions and tracks down all the clues to what produces excellence.

I've taught the best pistol marksmen in the U.S. Army to

shoot better by finding out the precise patterns of excellence in pistol shooting. I've learned the skills of a karate master by observing what they think and do. I've improved the performance of both professional and Olympic athletes. I did it by finding a way to precisely model what these men did when they produced their greatest results and then showing them how they could trigger those performances on cue.

Building from the successes of others is one of the fundamental aspects of most learning. In the world of technology, every advance in engineering or computer design follows naturally from earlier discoveries and breakthroughs. In the business world, companies that don't learn from the past, that don't operate with state-of-the-art information, are doomed.

But the world of human behavior is one of the few areas that continues to operate from outmoded theories and information. Many of us are still using a nineteenth-century model of how the brain works and how we behave. We put a label called "depression" on something, and guess what? We're depressed. The truth is, those terms can be self-fulfilling prophecies. This book teaches a technology that's readily available, a technology that can be used to create the quality of life you desire.

Bandler and Grinder found that there are three fundamental ingredients that must be duplicated in order to reproduce any form of human excellence. They are really the three forms of mental and physical actions that correspond most directly to the quality of results we produce. Picture them as three doors leading up to a spectacular banquet hall.

The first door represents a person's *belief system*. What a person believes, what he thinks is possible or impossible, to a great extent determines what he can or cannot do. There's an old phrase that says, "Whether you believe you can do something or you believe you can't, you're right." To a certain extent it's true, for when you don't believe you can do something, you're sending your nervous system consistent messages that limit or eliminate your ability to produce that very result. If, on the other hand, you are consistently delivering to your nervous system congruent messages that say you can do something, then they signal your brain to produce the result you desire, and that opens up the possibility for it. So if you can model a person's belief system, you've taken the first step toward acting as he does, thus producing a similar type of result. We'll look at belief systems further in chapter 4.

The second door that must be opened is a person's *mental syntax*. Mental syntax is the way people organize their thoughts. Syntax is like a code. There are seven digits in a phone number, but you have to dial them in the right order to reach the person you want. The same is true in reaching the part of your brain and nervous system that could most effectively help you get the outcome you desire. The same is true in communication. Many times people don't communicate well to each other because different people use different codes, different mental syntaxes. Unlock the codes, and you've gone through the second door toward modeling people's best qualities. We'll look at syntax in chapter 7.

The third door is *physiology*. The mind and body are totally linked. The way you use your physiology—the way you breathe and hold your body, your posture, facial expressions, the nature and quality of your movements—actually determines what state you are in. The state you're in then will determine the range and quality of the behaviors you're able to produce. We'll look further at physiology in chapter 9.

Actually, we're modeling all the time. How does a child learn to speak? How does a young athlete learn from an older one? How does an aspiring businessman decide to structure his company? Here's a simple modeling example from the business world. One way many people make a lot of money in this world is through what I call lag. We live in a culture that's consistent enough so that what works in one place will very often work in another. If someone has set up a successful business selling chocolate-chip cookies at a mall in Detroit, chances are the same thing will work at a mall in Dallas. If someone in Chicago runs a business supplying people in preposterous costumes to deliver messages, chances are the same thing will work in Los Angeles or New York.

All many people do to succeed in business is find something that works in one city and do the same thing somewhere else before the lag time is up. All you have to do is take a proven system and duplicate it—and maybe even better, improve upon it. People who do this are virtually guaranteed success.

The world's greatest modelers are the Japanese. What's behind the dazzling miracle of the Japanese economy? Is it brilliant innovation? Sometimes. However, if you'll check the industrial history of the past two decades, you'll find that very few of the major new products or technological advances began in Japan. The Japanese simply take ideas and products that begin here, ranging anywhere from cars to semiconductors, and, through meticulous modeling, they've retained the best elements and improved on the rest.

The man many people consider the richest in the world is Adnan Mohamad Khashoggi. How did he get that way? Simple: He modeled the Rockefellers, the Morgans, and others of like financial stature. He read everything he could about them, studied their beliefs, and modeled their strategies. Why was W. Mitchell able not just to survive, but to prosper from about as shattering an experience as a man could undergo? When he was in the hospital, friends read him examples of people who had overcome great obstacles. He had a model of possibility, and that positive model was stronger than the negative experiences he underwent. The difference between those who succeed and those who fail isn't what they have—it's what they choose to see and do with their resources and their experience of life.

Through this same modeling process, I began to get immediate results both for myself and for others. I continued to seek out other patterns of thought and action that produced outstanding results in short periods of time. I call these combined patterns *Optimum Performance Technologies.*® These strategies make up the body of this book. But I want to make something clear. My goal, my outcome for you, is not just that you master the patterns I'm describing here. What you need to do is develop your own patterns, your own strategies. John Grinder taught me never to believe anything too much, for if you believe it, there will always be a place where it doesn't work. NLP is a powerful tool, but it is just that—a tool you can use to develop your own approaches, your own strategies, your own insights. No one strategy works all the time.

Modeling is certainly nothing new. Every great inventor has modeled the discoveries of others to come up with something new. Every child has modeled the world around him.

But the trouble is that most of us model on an utterly haphazard, unfocused level. We pick up random bits and pieces from this person or that and then totally miss something much more important from someone else. We model something good here and something bad there. We attempt to model someone we respect but find we don't really know how to do what he/ she does.

> *"The meeting of preparation with opportunity generates the offspring we call luck."*
>
> —*Anthony Robbins*

Think of this as a guidebook for conscious modeling with greater precision, a chance for you to become conscious of something you've always been doing in your life.

There are phenomenal resources and strategies all around you. My challenge to you is to start thinking like a modeler, continuously being aware of the patterns and types of actions that produce outstanding results. If someone is able to do something outstanding, the immediate question that should pop into your mind is, "How does he create that result?" I'd hope you would continue to look for excellence, for the magic in everything you see, and learn how it's produced—so that you can create the same kinds of results whenever you desire.

The next thing we're going to explore is what determines our responses to the varying circumstances of life. Let us continue our studies of . . .

CHAPTER III

The Power
of State

"It is the mind that maketh good or ill,

That maketh wretch or happy, rich or poor."

—*Edmund Spenser*

Have you ever had the experience of being on a roll, the feeling that you could do no wrong? A time when everything seemed to go right? Maybe it was a tennis match when every shot hit the line or a business meeting where you had all the answers. Maybe it was a time when you amazed yourself by doing something heroic or dramatic you never thought you could do. You've probably had the opposite experience, too—a day when nothing went right. You can probably remember times you messed up things you usually do easily, when every step was wrong, every door was locked, everything you tried turned out wrong.

What's the difference? You're the same person. You should have the same resources at your disposal. So why do you produce dismal results one time and fabulous results the next? Why do even the best athletes have days when they do everything

35

right and follow them with days when they can't buy a basket or a base hit?

The difference is the neurophysiological state you're in. There are enabling states—confidence, love, inner strength, joy, ecstasy, belief—that tap great wellsprings of personal power. There are paralyzing states—confusion, depression, fear, anxiety, sadness, frustration—that leave us powerless. We all go in and out of good and bad states. Have you ever gone into a restaurant and had a waitress snarl, "Whaddya want?" Do you think she always communicates like that? It's possible that she's had such a difficult life that she's always like that. But it's more likely that she's had a bad day handling too many tables, maybe stiffed by a few customers. She's not a bad person; she's just in a terribly unresourceful state. If you can change her state, you can change her behavior.

Understanding state is the key to understanding change and achieving excellence. Our behavior is the result of the state we're in. We always do the best we can with the resources available to us, but sometimes we find ourselves in unresourceful states. I know there have been times in my life when, while in a particular state, I did or said things that later I regretted or was embarrassed about. Maybe you have, too. It's important to remember these times when someone treats you poorly. Thus, you create a sense of compassion instead of anger. After all, those who live in glass houses shouldn't throw stones. Remember, the waitress and other people are not their behaviors. The key, then, is to take charge of our states and thus our behaviors. What if you could snap your fingers and go into the most dynamic, resourceful state at will—a state in which you're excited, you're sure of success, your body is crackling with energy, your mind is alive? Well, you can.

By the time you finish this book, you're going to know how to put yourself into your most resourceful, empowering states and get yourself out of your disempowering states whenever you choose. Remember, the key to power is taking action. My goal is to share with you how to use the states that lead to decisive, congruent, committed action. In this chapter we're going to learn what states are, how they work. And we're going to learn why we can control our states to make them work for us.

A state can be defined as the sum of the millions of neurological processes happening within us, in other words, the sum total of our experience at any moment in time. Most of our states happen without any conscious direction on our part. We see something and we respond to it by going into a state. It may be a resourceful and useful state or an unresourceful and limiting state, but there's not much that most of us do to control it. The difference between those who fail to achieve their goals in life and those who succeed is the difference between those who cannot put themselves in a supportive state and those who can consistently put themselves in a state that supports them in their achievements.

Almost everything people want is some possible state. Make a list of the things you want in life. Do you want love? Well, love is a state, a feeling or emotion we signal to ourselves and feel within ourselves based on certain stimuli from the environment. Confidence? Respect? They're all things that we create. We produce these states within ourselves. Maybe you want money. Well, you don't care about having little pieces of green paper adorned with the faces of assorted deceased notables. You want what money represents to you: the love, confidence, freedom, or whatever states you think it can help provide. So the key to love, the key to joy, the key to the one power that man has sought for years—the ability to direct his life—is the ability to know how to direct and manage your states.

The first key to directing your state and producing the results you desire in life is to learn to effectively run your brain. In order to do this, we need to understand a little bit about how it works. We need to know what creates a state in the first place. For centuries, man has been fascinated by ways to alter his states and thus his experience of life. He has tried fasting, drugs, ritual, music, sex, food, hypnosis, chanting. These things all have their uses and their limitations. However, you are now going to be

DENNIS THE MENACE

"HOW COME DUMB STUFF SEEMS
SO SMART WHILE YOU'RE DOIN' IT ?"

Dennis the Menace® used by permission of Hank Ketcham and © by News
America Syndicate.

opened up to much simpler ways that are equally powerful and
in many cases quicker and more precise.

If all behavior is the result of the state we're in, we may
produce different communications and behaviors when we're in
resourceful states than we will when we are in an unresourceful
one. Then the next question is, What creates the state we're in?
There are two main components of state. The first is our internal
representations, and the second is the condition and use of our
physiology. What and how you picture things, as well as what
and how you say things to yourself about the situation at hand,
create the state you're in and thus the kinds of behaviors you
produce. For example, how do you treat your spouse or boyfriend or girlfriend when he or she comes home much later than
promised? Well, your behavior will greatly depend on the state
you're in when your loved one returns, and your state to a large
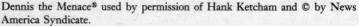

degree will be determined by what you have been representing
in your mind as the reason for the delay. If for hours you had
been picturing this person you care about in an accident, bloody,
dead, or hospitalized, as the person walks in the door you may
greet him or her with tears or a sigh of relief, or a big hug and
a question of what happened. These behaviors spring from a
state of concern. However, if instead you pictured your loved
one having a clandestine affair, or if you told yourself over and
over that this person is late simply because he or she just doesn't
care about your time or feelings, then when your loved one
arrives home, you will give him or her a far different reception
as a result of your state. Out of a state of feeling angry or feeling
used, a whole new set of behaviors results.

The next obvious question is, What causes one person to
represent things out of a state of concern, while another creates
internal representations that put her in a state of distrust or
anger? Well, there are many factors. We may have modeled the
reactions of our parents or other role models to such experiences.
If, for example, when you were a child, your mother always
worried when your father came home late, you may also represent things in a way that worries you. If your mother talked
of how she couldn't trust your father, you may have modeled
that pattern. Thus, our beliefs, attitudes, values, and past experiences with the particular person all affect the kinds of representations we will make about their behaviors.

There is an even more important and powerful factor in how
we perceive and represent the world, and that is the condition
and our pattern of use of our own physiology. Things like muscle tension, what we eat, how we breathe, our posture, our
overall level of biochemical functioning, all have a huge impact
on our state. Internal representation and physiology work together in a cybernetic loop. Anything that affects one will automatically affect the other. So changing states involves changing internal representation and changing physiology. If, when
your lover/spouse/child is supposed to be home, your body is
in a resourceful state, you will probably perceive that person as
being stuck in traffic or on the way home. If, however, you are

HOW WE CREATE OUR STATES AND BEHAVIORS

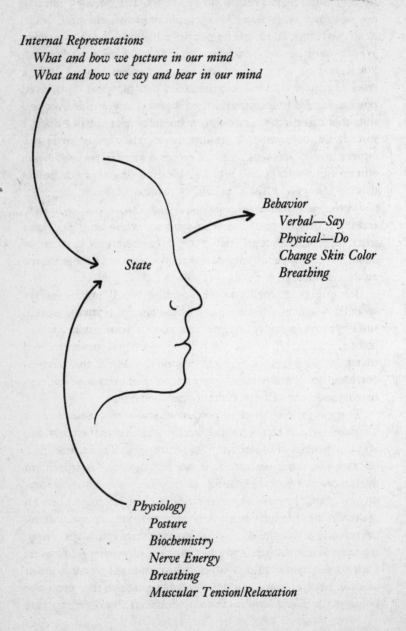

Internal Representations
   What and how we picture in our mind
   What and how we say and hear in our mind

State

Behavior
   Verbal—Say
   Physical—Do
   Change Skin Color
   Breathing

Physiology
   Posture
   Biochemistry
   Nerve Energy
   Breathing
   Muscular Tension/Relaxation

for various reasons in a physiological state of great muscular tension or extremely tired, or if you are experiencing pain or low blood sugar, you will tend to represent things to yourself in a way that may magnify your negative feelings. Think of it: When you're feeling physically vibrant and totally alive, don't you perceive the world differently than when you're tired or sick? The condition of your physiology literally changes the way you represent and thus experience the world. When you perceive things as being difficult or upsetting, doesn't your body follow suit and become tense? So these two factors, internal representations and physiology, are constantly interacting with each other to create the state we are in. And the state we are in determines the type of behavior we produce. Thus, to control and direct our behaviors, we must control and direct our states; and to control our states, we must control and consciously direct our internal representations and physiologies. Just imagine being able to be 100 percent in control of your state in any moment in time.

Before we can direct our experiences of life, we must first understand how we experience. As mammals, humans receive and represent information about their environment through specialized receptors and sense organs. There are five senses: gustation or taste, olfaction or smell, vision or sight, audition or hearing, and kinesthesis or feeling. We make most of the decisions that affect our behavior primarily using only three of these senses: the visual, auditory, and kinesthetic systems.

These specialized receptors transmit external stimuli to the brain. Through the process of generalization, distortion, and deletion, the brain then takes these electrical signals and filters them into an internal representation.

Thus, your internal representation, your experience of the event, isn't precisely what happened but rather a personalized internal re-presentation. The conscious mind of an individual can't use all the signals being sent to it. You would probably go stark raving mad if you consciously had to make sense of thousands of stimuli ranging from the pulse of blood through your left finger to the vibration of your ear. So the brain filters and stores the information it needs, or expects to need later, and allows the conscious mind of the individual to ignore the rest.

This filtering process explains the huge range in human perception. Two people can see the same traffic accident but give utterly different accounts of it. One may have paid more attention to what he saw, another to what he heard. They saw it from different angles. They both have different physiologies to begin the perception process with in the first place. One may have twenty-twenty vision while another may have poor physical resources in general. Perhaps one had been in an accident himself and had a vivid representation already stored. Whatever the case, the two will have very different representations of the same event. And they'll go on to store those perceptions and internal representations as new filters through which they will experience things in the future.

There's an important concept that's used in NLP—"The map is not the territory." As Alfred Korzybski noted in his *Science & Sanity*, "Important characteristics of maps should be noted. A map is not the territory it represents, but, if correct, it has a similar structure to the territory, which accounts for its usefulness." The meaning for individuals is that their internal representation is not a precise rendering of an event. It's just one interpretation as filtered through specific personal beliefs, attitudes, values, and something called metaprograms. Perhaps this is why Einstein once said, "Whoever undertakes to set himself up as a judge in the field of truth and knowledge is shipwrecked by the laughter of the gods."

Since we don't know how things really are, but only how we represent them to ourselves, why not represent them in a way that empowers ourselves and others, rather than creating limitations? The key to doing this successfully is memory management—the forming of representations that consistently create the most empowering states for an individual. In any experience, you have many things you can focus on. Even the most successful person can think of what isn't working and go into a state of depression or frustration or anger—or he can focus on all the things that work in his life. No matter how terrible a situation is, you can represent it in a way that empowers you.

Successful people are able to gain access to their most resourceful state on a consistent basis. Isn't that the difference between people who succeed and people who don't? Think back to W. Mitchell. It wasn't what happened to him that mattered. It was the way he represented what happened. Despite being terribly burned and then paralyzed, he found a way to put himself in a resourceful state. Remember, nothing is inherently bad or good. Value is how we represent it to ourselves. We can represent things in a way that puts us in a positive state, or we can do the opposite. Take a moment to think of a time when you have been in a powerful state.

That's what we do in the firewalk. If I asked you to put down this book and walk across a bed of hot coals, I doubt you would get up and do it. It's not something you believe you can do, and you may not have associated resourceful feelings and states with that task. So when I speak of it, you would probably not go into a state that would support you in taking that action.

The firewalk teaches people how to change their states and their behaviors in a way that empowers them to take action and produce new results in spite of fear or other limiting factors. People who walk on fire aren't different from the way they were when they came in the door thinking firewalking was impossible. But they've learned how to change their physiology, and they have learned to change their internal representations about what they can or cannot do, so that walking on fire is transformed from something terrifying to something they know they can do. They now can put themselves in a totally resourceful state, and from that state they can produce many actions and results that in the past they had labeled impossible.

The firewalk helps people form a new internal representation of possibility. If this thing that had seemed so impossible was only a limitation in their mind, then what other "impossibilities" are really very possible as well? It's one thing to talk about the power of state. It's another to experience it. That's what the firewalk does. It provides a new model for belief and for possibility, and it creates a new internal feeling or state association for people, one that makes their lives work better and enables them to do more than they ever thought "possible" before. It clearly demonstrates to them that their behavior is the result of the state they're in, for in one moment, by making a few changes in how they represent the experience to themselves, they can become so totally confident that they can take effective action. Obviously, there are many ways to do this. The firewalk is just one dramatic and fun way that people rarely forget.

The key to producing the results you desire, then, is to represent things to yourself in a way that puts you in such a resourceful state that you're empowered to take the types and qualities of actions that create your desired outcomes. Failure to do this will usually mean failure even to attempt that which you desire, or at best a feeble, halfhearted attempt that will produce like results. If I say to you, "Let's walk on fire," the stimuli I produce for you, in words and in body language, go to your brain, where you form a representation. If you picture people with rings through their noses taking part in some terrible rite, or people burning at the stake, you won't be in a very good state. If you form a representation of yourself burning, your state will be even worse.

However, if you were to picture people clapping and dancing and celebrating together, if you saw a scene of total joy and excitement, you would be in a very different state. If you saw a representation of yourself walking healthfully and joyously, and if you were to say, "Yes, I absolutely can do this," and move your body as if you were totally confident, then these neurological signals would put you in a state where you would most likely take action and walk.

The same is true for everything in life. If we represent to ourselves that things aren't going to work, they won't. If we form a representation that things will work, then we create the internal resources we need to produce the state that will support us in producing positive results. The difference between a Ted Turner, a Lee Iacocca, a W. Mitchell, and other people is that they represent the world as a place where they can produce any result they truly desire most. Obviously, even in the best state we do not always produce the results we desire, but when we create the appropriate state, we create the greatest possible chance for using all our resources effectively.

The next logical question is, If internal representations and physiology work together to create the state from which behaviors spring, what determines the specific kind of behavior we produce when we're in that state? One person in a state of love will hug you, while another will just tell you she loves you. The answer is, When we go into a state, our brain then accesses possible behavioral choices. The number of choices is determined by our models of the world. Some people, when they get angry, have one major model of how to respond, so they may lash out as they learned to do by watching their parents. Or maybe they just tried something, and it seemed to get them what they wanted, so that became a stored memory of how to respond in the future.

We all have world views, models that shape our perceptions of our environment. From people we know and from books and movies and television, we form an image of the world and what's possible in it. In W. Mitchell's case, one thing that shaped his life was the memory of a man he knew as a kid, a man who was paralyzed but made his life a triumph. So Mitchell had a model that helped him represent his situation as something that in no way prevented him from being utterly successful.

What we need to do in modeling people is to find out the specific beliefs that cause them to represent the world in a way that allows them to take effective action. We need to find out exactly how they represent to themselves their experience of the world. What do they do visually in their minds? What do they say? What do they feel? Once again, if we produce the same exact messages in our bodies, we can produce similar results. That's what modeling is all about.

One of the constants in life is that results are always being produced. If you don't consciously decide what results you want to produce and represent things accordingly, then some external trigger—a conversation, a TV show, whatever—may create states that create behaviors that do not support you. Life is like a river. It's moving, and you can be at the mercy of the river if you don't take deliberate, conscious action to steer yourself in a direction you have predetermined. If you don't plant the mental and physiological seeds of the results you want, weeds will grow automatically. If we don't consciously direct our own minds and states, our environment may produce undesirable haphazard states. The results can be disastrous. Thus it's critical that—on a daily basis—we stand guard at the door of our mind, that we know how we are consistently representing things to ourselves. We must daily weed our garden.

One of the most powerful examples of being in an undesirable state is the story of Karl Wallenda of the Flying Wallendas. He had performed aerial routines for years with great success, never considering the possibility of failure. Falling was just not part of his mental makeup. Then, a few years back, he suddenly began mentioning to his wife that he had started to see himself falling. For the first time, he had begun to consistently give himself a representation of falling. Three months after he first started talking about it, he fell to his death. Some people would say he had a premonition. Another viewpoint is that he gave his nervous system a consistent representation, a signal, that put him in a state that supported the behavior of falling—he created an outcome. He gave his brain a new path to follow, and eventually it did. This is why it is so critical to focus in life on what we want versus what we don't want.

If you continually focus on all bad things in life, all the things you don't want or all the possible problems, you put yourself in a state that supports those types of behaviors and results. For example, are you a jealous person? No, you are not. You may in the past have produced jealous states and the types of behaviors that spring from them. However, you are not your behavior. By making these kinds of generalizations about yourself, you create a belief that will govern and direct your actions in the future. Remember, your behavior is the result of your state, and your state is the result of your internal representations and your physiology, both of which you can change in a matter of moments. If in the past you have been jealous, that simply means that you have represented things in a way that created this state. You now can represent things in a new way and produce new states and accompanying behaviors. Remember, we always have a choice of how to represent things to ourselves. If you represent to yourself that your lover is cheating on you, pretty soon you will find yourself in a state of rage and anger. Bear in mind, you have no evidence this is true, but you experience it in your body as if it were, so that by the time the person you love comes home, you're suspicious or angry. In this state, how do you treat the person you love? Usually not very well. You may abuse or attack him or her verbally, or just feel bad inside and create some other retaliatory behavior later on.

Remember, the person you love may not have done anything, but the kind of behavior that you produce out of such a state will probably make him or her want to be with someone else! If you're jealous, you create that state. You can change your pictures of negativity to images of your loved one working hard to get home. This new picturing process will put you in a state where when your loved one does make it home, you will behave in a way that will make him or her feel wanted and will thus increase the desire to be with you. There may be times when a lover really is doing what you pictured, but why waste lots of emotion until you find out for sure? Most of the time it's highly unlikely that it's true yet you've created all kinds of pain for both of you, and for what?

> *"The ancestor of every action is a thought."*
> —*Ralph Waldo Emerson*

If we take control of our own communication with ourselves and produce visual, auditory, and kinesthetic signals of what we do want, outstanding positive results can be consistently produced, even in situations where the odds for success seem limited or nonexistent. The most powerful and effective managers, coaches, parents, and motivators are those who can represent the circumstances of life to themselves and to others in a way that signals success to the nervous system in spite of seemingly hopeless external stimuli. They keep themselves and others in a state of total resourcefulness so that they can continue to take action until they succeed. You've probably heard about Mel Fisher. He's the man who for seventeen years searched for an undersea buried treasure, finally discovering over 400 million dollars' worth of gold and silver bullion. In an article I read about him, one of the crew members was asked why he had stayed on so long. He replied that Mel just had the ability to get everyone excited. Every day Fisher told himself and the crew, Today's the day, and at the end of the day, Tomorrow's the day. But just saying it was not enough. He also said it congruently, in his tone of voice, the pictures in his mind, and his feelings. Every day he put himself in state so that he would continue to take action until he succeeded. He's a classic example of the Ultimate Success Formula. He knew his outcome, he took action, he learned from what worked—and if it didn't, he tried something else until he succeeded.

One of the best motivators I know is Dick Tomey, head football coach at the University of Hawaii. He truly understands how people's internal representations affect their performance. Once, in a game against the University of Wyoming, his team was being pushed all over the field. At halftime the score was 22–0, and his team didn't look as though it belonged on the same field with Wyoming.

You can imagine what kind of state Tomey's players were in when they trooped into the locker room at halftime. He took one look at their bowed heads and sunken expressions and realized that unless he changed their state, they didn't have a prayer in the second half. From the physiology they were in, they would be caught in a loop of feeling like failures, and out of that state they would not have the resources to succeed.

So Dick brought out a poster board of mimeographed articles that he had been collecting over the years. Each of the articles described teams that had been behind by a similar or larger margin and had rallied against these seemingly impossible odds to win the games. By having his players read the articles, he managed to instill a whole new belief, a belief that they really could come back—and that belief (internal representation) created a whole new neurophysiological state. What happened? Tomey's team came back in the second half and played the game of its life, holding Wyoming scoreless in the entire second half and winning 27–22. They did it because he was able to change their internal representations—their beliefs about what was possible.

Not long ago, I was on a plane with Ken Blanchard, the coauthor of *The One Minute Manager*. He'd just written an article for *Golf Digest*, entitled "The One Minute Golfer." He had hooked up with one of the top golf instructors in the United States, and a a result, he'd improved his score. He said he had learned all sorts of useful distinctions but was having trouble remembering them all. I told him he didn't have to grope for the distinctions. Instead, I asked him if he had ever hit a golf ball perfectly. He told me that of course he had. I asked if he had done this on many occasions. He said that of course he had. Then, I explained, that strategy or specific way of organizing his resources had clearly been recorded in his unconscious. All he needed to do was put himself back into the state where he made use of all that information he already had. I spent a few minutes teaching him how to get in that state and then how to retrigger it on cue. (You'll learn this technique in chapter 17.) What happened? He went out and played the best round he'd played in fifteen years, knocking fifteen strokes off his previous round. Why? Because there's no power like the power of a resourceful state. He didn't need to struggle to remember. He had access to everything he needed. He just had to learn to tap into it.

Remember, human behavior is the result of the state we're in. If you've ever produced a successful result, you can reproduce it by taking the same mental and physical actions you did then. Before the 1984 Olympics, I worked with Michael O'Brien, a swimmer who competed in the 1,500 freestyle. He had been practicing but felt as if he were not really putting his all into gearing up to succeed. He had developed a series of mental blocks that seemed to be limiting him. He had some fear about what success might mean, and thus his goal was the bronze or maybe the silver medal. He was not the favored swimmer to win the gold. The favorite, George DiCarlo, had beaten Michael on several occasions.

I spent an hour and a half with Michael and helped him to model his peak performance states—that is, to discover how he got himself into his most resourceful physiologies, what he had pictured, what he had said to himself, and what he had felt in the one match in which he'd beaten George DiCarlo. We began to break down what actions he took, mentally and physically, when he won matches. We linked the state he was in at these times to an automatic trigger, the sound of the starting gun firing. I found out that the one day he had beaten George DiCarlo he had been listening to Huey Lewis and the News right before starting. So the day of the Olympic finals he did everything the same, the same actions he had taken on the day he had won, even listening to Huey Lewis moments beforehand. And he beat George DiCarlo and won the gold medal by a full six seconds.

Did you ever see the film *The Killing Fields?* There was an amazing scene in it I'll never forget, involving a kid of perhaps twelve or thirteen living amid the awful chaos and destruction of war in Cambodia. At one point, in utter frustration, he picked up a machine gun and just blew someone away. It's a shocking scene. How in the world, you wonder, does a twelve-year-old kid reach the point where he can do something like that? Well, two things happen. The first is that he's so frustrated that he's gone into a state where he's tapped into terrible violent depths in his personality. The second is that he lives in a culture so permeated with war and destruction that picking up a machine gun seems an appropriate response. He's seen others do it, and he does it, too. It's a terrible negative scene. I try to concentrate on more positive states. But it's a dramatic summation of how we can do things in one state—good or bad—we'd never do in another. I'm emphasizing this over and over so it is embedded within you: *The kind of behavior people produce is the result of the* state they are in. *How they specifically respond out of that state is based on their models of the world*—that is, their stored neurological strategies. I could not have made Michael O'Brien win the Olympic gold medal. He had to work most of his life to store the strategies, the muscle responses, and so forth. But what I could do is find out how he could summon his most effective resources, his success strategies, on cue and in the key minutes he needed them.

Most people take very little conscious action to direct their states. They wake up depressed or they wake up energized. Good breaks lift them up, bad ones bring them down. One difference between people in any field is how effectively they marshal their resources. It's most clear in athletics. No one succeeds all the time, but there are certain athletes who have the ability to put themselves in a resourceful state almost on cue, who almost always rise to the occasion. Why did Reggie Jackson hit all those October home runs? How did Larry Bird or Jerry West develop the uncanny ability to hit all those shots at the buzzer? They were able to summon up their best when they needed it, when the pressure was the greatest.

State change is what most people are after. They want to be happy, joyous, ecstatic, centered. They want peace of mind, or they're trying to get away from states they do not like. They feel frustrated, angry, upset, bored. So what do most people do? Well, they turn on a TV set that gives them new representations they can internalize, so now they see something and laugh. They're no longer in their frustrated state. They go out and eat, or they smoke a cigarette or take a drug. On a more positive note, they might exercise. The only problem with most of these approaches is that the results are not lasting. When the TV show is over, they still have the same internal representations about their life. They remember them and feel bad again—after the excess food or drug has been consumed. There's now a price to pay for the temporary state change. By contrast, this book will show you how to directly change your internal representations and physiology, without the use of external devices, which many times create additional problems in the long run.

Why do people use drugs? Not because they like sticking needles in their arms, but because they like the experience and don't know any other way to get into that state. I've had kids who were hard-core drug users kick the habit after a firewalk, because they were given a more elegant model of how to achieve the same high. One kid who said he'd been on heroin for 6½ years finished the firewalk and told the group, "It's over. I never felt anything from a needle that even comes close to what I felt on the other side of those coals."

That didn't mean he had to walk on fire regularly. He just had to regularly access this new state. By doing something he thought was impossible, he developed a new model of what he could do to make himself feel good.

People who have achieved excellence are masters of tapping into the most resourceful parts of their brain. That's what separates them from the pack. The key thing to remember from this chapter is that your state has awesome power, and you can control it. You don't have to be at the mercy of whatever comes your way.

There is a factor that determines in advance how we will represent our experience of life—a factor that filters the way we represent the world to ourselves. A factor that determines the kinds of states we will consistently create in certain situations. If has been called the greatest power. Let us now investigate the magic power of . . .

CHAPTER IV

The Birth
of Excellence:
Belief

"Man is what he believes."

—*Anton Chekhov*

In his wonderful book, *Anatomy of an Illness*, Norman Cousins tells an instructive story about Pablo Casals, one of the great musicians of the twentieth century. It's a story of belief and renewal, and we can all learn from it.

Cousins describes meeting Casals shortly before the great cellist's ninetieth birthday. Cousins says that it was almost painful to watch the old man as he began his day. His frailty and arthritis were so debilitating that he needed help in dressing. His emphysema was evident in his labored breathing. He walked with a shuffle, stooped over, his head pitched forward. His hands were swollen, his fingers clenched. He looked like a very old, very tired man.

Even before eating, he made his way to the piano, one of several instruments on which Casals had become proficient. With great difficulty, he arranged himself on the piano bench.

It seemed a terrible effort for him to bring his clenched, swollen fingers to the keyboard.

And then something quite miraculous happened. Casals suddenly and completely transformed himself before Cousins's eyes. He went into a resourceful state, and as he did, his physiology changed to such a degree that he began to move and play, producing both in his body and on the piano results that should have been possible only for a healthy, strong, flexible pianist. As Cousins put it, "The fingers slowly unlocked and reached toward the keys like the buds of a plant toward the sunlight. His back straightened. He seemed to breathe more freely." The very thought of playing the piano totally changed his state and thus the effectiveness of his body. Casals began with Bach's *Wohltemperierte Klavier*, playing with great sensitivity and control. He then launched into a Brahms concerto, and his fingers seemed to race above the keyboard. "His entire body seemed fused with the music," Cousins wrote. "It was no longer stiff and shrunken but supple and graceful and completely freed of its arthritic coils." By the time he walked away from the piano, he seemed entirely different from the person who had sat down to play. He stood straighter and taller; he walked without a trace of a shuffle. He immediately walked to the breakfast table, ate heartily, and then went out for a stroll along the beach.

We usually think of beliefs in terms of creeds or doctrines, and that's what many beliefs are. But in the most basic sense, a belief is any guiding principle, dictum, faith, or passion that can provide meaning and direction in life. Unlimited stimuli are available to us. Beliefs are the prearranged, organized filters to our perceptions of the world. Beliefs are like commanders of the brain. When we congruently believe something is true, it is like delivering a command to our brain as to how to represent what is occurring. Casals believed in music and in art. That's what had given beauty and order and nobility to his life, and that's what could still provide daily miracles for him. Because he believed in the transcendent power of his art, he was empowered in a way that almost defies understanding. His beliefs transformed him daily from a tired old man to a vital genius. In the most profound sense, they kept him alive.

John Stuart Mill once wrote, "One person with a belief is equal to a force of ninety-nine who have only interests." That's precisely why beliefs open the door to excellence. Belief delivers a direct command to your nervous system. When you believe something is true, you literally go into the state of its being true. Handled effectively, beliefs can be the most powerful forces for creating good in your life. On the other hand, beliefs that limit your actions and thoughts can be as devastating as resourceful beliefs can be empowering. Religions throughout history have empowered millions of people and given them strength to do things they thought they couldn't. Beliefs help us tap the richest resources deep within us, creating and directing these resources in the support of our desired outcomes.

Beliefs are the compass and maps that guide us toward our goals and give us the surety to know we'll get there. Without beliefs or the ability to tap into them, people can be totally disempowered. They're like a motorboat without a motor or rudder. With powerful guiding beliefs, you have the power to take action and create the world you want to live in. Beliefs help you see what you want and energize you to get it.

In fact, there's no more powerful directing force in human behavior than belief. In essence, human history is the history of human belief. The people who have changed history— whether Christ, Mohammed, Copernicus, Columbus, Edison, or Einstein—have been the people who have changed our beliefs. To change our own behaviors, we have to start with our own beliefs. If we want to model excellence, we need to learn to model the beliefs of those who achieve excellence.

The more we learn about human behavior, the more we learn about the extraordinary power that beliefs have over our lives. In many ways, that power defies the logical models most of us have. But it's clear that even at the level of physiology, beliefs (congruent internal representations) control reality. A remarkable study was done on schizophrenia not long ago. One case involved a woman with a split personality. Normally, her blood sugar levels were completely normal. But when she believed she was a diabetic, her whole physiology changed to become that of a diabetic. Her belief had become her reality.

In a similar vein, there have been numerous studies in which a person in a hypnotic trance is touched with a piece of ice represented to him as a piece of hot metal. Invariably, a blister will develop at the point of contact. What counted was not reality but belief—the direct unquestioned communication to the nervous system. The brain simply does what it's told.

Most of us are aware of the placebo effect. People who are told a drug will have a certain effect will many times experience that effect even when given an empty pill with no active properties. Norman Cousins, who learned firsthand the power of belief in eliminating his own illness, concludes, "Drugs are not always necessary. Belief in recovery always is." One remarkable placebo study concerned a group of patients with bleeding ulcers. They were divided into two groups. People in the first were told they were being given a new drug that would absolutely produce relief. Those in the second were told they were being given an experimental drug, but that very little was known about its effects. Seventy percent of those in the first group experienced significant relief from their ulcers. Only 25 percent of the second group had a similar result. In both cases patients received a drug with no medicinal properties at all. The only difference was the belief system they adopted. Even more remarkable are the numerous studies of people who, given drugs known to have harmful effects, have experienced no ill effects at all when told they would experience a positive outcome.

Studies conducted by Dr. Andrew Weil have shown that the experiences of drug users correspond almost exactly to their expectations. He found he could lead a person given a dose of an amphetamine to feel sedated or a person given a barbiturate to feel stimulated. "The 'magic' of drugs resides within the mind of the user, not in the drugs," Weil concluded.

In all these instances, the one constant that most powerfully affected the results was belief, the consistent, congruent messages delivered to the brain and nervous system. For all its power, there is no abstruse magic involved in the process. Belief is nothing but a state, an internal representation that governs behavior. It can be an empowering belief in possibility—a belief that we will succeed in something or achieve something else. It can be a disempowering belief—a belief that we can't succeed, that our limitations are clear, intractable, and overwhelming. If you believe in success, you'll be empowered to achieve it. If you believe in failure, those messages will tend to lead you to experience that as well. Remember, whether you say you can do something or you say you can't, you're right. Both kinds of beliefs have great power. The question is what kinds of beliefs are best to have, and how do we develop them?

The birth of excellence begins with our awareness that our beliefs are a choice. We usually don't think of it that way, but belief can be a conscious choice. You can choose beliefs that limit you, or you can choose beliefs that support you. The trick is to choose the beliefs that are conducive to success and the results you want and to discard the ones that hold you back.

The biggest misconception people often have of belief is that it's a static, intellectual concept, an understanding that's divorced from action and results. Nothing could be further from the truth. Belief is the doorway to excellence precisely because there's nothing divorced or static about it.

It is our belief that determines how much of our potential we'll be able to tap. Beliefs can turn on or shut off the flow of ideas. Imagine the following situation. Someone says to you, "Please get me the salt," and as you walk into the next room, you say, "But I don't know where it is." After looking for a few minutes, you call out, "I can't find the salt." Then that someone walks up, takes the salt right off the shelf in front of you, and says, "Look, dummy, it's right here in front of you. If it was a snake, it would have bitten you." When you said, "I can't," you gave your brain a command not to see the salt. In psychology, we call it a schotoma. Remember, every human experience, everything you've ever said, seen, heard, felt, smelled, or tasted is stored in your brain. When you congruently say you cannot remember, you're right. When you congruently say you can, you give a command to your nervous system that opens up the pathways to the part of your brain that can potentially deliver the answers you need.

> *"They can because they think they can."*
>
> —*Virgil*

So again, what are beliefs? They are preformed, preorganized approaches to perception that filter our communication to ourselves in a consistent manner. Where do beliefs come from? Why do some people have beliefs that push them toward success while others have beliefs that only help them to fail? If we are going to try to model the beliefs that foster excellence, the first thing we need to find out is where those beliefs come from.

The first source is the environment. This is where the cycles of success breeding success and failure breeding failure are played out in the most relentless fashion. The real horror of ghetto life is not the daily frustrations and deprivations. People can overcome those. The real nightmare is the effect the environment has on beliefs and dreams. If all you see is failure, if all you see is despair, it's very hard for you to form the internal representations that will foster success. Remember, in the last chapter we said modeling is something we all do consistently. If you grow up in wealth and success, you can easily model wealth and success. If you grow up in poverty and despair, that's where your models of possibility come from. Albert Einstein said, "Few people are capable of expressing with equanimity opinions which differ from the prejudices of their social environment. Most people are even incapable of forming such opinions."

In one of my advanced courses in modeling, I do an exercise where we find people who live in the streets of big cities. We bring them in and model their belief systems and mental strategies. We offer them food and a great deal of love and simply ask if they would tell the group about their life, how they feel about where they are now, and why they believe things are that way. Then we contrast them with people who, in spite of great physical or emotional tragedies, have turned their lives around.

In a recent session, we had one man who was twenty-eight years old, strong, obviously intelligent, and physically fit, with a handsome face. Why was he so unhappy and living in the street while W. Mitchell—who, at least on the surface, had fewer resources available to change his life—was so happy? Mitchell grew up in an environment that provided examples, models of people who had overcome great odds to produce a life of joy. This created a belief in himself: "This was possible for me as well." By contrast, this other young man, call him John, grew up in an environment where no such models existed. His mother was a prostitute; his father went to jail for shooting someone. When he was eight years old, his father shot him up with heroin. That kind of environment certainly played a role in what he believed was possible—little more than survival— and how to achieve it: live in the streets, steal, attempt to erase your pain through drugs. He believed that people always take advantage of you if you don't watch them, that no one loves anyone, and so on. That night we worked with this man and changed his belief systems (as will be explained in chapter 6). As a result, he never went back to the streets. Since that night, he has been off drugs. He began working, and he now has new-found friends and is living in a new environment with new beliefs, producing new results.

Dr. Benjamin Bloom of the University of Chicago studied one hundred extraordinarily successful young athletes, musicians, and students. He was surprised to find that most of the young prodigies didn't begin by showing great flashes of brilliance.

Instead, most received careful attention, guidance, and support, and then they began to develop. The belief that they could be special came before any overt signs of great talent.

Environment may be the single most potent generator of belief, but it's not the only one. If it were, we'd live in a static world where the children of wealth would know only wealth, and the children of poverty would never rise above their origins.

Instead there are other experiences and ways of learning that
can also be incubators of belief.

Events, small or large, can help foster beliefs. There are certain
events in everyone's life that they will never forget. Where were
you the day John F. Kennedy was killed? If you are old enough
to remember it, I'm sure you know. For many people, it was a
day that forever altered their world-view. In the same way, most
of us have experiences we'll never forget, instances that had such
an impact on us that they were installed into our brains forever.
These are the kinds of experiences that form the beliefs that can
change our lives.

When I was thirteen, I was looking at what I wanted to do
with my life, and I decided that I would become a sportswriter/
caster. One day I read in the newspaper that Howard Cosell
would be autographing his new book at a local department store.
I thought, If I'm going to become a sportscaster, I need to start
interviewing professionals. Why not start at the top? I got out
of school, borrowed a tape recorder, and my mother drove me
to the department store. When I arrived, Mr. Cosell was getting
up to leave. I began to panic. He was also surrounded by reporters all fighting for his last comments. Somehow I ducked
under several reporters' arms and approached Mr. Cosell.
Speaking at lightning speed, I told him what I was doing and
asked for a brief taped interview. With dozens of reporters waiting, Howard Cosell gave me a personal interview. That experience changed my belief about what was possible, who in life
was approachable, and what the rewards were for asking for
what I wanted. Because of Mr. Cosell's encouragement, I went
on to write for a daily newspaper and developed a career in the
communications field.

A third way to foster belief is through knowledge. A direct experience is one form of knowledge. Another is gained through
reading, seeing movies, viewing the world as it is portrayed by
others. Knowledge is one of the great ways to break the shackles
of a limiting environment. No matter how grim your world is,
if you can read about the accomplishments of others, you can
create the beliefs that will allow you to succeed. Dr. Robert

Curvin, a black political scientist, wrote in *The New York Times* how the example of Jackie Robinson, the first black player in the major leagues, changed his life when he was a youngster. "I was enriched by my attachment to him; the level of my expectations was raised by his example."

A fourth way that results are created is through our past results. The surest way to create a belief that you can do something is to do it once, just once. If you succeed once, it's far easier to form the belief that you'll succeed again. I had to write the first draft of this book in less than a month in order to make the deadline. I wasn't sure if I could do it. But when I had to do a chapter in a single day, I found I could do it. And once I had succeeded with one, I knew I could do it again. I was able to form the belief that allowed me to finish this book on time.

Journalists learn the same thing about writing on deadline. There are few things in life as daunting as having to knock out a full story in an hour or less under daily deadline pressure. Most beginning journalists dread it more than any part of their job. But what they find is that if they succeed once or twice, they know they'll succeed in the future. They don't get smarter or quicker as they get older, but once empowered with the belief that they can knock out a story in whatever time is available, they find they can always do it. The same is true for comedians, businessmen, or people in just about any other walk of life. Believing it can be done becomes a self-fulfilling prophecy.

The fifth way to establish beliefs is through the creating in your mind of the experience you desire in the future as if it were here now. Just as past experiences can change your internal representations and thus what you believe is possible, so can your imagined experience of how you want things to be in the future. I call this *experiencing results in advance.* When the results you have around you are not supporting you in being in a powerful and effective state, you can simply create the world the way you want it to be and step into that experience, thereby changing your states, your beliefs, and your actions. After all, if you're a salesman, is it easier to make $10,000 or $100,000? The truth is it's easier to make $100,000. Let me tell you why. If your goal is to make $10,000, what you're really trying to do is make enough to pay the bills. If that's what your goal is, if that's what you represent to yourself about why you're working so hard, do you think that you will be in an excited, empowered, resourceful state as you work? Are you seething with excitement, thinking, Boy, oh, boy. I've got to get to work so I can make enough to pay my lousy bills? I don't know about you, but that doesn't get my motor running.

But selling is selling. You have to make the same calls, meet the same people, deliver the same products, no matter what you're hoping to achieve. So it's a lot more exciting, a lot more enticing, to go out with the goal of making $100,000 than $10,000. And that state of excitement is much more likely to activate your taking the kinds of consistent actions that will tap your higher potential than just hoping to go out and make a living.

Obviously, money is not the only way to motivate yourself. Whatever your goal may be, if you create in your mind a clear image of the result you want and represent it to yourself as if you've already achieved it, then you will go into the kind of states that will support you in creating the results you desire.

All these things are ways to mobilize belief. Most of us form our beliefs haphazardly. We soak up things—good and bad—from the world around us. But one of the key ideas of this book is that you're not just a leaf in the wind. You can control your beliefs. You can control the ways you model others. You can consciously direct your life. You can change. If there's a key word in this book, that's it—change. Let me ask you the most basic question I can. What are some of the beliefs you have about who you are and what you're capable of? Please take a moment and jot down five key beliefs that have limited you in the past.

1.
2.
3.

4.

5.

Now, make a list of at least five positive beliefs that can now serve to support you in achieving your highest goals.

1.

2.

3.

4.

5.

One of the premises we hold is that every statement you make is dated and is relative to the time that it's made. It's not a statement of universal truth. It's true only for a certain person at a certain time. It's subject to change. If you have negative belief systems, you should know by now what sort of harmful effects they have. But it's essential to realize that belief systems are no more immutable than the length of your hair, your affection for a particular kind of music, the quality of your relationship with a particular person. If you're driving a Honda and decide you would be happier with a Chrysler or Cadillac or Mercedes, it's in your power to change.

Your internal representations and beliefs work in much the same way. If you don't like them, you can change them. We all have a hierarchy, a ladder of beliefs. We have core beliefs, things that are so fundamental we would die for them. Those are things like our ideas about patriotism and family and love. But most of our lives are governed by beliefs about possibility or success or happiness that we've picked up unconsciously over the years. The key is to take those beliefs and make sure that they work for you, that they're effective and empowering.

We've talked about the importance of modeling. Modeling excellence begins with modeling belief. Some things take time to model, but if you can read and think and hear, you can model the beliefs of the most successful people on the planet. When J. Paul Getty started in life, he made up his mind to find out about the beliefs of the most successful people, and then he went out and modeled them. You can consciously model his beliefs and those of most great leaders by reading their autobiographies. Out libraries are teeming with answers to questions about how to produce practically any result you want.

Where do your personal beliefs come from? Do they come from the average man on the street? Do they come from TV and radio? Do they come from whoever talks the longest and the loudest? If you want to succeed, it would be wise for you to choose your beliefs carefully, rather than walking around like a piece of flypaper, picking up whichever belief sticks. An important thing to realize is that the potentials we tap, the results we get, are all part of a dynamic process that begins with belief. I like to think of the process in terms of the following diagram.

Let's say a person has a belief that he's ineffective at something. Let's say he's told himself that he's a bad student. If he has expectations of failure, how much of his potential is he going to tap? Not very much. He's already told himself that he doesn't know. He's already signaled his brain to expect failure. Having begun with those sorts of expectations, what sorts of actions will he probably take? Will they be confident, energized, congruent, and assertive? Will they reflect his real potential? Not likely. If you're convinced you're going to fail, why make the effort to try hard? So you've started with a belief system that stresses what you can't do, a system that subsequently signals your nervous system to respond in a certain way. You've tapped a limited amount of your potential. You've taken halfhearted, tentative actions. What sort of results come out of all this? Chances are they'll be pretty dismal. What will these dismal results do to your beliefs about subsequent endeavors? Chances are they'll reinforce the negative beliefs that started the whole chain. If this is a formula for success, the L.A. Raiders are a bunch of ballerinas.

What we have here is a classic downward spiral. Failure breeds failure. People who are unhappy and who live "broken lives" have often been without the results they desire for so long that they no longer believe they can produce the results that

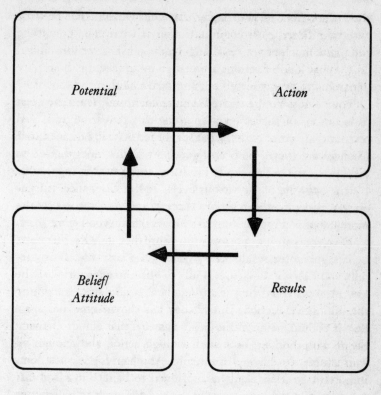

they want. They do little or nothing to tap their potential and begin to try to find out how they can get their life to where they're doing as little as possible. From such actions, what results do they achieve? Of course, they are miserable results that break down their beliefs even more, if that's possible.

> *"Good timber does not grow with ease; the stronger the wind, the stronger the trees."*
>
> —*J. Willard Marriott*

Let's look at this from another direction. Let's say you begin with great expectations. More than expectations—you believe

with every fiber of your being that you will succeed. Starting
with that direct, clear communication of what you know to be
true, how much of your potential will you use? Probably a good
deal. What kind of actions are you going to take this time? Are
you going to drag yourself out and take a halfhearted shot at it?
Of course not! You're excited, you're energized, you have great
expectations of success, you're going to go great guns. If you
put out that sort of effort, what sort of results will be generated?
Chances are they'll be pretty good. And what does that do to
your belief in your ability to produce great results in the future?
It's the opposite of the vicious cycle. In this case, success feeds
on success and generates more success, and each success creates
more belief and momentum to succeed on an even higher scale.

Do resourceful people screw up? Sure they do. Do affirmative
beliefs guarantee results every time? Of course not. If anyone
tells you he's got a magic formula to guarantee perpetual, flaw-
less success, you'd best grab your wallet and start walking in
the opposite direction. But history has shown time and again
that if people maintain the belief systems that empower them,
they'll keep coming back with enough action and enough resourcefulness to succeed eventually. Abraham Lincoln lost some
important elections, but he continued to believe in his ability
to succeed in the long term. He allowed himself to be empowered by success, and he refused to be cowed by his failures. His
belief system was geared toward excellence, and he finally
achieved it. When he did, he changed the history of this country.

Sometimes it's not necessary to have a tremendous belief or
attitude about something in order to succeed. Sometimes people
produce outstanding results simply because they don't know
something is difficult or impossible. Sometimes just not having
a limiting belief is enough. For example, there is a story of a
young man who fell asleep during math class. He woke up as
the bell rang, looked up at the blackboard, and copied the two
problems that were there. He assumed they were the homework
for the night. He went home and labored all day and all night.
He couldn't figure out either one, but he kept trying for the rest
of the week. Finally, he got the answer to one and brought it

to class. The teacher was absolutely stunned. It turned out the problem he'd solved was supposedly unsolvable. If the student had known that, he probably wouldn't have solved it. But since he didn't tell himself it couldn't be done—in fact, quite the opposite: he'd thought he had to solve it, and he was able to find a way to do it.

Another way to change your belief is to have an experience that disproves it. That's another reason why we do the firewalk. I don't care if people can walk on fire, but I do care that people can do something they thought was impossible. If you can do one thing you thought was utterly impossible, it causes you to rethink your beliefs.

Life is both subtler and more complex than some of us like to believe. So if you haven't done so already, review your beliefs and decide which ones you might change now and what you would change those beliefs to.

The next question is, Is the figure below concave or convex?

It's a silly question. The answer is, It depends on how you're looking at it.

Your reality is the reality you create. If you have positive

internal representations or beliefs, it's because that's what you have created. If you have negative ones, you've created them, too. There are any number of beliefs that foster excellence, but I've picked up seven that strike me as particularly important. I call them . . .

CHAPTER V

The Seven Lies
of Success

"The mind is its own place, and in it self Can make a
Heav'n of Hell, a Hell of Heav'n."

—John Molton

The world we live in is the world we choose to live in, whether consciously or unconsciously. If we choose bliss, that's what we get. If we choose misery, we get that, too. As we learned in the last chapter, belief is the foundation of excellence. Our beliefs are specific, consistent organizational approaches to perception. They're the fundamental choices we make about how to perceive our lives and thus how to live them. They're how we turn on or turn off our brain. So the first step toward excellence is to find the beliefs that guide us toward the outcomes we want.

The path to success consists of knowing your outcome, taking action, knowing what results you're getting, and having the flexibility to change until you're successful. The same is true of beliefs. You have to find the beliefs that support your outcome—the beliefs that get you where you want to go. If your beliefs don't do that, you have to throw them out and try something new.

People are sometimes put off when I talk about the "lies" of success. Who wants to live by lies? But all I mean is that we don't know how the world really is. We don't know if the line is concave or convex. We don't know if our beliefs are true or false. What we can know, though, is if they work—if they support us, if they make our lives richer, if they make us better people, if they help us and help others.

The word "lies" is used in this chapter as a consistent reminder that we do not know for certain exactly how things are. Once we know the line is concave, for example, we are no longer free to see it as convex. The word "lie" does not mean "to be deceitful or dishonest" but, rather, is a useful way to remind us that no matter how much we believe in a concept, we should be open to other possibilities and continuous learning. I suggest you look at these seven beliefs and decide whether they're useful for you. I've found them time and again in successful people I have modeled. To model excellence, we have to start with the belief systems of excellence. I've found that these seven beliefs have empowered people to use more, do more, take greater action, and produce greater results. I'm not saying they're the only useful beliefs of success. They are a start. They've worked for others, and I'd like you to see if they can work for you.

Belief #1: Everything happens for a reason and a purpose, and it serves us. Remember the story of W. Mitchell? What was the central belief that helped him overcome adversity? He decided to take what happened to him and make it work for him in whatever way he could. In the same way, all successful people have the uncanny ability to focus on what is possible in a situation, what positive results could come from it. No matter how much negative feedback they get from their environment, they think in terms of possibilities. They think that everything happens for a reason, and it serves them. They believe that every adversity contains the seed of an equivalent or greater benefit.

I can guarantee you that people who produce outstanding

results think this way. Think about it in your own life. There are an infinite number of ways to react to any situation. Let's say your business fails to get a contract you had counted on, one that you were certain you deserved. Some of us would be hurt and frustrated. We might sit home and mope or go out and get drunk. Some of us would be mad. We might blame the company that awarded the contract, figuring they were a bunch of ignorant individuals. Or we might blame our own people for ruining a sure thing.

All of that might allow us to let off some steam, but it doesn't help us. It doesn't bring us any closer to our desired outcome. It takes a lot of discipline to be able to retrace your steps, learn painful lessons, mend fences, and take a good look at new possibilities. But that's the only way to get a positive outcome from what seems like a negative result.

Let me give you a good example of possibility. Marilyn Hamilton, a former teacher and beauty queen, is a successful businesswoman in Fresno, California. She's also the survivor of a terrible accident. When she was twenty-nine, she fell down a rocky cliff in a hang-gliding accident that left her in a wheelchair, paralyzed below the waist.

Marilyn Hamilton certainly could have focused on a lot of things she could no longer do. Instead, she focused on the possibilities that were open to her. She managed to see the opportunity in tragedy. From the start she was frustrated with her wheelchairs. She found them too confining, too restrictive. Now you or I probably wouldn't have any idea how to judge the effectiveness of a wheelchair. But Marilyn Hamilton could. She figured she was uniquely equipped to design a better one. So she got together with two friends who built hang gliders and started working on a prototype for a better wheelchair.

The three went on to form a company called Motion Designs. It is now a multimillion-dollar success story that revolutionized the wheelchair industry and went on to become California's Small Business of the Year for 1984. They hired their first employee in 1981 and now have eighty employees and more than eight hundred dealers.

I don't know if Marilyn Hamilton ever consciously sat down and tried to figure out her beliefs, but she operated from a dynamic sense of possibility, a sense of what she could do. Virtually all great successes work from the same frame.

Take a moment to think again about your beliefs. Do you generally expect things to work out well or to work out poorly? Do you expect your best efforts to be successful, or do you expect them to be thwarted? Do you see the potential in a situation, or do you see the roadblocks? Many people tend to focus on the negative more than the positive. The first step toward changing that is to recognize it. Belief in limits creates limited people. The key is to let go of those limitations and operate from a higher set of resources. The leaders in our culture are the people who see the possibilities, who can go into a desert and see a garden. Impossible? What happened in Israel? If you have a strong belief in possibility, it's likely you'll achieve it.

Belief #2: There is no such thing as failure. There are only results. This is almost a corollary belief to number one, and it's equally important on its own. Most people in our culture have been programmed to fear this thing called failure. Yet, all of us can think of times when we wanted one thing and got another. We've all flunked a test, suffered through a frustrating romance that didn't work out, put together a business plan only to see everything go awry. I've used the words "outcome" and "results" throughout this book because that's what successful people see. They don't see failure. They don't believe in it. It doesn't compute.

People always succeed in getting some sort of results. The super successes of our culture aren't people who do not fail, but simply people who know that if they try something and it doesn't give them what they want, they've had a learning experience. They use what they've learned and simply try something else. They take some new actions and produce some new results.

Think about it. What is the one asset, the one benefit you have today over yesterday? The answer, of course, is experience. People who fear failure make internal representations of what might not work in advance. This is what keeps them from taking the very action that could ensure the accomplishment of their desires. Are you afraid of failure? Well, how do you feel about learning? You can learn from every human experience and can thereby always succeed in anything you do.

Mark Twain once said, "There is no sadder sight than a young pessimist." He's right. People who believe in failure are almost guaranteed a mediocre existence. Failure is something that is just not perceived by people who achieve greatness. They don't dwell on it. They don't attach negative emotions to something that doesn't work.

Let me share someone's life history with you. This was a man who

Failed in business at age 21.
Was defeated in a legislative race at age 22.
Failed again in business at age 24.
Overcame the death of his sweetheart at age 26.
Had a nervous breakdown at age 27.
Lost a congressional race at age 34.
Lost a congressional race at age 36.
Lost a senatorial race at age 45.
Failed in an effort to become vice-president at age 47.
Lost a senatorial race at age 49.
Was elected president of the United States at age 52.

The man's name was Abraham Lincoln. Could he have become president if he had seen these events of his life as failures? It's not likely. There's a famous story about Thomas Edison. After he'd tried 9,999 times to perfect the light bulb and hadn't succeeded, someone asked him, "Are you going to have ten thousand failures?" He answered, "I didn't fail. I just discovered another way not to invent the electric light bulb." He had discovered how another set of actions had produced a different result.

> *"Our doubts are traitors, And make us lose the good we oft might win, By fearing to attempt."*
>
> —*William Shakespeare*

Winners, leaders, masters—people with personal power—all understand that if you try something and do not get the outcome you want, it's simply feedback. You use that information to make finer distinctions about what you need to do to produce the results you desire. Buckminster Fuller once wrote, "Whatever humans have learned had to be learned as a consequence only of trial and error experience. Humans have learned only through mistakes." Sometimes we learn from our mistakes, sometimes from the mistakes of others. Take a minute to reflect on the five greatest so-called "failures" in your life. What did you learn from those experiences? Chances are they were some of the most valuable lessons you've learned in your life.

Fuller uses the metaphor of a ship's rudder. He says when the rudder of a ship is angled to one side or another, the ship tends to keep rotating beyond the helmsman's intention. He has to correct the rotation, moving it back toward the original direction in a never-ending process of action and reaction, adjustment and correction. Picture that in your mind—a helmsman on a quiet sea, gently guiding his boat toward its destination by coping with thousands of inevitable deviations from its course. It's a lovely image, and it's a wonderful model for the process of living successfully. But most of us don't think that way. Every error, every mistake, tends to take on emotional baggage. It's a failure. It reflects badly on us.

For example, many people get down on themselves because they're overweight. Their attitude about being overweight doesn't change anything. Instead, they could embrace the fact that they've been successful in producing a result called excess fat and that now they're going to produce a new result called being thin. They would produce this new result by producing new actions.

If you're not sure what actions to take to produce this result, take special note of chapter 10, or model someone who has produced the result called being thin. Find out what specific action that person produces mentally and physically to consistently remain thin. Produce the same actions, and you will produce the same results. As long as you regard your excess weight as a failure, you'll be immobilized. However, the minute you change it to a result you produced, therefore one you can change now, then your success is assured.

Belief in failure is a way of poisoning the mind. When we store negative emotions, we affect our physiology, our thinking process, and our state. One of the greatest limitations for most people is their fear of failure. Dr. Robert Schuller, who teaches the concept of possibility thinking, asks a great question: "What would you attempt to do if you knew you could not fail?" Think about it. How would you answer that? If you really believed you could not fail, you might take a whole new set of actions and produce powerful new desirable results. Wouldn't you be better off trying them? Isn't that the only way to grow? So I suggest you start realizing right now that there's no such thing as failure. There are only results. You always produce a result. If it's not the one you desire, you can just change your actions and you'll produce new results. Cross out the word "failure," circle the word "outcome" in this book, and commit yourself to learning from every experience.

Belief #3: Whatever happens, take responsibility. Another attribute great leaders and achievers have in common is that they operate from the belief that they create their world. The phrase you'll hear time and again is, "I am responsible. I'll take care of it."

It's not coincidental you hear the same viewpoint over and over. Achievers tend to believe that no matter what happens, whether it's good or bad, they created it. If they didn't cause it by their physical actions, maybe they did by the level and tenor of their thoughts. Now, I don't know if this is true. No scientist can prove that our thoughts create our reality. But it's a useful lie. It's an empowering belief. That's why I choose to believe in it. I believe that we generate our experiences in life—either by behavior or by thought—and that we can learn from all of them.

If you don't believe that you're creating your world, whether it be your successes or your failures, then you're at the mercy of circumstances. Things just happen to you. You're an object, not a subject. Let me tell you, if I had that belief, I'd check out now and look for another culture, another world, another planet. Why be here if you're just the product of random outside forces?

Taking responsibility is in my opinion one of the best measures of a person's power and maturity. It's also an example of beliefs supporting other beliefs, of the synergistic capabilities of a coherent system of beliefs. If you don't believe in failure, if you know you'll achieve your outcome, you have nothing to lose and everything to gain by taking responsibility. If you're in control, you'll succeed.

John F. Kennedy had this belief system. Dan Rather once said Kennedy became a true leader during the Bay of Pigs incident, when he stood before the American people and said that the Bay of Pigs was an atrocity that should never have happened—and then he took full responsibility for it. When he did that, he was transformed from an able young politician to a real leader. Kennedy did what every great leader must. Those who take responsibility are in power. Those who avoid it are disempowered.

The same principle of responsibility holds true on a personal level as well. Most of us have had the experience of trying to express a positive emotion to someone else. We try to tell someone we love them, or we understand a problem they're having. And instead of getting that positive message, they pick up a negative one instead. They get upset or hostile. Often our tendency is to get upset right back, to blame them, to hold them responsible for whatever ill will is generated. That's the easy way out, but not always the wisest. The fact is your communication may have been the trigger. You can still produce the communication result you desire if you remember your outcome—that is, the behavior you want to create. It's up to you to change your behavior, your tone of voice, your facial expressions, and so on. We say that the meaning of communication is the response you get. By changing your actions, you can change your communication. By retaining responsibility, you retain the power to change the result you produce.

Belief #4: It's not necessary to understand everything to be able to use everything. Many successful people live by another useful belief. They don't believe they have to know everything about something in order to use it. They know how to use what's essential without feeling a need to get bogged down in every detail of it. If you study people who are in power, you'll find they have a working knowledge about a lot of things but often have little mastery of each and *every* detail of their enterprise.

We talked in the first chapter about how modeling can save people one of our irreplaceable resources—time. By observing successful people to discover what specific actions they create to produce results, we are able to duplicate their actions—and thus their results—in much less time. Time is one of the things no one can create for you. But achievers invariably manage to be time misers. They exact the essence from a situation, take out what they need, and don't dwell on the rest. Of course, if they're intrigued by something, if they want to understand how a motor works or how a product is manufactured, they take the extra time to learn. But they're always aware of how much they need. They always know what's essential and what's not.

I'll bet that if I asked you to explain how electricity works, you would come up with something between a blank and a sketchy answer. But you're still happy to flick the switch and turn on the lights. I doubt that many of you are sitting at home right now reading this book by candlelight. Successful people are especially good at making distinctions between what is necessary for them to understand and what is not. In order to effectively use the information in this book, in order to effectively use all that you are in this life, you should discover that there's a balance between use and knowledge. You can spend all your time studying the roots, or you can learn to pick the fruit. Successful people aren't necessarily the ones with the most information, the most knowledge. There were probably plenty of scientists and engineers at Stanford and Cal Tech who knew more about computer circuitry than Steve Jobs or Steve Wozniak, but they were some of the most effective at using what they had. They were the ones who got results.

Belief #5: People are your greatest resource. Individuals of excellence—that is, people who produce outstanding results—almost universally have a tremendous sense of respect and appreciation for people. They have a sense of team, a sense of common purpose and unity. If there's any insight at the heart of the new generation of business books like *Innovation and Entrepreneurship*, *In Search of Excellence*, or *The One Minute Manager*, it's that there's no long-lasting success without rapport among people, that the way to succeed is to form a successful team that's working together. We've all seen reports on Japanese factories, where workers and management eat in the same cafeteria and where both have input into evaluating performance. Their success reflects the wonders that can be achieved when we respect people rather than trying to manipulate them.

When Thomas J. Peters and Robert H. Waterman, Jr., authors of *In Search of Excellence*, distilled the factors that made companies great, one of the key things they found was a passionate attention to people. "There was hardly a more pervasive theme in excellent companies than respect for the individual," they wrote. The companies that succeeded were the ones that treated people with respect and with dignity, the companies that viewed their employees as partners, not as tools. They note that in one study, eighteen out of twenty Hewlett-Packard executives interviewed said the company's success depended on HP's people-oriented philosophy. HP isn't a retailer dealing with the public or a service company dependent on goodwill. It's dealing at the most complex frontiers of modern technology. But even there, it's clear that dealing effectively with people is seen as the preeminent challenge.

Like many of the beliefs listed here, this one is easier to glibly mouth than to actually adopt. It's easy to pay lip service to the idea of treating people—whether in your family or your business—with respect. It's not always so easy to do it.

As you read this book, keep in mind an image of a helmsman readjusting his ship's path as it moves toward its destination. It's the same with life. We have to constantly remain alert, readjust our behavior, and recalibrate our actions to make sure we're going where we want to go. To say you treat people with respect and to do it are not the same thing. Those who succeed are the most effective in saying to others, "How can we do this better?" "How can we fix this?" "How can we produce greater results?" They know that one man alone, no matter how brilliant, will find it very difficult to match the collaborative talents of an effective team.

Belief #6: Work is play. Do you know any person who has achieved massive success by doing what he hates? I don't. One of the keys to success is making a successful marriage between what you do and what you love. Pablo Picasso once said, "When I work, I relax; doing nothing or entertaining visitors makes me tired."

Maybe we don't paint as well as Picasso, but we can all do our best to find work that invigorates and excites us. And we can bring to whatever we do at work many of the aspects of what we do at play. Mark Twain said, "The secret of success is making your vocation your vacation." That's what successful people seem to do.

We hear a lot about workaholics these days. And there are some people whose work has become something of an unhealthy obsession. They don't seem to get any pleasure out of their work, but they reach the point where they can't do anything else.

Researchers are finding surprising things about some workaholics. There are some people who seem maniacally focused on work because they love it. It challenges them, it excites them, it makes their life richer. These people tend to look at work the way most of us look at play. They see it as a way to stretch themselves, to learn new things, to explore new avenues.

Are some jobs more conducive to this than others? Of course

they are. The key is to work your way toward those jobs. One of those upward spirals is at work here. If you can find creative ways to do your job, it will help you to move toward work that's even better. If you decide work is mere drudgery, just a way to brink home a paycheck, chances are it will never be anything more.

We talked earlier about the synergistic nature of a coherent belief system, the way positive beliefs support other positive beliefs. This is another example. I don't think there are any dead-end jobs. There are only people who have lost the sense of possibility, people who have decided not to take responsibility, people who have decided to believe in failure. I'm not suggesting you have to become a workaholic. I'm not suggesting you should choose to orient your world around your work. But I am suggesting that you will enrich your world and enrich your work if you bring to it the same curiosity and vitality you bring to your play.

Belief #7: There's no abiding success without commitment. Individuals who succeed have a belief in the power of commitment. If there's a single belief that seems almost inseparable from success, it's that there's no great success without great commitment. If you look at successful people in any field, you'll find they're not necessarily the best and the brightest, the fastest and the strongest. You'll find they're the ones with the most commitment. The great Russian ballerina Anna Pavlova once said, "To follow, without halt, one aim: there's the secret of success." It's just another way of stating our Ultimate Success Formula—know your outcome, model what works, take action, develop the sensory acuity to know what you're getting, and keep refining it until you get what you want.

We see this in any field, even those where natural ability would seem to have the strongest hold. Take sports. What makes Larry Bird one of the best players in basketball? A lot of people are still wondering. He's slow. He can't jump. In a world of graceful gazelles, he sometimes looks like he's playing in slow motion. But when you come right down to it, Larry Bird succeeds because he has a massive commitment to success. He practices harder, he has more mental toughness, he plays harder, he wants it more. He gets more out of his skills than almost anyone else. Pete Rose has made his way into the record books the same way, by consistently using his commitment to excellence as a force driving him to put everything he's got into everything he does. Tom Watson, the great golfer, was nothing special at Stanford. He was just another kid on the team. But his coach still marvels about Watson, saying, "I never saw anyone practice more." The difference in pure physical skills between athletes seldom tells you anything. It's the quality of commitment that separates good from great.

Commitment is an important component of success in any field. Before he hit the big time, Dan Rather was a legend as the hardest-working television newsman in Houston. They still talk about the time he did a spot hanging on to a tree as a hurricane roared toward the Texas coast. I heard someone talking about Michael Jackson the other day, saying that Jackson was an overnight wonder. Overnight wonder? Does Michael Jackson have great talent? Sure he does. And he's been working at it since he was five years old. He's been entertaining since then, practicing his singing, perfecting his dancing, writing his songs. Sure he had some natural talent. He was also brought up in an environment that supported him; he developed belief systems that nurtured him; he had many successful models available to him; he had a family that guided him. Yet the bottom line was that he was willing to pay the price. I like to use the term W.I.T.—Whatever It Takes. Successful people are willing to do whatever it takes to succeed.* That, as much as anything else, is what separates them from the pack.

Are there other beliefs that foster excellence? Sure there are. When you think of them, so much the better. Throughout this book, you should be aware of additional distinctions or insights that you can add. Remember, *success leaves clues*. Study those

---

* It goes without saying you do whatever it takes to succeed without harming another person.

who succeed. Find out about the key beliefs they hold that enhance their ability to take effective action consistently and produce outstanding results. These seven beliefs have done wonders for others before you, and I believe they can do wonders for you if you can commit yourself to them consistently.

I can almost hear some of you thinking, Well, that's a big if. What if you have beliefs that don't support you? What if your beliefs are negative, not positive? How do we change beliefs? You've already taken the first step, awareness. You know what you want. The second step is action, learning to control your internal representations and beliefs, learning how to run your brain.

So far we've begun to put together the pieces that I believe lead to excellence. We started with the idea that information is the commodity of kings, that master communicators are those who know what they want and who take effective actions, varying their behavior until they achieve their outcomes. In chapter 2, we learned that the pathway to excellence is through modeling. If you can find people who have created massive success, you can model the specific actions they consistently take that produce results—their beliefs, mental syntax, and physiology— so you can produce similar results in a shorter learning time. In chapter 3, we talked about the power of state. We've seen how powerful, resourceful, and effective behavior neurophysiological state. In chapter 4, we learned about the nature of belief, how empowering beliefs unlock the door to excellence. In this chapter, we've explored the seven beliefs that are the cornerstone of excellence.

Now I'm going to share with you powerful techniques that can help you to make use of what you've learned. It's time to learn . . .

CHAPTER VI

Mastering Your Mind: How to Run Your Brain

"Don't find fault, find a remedy."

—Henry Ford

This chapter is about finding remedies. We've talked so far about what you should change if you wish to change your life, what kind of states empower you, and what kind of states leave you limp. In this section you're going to learn how to change your states so you can produce whatever you want, when you want it. People don't usually lack resources; they lack control over their resources. This chapter will teach you how to be in control, how to get more juice out of life, how to change your states, your actions, and thus the results you produce in your body—all in a matter of moments.

The model of change that I teach and that NLP teaches is very different from the one used in many schools of therapy. The therapeutic canon, a pastiche of assorted schools, is so familiar that it's become something of a cultural totem. A large number of therapists believe that in order to change, you have to go back to deep-seated negative experiences and experience them again. The idea is that people have negative experiences in life that build up inside them like a liquid, until finally there's no more room and they burst or overflow. The only way to get in touch with this process, the therapists say, is to reexperience the events and pain all over again and then to try to let it go once and for all.

Everything in my experience tells me that's one of the least effective ways to help people with their problems. In the first place, when you ask people to go back and reexperience some terrible trauma, you're putting them into the most painful, least resourceful state they can be in. If you put someone in an unresourceful state, their chances of producing new resourceful behaviors and results are greatly diminished. In fact, this approach may even reinforce the painful or unresourceful pattern. By continually accessing neurological states of limitation and pain, it becomes much easier to trigger these states in the future. The more you relive an experience, the more likely you are to use it again. Maybe that's why so many traditional therapies take so long to produce results.

I have some good friends who are therapists. They sincerely care about their patients. They believe that what they're doing is making a difference. It is. Traditional therapy does produce results. However, the question is, could these results be produced with less pain for the patient, and in a shorter period of time? The answer is yes—if we model the actions of the most effective therapists in the world, which is exactly what Bandler and Grinder did. In fact, by mastering a simple understanding of how your brain works, you can become your own therapist, your own personal consultant. You go beyond therapy to being able to change any feeling, emotion, or behavior for yourself in a matter of moments.

Producing more effective results begins, I believe, with creating a new model for the process of change. If you believe your problems store up inside you until they overflow, that's exactly what you'll experience. Instead of all the pain building up like some lethal fluid, I see our neurological activity as more like a jukebox. What really happens is that human beings keep having experiences that are being recorded. We store them in the brain like records in a jukebox. As with the records in a jukebox, our recordings can be played back at any time if the right stimulus in our environment is triggered, if the right button is pushed.

So we can choose to remember experiences or push buttons that play "songs" of happiness and joy, or we can push buttons that create pain. If your therapeutic plan involves hitting the button that creates pain time and again, you may be reinforcing the very negative state you wish to change.

I think you need to do something completely different. Perhaps you could simply reprogram your jukebox so it plays a completely different song. You hit the same button, but instead of playing the sad song, it brings up an ecstatic one instead. Or else you could rerecord over the disk—you could take the old memories and change them.

The point is, the records that aren't being played are not going to build up and explode. That's absurd. And just as it's a simple procedure to reprogram a jukebox, it's easy to change the ways we produce unresourceful feelings and emotions. We don't have to experience all that remembered pain to change our state. What we have to do is change the internal representation from a negative to a positive one that is automatically triggered and causes us to produce more effective results. We have to rev up the circuits to ecstasy and turn off the juice of the circuits to pain.

NLP looks at the structure of human experience, not the content. While we can be and are sympathetic from a personal point of view, we don't give a darn about what happened. What we do care very much about is how you put together in your mind what happened. What's the difference between how you produce the state of depression or the state of ecstasy? The main difference is the way you structure your internal representations.

> *"Nothing has any power over me other than that which I give it through my conscious thoughts."*
>
> —*Anthony Robbins*

We structure our internal representations through our five senses—sight, sound, touch, taste, and smell. In other words, we experience the world in the form of visual, auditory, kinesthetic, gustatory, or olfactory sensations. So whatever experiences we have stored in the mind are represented through these senses, primarily through the three major modalities—the visual, auditory, or kinesthetic messages.

These modalities are broad groupings of the way we form internal representations. You might consider your five senses or representational systems the ingredients from which you build any experience or result. Remember that if anyone is able to produce a particular result, that result is created by specific actions, both mental and physical. If you duplicate the exact same actions, you can duplicate the results that person produces. In order to produce a result, you must know what ingredients are necessary. The "ingredients" of all human experiences are derived from our five senses, or modalities. However, it's not enough just to know what ingredients are needed. To produce the precise result you want, you must know exactly how much of each ingredient is needed. If you put in too much or too little of any particular ingredient, you will not produce the kind and quality of result you want.

When human beings want to change something, they usually want to change one or both of two things: how they feel—that is, their state—and/or how they behave. For example, a smoker often wants to change how he physically and emotionally feels (state) and also his behavioral pattern of reaching for cigarette after cigarette. In the chapter on the power of state, we made it clear that there are two ways to change people's states and thus their behaviors—either to change their physiology, which will change how they feel and the kind of behavior they produce, or to change their internal representations. This chapter is about learning how to specifically change the way we represent things so that they empower us to feel and to produce the kinds of behavior that support us in the achievement of our goals.

There are two things we can change about our internal representations. We can change *what* we represent—thus, for ex-

ample, if we imagine the worst-possible scenario, we can change
to picturing the best-possible scenario. Or we can change *how*
we represent something. Many of us have certain keys within
our own mind that trigger our brain to respond in a particular
way. For example, some people find that picturing something
as being very, very large motivates them greatly. Other people
find that the tone of voice they use when they talk to themselves
about something makes a major difference in their motivation.
Almost all of us have certain key submodalities that trigger immediate responses within us. Once we discover the different
ways we represent things and how they affect us, we can take
charge of our own mind and begin to represent things in a way
that empowers rather than limits us.

If someone produces a result that we would like to model,
we need to know more than the fact that he pictured something
in his mind and said something to himself. We need sharper
tools to really access what's going on in the mind. That's where
submodalities come in. They are like the precise amounts of ingredients required to create a result. They're the smallest and
most precise building blocks that make up the structure of
human experience. To be able to understand and thus control
a visual experience, we need to know more about it. We need
to know if it's bright or dark, in black and white or in color,
moving or stationary. In the same way, we'd want to know if
an auditory communication is loud or quiet, near or far, resonant
or tinny. We'd want to know if a kinesthetic experience is soft
or hard, sharp or smooth, flexible or stiff. I've made a list of
submodalities below.

Another important distinction is whether an image is associated or disassociated. An associated image is one you experience as if you were really there. You see it through your own
eyes, hear and feel what you would if you were actually at that
time and place in your own body. A disassociated image is one
you experience as if you were watching it from outside yourself.
If you see a disassociated image of yourself, it's like watching a
movie of yourself.

Take a minute to remember a recent pleasant experience

CHECKLIST OF POSSIBLE SUBMODALITIES

Visual
 1. Movie or still frames
 2. Panorama or framed (if framed, the shape of frame)
 3. Color or black and white
 4. Brightness
 5. Size of picture (life size, larger or smaller)
 6. Size of central object(s)
 7. Self in or out of picture
 8. Distance of picture from self
 9. Distance of central object from self
10. 3-D quality
11. Intensity of color (or black and white)
12. Degree of contrast
13. Movement (if so, fast or slow tempo)
14. Focus (which parts—in or out)
15. Intermittent or steady focus
16. Angle viewed from
17. Number of pictures (shifts)
18. Location
19. Other?

Auditory:
 1. Volume
 2. Cadence (interruptions, groupings)
 3. Rhythm (regular, irregular)
 4. Inflections (words marked out, how)
 5. Tempo
 6. Pauses
 7. Tonality
 8. Timbre (quality, where resonating from)
 9. Uniqueness of sound (gravelly, smooth, and so on)
10. Sound move around—spatial
11. Location
12. Other?

Kinesthetic:
1. Temperature
2. Texture
3. Vibration
4. Pressure
5. Movement
6. Duration
7. Steady—Intermittent
8. Intensity
9. Weight
10. Density
11. Location
12. Other?

For Pain:
1. Tingling
2. Hot—Cold
3. Muscle tension
4. Sharp—Dull
5. Pressure
6. Duration
7. Intermittent (such as throbbing)
8. Location
9. Other?

you've had. Actually step into that experience. See what you saw through your own eyes: the events, images, colors, brightness, and so on. Hear what you heard: the voices, sounds, and so on. Feel what you felt: emotions, temperature, and so on. Experience what that's like. Now step out of your body and feel yourself stepping away from the situation but from a place where you can still see yourself over there in the experience. Imagine the experience as if you were watching yourself in a movie. What's the difference in your feelings? In which were the feelings most intense, the first example or the second? The difference between these is the difference between an associated experience and a disassociated experience.

By using submodality distinctions like association versus disassociation, you can radically change your experience of life. Remember, we've learned that all human behavior is the result of the state we're in, and that our states are created by our internal representations—the things we picture, say to ourselves, and so on. Just as a movie director can change the effect his movie has on an audience, you can change the effect any experience in life has upon yourself. A director can change the camera angle, the volume and type of music, the speed and amount of movement, the color and quality of the image, and thus create any state he wants in his audience. You can direct your brain in the same way to generate any state or behavior that supports your highest goals or needs.

Let me show you how. It's very important that you do these exercises, so you might want to read each one through, then stop and actually do it before reading on. It might be fun to do the exercises with someone else. Take turns giving the cues and responding to them.

I want you to think of a very pleasant memory. It can be recent or distant. Just close your eyes, relax, and think of it. Now take that image and make it brighter and brighter. As the image brightens, be aware of how your state changes. Next I want you to bring your mental picture closer to you. Now stop and make it bigger. What happens when you manipulate the image? It changes the intensity of the experience, doesn't it? For the vast majority of people, making an already pleasant memory bigger and brighter and closer creates an even more powerful image and more pleasant. It increases the power and pleasure of the internal representation. It puts you in a much more powerful, more joyous state.

All people have access to the three modalities or representational systems—visual, auditory, and kinesthetic. But people rely to different degrees on different representational systems. Many people access their brain primarily in a visual framework. They react to the pictures they see in their head. Others are primarily auditory. Others kinesthetic. These people react most strongly to what they hear or feel. So after you've varied the visual frames, let's try the same thing with the other representational systems.

Bring back the pleasant memory we've worked with so far. Raise the volume of the voices or sounds you hear. Give them more rhythm, more bass, a change in timbre. Make them stronger and more affirmative. Now do the same with the kinesthetic submodalities. Make the memory warmer and softer and smoother than it was before. What happens to your feelings about the experience now?

Not all people respond in the same ways. Kinesthetic cues in particular elicit different responses in different people. Most of you probably found that making the image brighter or larger enhanced it. It gave the internal representation more intensity, made it more appealing, and, most important, it put you in a more positive, more resourceful state. When I do these exercises in counseling sessions, I can see exactly what's happening in a person's mind just by watching his physiology. His breathing gets deeper, his shoulders straighten, his face relaxes, and his whole body seems more alert.

Let's try the same thing with a negative image. I want you to think of something that upset you and caused you pain. Now take that image and make it brighter. Bring it closer to you. Make it bigger. What's going on in your brain? Most people find that their negative state has intensified. The bad feelings they felt before are more powerful than ever. Now put the image back where it was. What happens if you make it smaller and dimmer and farther away? Try it and note the difference in your feelings. You'll discover that the negative feelings have lost their power.

Try the same thing with the other modalities. Hear your own internal voice, or whatever's going on in the experience, in a loud, staccato tone. Feel the experience as hard and firm. Chances are the same thing will happen—the negative feeling will be intensified. Again, I don't want you to understand this in an academic fashion. I want you to do these exercises in a focused, intense way, being careful to note which modalities and submodalities have the most power for you. You might want to run through these steps again in your mind, being aware of how the manipulation of the image changes your feelings about it.

Take the negative image you began with and now make it smaller. Be aware of what happens as the image shrinks. Now defocus it—make it fuzzier, dimmer, and harder to see. Now move it away from you—push it back so you can barely see it. Finally, take the image and push it back into an imaginary sun. Notice what you hear and see and feel as it disappears from the world.

Do the same thing with the auditory modality. Bring down the volume of the voices you hear. Make them more lethargic. Take away their rhythm and snap. Do the same thing with your kinesthetic perceptions. Make the image feel sort of wispy and insubstantial, flaccid. What happens to the negative image when you go through this process? If you're like most people, the image loses its power—it becomes less potent, less painful, or even nonexistent. You can take something that has caused great pain in the past and make it impotent, make it dissolve and disappear completely.

I think you can see from this brief experience just how powerful this technology can be. In just a few minutes, you've taken a positive feeling and made it stronger and more empowering. You've also been able to take a powerful negative image and strip it of its power over you. In the past, you've been at the mercy of the results of your internal representations. Now you should know that things don't have to work that way.

Basically, you can live your life one of two ways. You can let your brain run you the way it has in the past. You can let it flash you any picture or sound or feeling, and you can respond automatically on cue, like a Pavlovian dog responding to a bell.

Or you can choose to consciously run your brain yourself. You can implant the cues you want. You can take bad experiences and images and sap them of their strength and power. You can represent them to yourself in a way that no longer overpowers you, a way that "cuts them down" to a size where you know you can effectively handle things.

Haven't we all experienced a job or task so big that we didn't feel like we'd ever get done, so we didn't even begin? If you imagine that task as being a small picture, you'll feel like you can handle it, and you'll take the appropriate action instead of being overwhelmed. I know that may sound like a simplification, yet when you try this, you'll discover that changing your representations can change how you feel about a task and thus modify your actions.

And of course you now know that you can also take good experiences and enhance them. You can take the little joys of life and make them bigger, brighten up your vision of the day, and feel yourself become lighter and happier. What we have here is a way to create more juice, more joy, more ardor in life.

> *"There is nothing either good or bad, but thinking makes it so."*
>
> —*William Shakespeare*

Remember in the first chapter how we talked about the commodity of kings? The king had the ability to direct his kingdom. Well, your kingdom is your brain. Just as the king can run his kingdom, you can run yours—if you begin to take control of how you represent your experience of life. All the submodalities we've dealt with tell the brain how to feel. Remember, we don't know how life really is. We only know how we represent life to ourselves. So if we have a negative image that's presented in big, bright, potent, resonant form, the brain gives us a whopper of a big, bright, potent, resonant bad experience. But if we take that negative image and shrink it, darken it, make it a still frame, then we take away its power, and the brain will respond accordingly. Instead of it putting us in a negative state, we can just shrug it off or deal with it without giant upset.

Our language gives us many examples of the power of our representations. What do we mean when we say that a person has a bright future? How do you feel when a person says the future looks dim? What are you saying when you talk about shedding light on a subject? What do we mean when we say someone blew something out of proportion or has a distorted image of something? What do people mean when they say something weighs heavily on their mind or they feel they have a mental block? What do you mean when you say that something sounds about right or rings a bell; or that everything clicked?

We tend to assume those phrases are just metaphors. They're not. They're usually quite precise descriptions of what's going on inside the mind. Think back to a few minutes ago when you took an unpleasant memory and enlarged it. Remember how it accentuated the negative aspects of the experience and put you in a negative state? Can you find a better way to describe that experience than to say you blew it out of proportion? So we instinctively know how powerful our mental images are. Remember that we can control our brain; it doesn't have to control us.

Here's a simple exercise that helps many people. Have you ever been plagued by an insistent internal dialogue? Have you ever been in a position where your brain wouldn't shut up? Lots of times our brain runs dialogues over and over again. We debate points with ourselves or try to win old arguments or settle old scores. If that happens to you, just turn down the volume. Make the voice in your head softer, farther away, and weaker. That takes care of the problem for many people. Or do you have one of those internal dialogues that's always limiting you? Now hear it say the same things, only in a sexy voice, in an almost flirtatious tone and tempo: "You can't do that." How does it feel now? You may feel that you're even more motivated to do what the voice is telling you not to. Tyry it now and experience the difference.

———

Let's run through another exercise. This time think of something in your experience that you were totally motivated to do. Relax and form as clear a mental picture of that experience as possible. Now I'm going to ask you some questions about it. Pause and answer each question one by one. There are no right or wrong answers. Different people will respond in different ways.

As you look at the image, do you see a movie or a snapshot? Is it in color or black and white? Is it close or far away? Is it to the left, to the right, or in the center? Is it high, low, or in the middle of your field of vision? Is it associated—do you see it through your own eyes—or is it disassociated—do you see it like an outsider viewing it? Does it have a frame around it, or do you see a panorama that goes on forever? Is it bright or dim, dark or light? Is it focused or unfocused? As you do this exercise, be sure to note which submodalities are the strongest for you, which ones have the most power when you focus on them.

Now run through your auditory and kinesthetic submodalities. When you hear what's going on, do you hear your own voice, or do you hear the voices of others in the scene? Do you hear a dialogue or a monologue? Are the sounds you hear loud or quiet? Do they have varied inflections, or are they a monotone? Are they rhythmic or staccato? Is the tempo slow or rapid? Do the sounds come and go, or do they keep up a steady commentary? What's the main thing you're hearing or saying to yourself? Where is the sound located—where is it coming from? When you feel it, is it hard or soft? Is it warm or cool? Is it rough or smooth? Is it flexible or rigid? Is it a solid or a liquid? Is it sharp or dull? Where is the feeling located in your body? Is it sour or sweet?

Some of those questions may seem difficult to answer at first. If you have a tendency to form your internal representations primarily in a kinesthetic way, you may have thought to yourself, I don't make pictures. Remember, that's a belief, and as long as you hold it, it will be true. As you become more aware of your own modalities, you'll learn to improve your perceptions by something called overlap. That means if you're primarily auditory, for example, you'll do best by first hooking into all

the auditory cues you use to grasp and experience. So you might
first remember what you were hearing at that time. Once you're
in that state and you have a rich, powerful internal representation, it's much easier to ease into a visual frame to work on
visual submodalities or into a kinesthetic frame to experience
the kinesthetic submodalities.

Okay, you've just seen and experienced the structure of something that you once were strongly motivated to do. Now I want
you to think of something you would like to be strongly motivated to do, something that at present you have no special
feeling for, no real motivation to do. Once again, form a mental
image. Now run through the exact same question, being careful
to note the way your responses differ from those that you had
for the thing you were strongly motivated to do. For example,
as you look at the image, do you see a movie or a snapshot?
Then continue to run through all of the visual submodality questions. Now run through your auditory and kinesthetic modality
questions. As you do this, be sure to note which submodalities
are strongest for you, which ones have the most power to affect
your states.

Now take the thing you were motivated by—let's call it experience #1—and the thing you want to be motivated by—
experience #2—and look at them simultaneously. It's not hard
to do. Think of your brain as a split-screen TV, and look at
both images at the same time. There are differences in the submodalities, aren't there? We can predict this, of course, because
*different representations produce different types of results in the nervous
system.* Now take what we've learned about which kinds of submodalities motivate us and then, bit by bit, readjust the submodalities of the thing you were not yet motivated to do (experience #2) so that they match those of the thing you are
motivated to do (the submodalities of experience #1). Again,
these will be different for different people, but chances are the
image of experience #1 will be brighter than that of experience
#2. It will be clearer and closer. I want you to concentrate on
the differences between them, and manipulate the second representation so it becomes more and more like the first one.

Remember to do the same thing with the auditory and kinesthetic representations as well. Do this now.

How do you feel about experience #2 now? Are you more motivated by it? You should be if you matched the submodalities of experience #1 with those of #2 (for example, if experience #1 was a movie and experience #2 was a still frame, you made experience #2 into a movie) and continue the process with all the visual, auditory, and kinesthetic submodalities. When you find the specific triggers (submodalities) that cause you to go into a desirable state, than you can link these triggers to undesirable states and thereby change them in a moment.

Remember, similar internal representations will create similar states or feelings. And similar feelings or states will trigger similar actions. Also, if you find out what specifically makes you feel motivated to do just about anything, you then know exactly what you have to do with any experience to make yourself feel motivated. From that motivated state, you can get yourself to take effective action.

It's important to note that certain key submodalities affect us more than others. For example, I worked with a young boy who was unmotivated to go to school. Most of the visual submodalities did not seem to move him much. However, if he said certain words to himself in a certain tone of voice, he found himself immediately motivated to go to school. In addition, when he was motivated, he felt tension in his biceps. However, when he was not motivated or was angry, he had tension in his jaw and his tone of voice was quite different. Simply by changing these two submodalities alone, I could take him almost instantly from a state of being upset or unmotivated to a state of being motivated. The same thing can be done with food. One woman absolutely loved chocolate because of its texture, its creaminess, and its smoothness, yet she hated grapes because they were crunchy. All I had to do was have her imagine eating a grape slowly, biting into it slowly and feeling the texture as it rolled around in her mouth. I also had her say the same things with the same tonality. By doing this, she immediately began to desire and enjoy grapes and has ever since.

As a modeler, you always want to be curious about how someone is able to produce any result, mental or physical. For example, people will come to me for counseling and say, "I'm so depressed." I don't ask, "Why are you depressed?" and then ask them to represent to themselves and me why they are. That would just put them into a depressed state. I don't want to know why they're depressed; I want to know *how* they're depressed. I'll ask instead, "How do you do that?" Usually I get a startled look because the person doesn't realize that you have to do certain things in your mind and physiology to get depressed. So I'll ask, "If I were in your body, how would I get depressed? What would I picture? What would I say to myself? How would I say it? What tonality would I use?" These processes create specific mental and physical actions, and thus specific emotional results. If you change the structure of a process, it can become something else, something other than a depressed state.

Once you know how you do things with your new awareness, you can start running your own brain and creating the states that support you in living the quality of life you desire and deserve. Example: How do you get frustrated or depressed? Do you take something and make a towering image of it in your mind? Do you keep talking to yourself in a sad tone of voice? Now, how do you create ecstatic feelings, fun? Do you make bright pictures? Do they move fast or slow? What tone of voice do you use when you speak to yourself? Suppose someone seems to love work, and you don't—but would like to. Find out what he does to create that feeling. You'll be astonished at just how fast you're able to change. I've seen people who've been in therapy for years change their problem, states, their behaviors— often in only minutes. After all, frustration, depression, and ecstasy aren't things. They are processes created by specific mental images, sounds, and physical actions that you consciously or unconsciously control.

Do you realize how using these tools in an effective way could change your life? If you love the feeling of challenge that your work gives you but you hate to clean the house, you can do one of two things: hire a housekeeper or note the difference between how you represent work and how you represent cleaning house. By representing house cleaning and challenging work in the same submodalities, you will feel an immediate drive to clean. This might be a nice one to give your children!

What if you were to take all the things you hate to do but believe you must and attach to them the submodalities of pleasure? Remember, few things have any inherent feeling. You've learned what is pleasurable and you've learned what is uncomfortable. You can simply relabel these experiences in your brain and immediately create a new feeling about them. What if you took all your problems, shrank them down, and put a little distance between them and you? The possibilities are endless. You're in command!

It's important to remember that like any skill, this takes repetition and practice. The more often you consciously cue these simple submodality shifts, the better you'll get at quickly producing the result you want. You may find that changing the brightness or dimness of an image has a stronger effect on you than changing its location or size. Once you know this, you'll know that brightness should be one of the first things to manipulate when you want to change something.

Some of you may be thinking, These submodality changes are great, but what's going to keep them from changing back? I know I can change how I feel at the moment, and that's valuable, but it would be great if I had a way to make change more automatic, more consistent.

The way to do this is through a process we call the swish pattern. It can be used to deal with some of the most persistent problems and bad habits people have. A swish pattern takes internal representations that normally produce states of unresourcefulness and causes them to automatically trigger new internal representations that put you in the resourceful states you desire. When you find out, for example, what internal representations make you feel like overeating, with the swish pattern you can create a new internal representation of something else that is more powerful and would cause you, if you saw or heard it, to push food away. If you link the two representations, whenever you think of overeating, the first representation will instantly trigger the second and put you in a state of not desiring food. The best part of the swish pattern is that once you implant it effectively, you don't have to think of it ever again. The process will happen automatically, without any conscious effort. Here's how the swish pattern works.

Step #1: Identify the behavior you want to change. Now make an internal representation of that behavior as you see it through your own eyes. If you want to stop biting your fingernails, imagine a picture of you lifting your hand, bringing your fingers to your lips, and biting your nails.

Step #2: Once you have a clear picture of the behavior you want to change, you need to create a different representation, a picture of yourself as you would be if you made the desired change and what that change would mean to you. You might picture yourself taking your fingers away from your mouth, creating a little pressure on the finger you were going to bite, and seeing your nails perfectly manicured and yourself as well dressed, magnificently groomed, more in control, and more confident. The picture you make of yourself in that desired state should be disassociated. The reason for this is that we want to create an ideal internal representation, one that you will continue to be drawn to rather than one you feel you already have.

Step #3: "Swish" the two pictures so that the unresourceful experience automatically triggers the resourceful experience. Once you hook up this triggering mechanism, anything that used to trigger biting your nails will now trigger you into a state where you are moving toward that ideal picture of yourself. Thus, you're creating a whole new way for your brain to deal with what in the past may have upset you.

Here's how to do the swish: Start by making a big bright picture of the behavior you want to change. Then, in the bottom right-hand corner of that picture, make a small dark picture of the way you want to be. Now take that small picture, and in less than one second, have it grow in size and brightness and literally burst through the picture of the behavior you no longer desire. As you do this process, say the word "wooosh" with all the excitement and enthusiasm you can. I realize this may sound a bit juvenile. However, saying "wooosh" in an excited way sends a series of powerful, positive signals to your brain. Once you've set up the pictures in your mind, this whole process should only take about as long as it takes to say the word "wooosh." Now in front of you is a big, bright, focused, colorful picture of how you want to be. The old picture of how you were has been smashed to smithereens.

The key to this pattern is speed and repetition. You must see and feel that small dark picture become huge and bright and explode through the big picture, destroying it and replacing it with an even bigger, brighter picture of how you want things to be. Now experience the great feeling of seeing things the way you want them. Then open your eyes for a split second in order to break the state. When you close your eyes again, do the swish once more. Start by seeing the thing you want to change as large, and then have your small picture grow in size and brightness and explode through Wooosh! Pause to experience it. Open your eyes. Close your eyes. See what you want to change. See the original picture and how you want to change it. Wooosh it again. Do this five or six times, as fast as you can. Remember, the key to this is speed; and to have fun doing it. What you are telling your brain is, See this, "Wooosh!" Do this, see this, "Wooosh!" Do this, see this, "Wooosh!" Do this . . . until the old picture automatically triggers the new picture, the new states, and thus the new behavior.

Now make the first picture, and what happens? If, for example, you swished a pattern of biting your fingernails, then when you imagined yourself biting them, you would find it hard to do. It actually would feel unnatural. If not, you would run the pattern again. This time, you would do it more clearly and more rapidly, being certain to experience only for a moment the positive feeling you get from the new picture before opening your eyes and beginning the process again. It may not work if the picture you choose to move toward isn't exciting or desirous enough. It's very important that it be extremely attractive, something that puts you in a motivated or desirous state—something you really want or something that is more important to you than the old behavior. Sometimes it helps to add new submodalities, like smell or taste. The swish pattern produces results amazingly quickly because of certain tendencies of the brain. Our brain tends to move away from unpleasant things and toward pleasant ones. By making the picture of no longer needing to bite your fingernails much more appealing than the picture of needing to bite them, you've given your brain a powerful signal about which kind of behavior to move toward. I did this for myself to stop my fingernail biting. It had been a totally unconscious habit. The day after I did this swish pattern, I suddenly caught myself starting to chew my fingers. I could have looked at that as a failure. Instead, I saw my becoming conscious of my habit as progress. Then I simply did ten swish patterns, and I've never thought to bite my nails since.

You can also do this with fears or frustrations. Take something you're afraid to do. Now picture it working out the way you want it to. Make this picture really exciting. Now swish the two of them seven times. Now think of the thing you feared. How does it make you feel now? If the swish pattern has been done effectively, the moment you think of the things you feared, you should automatically switch to thinking of how you want things to be.

Another variation of the swish pattern is to imagine a slingshot in front of you. Between the two posts is a picture of the present behavior you want to change. Place a small picture of how you want to be in the sling. Then mentally watch this little picture being pulled farther and farther back until the sling is stretched as far as possible. Then let it go. Watch as it explodes right through the old picture in front of you and into your brain. It's important that when you do this, you mentally pull the sling all the way back before letting it go. You still say the word "wooosh" as you release it and break through the old limiting picture of yourself. If you've done this correctly, when you let go of the sling, the picture should come at you so fast that your head actually snaps back. Stop right now and take a moment to think of some limiting thought or behavior you would like to change, and use this slingshot swish pattern to change it.

Remember that your mind can defy the laws of the universe in one crucial way. It can go backward. Time can't, nor can events—but your mind can. Let's say you go into your office, and the first thing you notice is that an important report you needed was not written. The incomplete report tends to put you in a less-than-resourceful state. You feel mad. You feel frustrated. You're ready to go out and scream at your secretary. But screaming won't produce the result you want. It will only make a bad situation worse. The key is to change your state, to back up and put yourself in a state that will allow you to get things done. That's what you can do by rearranging your internal representations.

I've talked throughout the book of being a sovereign, being in control, running your own brain. Now you're seeing the way to do it. In just the few exercises we've done so far, you've seen that you have the ability to totally control your own state. Think what your life would be like if you remembered all your good experiences as looking bright, close, and colorful; as sounding joyous, rhythmic, and melodic; as feeling soft, warm, and nurturing. And what if you stored your bad experiences as fuzzy little still-framed images with almost inaudible voices and insubstantial forms you could not feel because they were far away from you? Successful people do this unconsciously. They know how to turn up the volume of the things that help them and turn off the sound of the things that don't. What you've learned in this chapter is how to model them.

I'm not suggesting you ignore problems. Some things need to be addressed. We all know people who can go through a day in which ninety-nine things worked out right and come home totally depressed. Why? Well, one thing went wrong. They may have turned the one thing that went wrong into a big, bright, blustery image and turned all the others into small, murky, quiet, insubstantial ones.

Lots of people spend their whole lives like this. I've had clients who tell me, "I'm always depressed." They almost say it with pride, because it's become so much a part of their world-view. Well, many therapists would begin with the long, arduous task of unearthing the causes of that depression. They'd let the patient talk for hours about his depression. They'd rummage through the patient's mental garbage bin to uncover seminal experiences of gloom and past emotional abuse. Of such techniques are very long and very expensive therapeutic relationships made.

No one is always depressed. Depression isn't a permanent condition like losing a leg. It's a state that people can pop into and out of. In fact, most people who are experiencing depression have had many happy experiences in their lives—maybe even as many or more than the average person. They just don't represent these experiences to themselves in a bright, large, associated way. They may also represent happy times as far away instead of close. Take a moment now and remember an event that happened last week and push it far away. Does it seem as recent an experience to you anymore? What if you bring it closer? Doesn't it now seem more recent? Some people take their happy experiences of the moment and push them far away so they seem like long ago, and store their problems up close. Haven't you ever heard a person say, "I just need to get some distance from my problems?" You don't have to fly to some distant land to do this. Just push them far away from you in your mind and notice the difference. People who feel depressed often have their brains filled to capacity with big, loud, close, heavy, insistent images of the bad times and only thin, gray wafers for the good times. The way to change isn't to wallow in the bad memories; it's to change the submodalities, the very structure of the memories themselves. Next, link what used to make you feel bad to new representations that make you feel like taking the challenges of life with vigor, humor, patience, and strength.

Some people say, "Wait a second, you can't change things

so quickly." Why not? It's often much easier to grasp something in a flash than over a long period of time. That's how the brain learns. Think of how you watch a movie. You view thousands of frames and put them together into a dynamic whole. What if you watched one frame and then an hour later looked at another and then a day or two later watched a third? You wouldn't get anything out of it, would you? Personal change can work the same way. If you do something, if you make a change in your mind right now, if you change your state and your behavior, you can show yourself in the most dramatic way what's possible. That's a more potent jolt than months of anguished thought. Quantum physics tells us that things do not change slowly over time—they make quantum leaps. We jump from one level of experience to another. If you don't like how you feel, change what you represent to yourself. It's that simple.

Let's look at another example—love. Love, for most of us, is a wonderful, ethereal, almost mystical experience. It's also important, from a modeling point of view, to note that love is a state, and like all states, all results, it is produced by specific sets of actions or stimuli when they are perceived or represented in certain ways. How do you fall in love? One of the most important perceptual ingredients of falling in love is associating with all the things you love about someone and disassociating from the things you don't. Falling in love can be such a heady, disorienting feeling because it's not a balanced one. You're not making a balance sheet of a person's good and bad qualities, running it through a computer and seeing what comes out. You're totally associated with a few elements of another person that you find intoxicating. You're not even aware, in that moment, at least, of that person's "faults."

What ruins relationships? There are, of course, many factors. One may be that you no longer associate with the things that attracted you to that person in the first place. In fact, you may have gone so far as to associate with all the unpleasant experiences you've had with them and to disassociate from the pleasant ones you've shared. How does this happen? A person may have noticed and made big pictures of his mate's habit of leaving the

cap off the toothpaste or strewing her stuff on the floor. Maybe
he no longer writes her love notes. Or possibly she remembers
what he said to her in the heat of an argument, and she listens
to that dialogue play over and over in her head, reexperiencing
how it felt. She doesn't remember the gentle way he touched
her that day or the special things he said the previous week or
what he did for her on their anniversary. The examples can go
on and on. Bear in mind, there's nothing "wrong" with doing
this. Just be clear that this pattern of representations will probably not empower your relationship. What if in the middle of
an argument you remembered the first time you kissed or held
hands—a time when your lover did something really special for
you—and you made that picture big and close and bright again?
From the state, how will you treat this person you love?

It's critical that we look at any pattern of communication and
ask ourselves regularly, "If I continue to represent things to
myself this way, what will likely be the final result in my life?
What direction is my present behavior taking me, and is that
where I want to go? Now is the time to examine what my mental
and physical actions are creating." You don't want to find out
later that something you could simply and easily have changed
led you down a path to a place you don't want to be.

It might be valuable to note if you have a particular pattern
of using association and disassociation. There are many people
who spend most of their time disassociated from most of their
representations. They seldom seem to be emotionally moved by
anything. Disassociation has its advantage; if you keep out of
too deep emotions about some things, you have more resources
in handling them. However, if this is your consistent pattern
of representing most of your experiences in life, you're really
missing what I like to call the juice of life, a tremendous amount
of joy. I've counseled conservative people who were limited in
expressing what they felt about their lives and set up new perceptual patterns for them. By greatly increasing their associated
internal representations, they have come alive and found life to
be a whole new experience.

On the other hand, if all or the vast majority of your internal representations are fully associated, you may find yourself an emotional misfit. You may have great difficulty coping with life because you feel every little thing, and life isn't always fun or easy or exciting. A person who is fully associated with everything in life is extremely vulnerable and will usually take things too personally.

The key to life is a balance in all things, including the perceptual filters of association and disassociation. We can associate with or disassociate from anything we want. The key is to associate consciously, so it helps us. We can control any representation we make in our brain. Remember when we learned about the power of our beliefs? We learned that we're not born with beliefs, that they can change. When we were little we believed some things that we think are ridiculous now. We finished the chapter on beliefs with a key question: How do we adopt the enabling beliefs and drop the negative ones? The first step was becoming aware of their powerful effects on our lives. You've been taking the second step throughout this chapter: changing the way you represent those beliefs to yourself. For if you change the structure of how you represent something to yourself, you will change how you feel about it and thus change what is true in your experience of life. You can represent things to yourself in a way that consistently empowers you—now!

Remember, a belief is a strong emotional state of certainty that you hold about specific people, things, ideas, or experiences of life. How do you create that certainty? Through specific submodalities. Do you think you'd be as certain about something that is dim, unfocused, tiny, and far away in your mind as you would be about something that is just the opposite?

Also, your brain has a filing system. Some people store the things they believe on the left, things they're not sure about on the right. I know this sounds ridiculous, yet you can change a person who has this coding system simply by having him, for example, take the things he's not sure of from the right and put them on the left, where his brain files things he believes. As soon as he does, he begins to feel certain. He begins to believe in an idea or concept that only a moment ago he was uncertain about!

This changing of beliefs is done simply by contrasting how you represent something you absolutely know to be true with something you're not sure of. Start with some belief you are totally sure of—that your name is John Smith, you are thirty-five years old, and you were born in Atlanta, Georgia, or that you love your kids with all your heart or that Miles Davis is the greatest trumpeter in history. Think of something you believe without reservation, something you're totally convinced is true. Now think of something you're not sure of, something you want to believe but don't feel quite certain of now. You might want to use one of the seven lies of success from chapter 5. (Do not pick something you don't believe in at all, because saying you don't believe in something really means you *believe* that it is not true.)

Now run your submodalities as we did earlier when we dealt with motivation. Run through all the visual, auditory, and kinesthetic aspects of the thing you totally believe. Then do the same for the thing you're not so sure of. Be aware of the differences between them. Are the things you believe in found in one location and the things you're not certain of in another? Or are the things you believe closer or brighter or larger than the things you're not certain of? Is one a still frame, the other moving? Is one moving faster than the other?

Now do what we did with motivation. Reprogram the submodalities of the thing you're not sure of so they match those of the thing you believe. Change the colors and the location. Change the voices, the tones, the tempos, the timbre of the sounds. Change the submodalities of texture, weight, and temperature. How do you feel when you're through? If you have accurately transformed the representation that used to cause uncertainty, you will be feeling certain about the very thing that only a moment ago you were not certain of.

The only difficulty that many people have is their belief that you just can't change things that fast. This may be a belief you'll want to change as well.

This same process can be used to discover the difference in your mind between things you're confused about and things you feel you understand. If you're confused about something, it may be because your internal representation is small, unfocused, dim, or far away, while the things you understand are represented as closer, brighter, and more focused. See what happens to your feelings when you change your representations to be exactly like those of the things you understand.

Of course, bringing things closer or making them brighter does not intensify the experience for everyone. The opposite may be true. Some people feel things intensify when they get darker or more unfocused. The point is to find out which submodalities are the key ones for you or for the person you want to help to create change, and then to have enough personal power to follow through and use these tools.

What we're really doing as we work with submodalities is relabeling the stimulus system that tells the brain how to feel about an experience. Your brain responds to whatever signals (submodalities) you give it. If you provide signals of one type, the brain will feel pain. If you provide different submodalities, you can feel fine in a matter of moments. For example, while I was conducting a Neuro-Linguistic Professionals Training in Phoenix, Arizona, I began to notice that a large number of people in the room showed a great deal of muscle tension in their faces, making expressions that I interpreted as expressing pain. I mentally reviewed what I had been talking about and found nothing that could have triggered such a response in so many people. So finally I asked someone, "What are you feeling right now?" He said, "I've got a massive headache." As soon as he said that, so did another person, and then another, and another. More than 60 percent of the people in the room had headaches. They explained that the bright lights needed for videotaping were shining in their eyes, and they found it irritating, even painful. In addition, we were in a room without windows, and the ventilation had broken down about three hours earlier, so it was very stuffy. All these things had created a physiological shift in these people. So, what could I do, send everyone out for an Excedrin?

Of course not. The brain delivers pain only when it receives stimuli that are represented in a way that tells it to feel pain. So I had the people describe the submodalities of their pain. For some, it was heavy and throbbing; for others, not. Some felt pain very large and bright (you can imagine how that felt), while for some it was small. I then had them change their submodalities of pain, by first of all disassociating themselves from the pain and putting it outside themselves. Then I got them out of their feelings by having them see the shape and size of the pain and place it about ten feet in front of them. Next I had them make their representation bigger and smaller, causing it to grow and explode through the ceiling and then shrink way down. Then I had them push the pain into the sun and watch it melt to nothing and then come down to earth as sunshine to feed the plants. Finally I asked them how they felt. In less than five minutes, 95 percent no longer had a headache. They had changed their internal representations of what they were signaling the brain to do, so the brain, now getting the new signals, was producing a new response. The remaining 5 percent took another five minutes to make more specific changes. One man had been experiencing a migraine, and even he was feeling fine again.

When I describe this process to some people, they have difficulty believing that they could eliminate their pain that quickly and easily. Yet haven't you yourself done this unconsciously many, many times? Can you remember a time when you were feeling pain but then got caught up in doing something else, or something exciting happened, and when you changed what you were thinking about or representing to your brain, you no longer felt the pain? Pain can simply go away and not come back again unless you start representing it to yourself. With a little bit of conscious direction of your internal representations, you can easily eliminate headaches at will.

In fact, once you learn the signals that produce specific results in your brain, you can cause yourself to feel whatever way you'd like to feel about virtually anything.

A final caveat: A larger set of filters on human experience can govern or affect your ability to maintain new internal representations—or even to make the changes in the first place. Those filters concern what we value most and what unconscious benefits we may be receiving from our present behavior. The issue and importance of values is a chapter in itself, and we will discuss unconscious secondary gain in chapter 16, on the process of reframing. If pain is sending you important signals about something you need to change in your body, then unless you address that need, the pain will most likely come back because it is serving you in an important way.

With what you've learned so far, you can already tremendously enhance your own life as well as the life of anyone you know. Let's look at another aspect of the way we structure our experience, a critical ingredient that can empower us to effectively model most anyone. Let's examine . . .

CHAPTER VII

The Syntax
of Success

"Let all things be done decently and in order."

—*1 Corinthians 14:40*

Throughout this book, we've talked about discovering how people do things. We've stated that people who are able to produce outstanding results consistently produce a set of specific actions, both mental and physical (internal things they do inside their minds and external things they do in the world). If we produce the same actions, we will create the same or similar results. However, there is another factor that affects the results—the syntax of action. The syntax—the way we order the actions—can make a huge difference in the kind of results we produce.

What's the difference between "The dog bit Jim" and "Jim bit the dog"? What's the difference between "Joe eats the lobster" and "The lobster eats Joe"? They're very different, particularly if you're Jim or Joe. The words are exactly the same. The difference is syntax, the way they're arranged. The meaning of the experience is determined by the order of the signals provided to the brain. The same stimuli are involved, the same words, yet the meaning is different. This is critical to understand if we are to effectively model the results of successful people. The order in which things are presented causes them to register in the brain in a specific way. It's like the commands to a computer. If you program the commands in the right order, the computer will use all its capabilities and produce the result you desire. If you program the correct commands in a different order, you will not get the outcome you wish.

We'll use the word "strategy" to describe all these factors—the kinds of internal representations, the necessary submodalities, and the required syntax—that work together to create a particular result.

We have a strategy for producing just about anything in life: the feeling of love, attraction, motivation, decision, whatever. If we discover what our strategy for love is, for example, we can trigger that state at will. If we discover what actions we take, and in what order, to make a decision, then if we're indecisive, we can become decisive in a matter of moments. We will know which keys to hit and how to produce the results we want in our internal biocomputer.

A nice metaphor for the components and use of strategies is that of baking. If someone makes the greatest chocolate cake in the world, can you produce the same quality results? Of course you can, if you have that person's recipe. A recipe is nothing but a strategy, a specific plan of what resources to use and how to use them to produce a specific result. If you believe that we all have the same neurology, then you believe we all have the same potential resources available to us. It is our strategy—that is, how we use those resources—that determines the results we produce. This is the law of business as well. One company may have superior resources, but the company with strategies that best use its resources will usually dominate the marketplace.

So what do you need to produce the same quality cake as the expert baker? You need the recipe, and you need to follow it explicitly. If you follow the recipe to the letter, you will produce the same results, even though you may never have baked such a cake before in your life. The baker may have worked through years of trial and error before finally developing the ultimate recipe. You can save years by following his recipe, by modeling what he did.

There are strategies for financial success, for creating and maintaining vibrant health, for feeling happy and loved throughout your life. If you find people who already have financial success or fulfilling relationships, you just need to discover their strategy and apply it to produce similar results and save tremendous amounts of time and effort. This is the power of modeling. You don't have to labor for years to do it.

What does a recipe tell us that empowers us to take effective action? Well, one of the first things it tells us is what ingredients are needed to produce the result. In the "baking" of human experience, the ingredients are our five senses. All human results are built or created from some specific use of the visual, auditory, kinesthetic, gustatory, and olfactory representational systems. What else does a recipe tell us that allows us to produce the exact same result as the person who created the recipe? It tells us the amounts we need. In reproducing human experience, we also need to know not only the ingredients, but also how much of each ingredient we need. In strategies, we can think of the submodalities as being the amounts. They tell us specifically how much we need. For example, how much visual input—how bright, how dark, how close is the experience? What's the tempo, the texture?

Is that all there is to it? If you know what the ingredients are and how much to use, can you now produce the same quality of cake? No, not unless you also know the syntax of the production—that is, when to do what, and in what order. What would happen if in baking the cake you put in first what the original baker put in last? Would you produce a cake of the same quality? I doubt it. If, however, you use the same ingredients, in the same amounts, in the same sequence, then you will of course produce similar results.

We have a strategy for everything—for motivation, for buying, for love, for being attracted to someone. Certain sequences of specific stimuli will always achieve a specific outcome. Strategies are like the combination to the vault of your brain's resources. Even if you know the numbers, if you don't use them in the right sequence, you won't be able to open the lock. However, if you get the right numbers and the right sequence, the lock will open every time. So you need to find the combination that opens your vault and those that open other people's vaults as well.

What are the building blocks of syntax? Our senses. We deal with sensory input on two levels—internal and external. Syntax is the way we put together the blocks of what we experience externally and what we represent to ourselves internally.

For example, you can have two kinds of visual experiences. The first is what you see in the outside world. As you read this book and look at the black letters on the white background, you're having a visual external experience. The second is visual internal. Remember when, in the previous chapter, we played with the visual modalities and submodalities in our mind? We really weren't there to see the beach or the clouds or the happy or frustrating times that were represented in our mind. Instead we experienced them in a visual manner.

The same is true of the other modalities. You can hear a train whistle outside your window. That's auditory external. Or you can hear a voice in your mind. That's auditory internal. If the tone of the voice is what is important, that is auditory tonal. If the words (meaning) conveyed by the voice are what is important, that's auditory digital. You can feel the texture of the armrest of the chair you're sitting in. That's kinesthetic external. Or you can have a deep feeling inside that something makes you feel good or bad. That's kinesthetic internal.

In order to create a recipe, we must have a system to describe what to do and when. So we have a notation system to describe strategies. We represent sensory processes in a shorthand notation, using V for visual, A for auditory, K for kinesthetic, i for internal, e for external, t for tonal, and d for digital. When you see something in the outside world (visual external), it can be represented as Ve. When you have a feeling inside, it's Ki.

Consider the strategy of someone who gets motivated by seeing something (Ve), then saying something to herself (Aid) that creates the driving feeling (Ki) inside. This strategy would be represented in the following way: Ve-Aid-Ki. You could "talk" all day to this person about why she should do something, and it's highly unlikely you'd succeed. However, if you "showed" her a result and mentioned what she would say to herself when she saw it, you could put that person into state almost on cue. In the next chapter, I'll show you how to elicit strategies that people use in specific situations. For now, I want to show you how those strategies work and why they're so important.

We have strategies for everything, representational patterns that consistently produce specific outcomes. Few of us know how to use those strategies consciously, so we go in and out of various states, depending on what stimuli hit us. All you need to do is figure out your strategy so you can produce your desired state on cue. And you need to be able to recognize other people's strategies so you can know exactly what they react to.

For example, is there a way in which you consistently organize your internal and external experiences to make a purchase? Most definitely. You may not know it, but the same syntax of experiences that attract you to a particular car may also attract you to a particular house. There are certain stimuli that, in the right sequence, will immediately put you in a state that's receptive to buying. We all have sequences we consistently follow to produce specific states and activities. Presenting information in another person's syntax is a powerful form of rapport. In fact, if it's done effectively, your communication becomes almost irresistible because it automatically triggers certain responses.

What other strategies are there? Are there persuasion strategies? Are there ways to organize material that you present to someone so that it becomes almost irresistible? Absolutely. Motivation? Seduction? Learning? Athletics? Selling? Absolutely. How about depression? Or ecstasy? Are there specific ways to represent your experience of the world in certain sequences that create these emotions? You bet. There are strategies for efficient management. There are strategies for creativity. When certain things trigger you, you go into that state. You just need to know what your strategy is in order to access a state on cue. And you need to be able to figure out the strategies others use so you can know how to give people what they want.

So what we need to find is the specific sequence, the specific syntax, that will produce a certain outcome, a certain state. If you can do that and you're willing to produce the action needed, you can create your world as you desire it. Other than the physical necessities of life, like food and water, almost everything else you might want is a state. All you have to know is the syntax, the right strategy, for getting yourself there.

One very successful modeling experience I had was with the U.S. Army. I was introduced to a general, with whom I began to communicate about *Optimum Performance Technologies®* like NLP. I told him I could take any training program he had, cut the time in half, and even increase the competency of the people in that shorter period of time. Pretty big claim, right? The general was intrigued but not convinced, so I was hired to teach NLP skills. After successful NLP training, the army gave me a contract to model training programs and simultaneously teach a group of its men how to model effectively. I would be paid only if I produced the results I had promised.

The first project they asked me to take on was a four-day program to teach enlisted men how to effectively and accurately fire a .45-caliber pistol. In the past, an average of only 70 percent of the soldiers who took the program qualified afterwards, and the general had been told that this was the best that could be expected. At this point, I began to wonder what I had gotten myself into. I had never shot a gun before in my life. I didn't even like the idea of firing one. Originally, John Grinder and I had been partners in the project, so I felt that with his background in shooting, we could work it out. Then, for various scheduling reasons, John suddenly canceled. Well, you can imagine what happened to my state! In addition, I heard a rumor that a couple of people in the training group were going to do anything they could to sabotage my work because they were angry about the amount of money I was to be paid. They were going to teach me a lesson. With no background in shooting, having lost my ace in the hole (John Grinder), and knowing there were people trying to make me fail, what did I do?

First I took this giant image of failure that I had been creating in my mind and literally shrank it down to size. Then I began to set up a new set of representations about what I could do. I changed my belief systems from "The best in the army can't do what they're asking, so obviously I can't" to "The pistol coaches are the best at what they do, but they know little or nothing about the effect of internal representations on performance or how to model the strategies of the best shooters." Having put myself in a state of total resourcefulness, I informed the general that I would need access to his best shooters so that I could find out specifically what they did—in their minds and physical actions—that produced the result of effective and accurate shooting. Once I discovered "the difference that made the difference," I could teach it to his soldiers in less time and produce the desired results.

Along with my modeling team, I discovered the key beliefs that some of the best shooters in the world shared, and I contrasted them with the beliefs of the soldiers who had not shot effectively. Next I discovered the common mental syntax and strategies of the best shooters and replicated them so I could teach them to a first-time shooter. This syntax was the result of thousands, maybe hundreds of thousands, of shots and minute changes in their techniques. Then I modeled the key components of their physiology.

Having discovered the optimum strategy for producing the result called effective shooting, I designed a one-and-a-half day course for first-time shooters. The results? When tested in less than two days, 100 percent of the soldiers qualified, and the number who qualified at the highest level—expert—was three times higher than after the standard four-day course. By teaching these novices how to produce the same signals to their brains the experts did, we made them experts in less than half the time. I then took the men I had modeled, the top shooters in the country, and taught them how to enhance their strategies. The result an hour later: One man scored higher than he had in six months, another shot more bull's-eyes than he had in any competition in recent memory, and the coach gave both of these men a run for their money. In his communication to the general, the colonel called it the first breakthrough in pistol shooting since World War I.

The point here is for you to realize that even when you have little or no background information and even when circumstances seem impossible, if you have an excellent model of how to produce a result, you can discover specifically what the model does and duplicate it—and thus produce similar results in a much shorter period of time than you may have thought possible.

A simpler strategy is one used by many athletes to model the best in their field. If you wanted to model an expert skier, you might first watch carefully to see what his technique is (Ve). As you watch, you might move your body in the same motions (Ke), until they feel like a part of you (Ki). (If you've ever watched skiing, you may have done this involuntarily. When the skier you are watching needs to turn, you turn for him as if you were the one skiing.) Next you would want to make an internal picture of an expert skiing (Vi). You've gone from visual external to kinesthetic external to kinesthetic internal. Then you would make a new visual internal image, this time a disassociated image of yourself skiing (Vi). It would be like watching a movie of yourself modeling the other person as precisely as possible. Next you would step inside that picture and, in an associated way, experience how it would feel to perform the same action precisely the way the expert athlete did (Ki). You would repeat that as often as it would take for you to feel completely comfortable doing it. Thus you would have provided yourself with the specific neurological strategy that could help you move and perform at optimum levels. Then you would try it in the real world (Ke).

You could map the syntax of this strategy as Ve-Ke-Ki-Vi-Vi-Ki-Ke. This is one of hundreds of ways you could model someone. Remember, there are many ways to produce results. There are no right ways or wrong ways—there are only effective or ineffective ways to produce your desires.

Obviously, you can produce more precise results by having more accurate and precise information about all the things a person does to produce a result. Ideally, in modeling someone, you would also model his internal experience, belief systems, and elemental syntax. However, just by watching a person you can model a great deal of his physiology. And physiology is the other factor (we'll talk about it in chapter 9) that creates the state we are in and thus the kinds of results we produce.

One crucial area where understanding strategies and syntax can make a major difference is teaching and learning. Why "can't" some kids learn? I'm convinced there are two main reasons. First, we often don't know the most effective strategy for teaching someone a specific task. Second, teachers seldom have an accurate idea of how different kids learn. Remember, we all have different strategies. If you don't know someone's learning strategy, you're going to have a great deal of trouble trying to teach him.

For example, some people are lousy spellers. Is it because they're less intelligent than good spellers? No. Successful spelling may have more to do with the syntax of your thoughts— that is, how you organize, store, and retrieve information in a given context. Whether you are able to produce consistent results is simply a matter of whether your present mental syntax supports the task you're asking of your brain. Whatever you've seen, heard, or felt is stored in your brain. Countless research projects have shown that people in a hypnotic trance can remember (that is, access) things they were unable to recall consciously.

If you are not spelling effectively, the problem is the way you are representing words to yourself. So what's the best strategy for spelling? It's certainly not kinesthetic. It's difficult to feel a word. It's not really auditory, because there are too many words you can't sound out effectively. So what does spelling entail? It entails the ability to store visual external characters in a specific syntax. The way to learn to spell is to make visual pictures that can be easily accessed at any time.

Take the word "Albuquerque." The best way to learn to spell it isn't to say the letters over and over again—it's to store the word as a picture in your mind. In the next chapter, we're going to learn some of the ways people access the different parts of their brain. For example, Bandler and Grinder, the founders of NLP, discovered that the location we move our eyes to determines which part of our nervous system we have clearest access to. We'll go into these "accessing cues" in detail in the next chapter. For now, just note that most people remember visual images best by looking up and to their left. The best way to learn to spell Albuquerque is to place the word up and to your left and form a clear visual image of it.

At this point I need to add another concept: chunking. Generally, people can consciously process only five to nine chunks of information at once. People who learn rapidly can master even the most complex tasks because they chunk information into small steps and then reassemble them into the original whole. The way to learn to spell Albuquerque is to break it down into three smaller chunks like this: *Albu/quer/que*. I want you to write the three parts on a piece of paper, hold them above and to the left of your eyes, see *Albu*, then close your eyes and see it in your mind. Open your eyes. See *Albu*. Do not say it, just see it; then close your eyes and see it in your mind. Continue to do this four or five or six times until you can close your eyes and clearly see *Albu*. Next take the second chunk, *quer*. Flash on the letters faster and follow the same process with it, and then with the *que* chunk, until the entire image *Albuquerque* is stored in your mind. If you have a clear picture, you'll probably have a feeling (kinesthetic) it's spelled right. Then you'll be able to see the word so clearly you can spell it not only forward but backward. Try it. Spell Albuquerque. Then spell it backward. Once you have that, you've got that word spelled forever. I guarantee it. You can do that with any word and become a superb speller, even if you've had trouble spelling you own name in the past.

The other aspect of learning is discovering other people's preferred learning strategies. As noted above, everyone has a particular neurology, a particular mental terrain they use most often. But we seldom teach to an individual's strength. We assume everyone learns the same way.

Let me give you an example. Not long ago a young man was sent to me. He brought along a six-and-a-half-page report saying he was dyslexic, he couldn't learn to spell, and he had psychological problems at school. I could tell right away that he preferred to process a great deal of his experience kinesthetically. Once I realized how he processed information, I was in a position to help him. This young man had the greatest grasp of the things he felt. However, much of the standard teaching process is visual or auditory. His problem wasn't that he had trouble learning. It was that his teachers had trouble teaching him in a way in which he could effectively perceive, store, and retrieve information.

The first thing I did was to take the report and rip it up. "This is a bunch of garbage," I told him. That got his attention. He was expecting the usual battery of questions. Instead I started talking with him about all the great ways he used his nervous system. I said, "I bet you're good in sports." He said, "Yeah, I'm pretty good." It turned out he was a great surfer. We talked about surfing a little, and he immediately got excited and attentive, in a state of feeling effective. He was in a more receptive state than his teachers had ever seen. I explained to him that he had a tendency to store information kinesthetically and that had great advantages in life. However, his learning style made spelling difficult for him. So I showed him how to do it visually and worked with his submodalities to give him the same feeling about spelling that he had about surfing. Within fifteen minutes, I had him spelling like a whiz kid.

What about learning-disabled kids? Many times, these young people are not so much learning-disabled as they are strategy-disabled. They need to learn how to use their resources. I taught these strategies to a schoolteacher who worked with learning-disabled kids, ages eleven to fourteen, who had never scored higher on a spelling test than 70 percent, most falling in the 25–50 percent range. She quickly realized that 90 percent of her "disabled" students had auditory or kinesthetic spelling strategies. Within a week after she began using the new spelling strategies, nineteen of twenty-six kids scored 100 percent, two scored 90 percent, two 80 percent, and the other three 70 percent. She says that there has been a major shift in the behavior problems— "As if by magic, they've disappeared." She will now be presenting this information to the school board for introduction to all the schools in her district.

I'm convinced that one of the greatest problems in education is that teachers don't know the strategies of their students. They don't know the combination to their students' vaults. The combination may be 2 to the left and 24 to the right, and the teacher is trying to use 24 to the right and 2 to the left. Up till now, our educational process has been geared to what students should learn, not how they can best learn it. *Optimum Performance Technologies*® teach us the specific strategies that different people use to learn and also the best ways to learn a specific subject, such as spelling.

Do you know how Albert Einstein was able to conceive the theory of relativity? He said that one crucial thing that helped him was his ability to visualize "what it would look like to be riding on the end of a light beam?" A person who can't see the same thing in his mind will have trouble learning about relativity. So the first thing he has to learn is the most effective way to run his brain. That's precisely what *Optimum Performance Technologies*® are all about. They teach us how to use the most effective strategies for producing most quickly and easily the results we want.

The same problems that we find in education occur in almost every other field. Use the wrong tool or the wrong sequence, and you get the wrong result. Use the right one, and you can work wonders. Remember, we have a strategy for everything. If you're a salesman, would it help to know your customer's buying strategy? You bet it would. If he's strongly kinesthetic, do you want to begin by showing him the beautiful colors of the cars he's looking at? I wouldn't. I'd want to zap him with a strong feeling. I'd want him to sit at the steering wheel, feel the upholstery, hook into the feelings he'd get zooming along the open road. If he were visual, you'd start with the colors and lines and the other visual submodalities that work for his strategy.

If you're a coach, would it help to know what motivates different players, what sorts of stimuli work best to get them in their most resourceful states? Would you want to be able to break down specific tasks into their most efficient syntax, just as I did with the best shooters in the U.S. Army? You bet you would. Just as there's a way to form a DNA molecule or a way to build a bridge, there's a syntax that's best for every task, a strategy that people can consistently use to produce the results they want.

Some of you may be saying to yourselves, "Well, this is great if you're a mind reader. But I can't just look at people and figure out their love strategies. I can't speak with someone for a few minutes and know what stimulates him to buy, or to do anything else." The reason you don't know is that you don't know what to look for—or how to ask for it. If you ask for almost anything in the world in the right way, with enough conviction and enough commitment, you'll get it. Some things take great conviction and energy to pursue: you can get them, though you really have to work at them. But strategies are easy. You can elicit a person's strategies in a matter of minutes. In the next chapter we're going to learn . . .

CHAPTER VIII

How to Elicit Someone's Strategy

"'Begin at the beginning,' the king said gravely, 'and go
till you come to the end; then stop.'"

—*Lewis Carroll*, Alice's Adventures in Wonderland

Ever see a master locksmith work? It looks like magic. He plays with a lock, hears things you aren't hearing, sees things you aren't seeing, feels things you aren't feeling, and somehow he manages to figure out the entire combination to a safe.

Master communicators work the same way. You can figure out anyone's mental syntax—you can open the combination to the vault of his mind or your own by thinking like a master locksmith. You have to look for things you weren't seeing before, listen for things you weren't hearing before, feel things you weren't feeling before, and ask the questions you didn't know to ask before. If you do that elegantly and attentively, you can elicit anyone's strategies in any situation. You can learn how to give people precisely what they want, and you can teach them how to do the same thing for themselves.

The key to eliciting strategies is knowing that people will tell you everything you need to know about their strategies. They'll tell you in words. They'll tell you in the way they use their body. They'll even tell you in the way they use their eyes. You can learn to read a person as skillfully as you can learn to read a map or a book. Remember, a strategy is simply a specific order of representations—visual, auditory, kinesthetic, olfactory, gustatory—that produces a specific result. All you need to do is get people to experience their strategy and take careful note of what they do specifically to get back into it.

Before you can effectively elicit strategies, you must know what to look for, what the clues are that tell which part of a person's nervous system he is using at any moment. It's also important to recognize some of the common tendencies people develop and to use them to create greater rapport and results. For example, people tend to use a particular part of their neurology—visual, auditory, or kinesthetic—more than others. Just as some people are right-handed and others are left-handed, people tend to favor one mode over the others.

But before eliciting someone's strategies, we need to find out his main representational system. People who are primarily visual tend to see the world in pictures; they achieve their greatest sense of power by tapping into the visual part of their brain. Because they're trying to keep up with the pictures in their brain, visual people tend to speak quickly. They don't care exactly how they get it out; they're just trying to put words to the pictures. These people tend to speak in visual metaphors. They talk about how things look to them, what patterns they see emerging, whether things look bright or dark.

People who are more auditory tend to be more selective about the words they use. They have more resonant voices, and their speech is slower, more rhythmic, and more measured. Since words mean a lot to them, they are careful about what they say. They tend to say things like "That sounds right to me" or "I can hear what you're saying" or "Everything clicks."

People who are more kinesthetic tend to be even slower. They react primarily to feelings. Their voices tend to be deep, and their words often ooze out slowly like molasses. Kinesthetic people use metaphors from the physical world. They're always "grasping" for something "concrete." Things are "heavy" and "intense," and they need to "get in touch" with things. They say things like, "I'm reaching for an answer, but I haven't got a hold on it yet."

Everyone has elements of all three modes, but most people have one system that dominates. When you're learning about people's strategies to understand how they make decisions, you also need to know their main representational system so you can present your message in a way that gets through. If you're dealing with a visually oriented person, you don't want to amble up slowly, take a deep breath, and speak at a snaillike pace. You'll drive him crazy. You've got to speak up so your message matches the way his mind works.

Just by watching people and listening to what they say, you can get an immediate impression of which systems they are using. And NLP utilizes even more specific indicators of what's going on in someone's mind.

It's long been said that the eyes are windows to the soul. Only recently, however, have we learned how true that is. There's no parapsychological mystery about it. Simply by being observant, by watching a person's eyes, you can immediately see which representational system he's using at a specific time: visual, auditory, or kinesthetic.

Answer this: What colors were the candles on your birthday cake when you were twelve years old? Take a moment and remember. . . . To answer that question, 90 percent of you looked up and to the left. That's where right-handed people and even some left-handed people access visual remembered images. Here's another question: How would Mickey Mouse look with a beard? Take a moment to picture this. This time your eyes probably went up and to the right. That's where people's eyes go to access constructed images. So, just by looking at people's eyes, it's possible to know what sensory system they're accessing. By reading their eyes, you can read their strategies. Remember, a strategy is the sequence of internal representations that allow a person to accomplish a particular task. The sequence tells you the "how" of what someone is doing. Memorize the following charts so you can understand and recognize eye-accessing clues.

Carry on a conversation with someone and observe his/her eye movements. Ask questions requiring him or her to remember images or sounds or feelings. Which way do her eyes go for each of the questions? Verify to yourself that the chart works.

Here are a few types of questions you could ask to get specific kinds of responses.

TO GET	YOU MIGHT ASK
Visual Remembered Pictures	"How many windows are there in your house?" "What is the first thing you see when you wake up in the morning?" "What did your boyfriend or girlfriend look like when you were sixteen?" "Which is the darkest room in your house?" "Which of your friends has the shortest hair?" "What was the color of your first bicycle?" "What was the smallest animal you saw on your last trip to the zoo?" "What was the color of your first teacher's hair?" "Think of all the different colors in your bedroom."
Visual Constructed	"How would you look if you had three eyes?" "Imagine a policeman with a lion's head and a rabbit's tail, with the wings of an eagle." "Imagine the skyline of your city going up in wisps of smoke." "Can you see yourself with golden hair?"
Auditory Remembered	"What was the first thing you said today?" "What was the first thing someone said to you today?" "Name one of your favorite songs from when you were younger." "What sounds of nature do you like best?" "What's the seventh word in

As people represent information internally, they move their eyes, even though that movement may be slight. With a normally organized right-handed person the following holds true, and the resultant sequences are systematic. (NOTE: There are some people who are organized in a right-to-left reverse manner.)

VISUAL (V)   AUDITORY (A)   KINESTHETIC (K)

Eye movements can allow you to know how a person is internally representing his external world. The person's internal representation of the external world is his "map" of reality and each person's map is unique.

the Pledge of Allegiance?" "What's the ninth word in the song 'Mary Had a Little Lamb'?" "Sing to yourself 'The Rose.'" "Listen in your mind to a small waterfall on a quiet summer day." "Listen in your mind to your favorite song." "Which door in your house slams the loudest?" "Which is softest, the slam of your car door or the slam of your trunk lid?" "Who of your acquaintances has the pleasantest voice?"

Auditory Constructed   "If you could ask any question of Thomas Jefferson, Abraham Lincoln, and John F. Kennedy, what question would you ask?" "What would you say if someone asked you how we could eliminate the possibility of nuclear war?" "Image the sound of a car horn becoming that of a flute."

Auditory Internal   "Repeat this question to yourself on the
Dialogue   inside: 'What's most important to me in my life now?'"

Kinesthetic Words   "Imagine the feeling of ice melting in your hand." "How did you feel this morning just after you got out of bed?" "Imagine the feeling of a block of wood changing to silk." "How cold was the ocean last time you tested it?" "Which carpet in your house is the softest?" "Imagine settling down to a nice hot bath." "Think of what it would feel like to slide your hand over a rough piece of bark onto a soft, cool piece of moss."

If, for example, a person's eyes go up to the left, he just pictured something from his memory. If they now go toward the left ear, he listened to something. When the eyes go down to the right, the person is accessing the kinesthetic part of his representational system.

In the same way, if you're having a difficult time remembering something, it's probably because you are not placing your eyes in a position that gives you clear access to the information you need. If you're trying to remember something you saw a few days ago, looking down to the right will not help you see that image. However, if you look up to the left, you'll discover that you'll be able to remember the information rapidly. Once you know where to look for information stored in your brain, you'll be able to get to it quickly and easily. (For about 5–10 percent of people, the direction of these accessing cues will be reversed. See if you can find a left-handed friend or an ambidextrous person with reversed accessing cues.)

Other aspects of people's physiologies give us clues about their modes. When people are breathing high in their chest, they're thinking visually. When breathing is even, from the diaphragm or the whole chest, they're in an auditory mode. Deep breathing low in the stomach indicates kinesthetic accessing. Observe three people breathing, and note the rate and location of their breathing.

The voice is equally expressive. Visual people speak in quick bursts and usually have high-pitched, nasal, or strained tonalities. Low, deep tonality and slow speech are usually kinesthetic. An even rhythm and clear, resonant tonality indicate auditory accessing. You can even read skin tone. When you think visually, your face tends to grow paler. A flushed face indicates kinesthetic accessing. When someone's head is up, he's in a visual mode. If it's balanced or slightly cocked (as in listening), he's in auditory. If it's down or the neck muscles are relaxed, he's in kinesthetic.

So even with the most minimal communication, you can get clear, unmistakable cues about how a person's mind works and what sorts of messages he uses and responds to. The simplest way to elicit strategies is simply to ask the right questions. Remember, there are strategies for everything—for buying and for

EYE-ACCESSING CUES

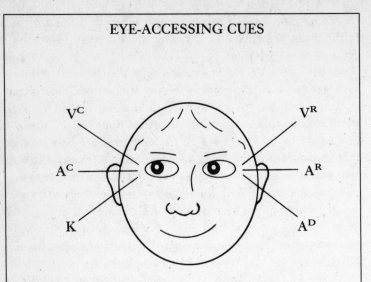

V^R *Visual remembered:* Seeing images of things seen before, in the way they were seen before. Sample questions that usually elicit this kind of processing include "What color are your mother's eyes?" and "What does your coat look like?"

V^C *Visual constructed:* Seeing images of things never seen before, or seeing things differently than they were seen before. Questions that usually elicit this kind of processing include "What would an orange hippopotamus with purple spots look like?" and "What would you look like from the other side of the room?"

A^R *Auditory remembered:* Remembering sounds heard before. Questions that usually elicit this kind of processing include "What's the last thing I said?" and "What does your alarm clock sound like?"

A^C *Auditory constructed:* Hearing words never heard in quite that way before. Putting sounds or phrases together in a new way. Questions that tend to elicit this kind of processing include "If you were to create a new song right now, what would it sound like?" and "Imagine a siren sound made by an electric guitar."

A^D *Auditory digital:* Talking to oneself. Statements that tend to elicit this kind of processing include "Say something to yourself that you often say to yourself" and "Recite the Pledge of Allegiance."

K Kinesthetic: Feeling emotions, tactile sensations (sense of touch), or proprioceptive feelings (feelings of muscle movement). Questions that elicit this kind of processing include "What does it feel like to be happy?" "What is the feeling of touching a pine cone?" and "What does it feel like to run?"

selling, for being motivated and for being in love, for attracting people and for being creative. I want to run through some of them with you. The best way to learn is not to observe, but to do. So do these exercises with someone else if at all possible.

The key to effective elicitation of a person's strategy is putting him in a fully "associated" state. Then he has no choice but to tell you exactly what his strategies are—if not verbally, then nonverbally, by eye movements, body change, and so forth. State is the hotline to strategy. It's the switch that opens the circuits to a person's unconscious. Trying to elicit strategy when a person isn't in a fully associated state is like trying to make toast when the toaster's not plugged in. It's like trying to start a car with no battery. You don't want an intellectual discussion; you want people to reexperience the state and thus the syntax that produced it.

Again, think of strategies as recipes. If you meet a cook who makes the greatest cake in the world, you may be disappointed to learn that he doesn't know exactly how he makes it. He does it unconsciously. He couldn't answer you if you asked the amounts of the ingredients. He might say, "I don't know—a pinch of this and a dash of that." So instead of asking him to tell you, have him show you. Put him in the kitchen, and have him bake the cake. You would note every step he took, and before he threw in that dash of this or that, you would immediately grab it and measure it. By following the cook through the entire process, noting the ingredients, the amounts, and the syntax, you would then have a recipe you could duplicate in the future.

Strategy elicitation is exactly the same. You must put the person back in the kitchen—back to the time when he was experiencing a particular state—and then find out what was the very first thing that caused him to go into that state. Was it something he saw or heard? Or was it the touch of something or someone? After he tells you what happened, watch him and ask, "What was the very next thing that caused you to be in that state? Was it . . . ?" and so on, until he's in the state you were pursuing.

Every strategy elicitation follows this pattern. You have to get the person in the appropriate state by having him remember a specific time when he was motivated, or felt loved, or felt creative, or whatever strategy you want to elicit. Then get him to reconstruct his strategy by asking clear, succinct questions about the syntax of what he saw, heard, and felt. Finally, after you have the syntax, get the submodalities of the strategy. Find out what specifically about the picture, sounds, and sensations caused the person to be in that state. Was it the size of the picture? The tone of the voice?

Try this technique for eliciting a motivation strategy with someone else. First, put the other person in a receptive state. Ask, "Can you remember a time when you were totally motivated to do something?" You're looking for a congruent answer, one in which the person's voice and body language give you the same message in a clear, firm, believable way. Remember, he won't be aware of much of his sequence. If it's been a part of his behavior for a while, he does it very quickly. In order to get each of his steps, you have to ask him to slow down and then pay careful attention to what he says and what his eyes and body tell you.

What does it mean if you ask a person, "Can you remember when you felt very motivated?" and the person shrugs and says, "Yeah"? It means he's not yet in the state you want. Sometimes someone will say yes and shake his head no. Same thing. He isn't really associated to the experience; he's not in state. So you have to make sure he's tapped into the specific experience that put him in the right state. So you ask, "Can you remember a specific time when you were totally motivated to do something? Can you go back to that time and step back into that experience?" That should do it almost every time.

When you get him in an involved state, ask, "As you remember that time, what was the very first thing that caused you to be totally motivated? Was it something you saw, something you heard, or was it the touch of something or someone?" If he answers that he once heard a powerful speech and immediately felt motivated to do something, his motivational strategy begins with auditory external (Ae). You wouldn't motivate him by showing him something or by having him do something physical. He responds best to words and sounds.

Now you know how to get his attention. But that's not the whole strategy. People respond to things both externally and internally. So you will need to find the internal part of his strategy. Next you ask, "After you heard that thing, what was the very next thing that caused you to be totally motivated to do something? Did you picture something in your mind? Did you say something to yourself? Or did you have a certain feeling or emotion?"

If he answers that he got a picture in his mind, the second part of his strategy is visual internal (Vi). After he hears something that motivates him, he immediately forms a mental picture that gets him more motivated. Chances are it's a picture that helps him focus on what he wants to do.

STRATEGY ELICITATION

Can you remember a time when you were totally X'd?
Can you remember a specific time?
Go back to that time and experience it . . . (get them in state)
As you remember that time . . . (keep them in state)
A. What was the very first thing that caused you to be X'd?
   Was it something you saw?
   Was it something you heard?
   Was it the touch of something or someone?
What was the very first thing that caused you to be totally X'd?
After you (saw, heard, or were touched), what was the very next thing that caused you to be totally X's?
B. Did you . . .
         make a picture in your mind?
         say something to yourself?
         have a certain *feeling* or *emotion*?
What was the very next thing that caused you to be X'd?
After you A'd and B'd (saw something, said something to yourself, and so on), what was the very next thing that caused you to be totally X'd?
C. Did you . . .
         make a picture in your mind?
         say something to yourself?
         have a certain *feeling* or *emotion*?
Or did something else happen?
What was the very next thing that caused you to be X'd?
Ask if the person was very X'd at this point (attracted, motivated, whatever).
If yes, elicitation is complete.
If no, continue eliciting syntax until congruent completion of state.
The next step is simply to elicit the specific submodalities of each representation in this person's strategy.
So if the first step of the strategy was visual, you would ask:
   What about what you *saw* (visual external)?
Then you would ask:
   What was it specifically about what you saw that motivated you?
      Was it the size of it?

> Brightness of it?
>
> The way it moved?
>
> Continue this process until you have all the submodalities for the strategy. Then simply talk about something you want to motivate that person to do by using the same syntax and the same key submodality words and then judge by the results you produce in that person's state.

You still don't have his whole strategy, so you need to keep asking, "After you heard something and then saw a picture in your mind, what was the very next thing that caused you to be totally motivated? Did you say something to yourself? Did you feel something inside, or did something else happen?" If at that point he gets a feeling that makes him totally motivated, he's completed his strategy. He has produced a series of representations, in this case Ae-Vi-Ki, which create the state of motivation. He has heard something, seen a picture in his mind, and then felt motivated. Most people need an external stimulus and either two or three internal ones before they're finished, although some people have strategies involving a sequence of ten or fifteen different representations before they reach the desired state.

Now that you know the syntax of his strategy, you need to find out the submodalities. So you ask, "What about the thing you heard motivated you? Was it the tone of the person's voice, the actual words themselves, the speed or rhythm of the voice? What did you picture in your mind? Was it a big picture, bright . . . ?" Once you have asked all this, you can test the responses by telling him in the same tone about something you want to motivate him to do, and then tell him what he'll picture in his mind and the feelings it will create. If you do all this accurately, you will see the person go into a motivated state right before your very eyes. If you doubt the importance of syntax, try changing the order subtly. Then tell him how it will feel and

what he'll say to himself, and you'll see him giving you an un-
interested stare. You've got the right ingredients in the wrong
order.

How long does it take to elicit a person's strategy? It depends
on the complexity of the activity you want to know about. Sometimes it takes only a minute or two to learn the precise syntax
that will motivate him to do just about anything you want.

Let's say you're a track coach. You want to motivate the
person in the example above to become a great long-distance
runner. Although he has some talent and some interest, he's not
really motivated to make a commitment. So how would you
start? Would you take him out and have him watch your best
runners at work? Would you show him the track? Would you
talk real fast to get his juices going, to show him how excited
you are? No, of course not. Every bit of that behavior would
work on a person with a visual strategy, and it would leave this
person cold.

Instead, you need to sell him by connecting with the auditory
stimuli that get him going. To start with, you wouldn't be talking a mile a minute like a visual person would, and you wouldn't
go into a slow, drooping kinesthetic rap. You would talk in a
well-modulated, steady, clear, resonant voice. You would speak
in the exact same submodalities of pitch and tempo that you
learned trigger the beginning of his motivation strategy. You
might say something like this: "I'm sure you've heard a lot about
how successful our track program has been. It's really the talk
of the school right now. We've been drawing great crowds this
year. It's amazing the noise they make. I've had kids say the
crowd noise has done wonders for them. It's kept them going
at levels they never expected they could reach. And the roar
when you hit the finish line is amazing. I've never heard anything like it in all my years of coaching." Now you're speaking
his language. You're using the same representational system he
does. You could spend hours showing him the big new stadium,
and he'd be nodding off. Let him really hear the roar of the
crowd as he crossed the finish line, and you've got him hooked.

That's only the first part of the syntax, the hook that gets him going. That by itself won't get him fully motivated. You need to put together the internal sequence as well. Depending on what descriptions he gives you, you might go from the auditory cues to something like this: "When you hear the roar of the hometown crowd, you'll be able to picture yourself running the best race of your life. Feeling absolutely motivated to run the race of your life."

If you have a business, motivating your employees is most likely a major concern. If it's not, you probably won't have the business for very long. But the more you know about motivational strategies, the more you realize how difficult it is to motivate well. After all, if each of your employees has a different strategy, it's hard to come up with a representation that will fill all their needs. If you simply run your own strategy, you're going to motivate only the people who are like you. You could give the most cogent and well-thought-out motivational lecture in the world, and unless it addressed the specific strategies of different people, it wouldn't do any good.

What can you do about it? Well, understanding strategy should give you two clear ideas. First, every motivational technique aimed at a group should have something for everyone— something visual, something auditory, and something kinesthetic. You should show them things, you should let them hear things, and you should give them feelings. And you should be able to vary your voice and intonations so you hook all three types.

Second, there's no substitute for working with people as individuals. You can provide the broad cues to a group that will give everyone something to work with. To tap into the full strategies different people use, it would be ideal to elicit individual strategies.

What we've looked at so far is the basic formula for eliciting anyone's strategy. To be able to use it effectively, you need to get more details about each step of the strategy. You need to add the submodalities to the basic pattern.

For example, if a person's buying strategy begins with something visual, what is it that catches his eye? Bright colors? Great size? Does he go bonkers at the sight of certain patterns or wild, splashy designs? If he's auditory, is he attracted to sexy voices or to powerful ones? Does he like loud clatter and rumbles or a finely tuned, efficient hum. Knowing someone's main modality is a great start. To be precise, to really punch the right buttons, you need to know more.

Understanding strategy is absolutely essential to success in sales. There are some salespeople who understand it instinctively. When they meet a potential client, they immediately develop rapport and elicit his decision-making strategies. They might begin, "I noticed you're using our competitor's copy machine. I'm curious. What was the first thing that caused you to want to buy that machine? Was it something you saw or read about it . . . or did someone tell you about it? Or was it the way you felt about the salesman or product itself?" These questions may seem a little strange, but a salesman who has established rapport will say, "I'm curious because I really want to fill your needs." The answer to such questions can well provide the salesman with invaluable information about how to present his product in the most effective way.

Clients have very specific buying strategies. I'm no different from anyone else when I shop. There are many ways to do things wrong—to try to sell me what I don't want in a way I don't want to hear. There aren't as many ways to get it right. So to be effective, a salesman must take his clients back to a time when they bought something they loved. He has to find out what caused them to decide to buy it. What were the key ingredients and submodalities? A salesman who learns how to elicit strategies will be learning his customer's exact needs. He will then be empowered to truly satisfy those needs and create a long-standing customer. When you elicit someone's strategy, you can learn in moments what might otherwise take days or weeks to learn.

What about limiting strategies—like overeating? I used to weight 268 pounds. How did I balloon to such a size? Easy. I developed a bingeing or overeating strategy. And it was running me. I found out what my strategy was by thinking about times when I wasn't hungry and yet became ravenous only moments later.

As I went back to those times, I asked myself, What caused me to feel like eating? Was it something I saw, something I heard, or the touch of something or someone? I realized it was something I saw. I would be driving and suddenly see signs for a certain fast-food chain. As soon as I did, I would make a picture in my mind of having my favorite food there, and then I would say to myself, "Boy, I'm hungry." That would create feelings of hunger, which I would then act on by stopping to order a meal. I may not have been even slightly hungry until I saw the signs that triggered this strategy. And those signs were everywhere. In addition, if someone else asked, "Do you want to get a bite to eat?" even if I wasn't hungry, I would begin to imagine (picture in my mind) eating certain foods. I would then say to myself, "Boy, I'm hungry," which would create the feeling of hunger, and I'd say, "Let's go eat." Then, of course, there were television commercials that kept showing me food after food and asking, "Aren't you hungry? . . . Aren't you hungry?" My brain would respond by making pictures, and I would say to myself, "Boy, I'm hungry," and that would create the feeling that would direct me into the nearest restaurant.

Finally I changed my behavior by changing my strategy. I set it up so that seeing the food signs triggered my picturing myself looking in the mirror at my fat, ugly body and saying to myself, "I look disgusting. I can pass on this meal." Then I imagined myself working out, seeing my body getting stronger, and saying to myself, "Great job! You're looking good," which created a desire to go work out. I linked all these through repetition—seeing the sign, immediately seeing the fat image of myself, hearing my internal dialogue, and so forth, over and over again—just like a swish pattern, until seeing the signs or hearing "Would you like to go to lunch?" automatically triggered my new strategy. The result produced by that new strategy is the body I now possess and the eating habits that support me to this day. You, too, can discover strategies with which your unconscious mind is creating results you do not desire. And you can change those strategies—now!

Once you discover someone's strategies, you can make him or her feel totally loved by triggering the exact stimuli that caused this feeling to occur within that person. You can also figure out what your own love strategy is. Love strategies are different from many other strategies in one key way. Instead of a three- or four-step procedure, there's usually only one step. There's one touch, one thing to say, or one way of looking at a person that makes him or her feel totally loved.

Does that mean everyone needs just one thing to feel loved? No. I like to have all three, and I'm sure you do, too. I want someone to touch me in the right way and tell me they love me and show me they love me. Just as one sense often dominates overall, one way of expressing love instantly unlocks your combination, making you feel totally loved.

How do you elicit someone's love strategy? You should already know. What's the first thing you do? What's the first thing you do whenever you're eliciting any strategy? You put the person in the state whose strategy you wish to elicit. Remember, state is the juice that gets the circuits going. So ask the other person, "Can you remember a time when you felt totally loved?" To make sure he or she is in the right state, follow up with, "Can you remember a specific time when you felt totally loved? Go back to that time. Remember how it felt? Reexperience those feelings in your body now."

So you have the person in the right state. Next you have to elicit strategy. Ask, "As you remember that time and feel those deep feelings of love, it it *absolutely necessary* that a person show you love by buying you things, taking you places, or looking at you in a certain way? Is it absolutely necessary that this person show love in this way for you to feel totally loved?" Note the answer and its congruency. Next, put the person back into state and say, "Remember that time when you felt totally loved. In order for you to feel these deep feelings of love, is it absolutely necessary for the person to express his or her love in a certain way, for you to feel totally loved?" Judge the verbal and non-

ELICITING LOVE STRATEGIES

Can you remember a time when you felt totally loved?
Can you remember a specific time?
As you go back to that time and experience it . . . (get
the person in state.)
V: In order for you to feel these deep feelings of love,
is it *absolutely necessary* for your partner to show you he/
she loves you by . . .

taking you places?
buying you things?
looking at you in a certain way? . . .

Is it *absolutely necessary* that your partner show you he/
she loves you in this way for you to feel totally loved?
(Judge by physiology.)
A: In order for you to feel these deep feelings of love,
is it *absolutely necessary* for your partner to . . .

tell you he/she loves you in a certain way? (Judge
by physiology.)
K: In order for you to feel these deep feelings of love,
is it *absolutely necessary* for your partner to . . .

touch you in a certain way? (Judge by physiology.)
Now elicit the submodality. How specifically? Show
me, tell me, demonstrate for me.
Test inside and outside the strategy. Judge by congruent physiology.

verbal responses for congruency. Finally, ask, "Remember how
it feels to be totally loved. In order for you to feel those deep
feelings of love, is it necessary that someone touch you in a
certain way for you to feel totally loved?"
Once you've discovered the key ingredient that creates these
deep feelings of love for a person, you need to discover the
specific submodalities. For example, ask, "How specifically

would someone need to touch you to make you feel totally loved?" Have the person demonstrate. And then test it. Touch him or her that way, and if you've done it accurately, you'll see an instantaneous shift in state.

I do this in seminars every week, and it never fails. We all have a certain look, a certain way of having our hair stroked, a certain tone of voice—a way of saying "I love you"—that reduces us to Jell-O. Most of us didn't know what it was before. But in state, we're able to come up with one thing that makes us feel absolutely, totally loved.

It doesn't matter that the people attending the seminars don't know me, that they're standing up in the middle of a room full of strangers. If I run through their love strategy, if I touch them in the right way or look at them in the right way, they just melt. They have very little choice because their brain is receiving the exact signal that creates for them the feeling of being totally loved.

A minority of people will at first come up with two love strategies instead of just one. They'll think of a touch, and they'll think of something they love to be told. So you have to keep them in the right state and get them to make a distinction. Ask them if they could have the touch but not the sound, would they feel totally loved? If they had the sound but not the touch, would they feel totally loved? If they're in the right state, they'll be able to make a clear distinction without fail. Remember, we need all three. But there's one that opens the vault. There's one that works magic.

Knowing the love strategy of your partner or your child can be one of the most powerful understandings you develop in supporting your relationship. If you know how to make that person feel loved at any moment, that's a pretty powerful tool to have available. If you don't know his/her love strategy, it can be pretty sad. I'm sure we've all been in the situation at least once in our lives when we loved someone and expressed our love, but we weren't believed; or someone expressed love to us, but we didn't believe it. The communication didn't work because the strategies didn't match.

There is an interesting dynamic that develops in relationships. In the very beginning of a relationship, the stage I call courting, we are very mobilized. So how do we let people know we love them? Do we just tell them that we love them? Do we just show them or just touch them? Of course not! During "courting," we do it all. We show each other, we tell each other, we touch each other all the time. Now as time goes on, do we still do all three? Some couples do. They are the exception, not the rule. Now, do we love the person any less? Of course not! We just aren't as mobilized anymore. We feel comfortable in the relationship. We know that person loves us, and we love that person. So how do we now communicate our feelings of love? Probably just as we would like to receive it. If so, what happens to the quality of the feelings of love in the relationship? Let's take a look.

If a husband has an auditory love strategy, how is he most likely to express his love to his wife? By telling her, of course. But what if she has a visual love strategy, so her brain causes her to feel deeply loved only after it receives certain visual stimuli? What will happen as time goes by? Neither member of this relationship is going to feel totally loved. When they were courting, they did it all—showed, told, and touched—and triggered each other's love strategies. Now the husband comes in and says, "I love you, honey," and she replies, "No, you don't!" He asks, "What are you 'talking' about? How can you 'say' that?" She may say, "Talk is cheap. You never bring me 'flowers' anymore. You never take me 'places' with you. You never 'look' at me in that special way." "What do you mean, look at you?" he may ask. "I'm 'telling' you I love you." She is no longer experiencing her deepest feelings of being loved because the specific stimulus that triggers that feeling is no longer being consistently applied by her husband.

Or consider the opposite: the husband is visual and the wife is auditory. He shows his wife he loves her by buying her things, taking her places, sending her flowers. One day she says, "You don't love me." He's upset: "How can you say that? Look at this home I've bought for you, all the places I take you." She

says, "Yeah, but you never say you love me." "I love you!" he
screams in a tonality not even close to her strategy. As a result,
she doesn't feel loved.

Or how about one of the greatest mismatches of all time—a
kinesthetic man and a visually oriented woman. He comes home
and wants to hug her. "Don't touch me," she says. "You're
always grabbing at me. All you ever want to do is hunker down
and hug. Why can't we go someplace? Look at me before you
touch me." Do any of these scenarios sound familiar? Can you
see now how a relationship you had in the past ended because
in the beginning you did it all, but as time went by you began
to communicate love in one way, and your partner needed it in
another, or vice versa?

Awareness is a powerful tool. Most of us think our map of
the world is the way it is. We think, I know what makes me
feel loved. That must be what works for everyone else. We forget
that the map in not the territory. It's only how we see the
territory.

Now that you know how to elicit a love strategy, sit down
with your partner and find out what makes him or her feel totally
loved. And having elicited your own love strategy, teach your
partner how to trigger your feeling totally loved. The changes
this understanding can make in the quality of your relationship
are worth your investment in this book many times over.

People have strategies for everything. If someone gets up in
the morning totally awake and alive, he has a strategy to do just
that, though he probably doesn't know what it is. But if you
ask him, he'll be able to tell you what he says or feels or sees
that gets him going. Remember, the way to elicit a strategy is
to put the cook in the kitchen. That is, get him to go into the
state you want, and then, while he's there, find out what he did
to create and maintain the state. You might ask a person who
wakes up easily in the morning to remember a specific morning
when he woke up quickly and easily. Ask him to recall the very
first thing he became conscious of. He may say he heard an
internal voice that said, "It's time to get up; let's go." Then ask
him to remember the very next thing that caused him to wake

up quickly. Did he picture something or feel something? He may say, "I pictured myself jumping out of bed and getting in the warm shower. I shook my body, and then I got out." Seems like a simple strategy. Next you want to find out the specific kinds and amounts of ingredients, so you would ask, "What was the voice like that said it's time to get out of bed? What was it about the quality of the voice that got you up?" He will probably answer, "The voice was loud, and it was talking very fast." Now ask, "What was the scene like that you pictured?" He may answer, "It was bright and moving fast." Now you can try this strategy for youself. I think you'll discover, as I did, that by speeding up your words and pictures, increasing volume and brightness, you can wake up in an instant.

Conversely, if you're having a hard time going to sleep, just slow down your own internal dialogue and create yawning, sleepy tones, and you'll feel yourself become very tired almost immediately. Try it right now. Talk very slowly like a very tired person in a yawning voice inside your head. Talk . . . about . . . how T-I-R-E-D—yawn—you are. Now speed it up. Feel the difference. The point is, you can model any strategy, as long as you put someone in state and find out specifically what he does, in what order and sequence. The key isn't to merely learn a few strategies and then use them. The most important thing is to constantly stay attuned to what people do well, and then to find out how they do it, what their strategies are. That's what modeling is all about.

NLP is like the nuclear physics of the mind. Physics deals with the structure of reality, the nature of the world. NLP does the same thing for your mind. It allows you to break things down into the component parts that make them work. People have spent a lifetime trying to find a way to feel totally loved. They've spent fortunes trying to get to "know themselves" with analysts and read dozens of books on how to succeed. NLP gives us the technology to accomplish these and many other goals elegantly, efficiently, and effectively—now!

As we've already seen, one way to get in a resourceful state is through syntax and internal representation. Another way is through physiology. Earlier, we talked about how mind and body are linked in a cybernetic loop. In this chapter, we discussed the mental side of state.

Now let's look at the other side. Let's look at . . .

CHAPTER IX

Physiology: The Avenue of Excellence

"Devils can be driven out of the heart by the touch of a hand on a hand or a mouth."

—*Tennessee Williams*

When I lead seminars, I always set off scenes of raucous, joyous, chaotic frenzy.

If you walked in the door at the right moment, you would come upon perhaps three hundred people jumping up and down, screeching and hollering, roaring like lions, waving their arms, shaking their fists like Rocky, clapping their hands, puffing up their chests, strutting like peacocks, giving the thumbs-up sign, and otherwise acting as if they had so much personal power they could light up a city if they wanted to.

What the heck is going on?

What's going on is the other half of the cybernetic loop: physiology. That bedlam is about one thing—acting as if you felt more resourceful, more powerful, happier than you ever felt before, acting as if you knew you were going to succeed. Acting as if you were totally energized as well. One way to get yourself into a state that supports your achieving any outcome is to act "as if" you were already there. Acting "as if" is most effective when you put your physiology in the state you'd be in if you were already effective.

Physiology is the most powerful tool we have for instantly changing states, for instantly producing dynamic results. There's an old saying: "If you would be powerful, pretend to be powerful." Truer words were never spoken. I expect people to get powerful results from my seminars, results that will change their lives. To do that, they have to be in the most resourceful physiology possible, for there's no powerful action without powerful physiology.

If you adopt a vital, dynamic, excited physiology, you automatically adopt the same kind of state. The biggest leverage we have in any situation is physiology—because it works so fast, and it works without fail. Physiology and internal representations are totally linked. If you change one, you instantly change the other. I like to say, "There is no mind, there is only body," and "there is no body, there is only mind." If you change your physiology—that is, your posture, your breathing patterns, your muscle tension, your tonality—you instantly change your internal representations and your state.

Can you ever remember a time when you felt totally rundown? How did you perceive the world? When you feel physically tired or your muscles are weak or you have pain somewhere, you perceive the world quite differently from when you feel rested, alive, and vital. Physiological manipulation is a powerful tool for controlling your own brain. So it's extremely important that we realize how strongly it affects us, that it's not some extraneous variable, but an absolutely crucial part of a cybernetic loop that's always in action.

When your physiology runs down, the positive energy of your state runs down. When your physiology brightens and intensifies, your state does the same thing. So physiology is the lever to emotional change. In fact, you can't have an emotion without a corresponding change in physiology. And you can't have a change in physiology without a corresponding change in state. There are two ways to change state, by changing internal representations or by changing physiology. So if you want to change your state in an instant—what do you do? *Zap!* You change your physiology—that is, your breathing, your posture, your facial expression, the quality of your movement, and so on.

If you start to grow tired, there are certain specific things you can do with your physiology to continue to communicate this to yourself: a slump in shoulder position, relaxation of many major muscle groups, and the like. You can become tired simply by changing your internal representations so that they give your nervous system a message that you are tired. If you change your physiology to the way it is when you feel strong, it will change your internal representations and how you feel at that moment. If you keep telling yourself that you're tired, you're forming the internal representation that keeps you tired. If you say you have the resources to be alert and on top of things, if you consciously adopt that physiology, your body will make it so. Change your physiology and you change your state.

In the chapter on belief, I showed you a little about the effects that beliefs have on health. Everything that scientists are finding today emphasizes one thing: sickness and health, vitality and depression are often decisions. They're things we can decide to do with our physiology. They're usually not conscious decisions, but they're decisions nonetheless.

No one consciously says, "I'd rather be depressed than happy." But what do depressed people do? We think of depression as a mental state, but it has a very clear, identifiable physiology. It's not hard to visualize a person who is depressed. Depressed people often walk around with their eyes down. (They're accessing in a kinesthetic mode and/or talking to themselves about all the things that make them feel depressed.) They drop their shoulders. They take weak, shallow breaths. They do all the things that put their body in a depressed physiology. Are they deciding to be depressed? They sure are. Depression is a result, and it requires very specific body images to create it. Even Charlie Brown understands this.

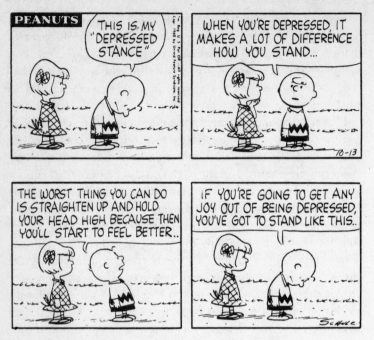

© 1960 United Feature Syndicate, Inc.

The exciting thing is that you can just as easily create the result called ecstasy by changing your physiology in certain specific ways. After all, what are emotions? They're a complex association, a complex configuration of physiological states. Without changing any of his internal representations, I can change the state of any depressed person in seconds. You don't have to look and see what pictures a depressed person is making in his mind. Just change his physiology, and zap, you change his state.

If you stand up straight, if you throw your shoulders back, if you breathe deeply from your chest, if you look upward—if you put yourself in a resourceful physiology—you can't be depressed. Try it yourself. Stand up tall, throw your shoulders back, breathe deeply, look up, move your body. See if you can feel depressed in that posture. You'll find that it's almost impossible. Instead, your brain is getting a message from your physiology to be alert and vital and resourceful. And that's what it becomes.

When people come to me and say they can't do something, I say, "Act as if you could do it." They usually reply, "Well, I don't know how." So I say, "Act as if you did know how. Stand the way you would be standing if you did know how to do it. Breathe the way you'd be breathing if you did know how to do it right now. Make your face look as if you could do it right now." As soon as they stand that way, breathe that way, and put their physiology in that state, they instantly feel they can do it. It works without fail because of the amazing leverage of being able to adapt and change physiology. Over and over again, simply by changing physiology, you can make people do things they could never do before—because the second they change their physiology, they change their state.

Think of something you imagine you can't do but would like to be able to do. Now how would you stand if you knew you could do it? How would you talk? How would you breathe? Right now, put yourself as congruently as possible in the physiology you would be in if you knew you could do it. Make your whole body give you the same message. Make your stance, breathing, and face reflect the physiology you'd have if you knew you could do it. Now note the difference between this state and the one you were in. If you are congruently maintaining the right physiology, you will feel "as if" you can handle what you didn't think you could before.

The same thing happens in the firewalk. When some people face the bed of coals, they're in a state of total confidence and readiness because of the combination of their internal representations and physiology. Therefore, they can stride confidently and healthfully across the hot coals. Some people, however, begin to panic at the last moment. They may have changed their internal representations of what is going to happen, so they now imagine the worst-possible scenario. Or the searing heat may take them out of their confident state as they approach the edge of the bed of coals. As a result, their bodies may be shaking with fear or they may be crying or they may freeze up, all their muscles locked, or they may have any number of other major physiological reactions. To help them break through their fear in a moment and take action in spite of seemingly impossible odds, I need to do only one thing—change their state. Remember, all human behavior is the result of the state we're in. When we feel strong and resourceful, we will attempt things we never would if we felt scared, weak, and tired. So the firewalk doesn't just teach people intellectually, it gives them an experience of changing their state and behavior in a moment to support their goals, regardless of what they had thought or felt previously.

What do I do with a shaking, crying, frozen person shrieking at the edge of the bed of coals? One thing I can do is change his internal representations. I can have him think of how he will feel after having walked successfully and healthfully to the other side of the coals. This causes him to create an internal representation that changes his physiology. In a matter of two to four seconds, the person is in a resourceful state—you can see him change his breathing and facial expression. I then tell him to go, and the same person who was paralyzed with fear a split second earlier now walks purposefully over the coals and celebrates on the other side. But sometimes people have clear internal pictures of burning or tripping that are bigger than their representations of being able to walk successfully and healthfully. So I need to have them change their submodalities—and this can take time.

My other choice—one that's more efficient when someone is totally panicked in front of the coals—is to change his physiology. After all, if he changes his internal representations, the nervous system has to signal the body to change its posture, breathing pattern, muscular tension, and so forth. So why not just go to the source—bypass all other communication and change the physiology directly? So I take this crying person and have him look up. By doing this, he begins to access the visual aspects of his neurology instead of his kinesthetic. Almost immediately, he stops crying. Try this for yourself; if you are upset or crying and want to stop, look up. Put your shoulders back and get into a visual state. Your feelings will change almost instantaneously. You can do this for your kids. When they get hurt, have them look up. The crying and pain will be stopped, or at least decrease tremendously, in a moment. I may then have the person stand the way he would if he were totally confident and knew he could walk successfully and healthfully across the coals, breathe the way he would be breathing, and say something in the tone of voice of someone who is totally confident. In this way, his brain gets a new message about how to feel, and in the resulting state the same person who was totally immobilized with fear a few seconds ago can produce the action that supports his goals.

The same technique can be practiced whenever we feel we can't do something—we can't approach that woman or man, we can't talk to the boss, and so on. We can change our states and empower ourselves to take action either by changing the pictures and dialogues in our minds or by changing how we are standing, how we are breathing, and the tone of voice we are using. The ideal is to change both physiology and tone. Having done this, we can immediately feel resourceful and be able to follow through with the actions necessary to produce the results we desire.

The same is true with exercise. If you work out hard and you're short of breath and you keep saying to yourself how tired you are or how far you've run, you will indulge in a physiology—like sitting down or panting—that supports that communication. If, however—even though you're out of breath—you consciously stand upright and direct your breathing into a normal rate, you will feel recovered in a matter of moments.

In addition to how we change our feelings, and thus our actions, by changing our internal representations and physiology, the biochemical and electrical processes of our bodies are also affected. Studies show that when people get depressed, their immune systems follow suit and become less efficient—their white blood cell count drops. Have you ever seen a Kirlian photograph of a person? It's the representation of the body's bioelectrical energy, and it changes remarkably as a person changes his state or mood. Because of the linking of mind and body, in intense states our whole electrical field can change, and we can do things that wouldn't otherwise seem possible. Everything I've experienced and read tells me that our bodies have far fewer limits—both positive and negative—than we have been led to believe.

Dr. Herbert Benson, who has written extensively about mind/body relationships, recounts some astonishing stories of the power of voodoo in different parts of the world. In one Australian aboriginal tribe, witch doctors practice a custom called "pointing the bone." It consists of casting a magic spell so potent that the victim knows with absolute certainty he will undergo some terrible disease and probable death. This is how Dr. Benson described one such occurrence in 1925:

"The man who discovers that he is being boned by an enemy is, indeed, a pitiable sight. He stands aghast, with his eyes staring at the treacherous pointer, and his hands lifted as though to ward off the lethal medium which he imagines is pouring into his body. His cheeks blanch and his eyes become glassy, and the expression of his face becomes horribly distorted. . . . He attempts to shriek, but usually the sound chokes in his throat, and all that one might see is froth at his mouth. His body begins to tremble and his muscles twist involuntarily. He sways backwards and falls to the ground, and after a short time appears to be in a swoon; but soon after he writhes as if in mortal agony, and covering his face with his hands, begins to moan. . . . His death is only a matter of a comparatively short time."

I don't know about you, but that's one of the most vivid and horrifying descriptions that I've ever read. I don't think I'll ask you to model it. But it's also one of the most telling examples imaginable of the power of physiology and of belief. In conventional terms, nothing was being done to that man, nothing at all. But the power of his own belief and the force of his own physiology created a terrifyingly potent negative force that utterly destroyed him.

Is that sort of experience limited to societies we consider primitive? Of course not. Exactly the same process goes on around us every day. Benson mentions that Dr. George L. Engel of the University of Rochester Medical Center has developed a lengthy file of newspaper items from all over the world concerning sudden deaths under unexpected circumstances. In each case, it was not that something awful happened in the outside world. Rather, the culprit was the victim's own negative internal representations. In each case, something made the victim feel powerless, helpless, and alone. The result was virtually the same as in the aboriginal rite.

What's interesting to me is that there seems to have been more research and more anecdotal emphasis on the harmful side of the mind/body relationship than on the helpful side. We always hear about the horrible effects of stress or about people losing the will to live after the death of a loved one. We all seem to know that negative states and emotions can literally kill us. But we hear less about the ways positive states can heal us.

One of the most famous stories on that side of the ledger is that of Norman Cousins. In his *Anatomy of an Illness*, he described how he made a miraculous recovery from a long, debilitating illness by laughing his way to health. Laughter was one tool Cousins used in a conscious effort to mobilize his will to live and to prosper. A major part of his regimen was spending a good deal of his day immersed in films, television programs, and books that made him laugh. This obviously changed the consistent internal representations he was making, and the laughter radically changed his physiology—and thus the messages to his nervous system of how to respond. He found that immediate, positive physical changes ensued. He slept better, his pain was lessened, his entire physical presence improved.

Eventually, he recovered completely, even though one of his doctors initially said he had a one-in-five-hundred chance of making a full recovery. Cousins concluded: "I have learned never to underestimate the capacity of the human mind and body to regenerate—even when prospects seem most wretched. The life force may be the least understood force on earth."

Some fascinating research that is beginning to surface may shed some light on Cousins's experience and others like it. The studies look at the way our facial expressions affect the way we feel and conclude it's not so much that we smile when we feel good or laugh when we're in good spirits. Rather, smiling and laughing set off biological processes that, in fact, make us feel good. They increase the flow of blood to the brain and change the level of oxygen, the level of stimulation of the neurotransmitters. The same thing happens with other expressions. Put your facial expression in the physiology of fear or anger or disgust or surprise, and that's what you'll feel.

> *"Our bodies are our gardens . . . our wills are gardeners."*
> —*William Shakespeare*

There are about eighty muscles in the face, and they act as tourniquets, either to keep the blood supply steady while the body is experiencing wild swings or to alter the brain's blood supply and thus, to some degree, the brain's functioning. In a remarkable paper written in 1907, a French physician named Israel Waynbaum theorized that facial expressions actually change feelings. Other researchers today are finding the same thing. As Dr. Paul Ekman, Professor of Psychiatry at the University of California in San Francisco, told the *Los Angeles Times* (June 5, 1985): "We know that if you have an emotion, it shows on your face. Now we've seen it goes the other way too. You become what you put on your face. . . . If you laugh at suffering, you don't feel suffering inside. If your face shows sorrow, you do feel it inside." In fact, Ekman says, the same principle is used regularly to beat lie detectors. People who put themselves in a physiology of belief, even when they're lying through their teeth, will register belief.

All this is exactly what I and others in the NLP community have been teaching for years. Now it looks as though the scientific community is finally verifying what we already found useful. There are a lot of other things in this book they'll be validating in upcoming years. But you don't have to wait for an academic researcher to confirm it for you. You can use it right away and produce the results you desire now.

We're learning so much now about mind/body correlations that some people teach that all you really have to do is take good care of your body. If your body is working at peak levels, your brain will work more effectively as well. The better you use your body, the better your brain is going to work. That's the essence of the work of Moshe Feldenkrais. He used movement to teach people how to think and how to live. Feldenkrais found that simply by working on a kinesthetic level, you can change your self-image, your state, and the overall functioning of your brain. In fact, he states that the quality of your life is the quality of your movement. His works are an invaluable source for creating human transformation through changing physiology in a very specific way.

An important corollary of physiology is congruency. If I'm giving you what I think is a positive message, but my voice is weak and tentative and my body language is disjointed and unfocused, I'm incongruent. Incongruity keeps me from being all I can be, from doing all I can do, and from creating my strongest state. Giving oneself contradictory messages is a subliminal way of pulling a punch.

You may have experienced times when you didn't believe a person, but you weren't sure why. What the person said made sense, but you somehow came away not really believing him. Your unconscious mind picked up what your conscious mind didn't. For example, when you asked a question, the person may have said, "Yes," but at the time his head may have been slowly shaking no. Or he may have said, "I can handle it," but you noted his shoulders were hunched over, his eyes were down, and his breathing was shallow—all of which told your unconscious that he was really saying, "I can't handle it." Part of him wanted to do what you were asking, and part of him didn't. Part of him was confident, and part of him wasn't. Incongruency worked against him. He was trying to go in two directions at once. He was representing one thing with his words and quite another with his physiology.

We've all experienced the price of incongruence when part of us really wants something but another part within seems to stop us. Congruence is power. People who consistently succeed are those who can commit all of their resources, mental and physical, to work together toward achieving a task. Stop a moment now and think of the three most congruent people you know. Now think of the three most incongruent people you know. What is the difference between them? How do congruent people affect you personally versus people who are incongruent?

Developing congruity is a major key to personal power. When I'm communicating, I'm emphatic—in my words, my voice, my breathing, my entire physiology. When my body and my words match, I'm giving clear signals to my brain that this is what I want to produce. And my mind responds accordingly.

If you say to yourself, "Well, yeah, I guess this is what I ought to be doing," and your physiology is weak and indecisive, what sort of a message does the brain get? It's like trying to view a television with a flickering tube. You can barely make out the picture. The same is true for your brain: if the signals your body provides are weak or conflicting, the brain doesn't have a clear sense of what to do. It's like a soldier going into battle with a general who says, "Well, maybe we ought to try this. I'm not sure if it will work, but let's go out and see what happens." What kind of a state does that put the soldier in?

If you say, "I absolutely will do that," and your physiology is unified—that is, your posture, your facial expression, your breathing pattern, the quality of your gestures and movements, and your words and your tonality match—you absolutely will do it. Congruent states are what we all want to move toward, and the biggest step you can take is to be sure you're in a firm, decisive, congruent physiology. If your words and your body don't match up, you're not going to be totally effective.

One way to develop congruency is to model the physiologies of people who are congruent. The essence of modeling is to discover which part of the brain an effective person uses in a given situation. If you want to be effective, you want to use your brain in the same way. If you mirror someone's physiology exactly, you will tap the same part of your brain. Are you in a congruent state now? If not, shift into one. What percentage of the time are you in incongruent states? Can you be congruent more often? Start to do so today. Stop and identify five people who have powerful physiologies that you would like to mirror. How do these physiologies differ from yours? How do the people it? Stand? Move? What are some of their key facial expressions and gestures? Take a moment and sit in the way one of these people sits. Make similar facial expressions and gestures. Notice how you feel.

In our seminars, we have people mirror other people's physiologies, and they find they'll access a similar state and get a similar feeling. So I want you to try an exercise. You need to do it with someone else. Have that person recall a specific intense memory and, without telling you about it, go back into that state. Now I want you to mirror that person exactly. Mirror the way he's sitting, how his legs are positioned. Mirror the position of his arms and hands. Mirror the amount of tension you see in his face and body. Mirror the position of the head and any movements you see in his eyes or legs or neck. Mirror his mouth, his skin tension, his rate of breathing. Try to put yourself in the exact same physiology he's in. If you do all this exactly, you'll succeed. By duplicating that person's physiology, you will be providing your brain with the same signal as he is giving his brain. You'll be able to feel similar or the same feelings. Often you'll see your version of the same pictures he's seeing and think your version of the same thoughts he's thinking.

After you've done this, note a couple of words to describe the state you're in—that is, what you feel while you are mirroring the person exactly. Then check with that person to find out what he was feeling. About 80–90 percent of the time, you will have used the same word to describe the state you were in. There are many people in every seminar who actually start seeing what the other person is seeing. They've described exactly where the person was or identified the people he was picturing in his mind. Some of the accuracies defy rational explanation. It's almost like a psychic experience—except there's no psychic training. All we do is deliver to our brains the exact same messages as the person we're mirroring.

I know this sounds hard to believe, but people in my seminars have learned that it can be done after five minutes of training. I can't guarantee you'll succeed the first time out, but if you ever come close, you'll find yourself in the same state of anger or pain or sadness or elation or joy or ecstasy that the other person is in. Yet you've had no conversation in advance as to what he was feeling.

Some recent research gives scientific support to this. According to a story in *Omni* magazine, two researchers have found that words have a characteristic electrical pattern in the brain. Neurophysiologist Donald York of the University of Missouri Medical Center and Chicago speech pathologist Tom Jenson found that the same patterns hold true from person to person. In one experiment, they were even able to find the same brain wave pattern in people who spoke different languages. They've already taught computers to recognize those brain wave patterns so they can interpret the words in a person's mind even before they're spoken! The computers can literally read minds, much the way we can when we precisely mirror physiology.

Some unique aspects of physiology—special looks or tonalities or physical gestures—can be found in people of great power, like John F. Kennedy, Martin Luther King, Jr., or Franklin Roosevelt. If you can model their specific physiologies, you'll tap into the same resourceful parts of the brain and start to process information the way they do. You'll literally feel the way they felt. Obviously, since breathing, movement, and tonality are critical factors in creating state, photos of these people do not provide as specific an amount of information as would be desirable. A movie or video of them would be ideal. For a moment mirror just their postures, facial expressions, and gestures as accurately as you can. You will begin to feel similar feelings. If you remember how that person's voice sounds, you might say something in that tone of voice.

Also note the level of congruency all these people share. Their physiology is delivering one single message, not conflicting messages. If you were incongruent when you mirrored their physiologies, you would not feel as they felt because you would not be delivering the same messages to the brain. If, for example, you were mirroring the physiology and simultaneously saying to yourself, "I look stupid," you would not fully experience the benefits of mirroring because you were not congruent. Your body would have been saying one thing and your mind another. Power comes from delivering one unified message.

If you can get a tape of a Martin Luther King, Jr., speech and speak as he speaks, duplicating his tonality, voice, and tempo, you may feel a sense of power and strength like never before. And one of the great advantages of reading a book by someone like John F. Kennedy or Benjamin Franklin or Albert Einstein is that it puts you in a state similar to theirs. You start thinking like the authors, creating the same kind of internal representations. But by duplicating their physiology, you can feel like them in the flesh and even behave as they did.

Would you like to immediately tap more of your inner power and magic? Start consciously modeling the physiology of people you respect or admire. You will begin to create the same states that they experience. It is often possible to achieve an exact experience. Obviously, you don't want to model the physiology of someone who is depressed. You want to model people who are in a powerful, resourceful state because duplicating them will give you a new set of choices, a way to access parts of your brain that you may not have effectively used in the past.

In one seminar, I met a kid I couldn't figure out. He was in the least resourceful physiology I'd ever seen, and I couldn't get him into a more powerful state. It turns out he'd had part of his brain destroyed in an accident. But I got him to act "as if"— to model me and put himself into a physiology he didn't think he had access to. And by modeling me, his brain started to work in a whole new way. By the end of the seminar, people almost couldn't recognize him. He was acting and feeling completely different from ever before. By mimicking another's physiology, he had begun to experience new choices of thought, emotion, and action.

If you were to model a world-class runner's belief sys mental syntax, and physiology, does that mean you, t be able to run a mile in less than four minutes shortly after modeling him? Of course not. You are not modeling the person exactly, because you have not developed the same consistent messages to your nervous system as he has through consistent practice. It's important to note that some strategies require a level of physiological development or programming that you do not yet have. You may have modeled the world's greatest baker, but if you try to bake his recipe in an oven that only gets up to 225 degrees, while his goes to 625, you are not going to produce the same result. However, by using his recipe, you can maximize the result you get even with your oven. And if you model the way he got his oven to increase its output over the years, you can create the same result if you're willing to pay the appropriate price. In order to increase your ability to produce results by modeling strategies, you may need to invest some time in increasing the power of your oven. This is something we'll talk a bit about in the next chapter.

Being attentive to physiology creates choices. Why do people take drugs, drink alcohol, smoke cigarettes, overeat? Aren't these all indirect attempts to change state by changing physiology? This chapter has provided you with the direct approach to quickly changing states. By breathing or moving body or facial muscles in a new pattern, you imediately change your state. It will produce the same results as food, alcohol, or drugs without harmful side effects to either your body or your psyche. Remember, in any cybernetic loop, the individual who has the most choice is in control. In any device, the most critical aspect is flexibility. All other things being equal, the system with the most flexibility has more choices and more ability to direct other aspects of the system. It's the same with people. The people with the most choices are the ones most in charge. Modeling is about creating possibility. And there's no faster, more dynamic way than through physiology.

The next time you see someone who is extremely successful, someone you admire and respect, copy gestures, feel the difference, and enjoy the change in thought patterns. Play. Experience it. New choices await you! Now let's take a look at another aspect of physiology—the foods we eat, the way we breathe, and the nutrients we supply to ourselves. They all are parts of . . .

CHAPTER X

Energy: The Fuel of Excellence

"The health of the people is really the foundation upon which all their happiness and all their powers as a state depend."

—*Benjamin Disraeli*

We've seen that physiology is the avenue to excellence. One way to affect physiology is to change the way you use your muscular system—you can change your posture, your facial expressions, and your breathing. Everything I talk about in this book also depends on a healthy level of biochemical functioning. It assumes that you're cleansing and nurturing your body, not clogging and poisoning it. In this chapter, we'll look at the underpinnings of physiology—what you eat and drink, and how you breathe.

I call energy the fuel of excellence. You can change your internal representations all day long, if your biochemistry is messed up, it's going to make the brain create distorted representations. It's going to throw off the whole system. In fact, it's ighly unlikely you'll even feel like using what you've learned. u could have the most beautiful race car in the world, but if you try to run it on beer, it's not going to work. You can have the right car and the right fuel, but if the spark plugs are not firing right, you won't get peak performance. In this chapter, I'm going to share some thoughts about energy and how to raise it to peak levels. The higher the energy level, the more efficient your body. The more efficient your body, the better you feel and the more you will use your talent to produce outstanding results.

I know firsthand the importance of energy and the magic that an abundance of it can unleash. I used to weigh 268 pounds. I now weigh 238. Before, I was not exactly looking for all the ways I could make my life work. My physiology didn't help me produce outstanding results. What I could learn and do and create was secondary to what I could eat and watch on TV. But one day I decided I was tired of living that way, so I started studying about what produced outstanding health, and then I modeled people who had consistently produced it in themselves.

The nutritional field was so contradictory and confusing, however, I didn't know what to do at first. I'd read one book, and it would say do this and this and this and you'll live forever. So I'd get all excited—until I got to the next book, which said if you did all those things, you'd die, so do this and that and this. Of course, as soon as I read the third book, it also contradicted the first two. All the authors were MDs, yet they couldn't even agree on the basics.

I wasn't looking for credentials. What I wanted was results. So I found people who were producing results in their body, people who were vibrant and healthy. I found out what they were doing, and I did the same. I compiled everything I learned into a set of commitments or principles for myself, and I set up a sixty-day program for healthy living. I applied these principles daily, and I lost thirty pounds in a little more than thirty days. More important, I finally found a way to live that was hassle free and not diet oriented (notice what the first three letters in the word "diet" spell)—a way that respected how my body worked.

I'll share with you here the principles I've lived by for the last five years. Before I do, though, let me give you an example of how they have transformed my physiology. I used to need eight hours of sleep. I also needed three alarm clocks to wake me up in the morning—one that rang, one that turned on a radio, and one that switched on the lights. Now, I can lead a seminar all evening, go to sleep at one or two in the morning, and wake up after five or six hours of sleep, feeling absolutely vibrant, strong, and energized. If my bloodstream were polluted, if my energy level were tainted, I'd be trying to make the most of a very limited physiology. Instead, I start with a physiology that allows me to mobilize all my physical and mental abilities.

In this chapter, I'm going to give you six keys to a powerful, indomitable physiology. Much of what I say will challenge things you've always believed. Some of it will go against the notions you now have of good health. But these six principles have worked spectacularly for me and the people I've worked with, as well as thousands of others who practice a science of health called natural hygiene. I want you to think carefully about whether they could work for you and whether your current health habits are the most effective way to take care of your body. Apply all six principles for ten to thirty days and judge their validity by the results they produce in your body rather than by what you may have been educated to believe. Understand how your body works, respect it, and take care of it, and it will take care of you. You've been learning to run your own brain. Now you must learn how to run your body.

Let's start with the first key to living health—the power of breath. The foundation of health is a healthy bloodstream, the system that transports oxygen and nutrients to all the cells of your body. If you have a healthy circulation system, you're going to live a long, healthy life. That environment is the bloodstream. What is the control button for that system? Breathing. It's the way you fully oxygenate the body and thus stimulate the electrical process of each and every cell.

Let's take a closer look at how the body works. Breathing not only controls the oxygenation of the cells. It also controls the flow of lymph fluid, which contains white blood cells to protect the body. What is the lymph system? Some people think of it as the body's sewage system. Every cell in your body is surrounded by lymph. You have four times as much lymph fluid in your body as you do blood. Here's how the lymph system works. Blood is pumped from your heart through your arteries to the thin, porous capillaries. The blood carries oxygen and nutrients to the capillaries, where they are then diffused into this fluid around the cells called lymph. The cells, having an intelligence or affinity for what they need, take oxygen and nutrients necessary for their health and then excrete toxins, some of which go back into the capillaries. But dead cells, blood proteins, and other toxic material must be removed by the lymph system. And the lymph system is activated by deep breathing.

The body's cells depend on the lymph system as the only way to drain off the large toxic materials and excess fluid, which restrict the amount of oxygen. The fluid passes through the lymph nodes, where dead cells and all other poisons except blood proteins are neutralized and destroyed. How important is the lymph system? If it were totally shut down for twenty-four hours, you would be dead as the result of trapped blood proteins and excess fluid around the cells.

The bloodstream has a pump, your heart. But the lymph system doesn't have one. The only way lymph moves is through deep breathing and muscular movement. So if you want to have a healthy bloodstream with effective lymph and immune systems, you need to breathe deeply and produce the movements that will stimulate them. Look carefully at any "health program" that doesn't first and foremost teach you how to fully cleanse your body through effective breathing.

Dr. Jack Shields, a highly regarded lymphologist from Santa Barbara, California, recently conducted an interesting study of the immune system. He put cameras inside people's bodies to see what stimulated cleansing of the lymph system. He found that a deep diaphragmatic breath is the most effective way to accomplish this. It creates something like a vacuum that sucks lymph through the bloodstream and multiplies the pace at which the body eliminates toxins. In fact, deep breathing and exercise can accelerate this process by as much as fifteen times.

If you get nothing else from this chapter but an understanding of the importance of deep breathing, you could dramatically increase the level of your body's health. It's the reason that health systems life yoga focus so much attention on healthy breathing. There's nothing like it to cleanse your body.

It doesn't take too much common sense to realize that of all the elements necessary for good health, oxygen is the most critical. Yet it's important to note just how important it is. Dr. Otto Warburg, Nobel Prize winner and director of the Max Planck Institute for Cell Physiology, studied the effect of oxygen on cells. He was able to turn normal, healthy cells into malignant cells simply by lowering the amount of oxygen available to them. His work was followed up here in the United States by Dr. Harry Goldblatt. In the *Journal of Experimental Medicine* (1953), Goldblatt described the experiments he conducted with a species of rats that had never been known to have malignant growths. He took cells out of newborn rats and divided them into three groups. One of the three groups of cells was put in a bell jar and deprived of oxygen for up to thirty minutes at a time. Like Dr. Warburg, Goldblatt discovered that after a few weeks many of these cells died, the movement of others slowed, and still others began to change their structure taking on the appearance of malignant cells. The other two groups of cells were maintained in bell jars whose oxygen content was consistently maintained at atmospheric concentrations.

After thirty days, Dr. Goldblatt injected all three groups of cells into three separate groups of rats. After two weeks, when the cells had been reabsorbed into the animals, nothing happened with the two normal groups. However, *all* the rats in the third group—those whose cells had been periodically deprived of oxygen—developed malignant growths. This work was followed up a year later. The malignant growths remained malignant, and the normal cells remained normal.

What does this tell us? The researchers came to believe that lack of oxygen seems to play a major role in causing cells to become malignant or cancerous. It certainly affects the quality of life of the cells. Remember that the quality of your health is really the quality of the life of your cells. Thus, fully oxygenating your system would seem to be a number-one priority, and breathing effectively is certainly the place to start.

The problem is that most people don't know how to breathe. One of three Americans gets cancer. Yet athletes experience only one case of cancer to every seven in average Americans. Why? These studies begin to give us an explanation. Athletes are giving the bloodstream its most important and vital element—oxygen. Another explanation is that athletes are stimulating their bodies' immune system to work at maximum levels by stimulating the movement of lymph.

Let me share with you the most effective way to breathe in order to cleanse your system. You should breathe in this ratio: inhale one count, hold four counts, exhale two counts. If you inhaled for four seconds, you would hold for sixteen and exhale for eight. Why exhale for twice as long as you inhale? That's when you eliminate toxins via your lymphatic system. Why hold four times as long? That's how you can fully oxygenate the blood and activate your lymphatic system. When you breathe, you should start from deep in your abdomen, like a vacuum cleaner that's getting rid of all toxins in the blood system.

How hungry do you feel after you exercise? Do you want to sit down and eat a big steak after you've just run four miles? We know in fact that people don't. Why not? Because through healthy breathing your body is already getting what it needs most. So here's the first key to healthy living. Stop and take ten deep breaths, in the above ratio, at least three times a day. What's the ratio? One count inhale, four counts hold, two counts exhale. For example, starting in the abdomen, take a deep breath through your nose while counting to seven (or pick a larger or smaller number based upon your ability). Hold your breath for a count four times that of your inhalation, or twenty-eight. Then exhale slowly through your mouth for a count two times the length of your inhalation, or fourteen. You should never strain yourself. See what numbers you can build up to by slowly developing greater lung capacity. Take ten of these deep breaths three times a day, and you'll experience a dramatic improvement in the level of your health. There is no food or vitamin pill in the world that can do for you what excellent breathing patterns can do.

The other essential component of healthy overall breathing is daily aerobic exercise.* Running is fine, though a little stressful. Swimming is excellent. But one of the best all-weather aerobic exercises is trampolining, which is easily accessible and puts minimal stress on your body.

It is important that this concentrated exercise of trampolining be done without undue stress. You can slowly and carefully work your way up until you can go for thirty minutes with no pain, no stress, and no fatigue. Build a solid foundation before you begin to jog or jump up and down. If you exercise properly, you will be able to breathe deeply and continue until you have had a good workout. There are many books on trampolining and how it strengthens every organ in the body. Please take the time to pursue this life-enhancing form of exercise. You'll be glad you did.

The second key is the principle of eating water-rich foods. Seventy percent of the planet is covered with water. Eighty percent of your body is made up of water. What do you think a large percentage of your diet should contain? You need to make certain that 70 percent of your diet is made up of foods that are rich in water. That means fresh fruits or vegetables, or their juices freshly squeezed.

Some people recommend drinking from eight to twelve glasses of water a day to "flush out the system." Do you know how crazy that is? In the first place, most of our water isn't so great. Chances are it contains chlorine, fluoride, minerals, and other toxic substances. Drinking distilled water is usually the best idea. But no matter what kind of water you drink, you can't cleanse your system by drowning it. The amount of water you drink should be dictated by thirst.

---

* Aerobic literally means "to exercise with air."

Instead of trying to flush your system by flooding it with water, all you have to do is eat foods that are naturally rich in water—water-content foods. There are only three kinds on the planet: fruits, vegetables, and sprouts. These will provide you with an abundance of water, the lifegiving, cleansing substance. When people live on a diet that is low in water-content foods, an unhealthy functioning of the body is almost guaranteed. As Alexander Bryce, M.D., states in *The Laws of Life and Health*, "When too little fluid is supplied, the blood maintains a higher specific gravity and the poisonous waste products of tissue or cell change are only cast off very imperfectly. The body is, therefore, poisoned by its own excretions, and it is not too much to say that the chief reason of this is because a sufficient amount of fluid has not been supplied to carry off in solution the waste matter the cells manufacture."

Your diet should be consistently assisting your body with the process of cleansing, rather than burdening it with indigestible food stuff. The buildup of waste products within the body promotes disease. One way to keep the bloodstream and body as free as possible from wastes and toxic poisons is to limit ingestion of those foods or nonfoods that strain the eliminative organs of the body; the other is to provide enough water to the system to assist in the dilution and elimination of such wastes. Dr. Bryce continues, "There is no fluid known to chemists which can dissolve as many solid substances as water, which is indeed the best solvent in existence. If, therefore, sufficient quantities of it are supplied, the whole process of nutrition is stimulated because the paralyzing effect of the toxic waste products is removed by their solution and subsequent excretion by the kidneys, skin, bowel, or lungs. If on the contrary these toxic materials are allowed to accumulate in the body, all sorts of diseases will arise."

Why is heart disease our biggest killer? Why do we hear about people keeling over and dropping dead on the tennis court at the age of forty? One reason may be that they've spent a lifetime clogging their system. Remember, the quality of your life is dependent upon the quality of the life of your cells. If the bloodstream is filled with waste products, the resulting environment does not promote a strong, vibrant, healthy cell life—nor a biochemistry capable of creating a balanced emotional life for an individual.

Dr. Alexis Carrel, a Nobel Prize winner in 1912 and then a member of the Rockefeller Institute, set out to prove this theory by taking the tissue from chickens (which normally live an average of eleven years) and keeping their cells alive indefinitely simply by keeping them free of their own wastes and by supplying them with the nutrients they needed. These cells were kept alive for thirty-four years, after which the Rockefeller Institute became convinced that they could keep them alive forever and thus decided to end the experiment.

What percentage of your diet is made up of water-rich foods? If you were to make a list of all the things you're ingested in the past week, what percentage would be rich in water? Would it be 70 percent? I doubt it. How about 50? Twenty-five? Fifteen? When I ask this in my seminars, I usually find that most people eat about 15–20 percent water-content foods. And that's definitely higher than the population as a whole. Let me tell you something. Fifteen percent is suicidal. If you don't believe me, just check out the statistics for cancer and heart disease and review what kinds of foods the National Academy of Sciences recommends you avoid, and the amount of water content available in those foods.

If you look to nature and you see the biggest and most powerful animals, you'll discover they're herbivores. Gorillas, elephants, rhinoceroses, and so on all eat only water-rich foods. Herbivores live longer than carnivores. Think of a vulture. Why do you think it looks that way? It doesn't eat water-rich foods. If you eat something that's dried and dead, guess what you're going to look like? I'm only half kidding on this point. A building can only be as strong and as elegant as its parts. The same is true of your body. If you want to feel fully alive, then common sense dictates that you eat water-rich, live foods. It's that simple. How can you make sure that 70 percent of your diet consists of water-content foods? It's actually very simple. Just be certain from now on to have a salad with each meal. Make fruit the snack you reach for instead of a candy bar. You'll feel the difference when you body runs more efficiently and thus allows you to feel as great as you are!

The third key to living health is the principle of effective food combining. Not long ago, a medical doctor named Steven Smith celebrated his one hundredth birthday. When he was asked what allowed him to live so long, he replied, "Take care of your stomach for the first fifty years, and it will take care of you for the next fifty." Truer words were never spoken.

Many great scientists have studied food combining. Dr. Herbert Shelton is the best known. But do you know who was the first scientist to study it extensively? It was Dr. Ivan Pavlov, the man best known for his groundbreaking work with stimulus/response. Some people turn food combining into something very complicated, but it's actually pretty simple: Some foods should not be eaten with others. Different types of foods require different types of digestive juices, and not all digestive juices are compatible.

For example, do you eat meat and potatoes together? How about cheese and bread, or milk and cereal, or fish and rice? What if I were to tell you that those combinations are totally destructive to your internal system and rob you of energy? You'd probably say that I'd made sense to this point, but now I'd lost my head.

Let me explain why these combinations are destructive and how you can save yourself large amounts of nerve energy you may currently be wasting. Different foods are digested differently. Starchy foods (rice, bread, potatoes, and so on) require an alkaline digestive medium, which is initially supplied in the mouth by the enzyme ptyalin. Protein foods (meat, dairy, nuts, seeds, and the like) require an acid medium for digestion—hydrochloric acid and pepsin.

Now it is a law of chemistry that two contrary mediums (acid and alkali) cannot work at the same time. They neutralize each other. If you eat a protein with a starch, digestion is impaired or completely arrested. Undigested food becomes soil for bacteria, which ferment and decompose it, giving rise to digestive disorders and gas.

Incompatible food combinations rob you of energy, and anything that produces a loss of energy is potentially disease-producing. It creates excess acid, which causes the blood to thicken and thus move more slowly through the system, robbing the body of oxygen. Remember how you felt after you dragged yourself from Thanksgiving dinner last year? How conducive is that to good health, to a healthy bloodstream, to an energetic physiology? To producing the results you desire for your life? What is the numnber-one-selling prescription drug in the United States? Do you know? It used to be the tranquilizer Valium. Now it's Tagamet, a drug for stomach disorders. Maybe there's a more sensible way to eat. That's what food combining is all about.

Here's a very simple way to think about it. Eat only one condensed food at a meal. What's a condensed food? It's any food that's not rich in water. For example, beef jerky is condensed, whereas watermelon is water-rich. Some people don't want to limit their intake of condensed foods, so let me tell you the least you can do. Make sure you don't eat starchy carbohydrates and protein at the same meal. Don't have those meat and potatoes together. If you feel you can't live without both, have one at lunch and the other at dinner. That's not so hard, is it? You can go to the finest restaurant in the world and say, "I'll have the steak without the baked potato, and I'll have a big salad and some steamed vegetables." That's no problem: the protein will mix with the salad and vegetables because they're water-content foods. You could also order the baked potato (or two) without the steak and have a huge salad and steamed vegetables. Will you leave a meal like this feeling hungry? Absolutely not.

Do you wake up tired in the morning, even after six or seven or eight hours of sleep? Know why? While you're sleeping, your body is working overtime to digest the incompatible combinations of food you've put in your stomach. For many people, digestion takes more nerve energy than almost anything else.

When foods are improperly combined in the digestive tract, the time it takes to digest them can be as much as eight, ten, twelve, or fourteen hours, even more. When foods are properly combined, the body is able to do its job effectively, and digestion lasts an average of three to four hours, so you don't have to waste your energy on digestion.*

An excellent source for a thorough treatment of the subject of food combining is Dr. Herbert Shelton's *Food Combining Made Easy*. Also, my former partners, Harvey and Marilyn Diamond have written an excellent book called *Fit for Life*. It's filled with great properly combined recipes. For immediate information, see the food-combining chart, and simply follow these principles in your eating.

Let's go on the fourth key, the law of controlled consumption. Do you love to eat? So do I. Want to learn how to eat a lot? Here it is: Eat a little. That way, you'll be around long enough to eat a lot.

Medical study after medical study has shown the same thing. The surest way to increase an animal's life span is to cut down on the amount of food it eats. Dr. Clive McCay conducted one famous study at Cornell University. In his experiment, he took laboratory rats and cut their food intake in half. It doubled their life span. One follow-up study done by Dr. Edward J. Masaro at the University of Texas was even more interesting. Masaro worked with three groups of rats: one group ate as much as it wanted; a second group had its food intake cut by 60 percent; and the third group was able to eat as much as it wanted, but its protein intake was cut in half. Want to know what happened? After 810 days, only 13 percent of the first group remained alive. Of the second group whose food consumption was cut by 60 percent, 97 percent were still alive. Of the third group where food intake remained high, but protein consumption was cut in half, 50 percent were still alive.

---

* After eating a properly combined meal, one must wait at least three and a half hours before ingesting any other foods. Also, it is important to note that the drinking of fluids at meals dilutes the digestive juices and slows the digestive process.

A FOOD COMBINING CHART FOR COMPLETE & EFFICIENT DIGESTION

This "Common Sense" chart will show you how fresh, vital foods properly combined will promote optimum digestion, energize & strengthen your body.

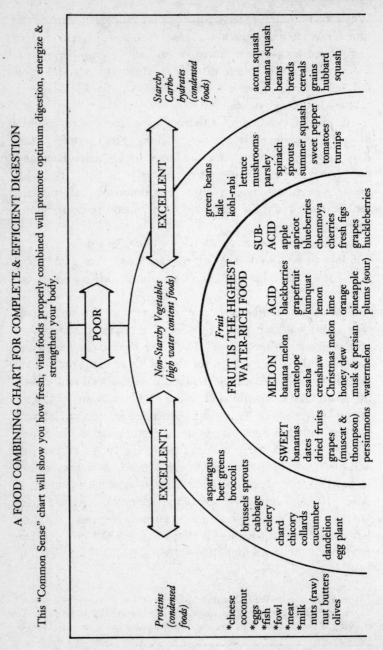

Proteins *(condensed foods)*

*cheese
coconut
*eggs
*fish
*fowl
*meat
*milk
nuts (raw)
nut butters
olives

EXCELLENT!

Non-Starchy Vegetables *(high water content foods)*

asparagus
beet greens
broccoli
brussels sprouts
cabbage
celery
chard
chicory
collards
cucumber
dandelion
egg plant

Fruit

FRUIT IS THE HIGHEST WATER-RICH FOOD

SWEET
bananas
dates
dried fruits
grapes
(muscat & thompson)
persimmons

MELON
banana melon
cantelope
casaba
crenshaw
Christmas melon
honey dew
musk & persian
watermelon

ACID
blackberries
grapefruit
kumquat
lemon
lime
orange
pineapple
plums (sour)

SUB-ACID
apple
apricot
blueberries
chenmoya
cherries
fresh figs
grapes
huckleberries

POOR

EXCELLENT

green beans
kale
kohl-rabi
lettuce
mushrooms
parsley
spinach
sprouts
summer squash
sweet pepper
tomatoes
turnips

Starchy Carbo-hydrates *(condensed foods)*

acorn squash
banana squash
beans
breads
cereals
grains
hubbard squash

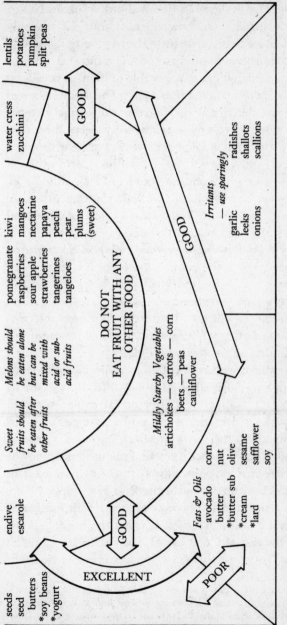

1. Protein & Carbohydrate foods should never be combined.
2. A leafy green salad can be eaten with any protein, carbohydrate, or fat.
3. Fats inhibit the digestion of protein. If you must have a fat with a protein, eat a mixed vegetable salad. It will offset the inhibiting effect on digestion.
4. You should never drink liquids with or immediately following a meal.
* Listed for clarification but not recommended.

Is there a message in this? Dr. Ray Walford, a famous UCLA researcher, concluded, "Undernutrition is thus far the only method we know of that consistently retards the aging process and extends the maximum life span of warm-blooded animals. These studies are undoubtedly applicable to humans because it works in every species studied thus far."* The studies showed that physiological deterioration, including the normal deterioration of the immune system, was markedly delayed by food restriction. So the message is simple and clear: Eat less, live more.† I'm like you. I love to eat. It can be a form of entertainment. But make sure your entertainment isn't killing you. If you want to eat large quantities of food, you can. Just make sure they're water-rich foods. You can eat a whole lot more salad than you can steak and remain vibrant and healthy.

The fifth key to the living health program is the principle of effective fruit consumption. Fruit is the most perfect food. It takes the least amount of energy to digest and gives your body the most in return. The only food your brain can work on is glucose. Fruit is primarily fructose (which can be easily converted into glucose), and it's most often 90–95 percent water. That means it's cleansing and nurturing at the same time.

The only problem with fruit is that most people don't know how to eat it in a way that allows the body effectively to use its nutrients. You must always eat fruit on an empty stomach. Why? The reason is that fruit is not primarily digested in the stomach. It digests in the small intestine. Fruit is designed to go right through the stomach in a few minutes and into the intestines, where it releases its sugars. But if there is meat or potatoes or starch in the stomach, the fruit gets trapped there and begins to ferment. Did you ever eat some fruit for dessert after a big meal and find yourself burping the uncomfortable aftertaste for the rest of the evening? The reason is you didn't eat it properly. You must always eat fruit on an empty stomach.

* From the "Informational News" Section of *Awake* (December 22, 1982), p. 3.
† When you eat is also important. It is best not to eat immediately before you go to bed. An excellent habit to develop is to eat no food other than fruit after 9:00 P.M.

The best kind of fruit is fresh fruit or freshly squeezed fruit juice. You don't want to drink juice right out of a can or glass container. Why not? Much of the time the juice has been heated in the sealing process, and its structure has become acidic. Do you want to make the most valuable purchase you can? Buy a juicer? Do you own a car? Sell the car and buy a juicer. The juicer will take you much farther. Or just buy the juicer now! You can ingest juice as you would the fruit itself, on an empty stomach. And juice is digested so fast that you can eat a meal fifteen or twenty minutes later.

This isn't just me talking. Dr. William Castillo, head of the famed Framington, Massachusetts, heart study, has stated that fruit is the finest food you could possibly eat to protect yourself against heart disease. He said fruit contains bioflavinoids, which keep the blood from thickening and plugging up the arteries. It also strengthens the capillaries, and weak capillaries often lead to internal bleeding and heart attacks.

Not long ago I talked with a marathon runner in one of the health seminars I promoted. He was pretty skeptical by nature, but he agreed to make the proper use of fruits in his diet. Know what happened? He took 9.5 minutes off his marathon time. He cut his recovery time in half, and he qualified for the Boston Marathon for the first time in his life.

Here's one final thing I want you to keep in mind about fruits. What should you start a day with? What should you have for breakfast? Do you think it's a smart idea to jump out of bed and clog your system with some huge mound of food you'll take all day to digest? Of course not.

What you want is something that is easy to digest, that provides fructose the body can use right away, and that helps cleanse the body. When you wake up, and for as long into the day as is comfortably possible, eat nothing but fresh fruit or freshly squeezed fruit juice. Keep this commitment until as least twelve noon each day. The longer you can go with just fruit in your body, the greater the opportunity for your body to cleanse itself. If you start to wean yourself from coffee and the other garbage you used to load your body down with at the start of the day, you'll feel a new rush of vitality and energy you won't believe. Try it for the next ten days and see for yourself.

The sixth key to living health is the protein myth. Have you ever heard it said that if you tell a big-enough lie loud enough and long enough, sooner or later people will believe you? Welcome to the wonderful world of protein. No bigger lie has ever been told than the one that human beings require a high-protein diet to maintain optimum health and well-being.

Chances are you're pretty conscious of your protein intake. Why is that? Some people are looking for an increased level of energy. Some think they need protein to help with endurance. Some eat it for strong bones. Excess protein has the exact opposite effect in every one of those cases.

Let's find a model of how much protein you might really need. When do you think people are most in need of protein? Probably when they're infants. Mother Nature has provided a food, mother's milk, that supplies the infant with everything it needs. Guess how much of mother's milk is protein—50 percent, 25 percent, 10 percent? Too high in every case. Mother's milk is 2.38 percent protein at birth and reduces to 1.2–1.6 percent protein in six months. That's all. So where do we get the idea that humans need massive amounts of protein?

No one really has any idea how much protein we need. After ten years of studying human protein ingestion needs, Dr. Mark Hegstead, past professor of nutrition at Harvard Medical School, confirmed the fact that most human beings seem to adapt to whatever protein intake is available to them. In addition, even people like Frances Lappé, who wrote *Diet for a Small Planet*, which for almost a decade promoted the concept of combining vegetables in order to get all the essential amino acids, now says that she was incorrect, that people do not have to combine their proteins, that if you eat a fairly balanced vegetarian diet, you will get all the protein you need. The National Academy of Sciences says that the adult American male needs fifty-six grams of protein a day. In a report by the International Union of Nutritional Sciences, we find that each country has adult male daily protein requirements that vary from 39 to 110 grams per day. So who really has any idea? Why would you need all that protein? Presumably to replace what you lose. But you lose only a tiny amount through excretion and respiration a day. So where do they get those numbers?

We called the National Academy of Sciences and asked how they arrived at the figure of fifty-six grams. In fact, their own literature says we only need thirty, but they recommend fifty-six. Now they also say that excess protein intake overworks the urinary tract and causes fatigue. So why do they recommend even more than they say we need? We're still waiting for a good answer. They simply told us they used to recommend eighty grams, but when they decided to lower it, they were met with a huge public outcry. From whom? Did you or I call in to complain? Not likely. The outcry came from vested interests who earn their livelihood through the sale of high-protein foods and products.

What's the greatest marketing plan on earth? It's making people think they'll die unless they use your product. That's exactly what has happened with protein. Let's analyze this correctly. What about the idea that you need protein for energy? What does your body use for energy? First it uses glucose from fruits, vegetables, and sprouts. Then it uses starch. Then it uses fat. The last thing it ever uses for energy is protein. So much for that myth. How about the idea that protein helps build endurance? Wrong. Excess protein provides the body with excess nitrogen, which causes fatigue. Body builders all pumped up with protein are not known for their marathon-running abilities. They're too tired. Well, what about protein building strong bones? Wrong again. It's the opposite. Too much protein has been linked continuously to osteoporosis, the softening and weakening of bones. The strongest bones on the planet belong to vegetarians.

I could give you a hundred reasons why eating meat for protein is one of the worst things you could do. One of the by-products of protein metabolism is ammonia, for example. Let me mention two points in particular. First, meat contains high levels of uric acid. Uric acid is one of the body's waste or excretory products resulting from the work of living cells. The kidneys extract uric acid from the bloodstream and send it on to the bladder to be passed out with the urea as urine. If uric acid is not promptly and thoroughly removed from the blood, the excess builds up in the tissues of the body, to later create gout or bladder stones, not to mention what it does to your kidneys. People with leukemia are usually found to have very high levels of uric acid in their bloodstream. The average piece of meat has fourteen grains of uric acid. Your body can only eliminate about 8 grains of uric acid in a day. In addition, do you know what gives meat its taste? Uric acid, from that now dead animal you're consuming. If you doubt this, try eating kosher-style meat before it's spiced. As the blood is drained out, so is most of the uric acid. Meat without uric acid has no flavor. Is that what you want to put in your body, the acid normally eliminated in the urine of an animal?

Moreover, meat is teeming with putrefactive bacteria. In case you're wondering what putrefactive bacteria are, they are colon germs. As Dr. Jay Milton Hoffman explained it in his book, *The Missing Link in the Medical Curriculum Which Is Food Chemistry in Its Relationship to Body Chemistry*, page 135: "When the animal is alive, the osmotic process in the colon keeps putrefactive bacteria from getting into the animal. When the animal is dead the osmotic process is gone and putrefactive bacteria swarm through the walls of the colon and into the flesh. They tenderize the meat." You notice meat has to age. What ages or softens the flesh are the putrefactive bacteria.

Other experts say of the bacteria in meat: "The bacteria in meats are identical in character with those of manure and more numerous in some meats than in fresh manure. All meats become infected with manure germs in the process of slaughtering and the number increases the longer the meat is kept in storage."*

* A. W. Nelson, bacteriologist of the Battle Creek Sanitarium and Hospital, from paper by Dr. J. H. Kellogg, read at National Nut Growers' Convention, Jacksonville, Florida, 1930, and printed in *Annual Proceedings* as quoted by Jay Milton Hoffman, N.D., Ph.D., in *The Missing Link in the Medical Curriculum Which Is Food Chemistry in its Relationship to Body Chemistry*, page 134, footnote #5, page 141, printed by Professional Press Publishing Company, 13115 Hunza Hill Terrace, Valley Center, CA 92802.

Is that what you want to eat?

If you absolutely must eat meat, this is what you should do. First, get it from a source that guarantees it's pasture grazed, that is, a source that guarantees it doesn't have growth hormones or DES. Second, drastically cut your intake. Make your new maximum one serving of meat per day.

I'm not saying that simply by not eating meat you will be healthy, nor am I saying if you do eat meat, you cannot be healthy. Neither of these two statements would be true. Many meat eaters are healthier than vegetarians simply because some vegetarians have a tendency to believe that if they don't eat meat, they can eat anything else. I'm certainly not advocating that.

But you should know you can be healthier and happier than you are now by deciding you no longer want to eat off the flesh and skin of other living beings. You know what Pythagoras, Socrates, Plato, Aristotle, Leonardo da Vinci, Isaac Newton, Voltaire, Henry David Thoreau, George Bernard Shaw, Benjamin Franklin, Thomas Edison, Dr. Albert Schweitzer, Mahatma Gandhi have in common? They were all vegetarians. Not a bad group of people to model, right?

Are dairy products any better? In some ways, they're even worse. Every animal has milk with the right balance of elements for that animal. Many problems can result from drinking the milk of other animals, including cows. For example, powerful growth hormones in cow's milk are designed to raise a calf from ninety pounds at birth to a thousand pounds at physical maturity two years later. By comparison, a human infant is born at six to eight pounds and reaches physical maturity at one hundred to two hundred pounds twenty-one years later. There is great controversy as to the effect this has on our population. Dr. William Ellis, a great authority on dairy products and how they affect the human bloodstream, states that if you want allergies, drink milk. If you want a clogged system, drink milk. The reason, he states, is that few adults can properly metabolize the protein in cow's milk. The principal protein in cow's milk is casein, which is what a cow's metabolism needs for proper health. However, casein is not what humans properly need. According to his studies, both infants and adults have a great deal of difficulty digesting casein. His studies show that, at least in infants, 50 percent or more of the casein is not digested. These partially digested proteins often enter the bloodstream and irritate the tissues, creating susceptibility to allergins. Eventually, the liver has to remove all these partially digested cow proteins, and that in turn places an unnecessarily heavy burden on the entire excretory system, and on the liver in particular. By contrast, lactalbumin, the primary protein in human milk, is easy for humans to digest. As for drinking milk for calcium, Ellis states that after doing blood tests on over 25,000 people, he found that those who drink three, four, or five glasses of milk a day had the lowest level of blood calcium.

According to Ellis, if you're concerned about getting enough calcium, simply eat plenty of green vegetables, sesame butters, or nuts—all of which are extremely rich in calcium and easy for the body to use. Also, it's important to note that if you consume too much calcium, it can accumulate in your kidneys and form kidney stones. Thus, to keep your blood concentrations relatively low, your body rejects about 80 percent of the calcium you eat. However, if you are concerned, there are sources other than milk. For example, turnip greens, weight for weight, contain twice as much calcium as milk. According to many experts, most people's concerns about calcium are unwarranted, anyway.

What's the main effect of milk on the body? It becomes a clogging, mucus-forming mass that hardens and clogs and sticks to everything inside the small intestine, making the body's job that much more difficult. How about cheese? It's just concentrated milk. Remember, it takes four to five quarts of milk to make one pound of cheese. The fat content alone is enough reason to limit its intake. If you really desire cheese, cut up a small amount in a big salad. That way you have plenty of water-rich food to counteract some of its clogging effects. For some, giving up cheese sounds awful. I know you love your pizza and brie. Yogurt? It's just as bad. Ice cream? It's not something that will support you in being your best. You don't have to give up that wonderful taste or texture, though. You can put frozen bananas through a juicer to create something that tastes and feels just like ice cream but is totally nurturing to your body. What about cottage cheese? Do you know what a large number of dairies use to thicken their cottage cheese and cause it to stick together? Plaster of Paris (calcium sulfate). No kidding. It's allowed within federal standards, although its use is against the law in California. (However, if the cottage cheese is made in a state where it is allowed, it can be shipped to California and sold there.) Can you imagine trying to create a clean, free-flowing bloodstream—and then filling it with Plaster of Paris?

Why haven't we heard these things about dairy products before? For many reasons, some having to do with past conditioning and belief systems. Another might have something to do with the fact that we (the federal government) spend about 2.5 billion dollars per year to handle dairy surpluses. In fact, according to *The New York Times* (11/18/83), the newest strategy is a government ad campaign to push the additional consumption of milk products, even though such ads are in direct opposition to other government campaigns that warn of the hazards of consuming too much fat. Government warehouses now bulge with 1.3 billion pounds of dried milk, 400 billion pounds of butter, and 900 million pounds of cheese. By the way, this is not meant as an attack on the dairy industry. I think dairy farmers are some of the hardest-working individuals in our culture. But that does not mean that I will continue to use their product if I find it does not support me in being my best physically.

I used to be just the way you may be now. Pizza was my favorite food. I didn't think I could give it up. But since I have, I've felt so much better there's not a chance in a million years I'll ever go back. Trying to describe the difference is like trying to describe the smell of a rose to someone who has never smelled one. Maybe you should try to smell that rose before you make a judgment about it. Try eliminating milk and limiting your intake of other dairy products for thirty days and judge by the results you feel in your body.

This whole book is designed for you to take in information, decide what you think is useful, and throw away what you find doesn't work. However, why not test all the principles before you judge them? Try the six principles of the living health system. Try them for the next ten to thirty days—or for your lifetime—and judge for yourself if they produce higher levels of energy and a feeling of vibrancy that supports you in all you do. Let me give you one small caveat. If you start breathing effectively in a way that stimulates your lymph system and you begin to combine your food correctly and eat 70 percent water-content foods, what's going to happen? Remember what Dr. Bryce stated about the power of water? Have you ever seen a fire start in a building with only a few exits? Everyone scrambles for the same exits. Your body works the same way. It will start cleaning out the garbage that's been piling up in your system for years, and it may use its newfound energy to do it as fast as it can. So you might suddenly start sneezing up excess mucus. Does that mean you've caught a cold? No, you ate a "cold." You created a "cold" by years of awful eating habits. Your body may now have the energy to use your eliminative organs to rid itself of excess waste products formerly stored in the tissues and bloodstream. A small number of people might release enough poisons from their tissues to the bloodstream to produce a slight headache. Should they reach for the Excedrin? No! Where do you want those poisons, out or in? Where do you want that excess mucus, in your handkerchief or in your lungs? It's a small price to pay for cleaning out years of awful health habits. Most people, though, will have no negative reaction at all but will feel a heightened sense of energy and well-being.

Obviously, there is only limited space in this book to discuss diet, so many subjects (like fats and oils, sugar, cigarettes, and so on) have been left out. So I hope this chapter will spur you on to your own personal health research. If you desire more information on my viewpoint, you can write the Robbins Research Institute in Del Mar, California, for a list of possible materials to support you (such as information or recipes). Or you can contact the American Natural Hygiene Society (813-855-6607), whose viewpoints I share and support.

Remember, the quality of our physiology affects our perceptions and behaviors. We see more evidence every day that the American diet of junk food, fast food, and additives and chemicals is causing "trapped" wastes in the body, and those wastes alter the level of oxygenation and electric energy of the body, contributing to everything from cancer to crime. One of the most horrifying things I ever read was the diet of a chronic juvenile delinquent, recounted by Alexander Schauss in his *Diet, Crime and Delinquency*.

For breakfast, the kid ate five cups of Sugar Smacks with a half teaspoon of added sugar, one glazed doughnut, and two glasses of milk. He snacked on a foot-long rope of licorice and 3 six-inch beef jerky sticks. Then for lunch he had two hamburgers, french fries, more licorice, a small serving of green beans, and little or no salad. He snacked on some white bread and chocolate milk before dinner. Then he had a peanut-butter-and-jelly sandwich on white bread, a can of tomato soup, and a ten-ounce glass of sweetened Kool-Aid. Later, he had a bowl of ice cream, a Marathon candy bar, and a small glass of water.

How much more sugar could a body take in, after all? What percentage of the food he ate was high in water content? Was it properly combined? A society that raises its young on a diet that even remotely resembles this is asking for trouble. Do you think these "foods" affected his physiology and thus his state and behavior? You bet. On a nutritions behavior inventory questionnaire, this fourteen-year-old-boy checked the following symptoms: After I fall asleep, I wake up and cannot get back to sleep. I get headaches—I have itching or crawling sensations on my skin—my stomach or intestines are upset—I get bruises or black-and-blue marks easily—I have nightmares or bad dreams—I get faint, dizzy, or have cold sweats or weak spells—I get hungry or feel faint if I do not eat often. I often forget things—I add sugar to most things I eat or drink—I am very restless—I cannot work under pressure—it's hard to decide things—I feel depressed—I constantly worry about things. I get confused. I get depressed or feel the blues over nothing. I blow little things out of proportion and easily lose my temper.

I get fearful. I feel very nervous. I am highly emotional. I cry for no apparent reason.

Do you wonder that, coming from this state, this young man created delinquent behaviors? Fortunately, he and many like him are now making radical changes in their behavior, not because they are being punished with long jail sentences, but because a major source of their behavior, their biochemical state, has been changed through diet. Criminal behavior is not just "in the mind." Biochemical variables influence state and thus behavior. In 1952, Dean James Simmons of the Harvard School of Public Health declared: "There is a special need for a fresh approach to the investigation of mental diseases. . . . May it not be possible that today we are spending too much time, energy, and money trying to clean up cesspools of the mind, and that we could more profitably try to discover and remove the specific biologic causes of mental diseases?"*

Your diet may not have made you a criminal, but why not develop a life-style that totally supports you in being in your most resourceful physiology most of the time?

I have enjoyed a disease-free life-style for many years. However, my younger brother has been constantly tired and ill a great deal during that same span of time. I spoke to him about this on several occasions, and having seen the changes in my health over the past seven years, he was willing to make a change. Yet the inevitable challenge occurred as he attempted to change his dietary patterns. He would develop cravings for less-than-desirable foods.

Stop and think. How do you get a craving? Well, first let's realize you don't get a craving, you create it by the way you represent things to yourself. Granted, much of this is usually unconscious. However, for you to go into the state of feeling an intense desire for some type of food, you had to create a specific kind of internal representation. Remember, things don't just happen. For every effect, there is a cause.

My brother's craving—or fetish, if you will—was for Ken-

* Quoted in *Diet, Crime and Delinquency* by Alexander Schauss.

tucky Fried Chicken. He would drive by one of the Colonel's places, and that would immediately trigger a memory of when he had some. He'd imagine the crunchy feeling (kinesthetic/gustatory submodalities) in his mouth, and he'd think of the warmth and the texture of the food as it went down his throat. Well, after a few moments of this, salad was definitely out—fried chicken was in! So one day, shortly after I had discovered how to use submodalities to create change, he finally requested that I assist him in getting control of this urge, which was sabotaging his dietary and health goals. I asked him to form an internal representation of eating Kentucky Fried Chicken. In a moment, he was salivating. Then I had him describe the visual, auditory, kinesthetic, and gustatory submodalities of his internal representation in detail. The image was up to the right. Life-size, a movie, focused, and in color. He could hear himself saying, "Mmmm, this is sooo good," as he ate it. He loved the crunchy feeling and warmth. Then I had him represent the one food he hated most, something that would make him sick to his stomach just to think of it—carrots. (I knew this in advance because every time I drank carrot juice he would turn green.) I had him describe in detail the submodalities of carrots. He didn't even want to think about them. He started to feel queasy. He said the carrots were down and on the left. They were dark, a little smaller than life, a still frame, and cold feeling. His auditory representation was, "These things are disgusting. I don't want to have to eat them. I hat them." His kinesthetic and gustatory submodalities were a limp feeling (usually over-cooked), lukewarm, mushy, rotten tasting. I told him to eat some in his mind. He started really feeling sick, said he couldn't. I asked, "If you did, what would it feel like going down your throat?" He said he'd be ready to throw up.

Having thoroughly elicited the differences between how he represented Kentucky Fried Chicken and carrots, I asked him if he'd like to switch his feelings about the two in order to support his eating in a way that produced healthful results. He said sure, with as pessimistic a tone as I'd heard in many a day. So I had him switch all the submodalities. I had him take his picture of the chicken and move it down and over to the left side. Immediately there was a reaction of disgust on his face. I had him make the picture dark and smaller than life, turn it into a still frame, and say to himself, "This stuff is disgusting. I don't want to have to eat it. I hate it," in the tonality he had previously used for carrots. I had him pick up the chicken in his mind, feel how limp it was, taste the lukewarm, rotten, mushy grease inside it. He began to look ill again. I told him to eat a piece, and he actually said no. Why? Because now chicken was giving his brain the same signals that carrots used to, so he was feeling the same way about it. Finally I got him to mentally take a bite of chicken, and he said, "I think I'm going to throw up."

I then took his representation of the carrots and did the opposite with it. I had him put it up on the right side, make the carrots life-size, bright, focused in color, and say to himself, "Mmmm, this is sooo good," as he ate it, feeling the warm, crunchy texture. Now he loved carrots. That night we went out to dinner, and he ordered carrots for the first time in his adult life. Not only did he enjoy them, but we passed by the Colonel to get there. He's maintained this dietary preference ever since.

In five minutes I was able to do something similar with my wife, Becky. I had her switch her submodalities of chocolate—rich, sweet, creamy—with those of a food that made her feel sick, oysters—wiggly, slithery, smelly . . . She has not touched chocolate since.

The six keys in this chapter can be yours to use to create the experience of health you desire. Take a moment and imagine yourself a month from now having actually followed the principles and concepts we've talked about. See the person you will be after having changed your biochemistry by eating and breathing effectively. What if you started your day by taking ten deep, clean, powerful breaths that invigorated your whole system? What if you began every day feeling alert and joyful and in control of your body? What if you started eating healthy, cleansing, water-content foods and stopped eating the meat and dairy products that were stressing and clogging up your system? What if you began combining foods properly so your energy was available for the things that really mattered? What if you went to bed every night feeling you had experienced the total vibrancy that allowed you to be all you could be? What if you felt as if you were living health—and you had energy you ever dreamed was possible?

If you look at that person and like what you see, then everything I'm offering you is easily within your grasp! It takes only a little discipline—not too much, because once you break your old habits, you'll never go back. For every disciplined effort there is a multiple reward. So if you like what you see, do it. Start today and it will change your life forever.

Now that you know how to put yourself in the finest state for producing results, let's discover . . .

The Ultimate
Success
Formula

CHAPTER XI

Limitation Disengage: What Do You Want?

"There is only one success—to be able to spend your life in your own way."

—Christopher Morley

In the first section of this book, I've shared with you what I believe are the tools of ultimate power. You now have the techniques and insights that will allow you to discover how people produce results and how to model their actions so that you can produce similar results. You've learned how to direct your mind and support your body. You now know how to achieve whatever you want and how to help others achieve what they want.

That leaves a major question. What do you want? What do the people you love and care about want? The second part of this book asks these questions, makes these distinctions, and finds these paths so you can use your abilities in the most elegant, effective, directed ways. You already know how to be an expert marksman. Now you need to find the right target.

Powerful tools aren't much use if you don't have a good idea what you want to use them for. You could find the greatest

chainsaw ever invented and wander out into the forest. What
are you going to do with it? If you know what trees you want
to cut down and why, you're in control of your situation. If you
don't, you have a fabulous tool that's all but worthless.

We learned earlier that the quality of your life is the quality
of your communication. In this section, we will talk about refining the communication skills that will allow you to use your
abilities in the most effective way for the situation at hand. It's
important to be able to map out a strategy so you know precisely
where you want to go—and know the things that can help get
you there.

Before we go on, let's review what we've learned thus far.
The main thing you now know is that there are no limits to
what you can do. Your key is power of modeling. Excellence
can be duplicated. If other people can do something, all you
need to do is model them with precision and you can do exactly
the same thing, whether it's walking on fire, making a million
dollars, or developing a perfect relationship. How do you
model? First you must realize that all results are produced by
some specific set of actions. Every effect has a cause. If you
exactly reproduce someone's actions—both internal and external—then you, too, can produce the same final result. You begin
by modeling someone's mental actions, starting with his belief
system, then you go on to his mental syntax, and finally you
mirror his physiology. Do all three effectively and elegantly,
and you can do just about anything.

You've learned that success or failure begins with belief.
Whether you believe you can do something or you believe you
can't, you're right. Even if you have the skills and resources to
do something, once you tell yourself you can't, you shut down
the neurological pathways that can make it possible. If you tell
yourself you can do something, you open up the pathways that
can provide you with the resources for achievement.

You've learned the Ultimate Success Formula: Know your
outcome, develop the sensory acuity to know what you're getting, develop the flexibility to change your behavior until you
find out what works—and you will reach your outcome. If you

don't get it, have you failed? Of course not. Like a helmsman guiding his boat, you just need to change your behavior until you get what you want.

You've learned about the power of being in a resourceful state, and you've learned how to adjust your physiology and your internal representations so they serve you, enable you, embolden you to achieve your desires. You know that if you're committed to success, you'll create it.

> *"People are not lazy. They simply have impotent goals—*
> *that it, goals that do not inspire them."*
>
> —*Anthony Robbins*

An important point worth adding is that there's an incredible dynamism inherent in this process. The more resources you develop, the more power you have; the more strength you feel, the more you can tap into even greater resources and even more powerful states.

There's an absolutely fascinating study that deals with something called the "100th monkey syndrome." In his book *Life-Tide*, published in 1979, biologist Lyall Watson recounted what happened in a monkey tribe on an island near Japan after a new food, freshly dug sweet potatoes covered with sand, was introduced into their midst. Since their other food required no preparation, the monkeys were reluctant to eat the dirty potatoes. Then one monkey solved the problem by washing the potatoes in a stream and teaching her mother and playmates to do the same. Then something remarkable happened. Once a certain number of monkeys—about one hundred of them—had acquired this knowledge, other monkeys who had no contact with them at all, even monkeys living on other islands, began to do the same thing. There was no physical way they could have interacted with the original monkeys. But somehow the behavior spread.

Now this is not unique. There are numerous cases where individuals with no way of coming in contact with one another act in remarkable unison. One physicist will get an idea, and simultaneously three physicists elsewhere will get the same idea. How does this happen? No one knows precisely, but many prominent scientists and brain researchers, such as physicist David Bohm and biologist Rupert Sheldrake, believe there is a collective consciousness we all can pull from—and that when we align ourselves through belief, through focus, through optimal physiology, we find a way to dip into this collective consciousness.*

Our bodies, our brains, and our states are like a tuning fork in harmony with that higher level of existence. So the better attuned you are, the better aligned you are, the more you can tap into this rich knowledge and feeling. Just as information filters to us from our unconscious, it may also filter in to us from completely outside of ourselves if we're in a resourceful-enough state to receive it.

A key part of this process is knowing what you want. The unconscious mind is constantly processing information in such a way as to move us in particular directions. Even at the unconscious level, the mind is distorting, deleting, and generalizing. So before the mind can work efficiently, we must develop our perception of the outcomes we expect to reach. Maxwell Maltz calls this "psycho-cybernetics" in his well-known book of the same title. When the mind has a defined target, it can focus and direct and refocus and redirect until it reaches its intended goal. If it doesn't have a defined target, its energy is squandered. It's like the person with the world's greatest chainsaw who has no idea why he's standing in the forest.

The difference in people's abilities to fully tap their personal resources is directly affected by their goals. A study of the 1953 graduates of Yale University clearly demonstrates this point. The graduates interviewed were asked if they had a clear, specific set of goals written down with a plan for achieving those goals. Only 3 percent had such written goals. Twenty years

* Rupert Sheldrake, a biologist who did graduate work at Harvard and earned his Ph.D. from Cambridge, has published his ideas in *A New Science of Life.* David Bohm, a physicist, is best known for his work on holographic paradigms. See his book, *Wholeness and the Implicate Order.*

later, in 1973, the researchers went back and interviewed the surviving members of the 1953 graduating class. They discovered that the 3 percent with written specific goals were worth more in financial terms that the entire other 97 percent put together. Obviously, this study measures only people's financial development. However, the interviewers also discovered that the less measurable or more subjective measures, such as the level of happiness and joy that the graduates felt, also seemed to be superior in the 3 percent with written goals. This is the power of goal setting.

In this chapter, you will learn how to formulate your goals and dreams and desires, how to fix firmly in your mind what you want and how to get it. Have you ever tried to put together a jigsaw puzzle without having seen the picture of what it represents? That's what happens when you try to put your life together without knowing your outcomes. When you know your outcome, you give your brain a clear picture of which kinds of information being received by the nervous system need high priority. You give it the clear messages it needs to be effective.

"Winning starts with beginning."

—Anonymous

There are people—we all know some of them—who seem constantly lost in a fog of confusion. They go one way, then another. They try one thing, then shift to another. They move down one path and then retreat in the opposite direction. Their problem is simple: They don't know what they want. You can't hit a target if you don't know what it is.

What you need to do in this chapter is dream. But it's absolutely essential that you do so in a totally focused way. If you just read this chapter, it's not going to do you any good. You need to sit down with a pencil and paper—or a word processor, if you're so inclined—and view this chapter as a twelve-step goal-setting workshop.

Settle into a place where you feel particularly comfortable—a favorite writing desk, a sunny corner table—someplace you find nurturing. Plan to spend an hour or so learning what you expect to be and do and share and see and create. It could be the most valuable hour you ever spend. You're going to learn to set goals and determine outcomes. You're going to make a map of the roads you want to travel on in your life. You're going to figure out where you want to go and how you expect to get there.

Let me start with one major warning: There is no need to put any limitations on what's possible. Of course, that doesn't mean throwing your intelligence and common sense out the window. If you're four feet eleven inches tall, there's no sense deciding your outcome is to win the NBA slam dunk contest next year. No matter what you try, it won't happen (unless you work well on stilts)*. More important, you'll be diverting your energy from where it can be most effective. But when viewed intelligently, there are no limits to the outcomes available to you. Limited goals create limited lives. So stretch yourself as far as you want in setting your goals. You need to decide what you want, because that's the only way you can expect to get it. Follow these five rules in formulating your outcomes.

1. *State your outcome in positive terms.* Say what you want to happen. Too often, people state what they don't want to happen as their goals.

2. *Be as specific as possible.* How does your outcome look, sound, feel, smell? Engage all of your senses in describing the results you want. The more sensory rich your description, the more you will empower your brain to create your desire. Also be certain to set a specific completion date and/or term.

3. *Have an evidence procedure.* Know how you will look, how you will feel, and what you will see and hear in your external world after you have achieved your outcome. If you don't know how you'll know when you've achieved your goal, you may already have it. You can be winning and feel like you're losing if you don't keep score.

* Since I wrote this, Spud Webb of the Atlanta Hawks, 5'7", won the slamdunk contest. So much for the limitations of stilts.

```
┌─────────────────────────────────────────────────────┐
│                 SETTING OUTCOMES                      │
│                 KEY COMPONENTS                        │
│                                                       │
│  Specific:              What exactly do you / we      │
│                         want?                         │
│                                                       │
│  Sensory Based:         What will you / we see?       │
│                         What will you / we hear?      │
│                         What will you / we feel?      │
│                         What will you / we smell?     │
│                         What will you / we taste?     │
│                                                       │
│  Desired State /        What do you / we want?        │
│  Present State:         What is happening now?        │
│                         What is the difference?       │
│                                                       │
│  Evidence Procedure:    How will you / we know        │
│                         the outcome has been          │
│                         realized?                     │
└─────────────────────────────────────────────────────┘
```

4. *Be in control.* Your outcome must be initiated and maintained by you. It must not be dependent upon other people having to change themselves for you to be happy. Make sure your outcome reflects things that you can affect directly.

5. *Verify that your outcome is ecologically sound and desirable.* Project into the future the consequences of your actual goal. Your outcome must be one that benefits you and other people.

I always ask a question in my seminars, and I want to ask it now: If you knew you could not fail, what would you do? If you were absolutely certain of success, what activities would you pursue, what actions would you take?

All of us have some idea of the things we want. Some are vague—more love, more money, more time to enjoy life. However, to empower our biocomputers to create a result, we need to become more specific than a new car, a new house, a better job.

As you create your list, some of the things you write down will be things you've thought about for years. Some will be things you've never consciously formulated before. But you need to consciously decide what you want, because knowing what you want determines what you will get. Before something happens in the external world, it must first happen in the internal world. There's something rather amazing about what happens when you get a clear internal representation of what you want. It programs your mind and body to achieve that goal. To go beyond our present limitations, we must first experience being more in our minds, and our lives will then follow suit.

Let me give you a simple physical metaphor for this. Try the following. Stand up, with your feet slightly apart and pointing forward. Bring both arms straight up in front of you so that they are parallel to the floor. Now turn to your left, pointing with your finger as far as you comfortably can as you turn. Take note of where you stop by the point on the wall opposite where your finger stops. Now turn back around, close your eyes, and in your mind make a picture of yourself turning again—only this time going much farther. Now again, and this time much farther still. Now open your eyes and again physically turn. Note what happens. Did you turn much farther? Of course you did. You created a new external reality by first programming your brain to go beyond its previous limits.

Think of this chapter as doing the same for your life. You're now going to create your life as you want it. Normally in life you could only go so far, but in your mind you're going to take the time to create a reality greater than what you've experienced in the past. Then you're going to externalize that internal reality.

1. *Start by making an inventory of your dreams, the things you want to have, do, be, and share.* Create the people, feelings, and

places you want to be a part of your life. Sit down right now, grab your paper and pen, and begin writing. The key is to commit to keeping your pen moving nonstop for no less than ten to fifteen minutes. Don't try to define how you're going to get this outcome now. Just write it down. There are no limits. Abbreviate whenever possible so you can immediately get on to the next goal. Keep your pen moving for the entire time. Take as long as you need to put together a broad sampling of outcomes having to do with work; family; relationships; mental, emotional, social, material and physical states; and anything else. Feel like a king. Remember that everything is within your grasp. Knowing your outcome is the first key to reaching it.

One key to goal setting is play. Let your mind roam free. Whatever limitations you have are limitations you've created. Where do they exist? Only in your mind. So whenever you start to place limitations on yourself, throw them off. Do it visually. Make a picture in your mind of a wrestler flipping his opponent out of the ring, and then do the same thing with whatever limits you. Take those limiting beliefs and toss them out of the ring, and be aware of the feeling of freedom you have when you do it. This is Step 1. Make your list now!

2. Let's do a second exercise. *Go over the list you made, estimating when you expect to reach those outcomes*: six months, one year, two years, five years, ten years, twenty years. It's helpful to see what sort of a time frame you're operating in. Note how your list came out. Some people find that the list they made is dominated by things they want today. Others find their greatest dreams are far in the future, in some imagined period of total achievement and fulfillment. If all your goals are short term, you need to start taking a longer view of potential and possibility. If all your goals are long term, you need to first develop some steps that can lead you in the direction you expect to go. A journey of a thousand miles begins with a single step. It's important to be aware of both the first steps and the final ones.

3. Now I want you to try something else: *Pick out the four*

most important goals for you for this year. Pick the things you're most committed to, most excited about, things that would give you the most satisfaction. Write them down. *Now* I want you to write down why you absolutely will achieve them. Be clear and concise and positive. Tell yourself why you're sure you can reach those outcomes, and why it's important that you do.

If you can find enough reasons to do something, you can get yourself to do anything. Our purpose for doing something is a much stronger motivator than the object that we pursue. Jim Rohn, my first personal-development teacher, always taught me that if you have enough reasons, you can do anything. Reasons are the difference between being interested versus being committed to accomplish something. There are many things in life we say we want, but really we're only interested in them for a time. We must be totally committed to whatever it takes to achieve. If, for example, you just say you want to be rich, well, that's a goal, but it doesn't tell your brain much. If you understand why you want to be rich, what being wealthy would mean to you, you'll be much more motivated to get there. Why to do something is much more important than how to do it. If you get a big-enough why, you can always figure out the how. If you have enough reasons, you can do virtually anything in this world.

4. *Now that you have a list of your key goals, review them against the five rules for formulating outcomes*. Are your goals stated in the positive? Are they sensory specific? Do they have an evidence procedure? Describe what you will experience when you achieve them. In even clearer sensory terms, what will you see, hear, feel, and smell? Also note if the goals are maintainable by you. Are they ecological and desirable for you and others? If they violate any of these conditions, change them to fit.

5. *Next, make a list of the important resources you already have at your disposal*. When you begin a construction project, you need to know which tools you have. To construct an empowering

vision of your future, you need to do the same thing. So make a list of what you have going for you: character traits, friends, financial resources, education, time, energy, or whatever. Come up with an inventory of the strengths, skills, resources, and tools.

6. *When you've done that, focus in on times you used some of those resources most skillfully.* Come up with three to five times in your life when you were totally successful. Think of the times in business or sports or financial matters or relationships when you did something particularly well. It can be anything from a killing in the stock market to a wonderful day with your kids. Then write them down. Describe what you did that made you succeed, what qualities or resources you made effective use of, and what about that situation made you feel successful.

7. *After you've done all that, describe the kind of person you would have to be to attain your goals.* Will it take a great deal of discipline, a great deal of education? Would you have to manage your time well? If, for example, you want to be a civic leader who really makes a difference, describe what kind of person gets elected and really has the ability to affect large numbers of people.

We hear a lot about success, but we don't hear as much about the components of success—the attitudes, beliefs, and behaviors that go into producing it. If you don't have a good grasp of the components, you may find it difficult to put together the whole, so stop now and write a couple of paragraphs or a page about all the character traits, skills, attitudes, beliefs, and disciplines you would need to have as a person in order to achieve all that you desire. Take some time on this.

8. *Next, in a few paragraphs, write down what prevents you from having the things you desire right now.* One way to overcome the limitations you've created is to know exactly what they are. Dissect your personality to see what's holding you back from achieving what you want. Do you fail to plan? Do you plan,

but fail to act? Do you try to do too many things at one time, or do you get so fixated on one thing that you don't do anything else? In the past, have you imagined the worst-possible scenario and then allowed that internal representation to stop you from taking action? We all have ways of limiting ourselves, our own strategies for failing, but by recognizing our past limitation strategies—recognizing your past limitation strategies—we can change them now.

We can know what we want, why we want it, who will help us, and a lot of other things, but the critical ingredient that in the end determines whether we succeed in achieving our outcomes is our actions. To guide our actions, we must create a step-by-step plan. When you build a house, do you just go out and get a pile of wood, some nails, a hammer, and a saw and then start to work? Would you start sawing and hammering and see what came out of it? Would that lead to success? It's not likely. To build a house you need a blueprint, a plan. You need a sequence and a structure so your actions complement and reinforce one another. Otherwise you will just have a wild assemblage of boards. It's the same with your life. So now you need to put together your own blueprint for success.

What are the necessary actions you must take consistently to produce the result you desire? If you're not sure, think of someone you can model who has already accomplished what you desire. You need to start with your ultimate outcomes, then work backward, step by step. If one of your major outcomes is to become financially independent, the step before that might to become president of your own company. The step before that might be becoming a vice-president or other important officer. Another step might be to find a smart investment counselor and/ or tax lawyer to help you manage your money. It's critical that you continue to work back until you find something you could do today to support the achievement of that goal. Maybe today you could open a savings account or get a book that teaches you some financial strategies of successful people in our culture. If you want to be a professional dancer, what do you have to do to reach that outcome? What are the major steps, and what are some things you can do today, tomorrow, this week, this month, this year to produce the results? If you want to be the greatest composer in the world, what are the steps along the way? By working backward, step by step, for outcomes in everything from business to personal life, you can map out the precise path to follow from your ultimate goal down to what you can do today.

Use the information in the last exercise to guide the design of your plan. If you're not sure what your plan should be, just ask yourself what prevents you from having what you want now. The answer to that question will be something you can work on immediately to change. The solving of that problem becomes a subgoal or stepping-stone to the achievement of your greater goals.

9. *Take the time now to take each of your four key goals and create your first draft of a step-by-step plan on how to achieve it.* Remember to start with the goal and ask yourself, What would I have to do first to accomplish this? or, What prevents me from having this now, and what can I do to change this? Make sure your plans include something you could do today.

So far we've completed the first part of the Ultimate Success Formula. You absolutely know your outcome. You've defined your outcomes over both the short and long terms, and you've defined which aspects of your personality help you and which hinder you in getting what you want. Now I want you to start developing a strategy of how to get there.

What's the surest way to achieve excellence? It's to model someone who has already done what you want to do.

10. *So come up with some models.* They can be people from your life or famous people who've achieved great success. Write down the names of three to five people who've achieved what you want to achieve, and specify in a few words the qualities and behaviors that made them successful. After you've done this, close your eyes and imagine for a moment that each of these

people is going to give you some advice about how to best go about accomplishing your goals. Write down one main idea that each would give you if he or she were speaking to you personally. Maybe it's how to avoid a roadblock or break through a limitation or what to pay attention to or look for. Just imagine they're talking to you and jot down under each of their names the first idea that comes to you about what you think each would say. Even though you may not know them personally, through this process they can become excellent advisers on your future.

Adnan Khashoggi modeled Rockefeller. He wanted to be a wealthy, successful businessman, so he modeled someone who had done what he wanted to do. Steven Spielberg modeled people at Universal Studios even before he was hired. Virtually everyone who has been a great success has had a model or a mentor or teachers who guided him in the right direction.

Now you have a clear internal representation of where you want to go. You can save time and energy and avoid traveling down wrong paths by following the example of people who've succeeded already. Who are the people in your life who can serve as models? There are resources in friends, family, national leaders, celebrities. If you don't know good models, you should make a point of going out and finding some.

What you've been doing is giving signals to your brain, forming a clear, concise pattern of outcomes. Goals are like magnets. They'll attract the things that make them come true. In chapter 6, you learned how to run your own brain, how to manipulate your submodalities to enhance positive images and decrease the power of negative ones. Let's apply that knowledge to your goals.

Take a dip into your personal history to a time when you were totally successful at something. Close your eyes and form the clearest, brightest possible image of that accomplishment. Take note of whether you put the image to the left or to the right, up, middle, or down. Again, notice all the submodalities—the size, shape, and quality of its movement as well as the type of sound and internal feelings that it creates. Now think about the outcomes you've written down today. Make a picture of how you would be if you achieved everything you've set down today. Put that image on the same side as the other one and make it as big and bright and focused and colorful as you can. Notice how you feel. You'll already feel very different, much more certain of success than you did when you first formulated your outcomes.

If you have trouble doing this, use the "swish" method we talked about earlier. Move the image of what you want to be to the other side of your mental frame. Make it defocused and black and white. Then quickly move it to the exact same spot as your successful image, having it break through any representations of possible failure that you may have perceived. Move it so that it takes on all the big, bright, colorful, focused qualities of the thing you've already accomplished. You should do these exercises on an ongoing basis so your brain gets an ever clearer, ever more intense picture of what you expect it to accomplish. The brain responds most to repetition and deep feelings, so if you can continually experience your life as you desire it, and if you experience this life with deep and intense feelings, you are almost certain to create what you desire. Remember, the road to success is always under construction.

11. It's great to have all kinds of different goals. However, what's even nicer is to be able to design what all of them together would mean for you. *Now create your ideal day.* What people would be involved? What would you do? How would it begin? Where would you go? Where would you be? Do it from the time you get up to the time you go to sleep. What kind of environment would you be in? How would you feel when you climbed into bed at the end of a perfect day? Use pen and paper and describe it in detail. Remember all results, actions, and realities we experience start from creations in our minds, so create your day the way you desire it most.

12. Sometimes we forget that dreams begin at home. We forget that the first step toward success is providing ourselves

with an atmosphere that nurtures our creativity, that helps us be everything we can be.

Finally, design your perfect environment. I want you to accentuate the sense of place. Let your mind go. No limitations. Whatever you want is what you should put in. Remember to think like a king. Design an environment that would bring out the best of all that you are as a person. Where would you be—in the woods, in the ocean, in an office? What tools would you have—an art pad, paints, music, a computer, a telephone? What support people would you have around you to make sure you achieved and created all that you desired in your life?

If you don't have a clear representation of what your ideal day would be, what are your chances of creating it? If you don't know what your ideal environment would be, how would you create it? How are you going to hit a target if you don't even know what it is? Remember, the brain needs clear, direct signals of what it wants to achieve. Your mind has the power to give you everything you want. But it can only do that if it's getting clear, bright, intense, focused signals.

> *"Thinking is the hardest work there is, which is the probable reason why so few engage in it."*
>
>   *—Henry Ford*

Doing the exercises in this chapter could be one of the most important steps you can take toward producing those unmistakable signals. You can't reach your outcome if you don't know what it is. If you get anything from this chapter, it should be this: Results are inevitable. If you don't provide your mind with the programming of the results you desire, someone else will provide that programming for you. If you don't have your own plan, someone else is going to make you fit into their plan. If all you do is read this chapter, you've wasted your time. It's imperative that you take the time to do each of these exercises. They may not be easy at first, but believe me, they're worth it; and as you begin to do them, they become more and more fun.

One of the reasons most people don't do well in life is because success is usually disguised behind hard work. And good setting, or outcome development, is hard work. It's easy for people to put things like this off and get trapped into making a living instead of designing their lives. Exert your personal power now and take the time to discipline yourself to fully complete these exercises. It's been said that there are only two pains in life, the pain of discipline or the pain of regret, and that discipline weighs ounces while regret weighs tons. There's a great deal of excitement to be gained from applying these twelve principles. Do this for yourself.

Also, it's important to review your outcomes on a regular basis. Sometimes we change, but our outcomes remain the same because we've never stopped to see if we still want to create the same things for our lives. Systematically update your outcomes every few months, and then perhaps once a year or every six months in a systematic way. One very useful thing is to keep a journal, which will provide you with an ongoing record of your goals at any time in your life. Journals are great to review, to study how your life has developed and how much you've grown. If your life is worth living, it's worth recording.

Does all this work? You bet is does. Three years ago I sat down and designed my ideal day and my ideal environment. I'm living both right now.

At that time I was living in a dinky place in Marina del Rey, California, but I knew I wanted something more. So I decided to do my own goal-setting workshop. I decided to design my perfect day and then program my subconscious to create that ideal life by daily experiencing in my imagination my life exactly as I desired it most. This is how I began. I knew I wanted to be able to get up and see the ocean in the morning, and then I wanted to be able to take a run on the beach. I had a picture— it wasn't perfectly clear—of a place that had both greenery and the beach.

After exercising, I wanted to have a great place to work. I saw it as someplace tall and spacious. I saw it as a cylindrical shape on the second or third floor of my home. I wanted a limousine and a driver. I wanted to have a business with four or five partners who were as strong and excited as I was, partners I could meet and brainstorm new ideas with on a regular basis. I dreamed of the ideal woman to be my wife. I didn't have any money, and I decided I wanted to be financially independent.

I got everything I programmed into my mind. Everything I imagined then has come to pass. My castle is exactly the kind of place I imagined when I was living in Marina del Rey. I met my ideal woman six months after I imagined her, and married her eighteen months after that. I've created an environment that totally nurtures my creativity, that constantly triggers my desire to be everything I can be and that creates for me a daily attitude of gratitude. Why? I gave myself a target, and every day I congruently gave my brain the clear, precise, direct message that this was my reality. Having a clear, precise target, my powerful unconscious mind guided my thoughts and actions to produce the results I desired. It worked for me, and it can work for you.

"Where there is no vision, people perish."
—Proverbs 29:18

Now you should do one final thing: make a list of the things you already have that were once goals—all the things in your ideal day you can already do, the activities and people of your life you are most grateful for, the resources you already have available to you. I call this a gratitude diary. Sometimes people get so fixated on what they want, they fail to appreciate or use what they already have. The first step toward a goal is seeing what you have, giving thanks for it, and applying it to future achievements. We all have ways to make our lives better at any moment. Achieving your wildest dreams should begin today with the everyday steps that can put you on the right path. Shakespeare once wrote, "Action is eloquence." Begin today with eloquent action that will lead to even more eloquent outcomes.

In this chapter, you've seen the importance of precision in

formulating your outcomes. It's the same in all our communications with ourselves and with others. The more precise we are, the more effective we are.

Now I'm going to share with you some tools for achieving that sort of precision.

CHAPTER XII

The Power
of Precision

"Human language is like a cracked kettle on which we beat
out tunes for bears to dance to, when all the time we are
longing to move the stars to pity."

—*Gustave Flaubert*

Think of a time when you heard words that seemed like magic.
Maybe it was a public event, like Martin Luther King, Jr.'s, "I
have a dream" speech. Maybe it was the words of your father
or mother or a special teacher. We can all remember moments
when someone spoke with so much force and precision and res-
onance that the words stayed with us forever. "Words are the
most powerful drug used by mankind," Rudyard Kipling once
said. We can all think of times when words did seem to have
that magical, intoxicating quality.

When John Grinder and Richard Bandler studied successful
people, they found many common attributes. One of the most
important was precise communication skills. A manager has to
manage information to be successful. Bandler and Grinder found
that the most successful managers seemed to have a genius for
getting to the heart of information rapidly and communicating

to others what they had learned. They tended to use key phrases and words that conveyed their most important ideas with great precision.

They also understood that they did not need to know everything. They distinguished between what they needed to know and what they didn't need to know, and focused on the former. Bandler and Grinder also observed that outstanding therapists like Virginia Satir, Fritz Perls, and Dr. Milton Erickson used some of the same phrases, phrases that many times enabled them to get immediate results with patients in one or two sessions instead of one or two years.

There is nothing surprising in what Bandler and Grinder found. Remember, we've learned that the map is not the territory. The words we use to describe experiences aren't the experiences. They're just the best verbal representation we can come up with. So it stands to reason that one of the measures of success is how accurately and precisely our words can convey what we want—how closely our map can approximate the territory. Just as we all can remember times when words moved us like magic, we can also remember times when our communication went utterly, hopelessly awry. Maybe we thought we were saying one thing, but the other person got the opposite message. So just as precise language has the ability to move people in useful directions, sloppy language can misdirect them. "If thought corrupts language, language can also corrupt thought," wrote George Orwell, whose *1984* is based on just that principle.

In this chapter, we're going to learn about tools that will help you communicate with more precision and effectiveness than you may have ever had before. You're going to learn how to guide others toward the same outcome. There are simple verbal tools that any of us can use to cut through the verbal fluff and distortion most of us are caught up in. Words can be walls, but they can also be bridges. It's important to use words to link people rather than divide them.

In my seminars, I tell the people there that I'm going to show them how to get whatever they want. In fact, I tell them to write just that at the top of a piece of paper—"How to get whatever I want." And after I go through a big long buildup, I give them the magic formula.

How to get whatever you want: "Ask," I say. "End of lecture."

Am I kidding? No. When I say, "Ask," I don't mean whine or beg or complain or plead or grovel. I don't mean expect a handout or a free lunch or an act of charity. I don't mean expect someone else to do your work for you. What I mean is learn to ask intelligently and precisely. Learn to ask in a way that helps you both define and achieve your outcome. In the last chapter, you began to learn to do that when you formulated the specific outcomes, goals, and activities you wanted to pursue. Now you need some more specific verbal tools. There are five guidelines for asking intelligently and precisely.

1. *Ask specifically.* You must describe what you want, both to yourself and to someone else. How high, how far, how much? When, where, how, with whom? If your business needs a loan, you'll get it—if you know how to ask. You won't get it if you say, "We need some more money to expand into a new product line. Please lend us some. You need to define precisely what you need, why you need it, and when you need it. You need to be able to show what you'll be able to produce with it. In our goal-setting seminars, people always say they want more money. I hand them a couple of quarters. They asked and they received, but they didn't ask intelligently, so they didn't get what they wanted.

2. *Ask someone who can help you.* It's not enough to ask specifically, you must ask specifically of someone who has the resources—the knowledge, the capital, the sensitivity, or the business experience. Let's say you're having trouble with your spouse. Your relationship is falling apart. You can pour out your heart. You can be as specific and as honest as is humanly possible. But if you seek help from someone who has as pitiful a relationship as you do, will you succeed? Of course not.

Finding the right person to ask brings us back to the importance of learning how to notice what works. Anything you want—a better relationship, a better job, a smarter program for investing your money—is something someone already has or something someone already does. The trick is to find those people and figure out what they do right. Many of us gravitate toward barroom wisdom. We find a sympathetic ear and expect that to translate to results. It won't unless the sympathy is matched by expertise and knowledge.

3. *Create value for the person you're asking.* Don't just ask and expect someone to give you something. Figure out how you can help him first. If you've had a business idea and need money to pull it off, one way to do it is to find someone who can both help and benefit. Show him how your idea can make money for you and for him as well. Creating value doesn't always have to be that tangible. The value you create may only be a feeling or a sensibility or a dream, but often that's enough. If you came up to me and said you needed $10,000, I'd probably say, "So do a lot of other people." If you said you needed the money to make a difference in people's lives, I might begin to listen. If you specifically showed me how you wanted to help others and create value for them and yourself, I might see how helping you could create value for me as well.

4. *Ask with focused, congruent belief.* The surest way to ensure failure is to convey ambivalence. If you aren't convinced about what you're asking for, how can anyone else be? So when you ask, do it with absolute conviction. Express that in your words and your physiology. Be able to show that you're sure of what you want, you're sure you'll succeed, and you're sure you will create value, not just for you but for the person you're asking as well.

Sometimes people do all four perfectly. They ask specifically. They ask someone who can help them. They create value for the person they're asking. They ask congruently. And even after that, they don't get what they want. The reason is they didn't do the fifth thing. They didn't "ask until." That's the fifth and most important part of asking intelligently.

(5. *Ask until you get what you want.*)That doesn't mean asking the same person. It doesn't mean asking in precisely the same way. Remember, the Ultimate Success Formula says you need to develop the sensory acuity to know what you're getting, and you have to have the personal flexibility to change. So when you ask, you have to change and adjust until you achieve what you want. When you study the lives of successful people, you'll find over and over again that they kept asking, kept trying, kept changing—because they knew that sooner or later they would find someone who could satisfy their needs.

What's the hardest part of the formula? For many people it's the part about asking specifically. We don't live in a culture that puts a great premium on precise communication. It may be one of our biggest cultural failings. Language reflects a society's needs. An Eskimo has several dozen words for "snow." Why? Because to be an effective Eskimo, you have to be able to make fine distinctions between different kinds of snow. There is snow you can fall through, snow you can build an igloo out of, snow you can run your dogs in, snow you can eat, snow that's ready to melt. I'm from California. I practically never see snow, so the one word I have for it is enough for me.

Many phrases and words used by people in our culture have little or no specific meaning. I call these generalized, nonsensory-based words "fluff." They're not descriptive language; they're more like vague guesswork. Fluff is "Mary looks depressed." Or, "Mary looks tired." Or even worse, "Mary is depressed." Or, "Mary is tired." Specific language is "Mary is a thirty-two-year-old woman with blue eyes and brown hair who is sitting to my right. She's leaning back in her chair, drinking a Diet Coke, with her eyes defocused and her breathing shallow." It's the difference between giving accurate descriptions of externally verifiable experience and making guesses about what no one can see. The speaker has no idea what's going on in

Mary's mind. He's taking his map and assuming he knows what her experience is.

> *"There is no expedient to which a man will not go to avoid the real labor of thinking."*
>
> —*Thomas Edison*

Making an assumption is the mark of a lazy communicator. It's one of the most dangerous things you can do in dealing with others. A good example is Three Mile Island. According to a report in *The New York Times*, many of the problems that led to the accident that shut down the nuclear plant had already been outlined in staff memorandums. As company officials later admitted, they'd all assumed someone else was dealing with the matter. Instead of taking the direct steps to ask who specifically was responsible and what specifically was being done, they'd assumed someone, somewhere, was taking care of things. The result was one of the worst nuclear accidents in American history.

Much of our language is nothing more than wild generalization and assumption. That sort of lazy language can suck the guts out of real communication. If people tell you with precision what specifically is bothering them, and if you can find out what they want instead, you can deal with it. If they use vague phrases and generalizations, you're just lost in their mental fog. The key to effective communication is to break through that fog, to become a fluff-buster.

There are countless ways we sabotage real communication by using lazy, overgeneralized language. If you want to communicate effectively, you have to be attuned to fluff when it pops up and know how to ask questions to gain specificity. The purpose of precision in language patterns is to find out as much useful information as possible. The closer you are to getting a full representation of the other person's internal experience, the more you can effect change.

One way to deal with verbal fluff is the precision model. It may best be pictured on your two hands. Take a few minutes

PRECISION MODEL

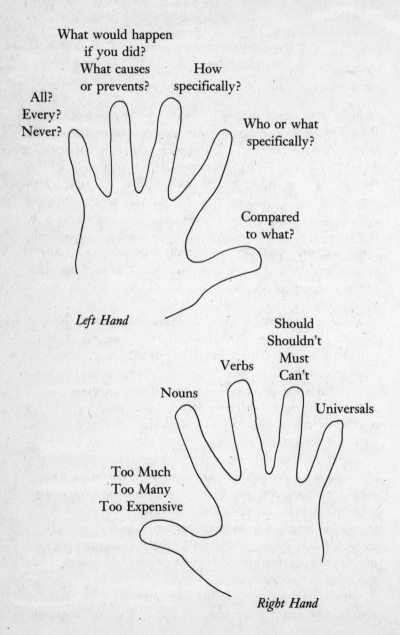

What would happen
   if you did?
      What causes   How
      or prevents?   specifically?
All?
Every?
Never?

                               Who or what
                               specifically?

                            Compared
                            to what?

Left Hand

                               Should
                               Shouldn't
                     Verbs   Must
                               Can't
         Nouns
                                  Universals

   Too Much
   Too Many
   Too Expensive

                            Right Hand

to memorize the diagram. Take your hands one at a time, and move them up and to the left of your eyes so that your eyes are in the position to best visually store this information. Look at your fingers one at a time, and say the words over and over again. Then go to the next finger and the next until you've memorized one hand. Then do the same for the other. Repeat this process with all your fingers, looking at the phrase and fixing it clearly in your mind. After you've done that, see if you can look at any finger and immediately think of the word or phrase at the end of it. Work on memorizing the chart until the associations are automatic.

Now that you have those words and phrases installed in your mind, here's what they mean. The precision model is a guide to overcoming some of the most common pitfalls in language. It's a map of some of the most pernicious wrong turns that people often take. The idea is to notice them when they pop up and redirect them in a more specific direction. It provides us with the means to qualify people's distortions, deletions, and generalizations while still maintaining a rapport with them.

Let's start with the pinkies. On the right hand, you should have the word "universals." On the left, the words, "all, every, never." Universals are fine—when they're true. If you say that *every* person needs oxygen or *all* the teachers in your son's school have graduated from college, you're just conveying facts. But more often, universals are a way of soaring into the fluff zone. You see a bunch of noisy kids on the street and you say, "Kids today have no manners." One of your employees messes up and you say, "I don't know why I pay these people. They *never* work." In both cases—and for much of the time we use universals—we've gone from a limited truth to a general untruth. Maybe those kids were noisy, but not all kids are ill-mannered. Maybe a particular employee seems incompetent, but not all are. So the next time you hear a generalization like that, simply go to the precision model. Repeat the statement, emphasizing the universal qualifier.

"All kids are ill-mannered?" Ask yourself: "All?"

"Well, I guess not. Just these particular kids."

"Your employees never work?" Your question: "Never?"

"Well, I guess that's not true. This one guy sure screwed up, but I can't say that's true for the rest of them."

Now bring the next two fingers together and examine the restrictive words "should, shouldn't, must, can't." If someone tells you he can't do something, what signal is he sending to the brain? A limiting one that makes sure, in fact, that he can't do it. If you ask people why they can't do something or why they have to do something they don't want to do, they usually have no shortage of answers. The way to break that cycle is to say, "What would happen if you were able to do that?" Asking that creates a possibility they were previously unaware of and gets them to consider the positive and negative by-products of the activity.

The same process works for you in internal dialogue. When you say to yourself, "I can't do that," the thing to do next is ask yourself, "What would happen if I could?" The reply would be a list of positive, enabling actions and feelings. It would create new representations of possibility and thus new states, new actions, and potentially new results. Just asking yourself that question will begin to change your physiology and your thinking to make it more possible.

In addition, you could ask, "What prevents me from doing this now?" and thereby become clear about what specifically you need to change.

Now go to your middle fingers, which stand for verbs, and ask "How specifically?" Remember, your brain needs clear signals to operate efficiently. Fluffy language and fluffy thought dull the brain. If someone says, "I feel depressed," he's just describing a stuck state. He's not telling you anything specific. He's not giving you any information you can work with in a positive way. Break the stuck state by breaking through the fluff. If someone says he's depressed, you need to ask him how specifically he's depressed, what specifically is causing him to feel that way.

When you get him to be more specific, you often must move from one part of the precision model to another. So if you ask the person to be more specific, he may say, "I'm depressed because I always mess up on the job." What's the next question? Is the universal true? It's not likely. So you would ask, "You *always* mess up on your job?" Most likely, the answer will be, "Well, no, not always, I guess." By breaking through the fluff, by getting to specifics, you're on the road to identifying a real problem and dealing with it. What usually happens is that a person has messed up in some small way and made it symbolize some big failing that exists only in his mind.

Now put your index fingers together, the ones that represent nouns and "who specifically, what specifically." Whenever you hear nouns—people, places, or things—in any generalized statement, respond with a phrase that includes "who [or what] specifically." It's precisely what you did with the verbs, going from unspecified fluff to the real world. You can't work with a generalized cloud that only exists in someone's head. You can deal with the real world.

Unspecified nouns are one of the worst kinds of fluff. How often have you heard someone say, "They don't understand me," or, "They're not going to give me a fair chance"? Well, just who specifically are "they"? If it's a big organization, there's probably one person who's going to make a decision. So instead of getting yourself stuck in this vague realm where "they" don't understand, you need to find a way to deal with the real-world person making the real-world decisions. Using an unspecified, nameless "they" can be the worst sort of copout. If you don't know who "they" are, you feel helpless and unable to change your situation. But if you focus on specifics, you can regain control.

If someone says, "Your plan just won't work," you need to find out what specifically they have a problem with. A rebuttal like "Yes, it will work" will not maintain the rapport or resolve the situation. Often, it's not the whole plan—it's a small part of it. If you try to rearrange your whole plan, you're like a plane flying without radar. You might fix everything but the one thing that's the problem. If you specify where the problem is and deal with it, you're on the road to bringing about valuable change. Remember, the closer the map approximates a real territory, the more valuable it is. The more you can discover what the territory is made of, the more power you have to change it.

Now press your thumbs together for the last part of the precision model. One thumb says, "too much, too many, too expensive." The other says, "compared to what?" When we say, "too much, too many, too expensive," we're using another form of deletion. Often it's based on an arbitrary construct that's lodged somewhere inside our brain. You might say that more than a week's vacation is too much time away from work. You might think that your kid's request for a $299 home computer is too expensive.

You can step outside your generalizations by making a comparison. Two weeks away from your job may be worth it if you'll come back totally relaxed and able to do your best work. That home computer may be too expensive if you don't think it will do any good. If you think it's a valuable learning tool, it could be worth many thousands of dollars down the line. The only way to make those judgments rationally is to have valid points of comparison. You'll find that when you start using the precision model, you'll end up using it naturally.

For example, occasionally someone tells me, "Your seminar is too expensive." When I respond, "Compared to what?" he might say, "Well, compared to other seminars I've gone to."

Then I find out what specific seminars he's referring to and ask about one of them, "How specifically is that seminar like mine?"

"Well," he replies, "it really isn't."

"That's interesting. What would happen if you felt my seminar was really worth the time and money?"

His breathing pattern changes, and he smiles and says, "I don't know . . . I'd feel good, I guess."

"What specifically could I do to help you feel that way about my seminar now?"

"Well, if you would spend more time on such and such a subject, I probably would feel good about it."

"All right. If I were to spend more time on that subject, would you feel the seminar was worth your time and money?"

He nods in agreement. What's happened in this conversation? We've found the real-world, specific points we needed to deal with. We've gone from a string of generalizations to a string of specifics. And once we got to the specifics, we were able to deal with them in a way that solved our problems. It's that way in almost any sort of communication. The road to agreement is paved with specific information.

During the next several days, begin to focus on the language other people use. Begin to identify things such as universals and unspecified verbs and nouns. How would you challenge these? Turn on your television and watch an interview program. Identify the fluff that is being used, and ask questions to the TV set that would enable you to get the specific information you need.

Here are some additional patterns to listen for. Avoid words like "good," "bad," "better," "worse"—words that indicate some form of evaluation or judgment. When you hear phrases like "That's a bad idea" or "It's good to eat everything on your plate," you can respond with "According to whom?" or "How do you know that?" Sometimes people will make statements linking cause and effect. They might say, "His comments made me mad," or "Your observations made me think." Now, when you hear those you'll know to ask, "How specifically does X cause Y?" and you will become a better communicator and a better modeler.

Another thing to be wary of is verbal mind reading. When someone says, "I just know he loves me," or, "You think I don't believe you," you need to ask, "How do you know that?"

The last pattern to learn is a little more subtle, which is a wonderful reason to give it your attention. What do words like "attention," "statement," and "reason" have in common? They are nouns, yes. But we can't find them in the external world. Have you even seen an attention? It's not a person, place, or thing. That's because it actually used to be a verb, describing the process of attending. Nominalizations are words that have lost their specificity. When you hear one, you want to turn it back into a process—which gives you the power to redirect and change your experience. If someone says, "I want to change my experience," the way to redirect it is to say, "What do you want to experience?" If he says, "I want love," you would respond with, "How do you want to be loved?" or "What is it to be loving?" Is there a difference in specificity in the two forms? There sure is.

There are other ways to direct communication by asking the right questions. One is the "outcome frame." If you ask someone what's bothering him or what's wrong, you'll get a long dissertation on just that. If you ask, "What do you want?" or "How do you want to change things?" you've redirected your conversation from the problem to the solution. In any situation, no matter how dismal, there's a desirable outcome to be achieved. Your goal should be to change direction toward that outcome and away from the problem.

Do this by asking the right questions. There are any number of them. In NLP they're referred to as "outcome questions."

"What do I want?"
"What is the objective?"
"What am I here for?"
"What do I want for you?"
"What do I want for me?"

Here's another important frame? Choose "how" questions over "why" questions. "Why" questions can get you reasons and explanations and justifications and excuses. But they usually don't come up with useful information. Don't ask your kid why he is having trouble with his algebra. Ask him what he needs to do to perform better. There's no need to ask an employee why he didn't get a contract you were bidding for. Ask him how he can change so you'll be certain to get the next one. Good communicators aren't interested in rationalizations of why something is going wrong. They want to find out how to do it right. The right questions will lead you in that direction.

Let me share with you a final point that goes back to the enabling beliefs we examined in chapter 5 ("The Seven Lies of Success"). All your communications with others and with yourself should stem from the principle that everything happens for a purpose and you can use it to serve your outcomes. That means your communication skills should reflect feedback, not failure. If you're putting together a jigsaw puzzle and a piece doesn't fit, you don't usually take that as failure and stop working on the puzzle. You take it as feedback and try another piece that looks more promising. It's to your advantage to use the same general rule in your communication. There is a specific question or a precise phrase that will transform almost any problem in communication. If you follow the general principles we've considered here, you'll be able to find it in every situation. ("Every situation"—start using your precision model now!)

In the next chapter, we're going to look at the underpinning of all successful human interaction, the glue that bonds people together. It's called . . .

CHAPTER XIII

The Magic
of Rapport

"The friend who understands you, creates you."

—*Romain Rolland*

Think of a time when you and another person were completely in sync. It could be a friend or a lover or a family member or someone you just met by chance. Go back to that time and try to think what it was about the person that made you feel so attuned to him/her.

Chances are that you found you thought alike or felt the same way about a certain movie or book or experience. You might not have noticed it, but maybe you had similar patterns of breathing or speech. Maybe you had a similar background or similar beliefs. Whatever you come up with will be a reflection of the same basic element—rapport. Rapport is the ability to enter someone else's world, to make him feel that you understand him, that you have a strong common bond. It's the ability to go fully from your map of the world to his map of the world. It's the essence of successful communication.

Rapport is the ultimate tool for producing results with other people. Remember, we learned in chapter 5 ("The Seven Lies of Success") that people are your most important resource. Well, rapport is the way you tap that resource. No matter what you want in your life, if you can develop rapport with the right people, you'll be able to fill their needs, and they will be able to fill yours.

The ability to establish rapport is one of the most important skills a person can have. To be a good performer or a good salesman, a good parent or a good friend, a good persuader or a good politician, what you really need is rapport, the ability to form a powerful common human bond and a relationship of responsiveness.

A lot of people make life very complicated and difficult. It doesn't have to be. All the skills you learn in this book are really ways to achieve greater rapport with people, and rapport with others makes almost any task simpler, easier, and more enjoyable. No matter what you want to do, see, create, share, or experience in life, whether it's achieving spiritual realization or earning a million dollars, there's someone else who can help you accomplish your goal more quickly and easily. Someone else knows how to get there quicker or more effectively or can do something to help you get where you want to go more rapidly. The way to enlist that person is to achieve rapport, the magic bond that unites people and makes them feel like partners.

Want to know the worst cliché ever coined? "Opposites attract." Like most things that are false, it has an element of truth. When people have enough in common, the elements of difference add a certain excitement to things. But overall, who is attractive to you? Whom do you want to spend time with? Are you looking for someone who disagrees with you on everything, has different interests, likes to sleep when you want to play, and likes to play when you want to sleep? Of course not. You want to be with people who are like you and yet unique.

When people are like each other, they tend to like each other. Do people form clubs of people who are different from them? No, they get together as fellow war veterans or stamp collectors or baseball card collectors, because having something in common creates rapport. Ever go to a convention? Isn't there an instant bond created among people who've never seen each other before? One of the staples of comedy is a fast-talking, back-slapping extrovert trying to interact with a quiet, self-effacing introvert. How do they get along? Terribly. They're just not enough alike to really like each other very much.

Whom do most Americans tend to feel better about, the English or the Iranians? Easy answer. And whom do we have the most in common with? Same answer. Think about the Middle East. Why do you think there are problems there? Are the Jews and Arabs alike in their religious beliefs? Do they have the same sort of justice system? Do they have the same language? You could go on and on. Their problems result from the ways they're different.

In fact, when we say that people are "having differences," we mean that the ways in which they're not alike are causing all sorts of problems. What about blacks and whites in the United States? Where do the problems begin? They begin when people focus on the ways they're different—the differences in color and culture and custom. Turmoil can result from a massive amount of difference. Harmony tends to result from similarity. It's been true throughout history. It's true on a global scale, and it's true on a personal scale.

Take any relationship between any two people, and you'll find the first thing that created their bond was something they had in common. They may have different ways of doing the same thing, but it was the commonalities that first brought them together. Think about someone you really like, and notice what makes him appealing. Isn't it the ways in which he's like you, or at least like the way you would like to be? You don't think, Wow, this guy thinks the opposite from me on every single issue. What a great guy! You think, What a smart guy. He's able to see the world much the way I do and even add to my perspective. Then think of someone you can't stand. Is he someone just like you? Do you think, God, what a rotten person. He thinks just the way I do?

Does this mean there's no way out of a vicious circle of difference creating conflict, creating more conflict, creating more difference? Of course not. Because in every case where there's difference, there's sameness, too. Do blacks and whites in America have a lot of differences? Sure, if you want to view things that way. But they have much more in common, don't they? We're all men and women, brothers and sisters, with similar fears and aspirations. The way to go from discord to harmony is to go from concentrating on differences to concentrating on similarities. The first step in real communication is learning to translate from your map of the world to someone else's. And what allows us to do that? Rapport skills.

> *"If you would win a man to your cause, first convince him that you are his sincere friend."*
>
> —*Abraham Lincoln*

How do we create rapport? We do it by creating or discovering things in common. In NLP language, we call this process "mirroring" or "matching." There are many ways to create commonality with another person and thus a state of rapport. You can mirror interests—that is, have a similar experience or style of dress or favorite activity. Or you can mirror association—that is, have similar friends or acquaintances. Or you can mirror beliefs. These are common experiences. They're the way we create friendships and relationships. All these experiences have one thing in common: They're communicated through words. The most common way to match others is through the exchange of information about each other through words. However, studies have shown that only 7 percent of what is communicated between people is transmitted through the words themselves. Thirty-eight percent comes through the tone of voice. I know when I was a kid and my mother raised her voice and said, "Anthony," in a certain tone, that meant much more than my name alone. Fifty-five percent of communication, the largest part, is a result of physiology or body language. The facial expressions, the gestures, the quality and type of movements of the person delivering a communication provides us with much more about what they're saying than the words do by themselves. This explains why a guy like Don Rickles can get up and attack you and say terrible things and make you laugh. Or how an Eddie Murphy can use four-letter words and make you laugh. Because it's not the words, it's the delivery—his tonality and physiology—that makes you laugh.

So if we are just trying to create rapport merely by the content of our conversation, we're missing out on the largest ways we could be communicating commonality to the brain of another person. One of the best ways to achieve rapport is through mirroring or creating a common physiology with that person. That's what the great hypnotherapist Dr. Milton Erickson did. He learned to mirror the breathing patterns, posture, tonality, and gestures of other people. And by doing that, he achieved a totally binding rapport in a matter of minutes. People who did not know him suddenly trusted him without question. So if you can develop rapport with just words, think of the incredible power of rapport you can develop with words and physiology linked together.

While the words are working on a person's conscious mind, the phyiology is working on the unconscious. That's where the brain is thinking, Hey, this person's like me. He must be okay. And once that happens, there's a tremendous attraction, a tremendous bond. And because it's unconscious, it's even more effective. You're not aware of anything but the bond that's been formed.

So how do you mirror another person's physiology? What kinds of physical traits can you mirror? Start with his voice. Mirror his tonality and phrasing, his pitch, how fast he talks, what sort of pauses he makes, his volume. Mirror favorite words or phrases. How about posture and breathing patterns, or eye contact, body language, facial expressions, hand gestures, or other distinctive movements? Any aspect of physiology, from the way a person plants his feet to the way he tilts his head, is something you can mirror. Now, this may sound absurd at first. What if you could mirror everything about another person?

Do you know what happens? People feel as though they've found their soulmate, someone who totally understands, who can read their deepest thoughts, who is just like them. But you don't have to mirror everything about a person to create a state of rapport. If you just start with the tone of voice or a similar facial expression, you can learn to build incredible rapport with anyone.

For the next several days, you should practice mirroring people you are with. Mirror their gestures and posture. Mirror the rate and location of their breathing. Mirror the tone, tempo, and volume of their voice. Do they feel closer to you, and do you feel closer to them?

Remember the mirroring experiment in the chapter on physiology? When a person mirrors someone else's physiology, he's able to experience not only the same state, but also the same sort of internal experiences and even the same thoughts. Now, what if you could do that in your daily life? What if you became such a skillful mirrorer that you could know what someone else was thinking? What sort of rapport would you have then, and what could you do with it? It's an awesome thing to contemplate, but professional communicators do it all the time. Mirroring is a skill like any other. It takes practice to develop. However, you can use it right now and get results.

When you break it down, there are two keys to mirroring— keen observation and personal flexibility. Here's an experiment to do when you're with someone else. Pick one person to be the mirrorer and the other to be the leader. Have the leader run through as many physical changes as possible in a minute or two. Change facial expressions, posture, and breathing. Change big things, like the way you hold your arms, and change small ones, like the tension in your neck. This is a great exercise to do with your children. They'll love it. When you're through, compare notes. See how well you did at mirroring the other person. Then change positions. You'll probably find you missed at least as many as you hit. Anyone can become an expert mirrorer, but you need to begin with the recognition that people use their bodies in hundreds of ways, and the more aware you are of these positions, the more successful you'll be. Even though

POSSIBLE COMPONENTS OF VOICE
TO MIRROR

Volume

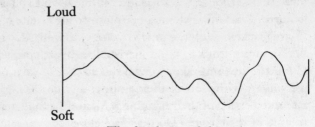

The loudness of the voice

Tempo

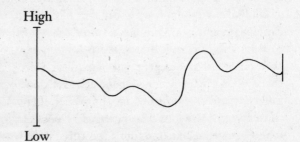

The pace or rhythm of the speech pattern

Tone

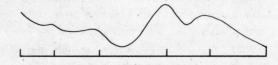

The pitch or frequency of the voice

Timbre

The individual characteristics or quality of the voice

there are unlimited possibilities, people in a sitting position, for example, usually make a limited number of movements. After some practice, you won't even have to think consciously about doing it. You'll just automatically mirror the postures and physiologies of the people around you.

There are infinite subleties to effective mirroring, but the foundation is something we touched on in the chapter on eliciting strategy: the three basic representational systems. Remember, everyone uses all three representational systems. But most of us have strong preferences, representational systems that we lean on time and time again. We're often primarily visual, or auditory, or kinesthetic. Once you've figured out a person's primary representational system, you've radically simplified the job of developing rapport with him.

> *"To effectively communicate, we must realize that we are all different in the way we perceive the world and use this understanding as a guide to our communication with others."*
>
> *—Anthony Robbins*

If behavior and physiology were made of a random set of factors, you would have to painstakingly pick up every cue and then put them all together. But representational systems are like the keys to a secret code. Knowing one fact gives you a clue to a dozen more. As we saw in chapter 8, there is a whole constellation of behaviors that go along with being primarily visual. There are verbal cues, phrases like "This is how it looks to me" or "I just can't picture myself doing that." Speech is usually fast, and breathing is high in the chest. The vocal tone is high-pitched, nasal, and/or often strained. There's usually muscle tension, particularly in the shoulders and abdomen. Visually oriented people tend to point a lot. They often have hunched shoulders and an extended neck.

Auditory people use phrases like "It sounds good to me" and "That doesn't ring a bell." Speech is more modulated, the tempo is balanced, and the voice tends to have a clear, resonant tonality.

HOW PEOPLE PERCEIVE COMMUNICATION

GENERIC	VISUAL	AUDITORY	KINESTHETIC
I understand you.	I see your point.	I hear what you are saying.	I feel that I am in touch with what you're saying.
I want to communicate something to you.	I want you to take a look at this.	I want to make this loud and clear.	I want you to get a grasp on this.
Do you understand what I am trying to communicate?	Am I painting a clear picture?	Does what I am saying sound right to you?	Are you able to get a handle on this?
I know that to be true.	I know beyond a shadow of a doubt that that is true.	That information is accurate word for word.	That information is as solid as a rock.
I am not sure about that.	That is pretty hazy to me.	That doesn't really ring a bell.	I am not sure I'm following you.
I don't like what you are doing.	I take a dim view of your perspective.	That does not resonate with me at all.	What it boils down to is that what you're doing doesn't feel right to me.
Life is good.	My mental image of life is sparkling and crystal clear.	Life is in perfect harmony.	Life feels warm and wonderful.

Breathing tends to be even and deep, coming from the diaphragm or the whole chest. There tends to be balanced muscle tension. When people fold their hands or arms, it usually indicates auditory accessing. There's a tendency for shoulders to slouch somewhat and for the head to tilt slightly to one side.

Kinesthetic people use phrases like "It doesn't feel right" or "I'm just not in touch with things." They speak in a slow tempo. Many times they take long pauses between words and have a low, deep tonality. A lot of body movement tends to indicate tactile or external kinesthetic accessing. Muscle relaxation indicates internal, visceral kinesthetic accessing. A position characterized by upturned palms with arms bent and relaxed is kinesthetic. Posture tends to be solid, with the head sitting squarely on the shoulders.

There are other cues, and things vary somewhat from person to person, so careful observation is always needed. Each person is unique. But when you know someone's main representational system, you've taken a huge step toward learning how to enter his world. All you have to do is match it.

Consider someone who is primarily in an auditory state. If you are trying to persuade him to do something by asking him to picture how it will look, and you talk very, very rapidly, you probably won't get through to him. He needs to hear what you have to say, needs to listen to your proposal and notice if it clicks for himself. In fact, he may not even "hear" you, simply because your tone of voice may turn him off from the very start. Another person may be in a primarily visual state, and you approach him kinesthetically, talking very slowly about how you feel about something, he will probably become irritated at your slow pace and ask you to please get to the point.

To illustrate these differences, I like to give the example of a residential neighborhood I know. One house is located on a quiet, peaceful street. Almost any time of day you can walk out and hear the birds singing. It has a storybook interior that speaks so eloquently, it's hard not to ask yourself how anyone could pass it by. Around twilight, you wander out to the garden just to listen to the birds, the breeze rustling through the branches, and the sound of the wind chimes on the front porch.

Another house is amazingly picturesque. You get excited just looking at it. It's visually stunning, from the long white porch out front to the beautifully detailed wainscoting on the peach-colored walls. There are windows everywhere, so it has beautiful light at almost any time of the day. There's so much to look at, from its winding stairways to its elegant carved oak doors, you could spend a day just exploring every nook and cranny, finding out what new things there are to see.

The third house is harder to describe. You have to go and experience it yourself; you just have to feel it. Its construction is solid and reassuring. Its rooms have a distinctive warmth. In a totally undefinable way, it touches something very fundamental in you. It's almost nurturing. You feel like sitting in a corner and soaking up whatever vapors are making you feel so serene.

In all three cases, I'm talking about the same house. The first is from an auditory, the second from a visual, and the third from a kinesthetic point of view. If you were showing the house to a group of people, to fully bring alive its richness, you would tap into all three modes. Each person's main representational system will determine which of the three descriptions sounds most enticing. But remember, people use all three. The most elegant way to communicate is to tap them all, while focusing on the system the other person uses most.

Begin to make a list of visual, auditory, and kinesthetic words.

For the next several days, listen to the people you are talking with and determine what kind of words they use most. Then speak to them using the same kind of words. What happens? Then speak for a while using a different representational system. What happens this time?

Let me give you an example of just how potent effective mirroring can be. I was in New York recently, and I wanted to relax, so I went to Central Park. I walked over and sat on a bench to watch what was going on. Pretty soon, I noticed this

PREDICATE WORDS

Visual	Auditory	Kinesthetic	Unspecified
see	hear	feel	sense
look	listen	touch	experience
view	sound(s)	grasp	understand
appear	make music	get hold of	think
show	harmonize	slip through	learn
dawn	tune in/out	catch on	process
reveal	be all ears	tap into	decide
envision	rings a bell	make contact	motivate
illuminate	silence	throw out	consider
twinkle	be heard	turn around	change
clear	resonate	hard	perceive
foggy	deaf	unfeeling	insensitive
focused	mellifluous	concrete	distinct
hazy	dissonance	scrape	conceive
sparkling	attune	unbudging	be conscious
crystal clear	overtones	get a handle	know
flash	unhearing	solid	
imagine	question	suffer	

guy sitting across from me. And I just began to mirror him. (Once you get in the habit, it's tough to stop.) I mirrored him exactly. I'm sitting the way he is, breathing the way he is, doing the same thing with my feet. He starts throwing bread crumbs to the birds. I start throwing bread crumbs to the birds. He's swaying his head a little. I start swaying my head a little. Then he glances up, and I glance up. He looks at me, and I look at him.

Before too long he gets up and walks over to me. No surprise. I'm totally attractive to him because he thinks I'm just like him. We start talking, and I'm mirroring his tone of voice and his

PREDICATE PHRASES

Predicates are the process words (verbs, adverbs, adjectives) people use in their communication to represent their experiences internally through the visual, auditory, or kinesthetic modality. Listed below are some of the more commonly used predicate phrases*

Visual (see)	*Auditory (hear)*	*Kinesthetic (feel)*
An eyeful	Afterthought	All washed up
Appears to me	Blabbermouth	Boils down to
Beyond a shadow of a doubt	Clear as a bell	Chip off the old block
Bird's-eye view	Clearly expressed	Come to grips with
Catch a glimpse of	Call on	Control yourself
Clear cut	Describe in detail	Cool/calm/collected
Dim view	Earful	Firm foundations
Eye to eye	Express yourself	Floating on thin air
Flashed on	Give an account of	Get a handle on
Get a perspective on	Give me your ear	Get a load of this
Get a scope on	Grant an audience	Get in touch with
Hazy idea	Heard voices	Get the drift of
Horse of a different color	Hidden message	Get your goat
In light of	Hold your tongue	Hand in hand
In person	Idle talk	Hang in there
In view of	Inquire into	Heated argument
Looks like	Keynote speaker	Hold it!
Make a scene	Loud and clear	Hold on!
Mental image	Manner of speaking	Hot-head
Mental picture	Pay attention to	Keep your shirt on!
Mind's eye	Power of speech	Know-how
Naked eye	Purrs like a kitten	Lay cards on table
Paint a pictue	Outspoken	Light-headed
Photographic memory	Rap session	Moment of panic
Plainly see	Rings a bell	Not following you
Pretty as a picture	State your purpose	Pain in the neck

Visual (see)	Auditory (hear)	Kinesthetic (feel)
See to it	Tattletale	Pull some strings
Short-sighted	To tell the truth	Sharp as a tack
Showing off	Tongue-tied	Slipped my mind
Sight for sore eyes	Tuned in/tuned out	Smooth operator
Staring off into space	Unheard-of	So-so
Take a peek	Utterly	Start from scratch
Tunnel vision	Voiced an opinion	Stiff upper lip
Under your nose	Well informed	Stuffed shirt
Up front	Within hearing range	Too much of a hassle
Well defined	Word for word	Topsy-turvey
		Underhanded

* The objective in matching predicates is to match the language in which your listener speaks, thus creating an atmosphere of rapport and understanding.

phraseology exactly. After a few moments he says, "It's obvious you're a very intelligent man." Why does he believe that? Because he feels I'm just like him. Before too long he's telling me he feels he knows me better than people he's known for twenty-five years. And not long after that, he offers me a job.

I know that some people I talk to about mirroring get all uptight and say that it's unnatural, it's manipulative. But the idea that it's unnatural is absurd. Anytime you are in rapport with someone, it's natural for you to begin mirroring him in physiology, tonality, and so on. Whenever I teach seminars, usually someone present is upset about mirroring. I simply point out that if he will look over at the person next to him, he will notice that they are sitting just the same way. They both have their legs crossed, their heads are tilted at the same angle, and so forth. Invariably, they are mirroring each other because they have developed rapport over the course of several days. I then ask the one how he feels about the other, and he will say, "Great," or, "Close." Then I have the other person change his physiology and sit in a completely different posture. When I ask the first person how he feels about the other person now, the answers I receive are, "Not as close," or, "Distant," or, "I'm not sure anymore."

So mirroring is a natural process of rapport. You already do it unconsciously. In this chapter, we're learning what we do— the recipes for rapport—so that we can create that result anytime we wish, with anyone, even a stranger. As for mirroring being manipulative, tell me which requires more conscious effort, just to speak at your normal pace and tone or truly to find out how another person communicates best and to enter his world? And remember that while you're mirroring another person, you truly experience how he feels. If your intent were to manipulate someone else, once you begin to mirror, you in fact begin to feel more like him—so the question becomes, Are you willing to manipulate yourself?

You're not giving up your identity when you mirror another person. You are not exclusively a visual, auditory, or kinesthetic person. We should all strive to be flexible. Mirroring simply creates a commonality of physiology that underscores our shared humanity. When I'm mirroring, I can get the benefits of another person's feelings and experiences and thoughts. That's a powerful, beautiful, and empowering lesson to experience about how to share the world with other human beings.

Massive cultural success results from rapport with the masses. The most effective leaders are strong in all three representational systems. We tend to trust people who appeal to us on all three levels and who give off a sense of congruity—all the parts of their personality convey the same thing. Think of the past presidential election. Do you think Ronald Reagan, for his age, is an attractive man visually? Does he have an attractive tone of voice and manner of speaking? Can he move you emotionally with feelings of patriotism and possibility? Most people—even those who disagree with his policies—would give a resounding "Yes!" to all three questions. No wonder they call him the Great Communicator. Now think of Walter Mondale. Is he an attractive man visually? When I ask this question in seminars, I'm lucky if I get a 20 percent "yes" response. Does he have an attractive tone of voice and manner of speaking? I get an even smaller number of people who believe he does. Even those who agree with everything Mondale says seldom answer yes to this question. Can he move you emotionally with feelings of patriotism and possibility? I usually get a laugh at this point. That was one of his biggest failings. So was it any surprise that Reagan won in a landslide?

Think of what happened to Gary Hart. He was fairly attractive on all three levels. Mondale had more money and had been in the White House, so he seemed the logical choice. Yet Hart was in the running—but only for a short time. What happened? For one thing, Hart was incongruent. When people asked him why he had changed his name, he said it wasn't important—but his body language and tone of voice said otherwise. He could have stood in front of the press and said, "Yes, I changed my name. But I did it so that you wouldn't judge me by my name, but rather by the quality of the job that I do." Instead, he was wishy-washy. Then he had to be pressed to discuss his "new ideas," and when he did, many people felt there was no substance to them. They were just fluff.

What about Geraldine Ferraro? Do you think she's an attractive woman visually? About 60 percent of the people I interviewed thought so. Do you feel she has an attractive tone of voice? Here is where Ferraro loses, and loses big. Between 80 and 90 percent of the audience I interviewed said that her voice was not only unattractive but irritating. (The only exceptions were people from New York City.) And only 10 percent said she could move them emotionally. Can you imagine how difficult it would be for you to be popular—even if you have the greatest ideas in the world—if people are irritated every time you open your mouth? Being a woman and being on the same ticket with Mondale didn't help Ms. Ferraro in some people's eyes. Yet they may not have been the major reasons she didn't get support. Her tone of voice, her inability to move people emotionally, and, finally, her incongruency cost her. Many issues arose where it appeared she was delivering mixed messages—about abortion, nuclear first strike, her husband's fi-

nances, and more. The personal communication skills of the
Democratic candidates alone made defeat almost inevitable.

Think now of a major cultural success like Bruce Springsteen.
His concerts are packed, and he offers everything for the eyes
and ears. Visually attractive, he talks to his audiences in a voice
deep with feeling, and he develops tremendous rapport. He appears totally congruent.

Think of a president from modern history who stands out in
your mind as being powerful, charismatic, able to make a difference. . . . Did you think of John F. Kennedy? Ninety-five
percent of the people I poll do. Why? Well, there are many
reasons, but let's check a few. Did you feel that Kennedy was
an attractive man visually? You bet. I rarely find someone who
didn't think he was. How about from an auditory point of view?
Ninety percent of the people I polled agreed he was attractive
in this way, too. Could he move you emotionally with statements like "Ask not what your country can do for you, ask what
you can do for your country"? He was a master of using communication to affect people. Was he congruent? Khruschev must
have thought so. The Cuban missile crisis was a test of congruency between Kennedy and Khruschev. They were both
staring at each other eye to eye, and as one writer put it,
"Khrushchev blinked."

Studies of successful people have shown over and over again
that they have a great talent for creating rapport. Those who
are flexible and attractive in all three modes can affect large
numbers of people whether as a teacher, a businessman, or a
world leader. But you don't need any sort of natural gift to do
it. If you can see and hear and feel, you can create rapport with
anyone just by doing what he does. You're looking for the things
you can mirror as unobtrusively and as naturally as possible. If
you mirror a person who is asthmatic or has a terrible twitch,
instead of achieving rapport, you'll lead him to think you're
mocking him.

By practicing consistently, you enter the world of whomever
you're with and speaking in that person's mode. It will soon
become second nature. And you will do it automatically without

any conscious thought. When you begin to mirror effectively, you'll learn that the process does more than just allow you to achieve rapport and understand the other person. Because of what's known as pacing and leading, you are able to get them to follow you. It doesn't matter how different you are. It doesn't matter how you meet. If you can establish enough rapport with someone, before too long you can change his behavior to begin matching yours.

Let me give you an example. A few years ago, my nutrition business began to develop a relationship with a very powerful doctor in Beverly Hills. We got off on the wrong foot. He wanted an immediate decision on a proposal, but I was out of town, and I was the only one who could make the decision. He didn't like having to wait for someone as young as I was— twenty-one at the time—and he was in a pretty antagonistic state when I finally met him.

I found him sitting in his office in a very rigid position, his muscles tensed. I sat in the chair opposite him in exactly the same posture and began to mirror the rhythm of his breathing. He spoke rapidly, so I spoke rapidly. He had an unusual way of gesturing, waving his right arm in a circle. I picked up the same thing.

Despite the bad circumstances of our meeting, we began to get along. Why? Because by matching him, I'd established rapport. Before too long, I began to see if I could lead him. First, I slowed down the pace of my speech. He slowed down, too. Then I sat back in my chair. He did the same thing. At the beginning, I was matching and mirroring him. But as our rapport developed, I was able to lead him to match and mirror me. Then he asked me out to lunch, and we ended up having a really friendly meal together, as if we were the best of buddies. Now this was a guy who hated my guts when I walked in the door. So you don't need to have ideal circumstances to mirror well. You just need the skill to adapt your behavior to that of someone else.

What I was doing with this man was pacing and leading. Pacing is just graceful mirroring, moving the way a person moves, changing gestures as he changes gestures. Once you attain great skill in mirroring someone else, you can change your physiology and behavior almost instinctively as the other person changes. Rapport is not static; it's not something that remains stable once achieved. It's a dynamic, fluid, flexible process. Just as the key to establishing a truly resonant, lasting relationship is the ability to change and adjust to what someone else is going through, the key to pacing is an ability to elegantly and accurately change gears when someone else does.

Leading follows directly from pacing. As you establish rapport with someone, you create a link that can almost be felt. Leading comes just as naturally as pacing. You reach a point where you start to initiate change rather than just mirroring the other person, a point where you have developed so much rapport that when you change, the other person will unconsciously follow you. You've probably experienced being with friends late at night when you're not tired at all, but you're in such deep rapport that when they yawn, you yawn, too. The best salesmen do exactly the same thing. They enter another person's world, achieve rapport, and then use that rapport to lead.

An obvious question comes up when we talk about rapport this way: What if someone's mad? Do you mirror his madness or his anger? Well, that's certainly one choice. However, in the next chapter we're going to talk about how to break someone's pattern, whether it be one of anger or frustration, and how to do it quickly. It might be best to break someone's pattern rather than to mirror that anger. Sometimes, by mirroring someone's anger, you can enter his world so strongly that when you begin to relax, he begins to relax also. Remember, rapport doesn't just mean you're smiling. Rapport means responsiveness. Street people, for instance, sometimes find that mirroring the anger right back is absolutely essential. Occasionally you may need to be just as intense in your communication to a person, since his challenge to you is one of the many ways respect is developed in this part of our culture.

Here's another experiment. Engage someone in conversation. Mirror him in posture, voice, and breathing. After a while,

PACING AND LEADING

Digital Pacing:
- Match Predicates
- Match Sequence of Accessing Cues
- Match Tonality
- Match Pitch

Analogical Pacing or Mirroring:
- Breathing
- Pulse
- Moisture on the Skin
- Head Position
- Facial Movements
- Movement of Eyebrows
- Pupil Size
- Muscle Tension
- Weight Shifts
- Movement of Feet
- Placement of Body Parts
- Spacial Relationships
- Hand Gestures
- Body Movements through Space
- Body Posture

gradually change your posture or tone of voice. Does the other person follow you after a few minutes? If he does not, simply go back and pace again. Then try a different lead and make the change less radical. If, when you attempt to lead someone, he does not follow, it simply means you do not have enough rapport yet. Develop more rapport and try again.

> *"I bid him look into the lives of men as though into a mirror, and from others to take an example for himself."*
> —*Terence*

What's the key to establishing rapport? Flexibility. Remember, the biggest barrier to rapport is thinking that other people have the same map you do, that because you see the world one way, they do, too. Excellent communicators rarely make this mistake. They know they have to change their language, their tonality, their breathing patterns, their gestures, until they discover an approach that is successful in achieving their outcome.

If you fail to communicate with someone, it's tempting to assume that he is a hopeless fool who refuses to listen to reason. But that virtually guarantees you'll never get through. It's better to change your words and behaviors until they match his model of the world.

One essential tenet of NLP is that the meaning of your communication is the response you elicit. The responsibility in communication rests upon you. If you try to persuade someone to do one thing, and he does the other, the fault was in your communication. You didn't find a way to get your message through.

This is absolutely crucial in anything you do. Let's look at teaching. The greatest tragedy in education is that most teachers know their subjects, but they don't know their students. They don't know how their students process information, they don't know their students' representational systems, they don't know how their students' minds work.

The best teachers instinctively know how to pace and lead. They're able to establish rapport, so their message gets through. But there's no reason why all teachers can't learn the same thing. By learning to pace their students, by learning to present information in the forms their students can effectively process, they can revolutionize the educational world.

Some teachers think that since they know their subjects, any failure in communication rests with the students who can't learn. But response, not content, is the meaning of communication. You can know everything in the world about the Holy Roman Empire, but if you can't establish rapport, if you can't translate that information from your map to someone else's, your knowledge is meaningless. That's why the best teachers are the ones who establish rapport. There's a story about a classroom in which all the kids—as a prank—arranged to drop their books at exactly nine A.M. so as to throw the teacher off. Without missing a beat, she put down her chalk, picked up a book, and dropped it, too. "Sorry I'm late," she said. After that, she had the kids eating out of her hand.

The founders of NLP give a fascinating example of just how education should work. There was a young engineering student whose primary representational system was kinesthetic. At first he had terrible problems learning to read electrical schematics. He found the subject difficult and boring. Basically, he was having trouble making sense of concepts that were being presented visually.

Then one day he began to imagine what it would feel like to be an electron floating through the circuit he saw diagramed in front of him. He imagined his various reactions and changes in behavior as he came in contact with the components in the circuit, symbolized by characters on the schematic. Almost immediately, the diagrams began to make more sense to him. He even began to enjoy them. Each schematic presented him with a new odyssey. It was so enjoyable that he ended up becoming an engineer. He succeeded because he was able to learn through his favored representational system. Nearly all the kids who wash out of our educational systems are capable of learning. We just never learned how to teach them. We never established rapport with them and never matched their learning strategies.

I've been emphasizing teaching because, in the end, it's something we all do, whether at home with our kids or at work with our employees or peers. What works in a classroom works in a boardroom or a living room as well.

There's a final wonderful thing about the magic of rapport. It's the most accessible skill in the world. You don't need textbooks, and you don't need courses. You don't need to travel to study at the feet of a master, and you don't need to earn a degree. The only tools you need are your eyes, your ears, you senses of touch, taste, and smell.

You can begin cultivating rapport right now. We are always communicating and interacting. Rapport is simply doing both in the most effective ways possible. You can study rapport when you're waiting for a plane by mirroring the people in line with you. You can use rapport at the grocery store. You can use it at your job and at home. If, when you go in for a job interview, you match and mirror the interviewer, he'll like you immediately. Use rapport in your business to create an immediate connection with clients. If you want to become a master communicator, all you need to do is learn how to enter other people's worlds. You already have everything you need to do it now.

There's another way to establish rapport, sets of distinctions that help determine the choices people make. They're called . . .

CHAPTER XIV

Distinctions of Excellence: Metaprograms

"In the right key one can say anything. In the wrong key, nothing: the only delicate part is the establishment of the key."

—*George Bernard Shaw*

One of the best ways to become aware of the astonishing diversity of human reactions is to speak to a group of people. You can't help noticing how differently people react to the same thing. You tell a motivational story, and one person will be transfixed, another bored to tears. You tell a joke, and one person howls while another doesn't move a muscle. You'd think each person was listening in a different mental language.

The question is why people react so differently to identical messages. Why does one person see the glass as half-empty and another see it as half-full? Why does one person hear a message and feel energized, excited, and motivated while another hears the exact same message and doesn't respond at all? Shaw's quote is precisely right. If you address someone in the right key, you can do anything. If you address him in the wrong one, you can do nothing. The most inspiring message, the most insightful thought, the most intelligent critique, are absolutely meaningless unless they're understood both intellectually and emotionally by the person to whom they're being addressed. They're major keys not just to personal power, but to many of the broader issues we must confront collectively. If you want to be a master persuader, a master communicator, in both business and in personal life, you have to know how to find the right key.

The path is through metaprograms. Metaprograms are the keys to the way a person processes information. They're powerful internal patterns that help determine how he forms his internal representations and directs his behavior. Metaprograms are the internal programs (or sorts) we use in deciding what to pay attention to. We distort, delete, and generalize information because the conscious mind can only pay attention to so many pieces of information at any given time.

Our brain processes information much the way a computer does. It takes fantastic amounts of data and organizes them into a configuration that makes sense to that person. A computer can't do anything without software, which provides the structure to perform specific tasks. Metaprograms operate much the same way in our brain. They provide the structure that governs what we pay attention to, how we make sense of our experiences, and the directions in which they take us. They provide the basis on which we decide that something is interesting or dull, a potential blessing or a potential threat. To communicate with a computer, you have to understand its software. To communicate effectively with a person, you have to understand his metaprograms.

People have patterns of behavior, and they have patterns by which they organize their experience to create those behaviors. Only through understanding those mental patterns can you expect to get your message across, whether it's trying to get someone to buy a car or to understand that you really love him/her. Even though the situations may vary, there is a consistent structure to how people understand things and organize their thinking.

The first metaprogram involves moving toward something or moving away. All human behavior revolves around the urge to gain pleasure or avoid pain. You pull away from a lighted match in order to avoid the pain of burning your hand. You sit and watch a beautiful sunset because you get pleasure from the glorious celestial show as day glides into night.

The same is true of more ambiguous actions. One person may walk a mile to work becausse he enjoys the exercise. Another may walk because he has a terrible phobia about being in a car. One person may read Faulkner, Hemingway, or Fitzgerald because he enjoys their prose and insight. He's moving toward something that gives him pleasure. Another might read the same writers because he doesn't want people to think of him as an uneducated dunce. He's not so much seeking pleasure as avoiding pain; he's moving away from something, not toward it.

As with the other metaprograms I'll discuss, this process is not one of absolutes. Everyone moves toward some things and away from others. No one responds the same way to each and every stimulus, although everyone has a dominant mode, a strong tendency toward one program or another. Some people tend to be energetic, curious risk takers. They may feel most comfortable moving toward something that excites them. Others tend to be cautious, wary, and protective; they see the world as a more perilous place. They tend to take actions away from harmful or threatening things rather than toward exciting ones. To find out which way people move, *ask them what they want in a relationship—a house, car, job, or anything else.* Do they tell you want they want or what they don't want?

What does this information mean? Everything. If you're a businessman selling a product, you can promote it two ways, by what it does or by what it doesn't do. You can try to sell cars by stressing that they're fast, sleek, or sexy, or you can emphasize that they don't use much gas, don't cost much to maintain, and are particularly safe in crashes. The strategy you use should depend entirely upon the strategy of the person you're dealing with. Use the wrong metaprogram with a person, and you might as well have stayed home. You're trying to move him toward something, and all he wants to do is find a good reason to back away.

Remember, a car can travel along the same path in forward or reverse. It just depends on what direction it's facing. The same is true on a personal basis. Let's say you want your child to spend more time on his schoolwork. You might tell him, "You better study or you won't get into a good college." Or "Look at Fred. He didn't study, so he flunked out of school, and he's going to spend the rest of his life pumping gas. Is that the kind of life you want for yourself?" How well will that strategy work? It depends on your child. If he's primarily motivated by moving away, it might work well. But what if he moves toward things? What if he's motivated by things that excite him, by moving toward things he finds appealing? If that's how he responds, you're not going to change his behavior by offering the example of something to move away from. You can nag until you're blue in the face, but you're talking in the wrong key. You're talking Latin, and the kid understands Greek. You're wasting your time, and you're wasting his. In fact, people who move toward are often angered by or resentful of those who present things to be moved away from. You would motivate your child better by saying, "If you do this, you can pick and choose any college you want to."

The second metaprogram deals with external and internal frames of reference. Ask someone else how he knows when he's done a good job. For some people, the proof comes from outside. The boss pats you on the back and says your work was great. You get a raise. You win a big award. Your work is noticed and applauded by your peers. When you get that sort of external approval, you know your work is good. That's an external frame of reference.

For others, the proof comes from inside. They "just know inside" when they've done well. If you have an internal frame of reference, you can design a building that wins all sorts of architectural awards, but if you don't feel it's special, no amount of outside approval will convince you it is. Conversely, you might do a job that gets a lukewarm reception from your boss or peers, but if you feel it's good work, you'll trust you own instincts rather than theirs. That's an internal frame of reference.

Let's say you're trying to convince someone to attend a seminar. You might say, "You've got to attend this seminar. It's great. I've gone and all my friends have gone, and they've all had a terrific time and raved about it for days. They all said it changed their lives for the better." If the person you're talking to has an external frame of reference, chances are you'll convince him. If all those people say it's true, he'll often assume it's probably true.

But what if he has an internal frame of reference? You'll have a difficult time convincing him by telling him what others have said. It doesn't mean anything to him. It doesn't compute. You can only convince him by appealing to things he knows himself. What if you told him, "Remember the series of lectures you went to last year? Remember how you said it was the most insightful experience you'd had in years? Well, I know about something that's maybe like that; I think if you check it out, you may find you'll have the same kind of experience. What do you think?" Will that work? Sure it will, because you're talking to him in his language.

It's important to note that all these metaprograms are *context- and stress-related*. If you've done something for ten or fifteen years, you probably have a strong internal frame of reference; if you're brand new, you may not have as strong an internal frame of reference about what is right or wrong in that context. So you tend to develop preferences and patterns over time. But even if you're right-handed, you still use your left hand in various situations where it is useful to do so. The same is true of metaprograms. You're not just one way. You can vary. You can change.

What kind of frame of reference do most leaders have—internal or external? A truly effective leader has to have a strong internal frame. He wouldn't be much of a leader if he spent all his time asking people what they thought of something before he took any action. And, as with metaprograms, there's an ideal balance to be struck. Remember, few people operate strictly at one extreme. A truly effective leader has to be able to take in information effectively from the outside as well. When he doesn't, leadership becomes megalomania.

After one of my recent seminars open to guests, a man came up with three friends and sternly told me, "I'm not sold!" He was doing everything he could to egg me on. It quickly became obvious he was sorting by an internal frame of reference. (Externally oriented people rarely come up and just tell you what you should do and how you should do it.) And from his conversation with his friends, it also became clear that he moved away from things. So I told him, "I can't convince you to do anything. You're the only one who can convince you." He didn't know how to handle this response. He was waiting for me to strut my stuff and have him reject it. Now he had to agree with what I said, because he knew it was true inside. Then I said, "You're the only person who knows who would lose if you didn't attend the course." Normally such a remark would have sounded terrible to me. But I was speaking in his language, and it worked. Notice, I didn't say he would lose if he didn't attend. If I'd said that, he never would have. Instead I said, "You're the only one who knows" (internal frame of reference) "who would lose" (moving away from) "if you didn't go." He said, "Yeah, that's true," and he went to the back of the room and signed up. Before I learned about metaprograms, I would have tried to persuade him by having him talk to other people (external frame of reference) who had taken the course, and I would have told him about all the benefits he would derive (moving toward). But that would have been the way to get me interested, not him.

The third set of metaprograms involves sorting by self or sorting by others. Some people look at human interactions primarily in terms of what's in it for them personally, some in terms of what they can do for themselves and others. Of course, people don't always fall into one extreme or the other. If you sort only by self, you become a self-absorbed egotist. If you sort only by others, you become a martyr.

If you're involved in hiring people, wouldn't you want to know where an applicant fits on this scale? Not long ago a major airline found that 95 percent of its complaints involved 5 percent of its employees. These 5 percent sorted strongly by self; they were most interested in looking out for themselves, not others. Were they poor employees? Yes and no. They were obviously in the wrong jobs and obviously doing a poor job, though they might have been smart, hardworking, and congenial. They may have been the right people put in the wrong slots.

What did the airline do? It replaced them with people who sorted by others. The company determined this through group interviews in which prospective employees were asked why they wanted to work for the airline. Most of the individuals thought they were being judged by the answers they gave in front of the group, when in fact they were being judged by their behavior as members of the audience. That is, individuals who paid the most attention and gave the most eye contact, smiles, or support to the person who was doing the speaking at the front of the room were given the highest rating, while those who paid little or no attention and were in their own world while others were talking were considered to be primarily self-sorting and were not hired. The company's complaint ratio dropped over 80 percent as a result of this move. That's why metaprograms are so important in the business world. How can you evaluate a person if you don't know what motivates him? How can you match the job you have available with the correct person, in terms of required skills, ability to learn, and internal makeup? A lot of very smart people spend their careers totally frustrated because they're doing jobs that don't make the best use of their inherent capabilities. A liability in one context can be a valuable asset in another.

In a service business, like an airline, you obviously need people who sort by others. If you're hiring an auditor, you might want someone who would sort by self. How many times have you dealt with someone who left you in a confused state because he did his job well intellectually but poorly emotionally? It's like a doctor who sorts strongly by self. He may be a brilliant diagnostician, but unless you feel he cares about you, he won't be totally effective. In fact, someone like that would probably be better off as a researcher than as a clinician. Putting the right person in the right job remains one of the biggest problems in American business. But it's a problem that could be dealt with if people knew how to evaluate the ways that job applicants processed information.

At this point, it's worth noting that not all metaprograms are created equal. Are people better off moving toward things rather than away from them? Perhaps. Would the world be a better place if people sorted more by others and less by self? Probably. But we have to deal with life the way it is, not the way we wish it were. You may wish your son moved toward things rather than away. If you want to effectively communicate with him, you have to do it in a way that works, not in a way that plays to your idea of how the world should work. The key is to observe a person as carefully as possible, listen to what he says, what sort of metaphors he uses, what his physiology reveals, when he's attentive and when he's bored. People reveal their metaprograms on a consistent, ongoing basis. It doesn't take much concentrated study to figure out what people's tendencies are or how they are sorting at the moment. To determine if people sort by self or others, see how much attention they pay to other people. Do they lean toward people and have facial expressions that reflect concern for what others are saying, or do they lean back and remain bored and unresponsive? Everyone sorts by self some of the time, and it's important to do so sometimes. The key is what you do consistently and whether your sorting procedure enables you to produce the results you desire.

The fourth sorting program involves matchers and mismatchers. I want to try an experiment with you. Look at these figures and tell me how they relate to each other.

If I asked you to describe the relationship between the three figures, you could answer in many ways. You could say they're all rectangles. You could say they all have four sides. You could say two are vertical and one is horizontal, or that two are standing up and one is lying down, or that no one figure has precisely the same relationship to the other two. Or that one is different and the other two are alike.

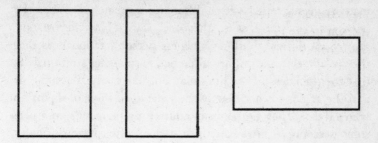

I'm sure you can think of more descriptions. What's going on here? They're all descriptions of the same picture, but they take completely different approaches. So it is with matchers and mismatchers. This metaprogram determines how you sort information to learn, understand, and the like. Some people respond to the world by finding sameness. They look at things and see what they have in common. They're matchers. So when they look at our figures they might say, "Well, they're all rectangles." Another kind of matcher finds sameness with exceptions. He might look at the figures and say, "They're all rectangles, but one is lying down and the other two are standing up."

Other people are mismatchers—difference people. There are two kinds of them. One type looks at the world and sees how things are different. He might look at the figures and say they are all different and have different relationships to one another. They're not alike at all. The other kind of mismatcher sees differences with exceptions. He's like a matcher who finds sameness with exceptions in reverse—he sees the differences first, and then he'll add the things they have in common. To determine whether someone is a matcher or mismatcher, ask him about the relationship between any set of objects or situations and note whether he focuses first on the similarities or the differences. Can you imagine what happens when a sameness matcher gets together with a difference mismatcher? When the one says they're all alike, the other says, "No, they're not, they're all different!" The sameness person's rationale is that they're all rectangles. The difference mismatcher's rationale is that the thickness of the lines may not be exactly the same, or that the angles are not exactly the same in all three of them. So who's right? They both are, of course; it all depends on a person's perception. However, mismatchers often have difficulty creating rapport with people because they are always creating differences. They can more easily develop rapport with other mismatchers.

How is understanding these distinctions important? Let me give an example from my business. I have five partners, and all but one of us are matchers. For the most part, this is terrific. We're alike, so we like each other. We think the same way and see the same things, so in our meetings we can achieve a wonderful synergy; we're all talking and coming up with ideas, and they all look better and better because we're matching one another, seeing what the others are seeing, building on their insights, getting more and more excited.

Until our mismatcher weighs in, that is. Without fail, he sees things differently from the way we do. While we see the way things fit together, he sees the way they don't. While we get enthusiastic and move along, he jumps in and tells us it's not going to work, then sits back like a bump on a log—not paying attention to what we see and instead seeing all sorts of problems we don't want to worry about. We want to soar into the mental ozone. He wants to get back to square one and say, "Oh, yeah? What about this? What about that?"

Is he a pain in the neck? You bet he is. Is he a valuable partner? He sure is. What we need to do is use him at the appropriate time in the planning process. We don't want him harping on details and ruining our brainstorming. The synergy we get from planning together is more valuable than his nitpicking at the time. Then after we've slowed down, we desperately need someone who sees the holes, sees the incongruities, sees how things don't fit, how they don't match. That's the function he plays, and it often saves us from ourselves.

Mismatchers are in the minority. The generalizations offered by survey show that about 35 percent of the people interviewed were mismatchers. (If you're a mismatcher, you'll probably say the surveys are not accurate.) However, mismatchers are extremely valuable because they tend to see what the rest of us don't. Mismatchers aren't usually the souls of poetic inspiration. Many times, even when they get excited, they'll start mismatching and find a way to get unexcited. But their critical, analytical sensibilities are important to any business. Think of a titanic business failure like the movie *Heaven's Gate*. If you'd been able to look behind the scenes, you might have found a bunch of creative matchers with internal frames of reference—all moving toward the goal and not looking at anything they need to move away from. They desperately needed a mismatcher to say, "Wait a second. What about this?" and communicate it in a way that could be accepted by the creative people's internal frames of reference.

Matching or mismatching modes are extremely important because they can play out in so many ways, even in nutrition. Extreme matchers can often end up eating food that's bad for them, because they want food that is always the same. They wouldn't want an apple or a plum. There's too much variety in ripeness, texture, tastes, shelf time, and other assorted variables. Instead they might eat a lot of junk food because it doesn't change. It might be lousy food, but it warms a matcher's unvarying soul.

If you have a job that requires the same repetitive work, year after year, would you want to hire a difference person? Of course not. You want to hire a sameness person—he'd be very, very happy in such a job for as long as you needed him there. If, however, you have a job that requires a great deal of flexibility or constant change, would you want to hire a sameness person in that position? Obviously not. These distinctions can be very useful in discovering what kind of jobs people would be most happy at for the longest period of time.

Consider the case of a football field goal kicker. A few years back, he began the season with great success, kicking with remarkable accuracy. But since he was a mismatcher, he soon felt obligated to begin varying his routine, and he went into a slump. He was persuaded to concentrate on the different kinds of fans behind the goal post in each different stadium. By focusing on how different they were, he could mismatch to his heart's content on something trivial while still performing his best in the same way in what really mattered.

Would you use the same persuasion techniques on a matcher and a mismatcher? Would you want them in the same job? Would you treat two kids with different matching strategies in the same way? Of course not. This is not to say that strategies are immutable. People are not Pavlovian dogs. They can modify their strategies to some extent, but only if someone talks to them in their own language about how to do that. It takes tremendous effort and patience to turn a lifelong mismatcher into a matcher, but you can help him make the most of his approach and be a little less churlish and doctrinaire in the process. That's one of the secrets of living with people who are different from you. On the other hand, it's useful for matchers to see more differences, for they have a tendency to generalize. It might be useful for a matcher to notice all the differences between this week and last week, or between the cities they visit (instead of saying Los Angeles is very much like New York). Focus a little on the *differences*, too—they are part of the spice of life.

Can a matcher and a mismatcher live happily together? Sure—just as long as they understand each other. That way, when differences occur they'll just realize the other person isn't bad or wrong, he/she just perceives things in a different way. You don't have to be totally alike to establish rapport. You do need to remember the differences in the ways you both perceive things and learn how to respect and appreciate each other.

The next metaprogram involves what it takes to convince someone of something. The convincer strategy has two parts. To figure out what consistently convinces someone, you must first find out what sensory building blocks he needs to become convinced, and then you must discover how often he has to receive these stimuli before becoming convinced. To discover someone's convincer metaprogram, ask, "How do you know when someone else is good at a job? Do you have to a) see them or watch them do it, b) hear about how good they are, c) do it with them, or d) read about their ability?" The answer may be a combination of these. You may believe someone's good when you see him do a good job and when other people tell you he's good. The next question is, "How often does someone have to demonstrate he's good before you're convinced?" There are four possible answers: a) immediately (for example, if they demonstrate that they're good at something once, you believe them, b) a number of times (two or more), c) over a period of time (say, a few weeks or a month or a year), and d) consistently. In the last case, a person has to demonstrate that he's good each and every time.

If you're the head of an organization, one of the most valuable states you can achieve with your key workers is trust and rapport. If they know you care about them, they'll work harder and better for you. If they don't trust you, they won't deliver for you. But part of establishing that trust is being attentive to the different needs of different people. Some people will establish a relationship and maintain it. If they know that you play fair and that you care about them, you can establish a bond that will last until you do something to betray it.

This doesn't work for everyone. Some workers need more than that, whether it's a kind word, an approving memo, a show of public support, or an important task to perform. They may be just as loyal and just as talented, but they need more verification from you than other people do. They need more proof that the bond between you still holds. Likewise, any good salesman knows customers he only had to sell once, and they were customers forever. Other people have to see the product two or three times before they decide to buy, while for others maybe six months can pass before there is a need to sell to them again. Then of course there is the salesman's "favorite"—the man who has used your product for years, and every time you come in he wants to know again why he should use it. He has to be shown every time. The same process plays out with even greater intensity in personal relationships. With some people, if you can prove your love once, you've proved it forever. With others, you have to prove it every day. The value of understanding these metaprograms is that they provide you with the game plan for convincing someone. You know in advance what it will take to convince him, and you're no longer upset by the person you have to show every time. You expect that behavior from him.

Another metaprogram is possibility versus necessity. Ask someone why he went to work for his present company or why he bought his current car or house. Some people are motivated primarily by necessity, rather than by what they want. They do something because they must. They're not pulled to take action by what is possible. They're not looking for infinite varieties of experience. They go through life taking what comes and what is available. When they need a new job or a new house or a new car or even a new spouse, they go out and accept what is available.

Others are motivated to look for possibilities. They're motivated less by what they have to do than by what they want to do. They seek options, experiences, choices, paths. The person who is motivated by necessity is interested in what's known and what's secure. The person who is motivated by possibility is equally interested in what's not known. He wants to know what can evolve, what opportunities might develop.

If you were an employer, which kind of a person would you most want to hire? Some people would probably answer, "The person who is motivated by possibility." After all, having a rich sense of potential makes for a richer life. Instinctively, most of us (even a lot of people who are motivated by necessity) would advocate the virtues of remaining open to an infinite variety of new directions.

In reality, it's not that cut-and-dried. There are jobs that require attention to detail, steadfastness, and consistency. Let's say you're a quality-control inspector at an auto plant. A sense of possibility is nice. However, what you might need most is a sense of necessity. You need to know exactly what's needed, and you have to verify it's being done. Someone motivated by possibility would probably be bored stiff in a job like that, while someone motivated by necessity would feel perfectly attuned to it.

People who are motivated by necessity have other virtues as well. Some jobs place a particular virtue on permanence. When you fill them, you want someone who'll last for a long time. A person motivated by possibilities is always looking for new options, new enterprises, new challenges. If he finds another job that seems to offer more potential, there's a good chance he'll leave. Not so the somewhat plodding soul who is motivated by necessity. He takes a job when he needs one. He sticks with it because working is a necessity of life. There are many jobs that cry out for a dreamy-eyed, swashbuckling, risk-taking believer in possibility. If your company were diversifying into a whole new field, you'd want to hire someone who'll be attuned to all the possibilities. And there are other jobs that place a premium on solidity, consistency, and longevity. For those jobs you need someone who is motivated most by what he needs. It's equally important to know what your own personal metaprograms are so that if you're looking for a job, you can select one that will best support your needs.

The same principle works in motivating your children. Let's say you're trying to stress the virtues of education and going to a good college. If your child is motivated by necessity, you have to show her why she needs a good education. You can tell her about all the jobs that absolutely require a degree. You can explain why you need a foundation in math to be a good engineer or in language skills to be a good teacher. If your kid is motivated by possibility, you would take a different approach. She's bored by what she has to do, so you'd stress the infinite possibilities open to those with a good education. Show her how learning itself is the greatest avenue for possibility—fill her brain with images of new avenues to be explored, new dimensions to be opened, new things to be discovered. With each child the result will be the same, although the way you lead her there is very different.

Another metaprogram is a person's working style. Everyone has his own strategy for work. Some people are not happy unless they're *independent*. They have great difficulty working closely with other people and can't work well under a great deal of supervision. They have to run their own show. Others function best as part of a group. We call their strategy a *cooperative* one. They want to share responsibility for any task they take on. Still others have a *proximity* strategy, which is somewhere in between. They prefer to work with other people while maintaining sole responsibility for a task. They're in charge but not alone.

If you want to get the most out of your employees, or your children, or those you supervise, figure out their work strategies, the ways in which they're most effective. Sometimes you'll find an employee who is brilliant but a pain in the neck. He always has to do things his way. Now he just might not be cut out to be an employee. He may be the kind of person who has to run his own business, and sooner or later he probably will if you do not provide an avenue of expression. If you have a valuable employee like this, you should try to find a way to maximize his/her talents and give him/her as much autonomy as possible. If you make him a part of a team, he'll drive everyone crazy. But if you give him as much independence as possible, he can prove invaluable. That's what the new concepts of entrepreneurship are all about.

You've heard of the Peter Principle, the idea that all people are promoted to the level of their incompetence. One reason this happens is that employers are often insensitive to their employees' work strategies. There are people who work best in a cooperative setting. They thrive on a large amount of feedback and human interaction. Would you reward their good work by putting them in charge of some new autonomous venture? Not if you want to make use of their best talents. That doesn't mean you have to keep a person at the same level. But it does mean you should give promotions and new work experiences that utilize a person's best talents, not his worst ones.

Likewise, many people with proximity strategies want to be part of a team but need to do their own work alone. In any structure there are jobs that nurture all three strategies. The key is to have the acuity to know how people work best and then find a task they thrive in.

Here's an exercise to do today. After reading this chapter, practice eliciting people's metaprograms. Ask them: What do you want in a relationship (or house or car or career)? How do you know when you have been successful at something? What is the relationship between what you are doing this month and what you did last month? How often does someone have to demonstrate something to you before you are convinced it's true? Tell me about a favorite work experience and why it was important to you.

Does the person pay attention to you while you are asking these questions? Is he interested in your response, or is he occupied elsewhere? These are only a few of the questions you can ask to successfully elicit the metaprograms we've discussed. If you don't get the information you need, rephrase the question until you do.

Think of almost any communication problem you have, and you'll probably find that understanding the person's metaprograms will help you adjust communications so that the problem disappears. Think of a frustration in your life—someone you love who doesn't feel loved, someone you work for who manages to rub you the wrong way, or someone you've tried to help who hasn't responded. What you need to do is identify the operating metaprogram, identify what you are doing, and identify what the other person is doing. For example, suppose you need verification only once that you have a loving relationship, and your partner needs it consistently. Or you put together a proposal that shows how things are alike, and your supervisor only wants to hear about the ways they're different. Or you try to warn someone about something he needs to avoid, and he's only interested in hearing about something he wants to go after.

When you speak in the wrong key, the message that comes through is the wrong one. It's as much a problem for parents dealing with their children as it is for executives dealing with their employees. In the past, many of us have not developed the acuity to recognize and calibrate the basic strategies that others use. When you fail to get your message through to someone, you don't need to change the content. You do have to develop the flexibility to be able to alter its form to fit the metaprograms of the person with whom you're trying to communicate.

You can often communicate most effectively when you use several metaprograms together. My partners and I once had a business disagreement with a man who did some work for us. We got together, and I began the meeting by trying to set a positive frame, saying I wanted to create an outcome that would satisfy both of us. He immediately said, "I'm not interested in any of that. I have this money, and I'm going to hang on to it. I just don't want your attorney calling and bugging me anymore." So he began by moving away. I said, "We want to make this work because we're all committed to helping people and ourselves experience a better quality of life, and by working together we can do that." He said, "We're not all committed to helping other people. I don't give a damn about you. All I care about is that I leave here happy." As the meeting continued with very little progress, it became clear that he moved away from, that he sorted by self, that he mismatched, that he had an internal frame of reference, and he didn't believe things unless he saw them, heard them, and had them continually reinforced.

These metaprograms did not add up to a blueprint for perfect communication, especially since I'm the opposite of almost all these things. We talked for almost two hours with no progress, and I was almost ready to give up. And then a light bulb finally lit up in my head, and I changed gears. I said, "You know that idea you have in your mind, I have it right here." Then I made a fist. So I took his internal frame of reference, which I couldn't manipulate with words, and I externalized it, so I could control it. Then I said, "I have it right here and you've got sixty seconds. Make your decision or you're about to lose and lose big. I'm not going to lose, but you're going to lose personally." That gave him something new to move away from.

I went on from there. I said, "You're [self] going to lose [move away from] because you don't believe there's a solution that can be worked out." Well, he was a mismatcher, so he started to think the opposite, that there was a solution. Then I went on, "You better check inside yourself and see [internal frame of reference] if you're really willing to pay the price that you're going to have to pay, day after day, as a result of your decisions today. Because I'm going to continually tell people [his convincer strategy] about how you behaved here and what you did. You've got one minute to decide. You can decide now that you want to work this thing out or otherwise you're going to lose everything—you personally, forever. Check me out. See if I'm congruent."

It took him twenty seconds to jump up and say, "Look, guys, I always wanted to work with you. I know we can work things out." He didn't do it grudgingly. He got up enthusiastically, as though we were true pals. He said, "I just wanted to know we could talk." Why so positive after two hours? Because I'd used his metaprograms, not my model of the world, to motivate him.

What I'd said would have been an insult to me. I used to get frustrated with people when they behaved in ways that were the opposite of mine until I learned that different people have different metaprograms and patterns.

The metaprogram-sorting principles we've dealt with so far are important and powerful. However, the crucial thing to remember is that the number of metaprograms you're aware of is limited only by your sensitivity, awareness, and imagination. One of the keys to success in anything is the ability to make new distinctions. Metaprograms give you the tools to make crucial distinctions in deciding how to deal with people. You are not limited to the metaprograms discussed here. Become a student of possibility. Constantly gauge and calibrate the people

around you. Take note of specific patterns they have for per-
ceiving the world and begin to analyze if others have similar
patterns. Through this approach you can develop a whole set
of distinctions about people that can empower you in knowing
how to communicate effectively with all types of people.

For example, some people sort primarily by feelings and others sort by logical thoughts. Would you try to persuade them
in the same way? Of course not. Some people make decisions
based only on specific facts and figures. First they have to know
if the parts will work—they'll think about the broader picture
later. Others are convinced first by an overall concept or idea.
They react to global chunks. They want to see the big picture
first. If they like it, then they'll think about the details. Some
people are turned on by beginings. They're most excited when
they get a new idea off the ground, and then they soon tend to
lose interest in it and go on to something else. Others are fixated
on completion. Anything they do they have to see all the way
to the end, whether it's reading a book or doing a task at work.
Some people sort by food. That's right, by food. Almost anything they do or consider doing is evaluated in terms of food.
Ask them how to get someplace, and they'll say, "Go down the
road till you get to Burger King, make a left, and then continue
down until you get to McDonald's and make a right, and then
make a left at Kentucky Fried Chicken until you get down to
that chocolate-brown building." Ask about a movie they went
to, and they immediately begin telling you about how bad the
concession stand was. Ask about the wedding, and they'll tell
you about the cake. A person who sorts primarily by people
will talk mostly about the people at the wedding or the people
in the film. A person who sorts primarily by activities will talk
about what actually happened at the wedding, what happened
in the film, and so on.

The other thing an undertaking of metaprograms provides is
a model for balance. We all follow one strategy or another for
using metaprograms. For some metaprograms we may lean
slightly more to one side than to another. For others we may
swing wildly to one strategy instead of the other. But there's

nothing carved in stone about any of those strategies. Just as you can make the decision to put yourself in an empowering state, you can choose to adopt metaprograms that help rather than hinder you. What a metaprogram does is tell your brain what to delete. So if you're moving toward, for example, you're deleting the things to move away from. If you're moving away from, you're deleting the things you could be moving toward. To change your metaprograms, all you have to do is become aware of the things you normally delete. And begin to focus your attention on them.

Don't make the mistake of confusing yourself with your behaviors or doing the same thing with someone else. You say, "I know Joe. He does this and this and this." Well, you don't know Joe. You know him through his behaviors. But he isn't his behaviors any more than you are yours. If you're someone who tends to move away from everything, maybe that's your pattern of behavior. If you don't like it, you can change. In fact, there's no excuse for you not to change. You have the power now. The only question is whether you have enough reasons to make yourself use what you know.

There are two ways to change metaprograms. One is by Significant Emotional Events—"SEEs." If you saw your parents constantly moving away from things and not being able to achieve their full potential as a result, it might influence the way you move toward or away. If you only sorted by necessity and missed out on some great job opportunity because the company was looking to someone with a dynamic sense of possibility, you might be shocked into changing your approach. If you tend to move toward everything and get taken in by a flashy-looking investment scam, it would probably affect the way you looked at the next proposal that came your way.

The other way you can change is by consciously deciding to do so. Most of us never give a thought to which metaprograms we use. The first step toward change is recognition. The awareness of exactly what we are currently doing provides the opportunity for new choices and thus for change. Let's say you realize that you have a strong tendency to move away from things. How do you feel about it? Sure, there are things you want to move away from. If you put your hand on a hot iron, you would want to move it away as soon as you could. But aren't there things you really want to move toward? Isn't a part of being in control making a conscious effort to make a move toward something? Don't most great leaders and great successes move toward things rather than away? So you might want to begin to stretch a little. You can start thinking about things that appeal to you and actively move toward them.

You could also think of metaprograms on a higher level. Do nations have metaprograms? Well, they have behaviors, don't they? So they have metaprograms, too. Their collective behavior many times forms a pattern, based upon metaprograms of their leaders. The United States for the most part has a culture that seems to move toward. Does a country like Iran have an internal or external frame of reference? Think of the last election. What was Walter Mondale's basic metaprogram? Many people perceived him as moving away. He talked about doom and gloom and how Reagan wasn't telling the truth and would raise your taxes. He told us, "At least I'll tell you now we have to raise taxes or disaster is certain." I'm not saying he was right or wrong; just note the pattern. Ronald Reagan was sounding nothing but positive notes, while Mondale was perceived as invoking dark issues. Mondale might have made a lot of sense. There were some major issues the nation needed to confront. But on an emotional level—which is where much of politics is played out—Reagan's metaprogram seems to have more effectively matched that of the nation.

Like everything else in this book, metaprograms should be used on two levels. The first is as a tool to calibrate and guide our communication with others. Just as a person's physiology will tell you countless stories about him, his metaprograms will speak eloquently about what motivates him and frightens him off. The second is as a tool for personal change. Remember, you are not your behaviors. If you tend to run any kind of pattern that works against you, all you have to do is change it.

Metaprograms offer one of the most useful tools for personal calibration and change. And they provide keys to some of the most useful communication tools available.

In the next chapter, we'll look at other invaluable communication tools—tools that will show you . . .

CHAPTER XV

How to Handle
Resistance and
Solve Problems

"One can stand still in a flowing stream,

but not in the world of men."

—*Japanese Proverb*

Earlier, you learned how to model, to elicit decisive patterns of human actions that produce desirable results, to direct your own actions to take control of your life. The underlying idea was that you didn't need to choose your behavior by trial and error—you could become a sovereign by learning the most effective way to run your own brain.

When you deal with others, a certain amount of trial and error is inevitable. You can't direct the behavior of others with the speed, certainty, and effectiveness with which you control your own results. But a key to personal success is learning how to speed up that process. You can do it by developing rapport, by understanding metaprograms, by learning how to calibrate others so you can deal with them on their terms. This chapter is about taking the trial and error that's inherent in human in-

276

teraction and increasing the pace of discovery—by learning to handle resistance and solve problems.

If there was a key word in the first half of the book, it was "modeling." Modeling excellence is crucial to learning to rapidly create the results you desire. If there's a key word for the second half of this book, it's "flexibility"—the one thing effective communicators have in common. They learn how to calibrate someone and then keep changing their own behavior—verbal or nonverbal—until they create what they want. The only way to communicate well is to begin with a sense of humility and a willingness to change. You can't communicate by force of will; you can't bludgeon someone into understanding your point of view. You can only communicate by constant, resourceful, attentive flexibility.

Often, flexibility doesn't come naturally. Many of us follow the same patterns with numbing regularity. Some of us are so sure we're right about something, we assume mere forceful repetition will get us through. There's a combination of ego and inertia at work. Many times it's easiest to do exactly what we've done before. But the easiest is often the worst thing to do. In this chapter, we're going to look at ways to change directions, break patterns, redirect communication, and profit from confusion. The mystic poet William Blake once wrote, "The man who never alters his opinion is like standing water and breeds reptiles of the mind." The man who never alters his communication patterns finds himself in the same dangerous ooze.

We learned earlier that in any system, the machine with the greatest number of options, the most flexibility, will have the greatest effect. It's the same with people. The key to life is opening up as many avenues as possible, trying as many doors, using as many different approaches as it takes to solve a problem. If you run on one program, work from one strategy, you'll be about as effective as a car that runs in one gear.

I once watched a friend try to convince a desk clerk at a hotel to let her keep her room for several hours after checkout time. Her husband had been injured in a skiing accident, and she wanted him to be able to rest until transportation was arranged. The clerk politely and persistently kept giving her all the excellent reasons why it simply wasn't possible. My friend listened respectfully and then kept coming up with even more compelling counterreasons.

I watched her run the gamut from charm and feminine persuasion to reason and logic. Without ever being haughty or bringing outside pressure to bear, she simply hung in there, pursuing her desired outcome. Finally, the clerk gave her a rueful smile and said, "Madam, I think you're winning." How did she get what she wanted? Because she was flexible enough to keep producing new behavior and new maneuvers until the clerk was unwilling to oppose her any longer.

Most of us think of settling a dispute as something akin to verbal boxing. You pound through your arguments until you get what you want. Much more elegant and effective models are the Oriental martial arts, like aikido and t'ai chi. There, the goal is not to overcome force, but to redirect it—not to meet force with force, but to align yourself with the force directed at you and guide it in a new direction. That's precisely what my friend did, and it's what the best communicators do.

Remember that there is no such thing as resistance, there are only inflexible communicators who push at the wrong time and in the wrong direction. Like an aikido master, a good communicator, instead of opposing someone's views, is flexible and resourceful enough to sense the creation of resistance, find points of agreement, align himself with them, and then redirect communication in a way he wants to go.

> *"The best soldier does not attack. The superior fighter*
> *succeeds without violence. The greatest conqueror wins*
> *without a struggle. The most successful manager leads*
> *without dictating. This is called intelligent*
> *nonaggressiveness. This is called mastery of men."*
> —*Lao-Tsu, Tao Teh King*

It's important for us to remember that certain words and

phrases create resistance and problems. Great leaders and communicators realize this and pay close attention to the words they use and the effect they have. In his personal autobiography, Benjamin Franklin describes his strategy for communicating his opinions and yet maintaining rapport: "I develop the habit of expressing myself in terms of modest diffidence, never using, when I advanced anything that may possibly be disputed, the words certainly, undoubtedly, or any other that give the air of positiveness to an opinion, but rather say, I conceive or apprehend a thing to be so and so: It appears to me or I should not think it, so or so, for such and such reasons; or, I imagine it to be so; or it is so, if I am not mistaken. This habit I believe has been of great advantage to me when I have had oocasion to inculcate my opinion and persuade men into measures that I have been, time to time, engaged in promoting."

Old Ben Franklin knew how to persuade by being certain not to create any resistance to his proposals through the use of words that trigger negative responses. There are other words. Let me give you the example of one ever-present, three-letter word—"but." Used unconsciously and automatically, it can be one of the most destructive words in our language. If someone says, "That's true, but . . . " what is he saying? He's saying it's not true, or it's irrelevant. The word "but" has negated everything said before it. How do you feel if someone says to you that they agree with you, but . . . ? What if you simply substitute the word "and" instead? What if you say, "That's true, and here's something else that's also true"? Or, "That's an interesting idea, and here's another way to think about it." In both cases, you start with agreement. Instead of creating resistance, you've created an avenue of redirection.

Remember, there are no resistant people, only inflexible communicators. Just as there are phrases and words that automatically trigger feelings or states of resistance, there are also ways to communicate that keep people involved and open.

For example, what would happen if you had a communication tool you could use to communicate exactly how you felt about an issue, without compromising your integrity in any way, and

yet you never had to disagree with the person, either? Would
that be a fairly powerful tool? Well, here it is. It's called the
agreement frame. It consists of three phrases you can use in any
communication to respect the person you're communicating
with, maintain rapport with him, share with him what you feel
is true, and yet never resist his opinion in any way. Without
resistance there is no conflict.

Here are the three phrases:

"I appreciate and . . . "
"I respect and . . . "
"I agree and . . . "

In each case, you're doing three things. You're building rapport by entering the other person's world and acknowledging
his communication rather than ignoring or denigrating it with
words like "but" or "however." You're creating a frame of agreement that bonds you together. And you're opening the door to
redirecting something without creating resistance.

Let me give you an example. Someone says to you, "You're
absolutely wrong," about something. If you say, "No, I'm not
wrong," just as strongly, are you going to remain in rapport?
No. There will be a conflict, and there will be resistance. Instead, say to that person, "I respect the intensity of your feelings
about this, and I think if you were to hear my side of it you
might feel differently." Notice, you don't have to agree with the
content of the person's communication. You can always appreciate, respect, or agree with someone's feeling about something.
You can appreciate his feeling because if you were in the same
physiology, if you had the same perception, you would feel the
same way.

You can also appreciate someone else's intent. For example,
many times two people on opposite sides of an issue don't appreciate each other's points of view, so they don't even hear each
other. But if you use the agreement frame, you will find yourself
listening more intently to what the other person is saying—and
discovering new ways to appreciate people as a result. Let's

assume you're having a discussion with someone on the nuclear issue. He is for a buildup of nuclear arms, while you are for a nuclear freeze. The two of you might see yourselves as rivals, yet you may have the same intent—more security for your families and yourselves, and a world with peace. So if the other person says, "The only way to take care of this nuclear problem is to nuke the Russians," rather than arguing with him, you could enter his world and say, "I really appreciate your commitment and desire to create security for our children, and I think there may be a more effective way than nuking the Russians that will accomplish this. What about the possibility of . . . " When you communicate in this way, the other person feels respected. He feels heard, and he has no fight. There is no disagreement, yet new possibilities are also simultaneously introduced. This formula can be used with anyone—no matter what the other person says, you can find something to appreciate, respect, and agree with. You're impossible to fight, because you won't fight.

> *"One who is too insistent on his own views, finds few to agree with him."*
>
> —*Lao-Tsu, Tao Teh King*

In my seminars I do a simple little experiment that provides most people with memorable results. I have two people take different sides of a question and debate it without ever using the word "but" and without ever trying to denigrate the other's point of view. It's something akin to verbal aikido. People find this a liberating experience. They learn more because they're able to appreciate the other person's point of view rather than feeling they have to destroy it. They can argue without getting belligerent or upset. They can make new distinctions. And they can reach points of agreement.

Try the same thing with someone. Pick a topic you can take opposite sides on and argue it precisely the way I described above—as a game of finding commonality and then leading in the direction you want to go. I don't mean you should sell out your beliefs; I don't want you to be an intellectual jellyfish. But you'll find you can reach your outcome more effectively by gently aligning and then leading rather than by pushing violently. And you'll be able to develop a richer, more balanced point of view by being open to another perspective. Most of us look at discussion as a win-lose game. We're right, and the other guy's wrong. One side has a monopoly on truth, and the other resides in utter darkness. I've found time and again I learn more and get where I want to go much more quickly by finding an agreement frame. Another worthwhile exercise is to argue for something you don't believe. You'll surprise yourself by coming up with new perspectives.

The best salesmen, the best communicators, know it's very hard to persuade someone to do something he doesn't want to do. It's very easy to get him to do what he does want to do. By creating an agreement frame, by leading him naturally rather than through conflict, you do the latter, not the former. The key to effective communication is to frame things so that a person is doing what he wants to do, not what you want him to do. It's very hard to overcome resistance. It's much easier to avoid it by building on agreement and rapport. This is one way to turn resistance into assistance.

One way to solve problems is to redefine them—to find a way to agree rather than to disagree. Another way is to break their patterns. We've all found ourselves in stuck states, in which we recycle our own mental dirty dishwasher. It's like a record stuck in a scratched groove, playing the same tired refrain over and over again. The way to get the record unstuck is to give the needle a nudge or pick it up and put it somewhere else. The way to change a stuck state is the same: you need to interrupt the pattern—the tired old refrain—and start anew.

I'm always amused at what happens when I conduct a therapy session at my home in California. It's on a beautiful piece of property overlooking the ocean, and when people arrive, the surroundings tend to put them in a positive state. I like to watch them from the turret above the house. I can see them drive up to the house, get out of the car, look around in obvious excitement, and proceed to the front door. It's apparent that everything they see is putting them in an alive, positive state.

So what happens? They come upstairs, and we talk a little—it's all very pleasant and positive—and then I'll ask, "Well, okay, what brings you here?" Immediately, I can see their shoulders slump, their facial muscles droop, their breathing become more shallow, their voice take on a tone of self-pity as they begin their tale of woe and decide to enter their "troubled" state.

The best way to deal with that pattern is to show how easy it is to break. What I usually do is say very forcefully, almost in an angry or upset manner, "Excuse me. We haven't started yet!" What happens? Immediately they say, "Oh, I'm sorry," sit straight up, resume normal breathing, posture, and facial expressions, and go back to feeling fine. The message comes through loud and clear. They already know how to be in a good state. They also know how to choose to be in a bad one. They have all the tools for changing their physiology, changing their internal representations, and changing their state in order to change behavior right on the spot. How fast can they do it? In an instant.

I've found that confusion is one of the greatest ways to interrupt patterns. People fall into patterns because they don't know how to do anything else. They might mope around and become depressed because they think they'll evoke sensitive, caring questions about what's troubling them. It's their way of getting attention and using their resources in the best way they know how to change their state.

If you knew someone like that, how would you react? Well, you could do the expected. You could sit down and begin a long, sensitive, anguished discussion. That might make the person feel a little better, but it also reinforces the pattern. It tells the person that if he mopes around, he'll get all the attention he wants. What if you did something else? What if you began tickling him, or ignoring him, or barking like a dog in his face? You'll find that this person won't know how to respond to you, and out of his confusion or laughter will emerge a new pattern of how to perceive his experience.

Now clearly there are times when we all need someone to talk to, when we need a friend. There are real instances of grief and pain that require a caring, sensitive ear. But I'm talking about patterns and stuck states, repeated behavioral sequences that are self-perpetuating and destructive. The more you reinforce them, the more harm you do. The real aim is to show people they can change these patterns, that they can change behaviors. If you believe that you're the ball on the tether, waiting for someone to hit it, that's how you'll behave. If you believe that you're in control, that you can change your patterns, you'll be able to.

The trouble is that many times our culture tells us otherwise. It says we don't control our behaviors, we don't control our states, we don't control our emotions. Most of us have adopted a therapeutic model that says we're at the mercy of everything from childhood traumas to raging hormones. So the lesson to learn is that patterns can be interrupted and changed—in an instant.

When Richard Bandler and John Grinder were doing private therapies, they were known as masters of the pattern interrupt. Bandler tells one story about visiting a mental institution and dealing with a man who insisted he was Jesus Christ—not metaphorically, not in spirit, but in the flesh. One day Bandler walked in to meet this man. "Are you Jesus?" he said. "Yes, my son," the man replied. Bandler said, "I'll be back in a minute." This left the man a little bit confused. Within three or four minutes, Bandler came back, holding a measuring tape. Asking the man to hold out his arms, Bandler measured the length of his arms and his height from head to toe. After that, Bandler left. The man claiming to be Christ became a little concerned. A little while later, Bandler came back with a hammer, some large spiked nails, and a long set of boards. He began to pound them into the form of a cross. The man asked, "What are you doing?" As Richard put the last nails in the cross, he asked, "Are you Jesus?" Again the man said, "Yes my son." Bandler said,

"Then you know why I'm here." Somehow, the man suddenly recalled who he really was. His old pattern didn't seem like such a good idea. "I'm not Jesus. I'm not Jesus!" the man started yelling. Case closed.

A more positive pattern interrupt is an antismoking campaign that began a few years ago. It suggested that anytime someone you love reaches for a cigarette, give him/her a kiss instead. In the first place, it interrupts the automatic pattern of reaching for a cigarette. At the same time, it produces a new experience that can cast doubts on the wisdom of the old one.

Pattern interrupts are also valuable in business. One executive used them to get his factory workers to change the way they looked at their work. When he first took over, he went to the plant where they were building his personal model of the company's product. But when it came off the line, instead of taking it, he chose another model that was made for the general public. It wouldn't even start. He flew into a range and made it clear he wanted every one of the plant's products built as if it were for his personal use. He said he might show up at any time to check out the quality of any product. This news spread like wildfire, and the experience interrupted the pattern of poor workmanship and caused many people to reexamine what they were doing. A master of rapport, the executive was able to pull this off without causing the workers to resent him because he appealed to their pride.

Pattern interrupts can be particularly useful in politics. There was a good example recently in Louisiana. Kevin Reilly, a state legislator there, lobbied throughout the legislative session for more money for the state's colleges and universities. All his efforts turned out to be in vain: no more money was appropriated. As he stomped out of the state Capitol, a reporter asked him his thoughts. He launched into a tirade, declaring Louisiana was nothing but a "banana republic." He said, "What we ought to do is declare bankruptcy, secede from the union, and file for foreign aid. . . . We lead in all the good stuff—illiteracy, unwed mothers—and we're last in education."

At first his remarks set off a storm of criticism, because they went so far beyond the usual circumspect level of political discourse. But soon he became something of a hero. He probably did more to change the state's thinking about funding education by that one tirade than through all his ardent politicking.

You can use pattern interrupts in daily life. We've all been in arguments that take on a life of their own. The original reason behind the dispute may have long since been forgotten, but we rage on, getting madder and madder, more and more intent on "winning"—on proving our point. Arguments like this can be the most destructive thing a relationship can face. When they're over, you may think, How in the world did that get so far out of hand? But while the argument is still going on, you have no perspective whatsoever. Think of situations you have been in lately where you or others were stuck. What pattern interrupts could you have used? Take a moment now to create five pattern interrupts you could use in the future and think of situations where they would be useful.

> *"Respond intelligently even to unintelligent treatment."*
> —Lao-Tsu, *Tao Teh King*

What if you had a pattern interrupt set up in advance, like an early-warning alarm, to short-circuit an argument before it got out of hand? I've found humor is one of the best pattern interrupts. It's hard to be angry when you're laughing. My wife, Becky, and I have one in place that we use all the time. Have you ever seen the *Saturday Night Live* skit based on the phrase "I hate it when that happens"? It's pretty hilarious. The actors tell each other about awful things they do to themselves, like rubbing sandpaper across their lips and then pouring rubbing alcohol on them or grinding a carrot scraper up their nose and then sticking a menthol cough drop there, and then they say, "Yeah, I know what you mean, I hate it when that happens."

So Becky and I have an agreement that when one of us feels an argument is becoming destructive, that partner can say, "I hate it when that happens," and the other has to let go. It forces us to break the negative state we're in by thinking of something that makes us laugh. And it also reminds us that we do hate it when we do that. It's about as smart to get in a vicious argument with a person you love as it is to rub sandpaper across your lips and then pour alcohol on them.

> *"Everything that enlarges the sphere of human powers, that shows man he can do what he thought he could not do, is valuable."*
>
> —*Ben Jonson*

There are two main ideas in this chapter, and they both go against the grain of what many of us have been taught. The first is that you can persuade better through agreement than through conquest. We live in a society that revels in competition, that likes to make clear distinctions between winners and losers, as if every interaction must have both. Remember the cigarette ads from a few years back that carried the message, "I'd rather fight than switch"? They featured a person proudly sporting a black eye as proof that he stuck to his guns, no matter what.

But everything I know about communication tells me the competition model is very limited. I've already talked about the magic of rapport and how essential it is to personal power. If you see someone as a competitor, someone to be vanquished, you're starting out with the exact opposite framework. Everything I know about communication tells me to build from agreement, not from conflict; to learn to align and lead rather than to try and overcome resistance. This is easier said that done. However, through conscious and consistent awareness, we can change our patterns of communication.

The second idea is that our behavior patterns aren't indelibly carved into our brain. If we repeatedly do something that limits us, we're not suffering from some abstruse mental ailment. We're just running a terrible pattern over and over again. It may be a way we relate to others or a way we think. The solution is simply to interrupt the pattern, stop what you're doing, and try something new. We're not robots wired into barely remembered personal traumas. If we do something we don't like, all we have to do is recognize it and change it. What does the Bible say? "We shall all be changed in an instant. In the twinkling of an eye." We will be if we want to be.

In both cases, the common ground is the idea of flexibility. If you have trouble putting together a puzzle, you won't get anywhere by trying the same solution time and time again. You'll solve it by being flexible enough to change, to adapt, to experiment, to try something new. The more flexible you are, the more options you create, the more doors you can open, and the more successful you will be.

In the next chapter, we'll look at another crucial tool to personal flexibility. It's called . . .

CHAPTER XVI

Reframing: The Power of Perspective

"Life is not a static thing. The only people who do not
change their minds are incompetents in asylums
who can't and those in cemeteries."

—*Everett Dirksen*

Consider the sound of a footstep. If I asked you, "What does a footstep mean?" you would probably answer, "It doesn't mean anything to me." Well, let's think about that. If you're walking along a busy street, there are so many footsteps you don't even hear them. In that situation, they don't have any effective meaning. But what if you're sitting home alone late at night, and you hear footsteps downstairs? A moment later, you hear the steps moving toward you. Do the footsteps have meaning then? They sure do. That same signal (the sound of footsteps) will have many different meanings depending upon what it has meant to you in similar situations in the past. Your past experience may provide you with a context for that signal and thus determine whether it relaxes or frightens you. For example, you may classify the sound as that of your spouse coming home early. People who have experienced a burglary may think it means an intruder. Thus the meaning of any experience in life depends upon the frame we put around it. If you change the frame, the context, the meaning changes instantly. One of the most effective tools for personal change is learning how to put the best frames on any experience. This process is called reframing.

On a piece of paper, describe the figure below. What do you see?

There are many things you could see. You might see what you consider to be a hat on its side, a monster, an arrow pointing down, and so on. Describe to yourself what you see right now. Do you also see the word "fly"? You may have seen it right away because this example has been used for bumper stickers and other promotional items. So your previous frame of reference helped you to see it as fly immediately. If you didn't see it, why didn't you? Do you even see it now? If you didn't see the word, it's probably because your habitual perceptual frame leads you to expect words on white paper to be written in black ink. So as long as you use this frame to interpret this situation, you will not see the word "fly." In this case, fly is written in white. You must be able to reframe your perception in order to see it. The same is true in life. Many times there are opportunities all around for us to make our lives exactly as we wish them to be. There are ways to see our biggest problems as our greatest opportunities—if only we can step out of our trained patterns of perception.

Again, as we've discussed over and over in this book, nothing in the world has any inherent meaning. How we feel about something and what we do in the world are dependent upon

Figure A

Figure B

our perception of it. A signal has meaning only in the frame or context in which we perceive it. Misfortune is a point of view. Your headache may feel good to an aspirin salesman. Human beings tend to attach specific meanings to experiences. We say this happened, so "this" means "that," when in actuality there may be an infinite number of ways to interpret any experience. We tend to frame things based upon how we have perceived them in the past. Many times, by changing these habitual perception patterns, we can create greater choices for our lives. It's important to remember that perceptions are creative. That is, if we perceive something as a liability, that's the message we deliver to our brain. Then the brain produces states that make it the reality. If we change our frame of reference by looking at the same situation from a different point of view, we can change the way we respond in life. We can change our representation or perception about anything and in a moment change our states and behaviors. This is what reframing is all about.

Remember, we do not see the world as it is because how things are can be interpreted from many points of view. How we are, our frames of reference, our "maps" define the territory.

For example, take a look at figure A. What do you see? Of course you see an old, ugly woman. Take a look at figure B. As you can see, this is a drawing of a similar ugly old woman, with her chin buried in her fur coat. Look at it carefully and try to figure out what kind of old woman she is. Is she happy or sad? What do you think she's thinking about? Yet there's something interesting about this old woman. The artist who drew it claims it's a drawing of her pretty young daughter. If you change your frame of reference, you should be able to see this beautiful young woman. Here's some help. The old woman's nose becomes the chin and jawline of the younger woman's face. The older woman's left eye becomes the younger woman's left ear. The older woman's mouth becomes a necklace around the younger woman's neck. If you still have difficulty, I'll provide you with a drawing that will help you pull it out. Take a look at figure C.

The obvious question is, Why did you see the ugly old woman in figure B, instead of the beautiful young girl? The answer? You were conditioned in advance to see the old woman. Many times in my seminars I will show half the group figure A and half the group figure C. Then I will show them the composite drawing of figure B. When the two groups begin to interact with each other, arguments will often break out over who is right. Those who saw A first have difficulty seeing the young woman, and vice versa for those who saw C first.

It is important to note that our past experiences regularly filter our ability to see what is really happening in the world. But there are multiple ways to see or experience any situation. The enterpreneur who buys advance tickets to a concert and then sells them at a higher price at the gate can be seen as a despicable person who takes advantage of others—or he can be seen as adding value to those who could not get tickets or did not want to wait in line. The key to success in life is to consistently represent your experience in ways that support you in producing even greater results for yourself and others.

> *"If you see what is small as it sees itself, and accept what is weak for what strength it has, and use what is dim for the light it gives then all will go well? This is called Acting Naturally."*
>
> —*Lao-Tsu, Tao Teh King*

Figure C

Reframing in its simplest form is changing a negative statement into a positive one by changing the frame of reference used to perceive the experience. There are two major types of reframes, or ways to alter our perception about something: context reframing and content reframing. Both alter your internal representations by resolving internal pain or conflict, therefore putting you in a more resourceful state.

Context reframing involves taking an experience that seems to be bad, upsetting, or undesirable and showing how the same behavior or experience is actually a great advantage in another context. Children's literature is filled with examples of context reframing. Rudolph's nose, which made people make fun of him, was actually an advantage and made him a hero in the context of a dark and snowy night. The ugly duckling suffered great pain because he was so different, but his difference was his beauty as a full-grown swan. Context reframing is invaluable in business. Our mismatching partner was a liability until we realized after the brainstorming process that he could be a great asset as a backup, as the one to note in advance any potential problems.

Great innovations are made by those who know how to reframe activities and problems into potential resources in other contexts. For example, oil was once considered something that destroyed the value of land for crop usage. Yet look at its value today. Several years ago, lumber yards had difficulty disposing of large amounts of waste sawdust from their mills. One guy took that waste and decided to put it to use in another context. He pressed it together with glue and lighter fluid and created something called Presto Logs! After contracting to take away all the "worthless" sawdust from these mills, in two years he developed a multimillion-dollar business, with his major resource costing him nothing! But that's all an entrepreneur is: someone who endows resources with new wealth-producing capacity. In other words, someone who is an expert reframer.

Content reframing involves taking the exact same situation and changing what it means. For example, you might say your son never stops talking. He never shuts up! After content reframe, you might say that he certainly must be a very intelligent young man to have so much to say. There's the story of a famous army general who was known to have reframed his troops during a heavy enemy attack by saying, "We're not retreating, we're just advancing in another direction." When a person close to us dies, most people in our culture are sad. Why? Many reasons—feelings of loss, for instance. Yet some people are joyous. Why? They reframe death to mean that the deceased is always with them, that nothing in the universe is ever destroyed, that things just change form. Some consider death as graduation to a higher level of existence, so they are joyous.

Another kind of content reframe is to actually change the way you see, hear, or represent a situation. If you're upset about what someone said to you, you may envision yourself smiling as he says the same negative words expressed in the tonality of your favorite singer. Or you may see the same experience in your brain, only this time with the speaker surrounded by your favorite color. Or you may even change what he says to you in the first place. As you reexperience it in your mind, you may hear him apologize to you. Or you could see him speaking to you from a perspective that puts you very high above him. Reframing the same stimulus changes the meaning sent to the brain and thus the states and behaviors associated with it. This book is full of reframes. "The Seven Lies of Success" is a whole chapter of reframes.

"Ten salads."

There was a touching and powerful article in the *Baltimore Sun* not long ago. Republished by *Reader's Digest*, it was entitled, "A Boy of Unusual Vision." It was about a young boy named Calvin Stanley. It seems Calvin rides a bike, plays baseball, goes to school, and does just about everything else that eleven-year-olds do—except see.

How could this little boy do all these things, while many people in the same situation just give up on life or live in sorrow? As I read the article, it became clear that Calvin's mother is a master reframer. She has turned every experience Calvin has—experiences that others would have classified as "limitations"—into advantages in Calvin's mind. Since that's what he represents to himself, that's what Calvin experiences. Here are some examples of her communication to him:

Calvin's mother remembers the day her son asked why he was blind. "I explained he was born that way and it was nobody's fault. He asked. 'Why me?' I said, 'I don't know why, Calvin. Maybe there's a special plan for you.'" Then she sat her son down and told him, "You're seeing, Calvin. You're just using your hands instead of your eyes. And remember, there's nothing you can't do."

One day Calvin was very sad because he realized he'd never see his mother's face. "But Mrs. Stanley knew what to tell her ony child," the article continued. "'I said, Calvin you can see my face. You can see it with your hands and by listening to my voice, and you can tell more about me that way than somebody who can use his eyes.'" The article went on to say that Calvin moves in the sighted world with trust and faith and the unshakable confidence of a child whose mother has always been there for him. Calvin wants to become a computer programmer and someday design programs for the blind.

The world is full of Calvins. We need more people who use reframing as effectively as Mrs. Stanley did. I had the good fortune of recently meeting another master reframer. His name is Commander Jerry Coffey. He is an incredible man who used reframing to keep his sanity while he spent seven years in solitary confinement in a POW camp in Vietnam. Our first reaction to hearing this is probably to wince a bit. However, nothing is good or bad in the world except in the way we represent it to ourselves. Jerry decided to represent it to himself as a great opportunity, a challenge to stay strong, an opportunity to learn more about himself than ever before. A chance to become closer to God. Something that someday would make him proud of the way he handled himself. With that frame, he saw everything that happened as part of a personal development experience, and he came out totally and positively transformed by the experience. He wouldn't give up the experience for a million dollars, he says.

Think of a major mistake you've made in the last year. You

might feel an instant rush of gloom. But chances are the mistake was part of an experience with more successes than failures. And, as you consider it, you'll begin to realize you probably learned more from that mistake than from anything else you did that month.

So you can zero in on what you did wrong, or you can reframe the experience in a way that focuses beyond it to what you have learned. There are multiple meanings to any experience. The meaning is whatever you choose to emphasize, just as its content is what you choose to focus on. One of the keys to success is finding the most useful frame for any experience so you can turn it into something that works for you rather than against you.

Is there any experience you can't change? Is there any behavior that's an immutable part of your being? Are you your behaviors, or are you in charge of them? The one thing I've stressed in every part of this book is that you're in control. You run your brain. You produce the results of your life. Reframing is one of the most powerful ways you can change the way you think about an experience. You already put frames on experiences. Sometimes you change that frame as events change.

Take a moment and reframe these situations:

1. My boss yells at me all the time.
2. I had to pay $4,000 more in income tax this year than last year.
3. We have little or no extra money to buy Christmas presents this year.
4. Every time I begin to succeed in a big way, I sabotage my success.

Here are some possible reframes:

1a. It's great that he cares enough to tell you how he really feels. He could have just fired you.
2a. That's great. You must have made a lot more money this year than last year.
3a. Great! Then you can become much more ingenious and

make something people will never forget instead of buying run-of-the-mill gifts. Your gifts will be personal.

4a. It's great that you're so aware of what your pattern has been in the past. Now you can figure out what triggered it and change it forever!

Reframing is crucial to learning how to communicate with ourselves and with others. On the personal level, it's how we choose to put meaning on events. On a broader level, it's one of the most effective communication tools available. Think of selling. Think of any form of persuasion. The person who sets the frame, the person who defines the turf, is the one with the most influence. Most of the major successes you can think of, in fields ranging from advertising to politics, are the result of artful reframes—changing people's perceptions so that their new representations about something put them in a state that makes them feel or act differently. A friend of mine sold his health-restaurant chain to General Mills for 167 times his earnings. That's almost unheard of in the industry. How did he do it? He got General Mills to decide the value of his company based upon what it would be worth if they did not buy it within five years and it continued to expand. He could easily wait to sell it to them. But they needed it now to achieve their corporate goals, so they agreed to his frame. All persuasion is an altering of perception.

Most reframing is done for us, not by us. Someone else changes the frame for us and we react to it. What is advertising, after all, but a huge industry with the sole purpose of framing and reframing mass perceptions? Do you really think there's anything particularly macho about a specific brand of beer or particularly sexy about a particular cigarette? If you give an aborigine a Virginia Slims cigarette, he wouldn't say, "Hey, this is kinda sexy." But the pitchmen put on the frame, and we respond. If they don't think we're responding well enough, they put on a new frame and see if it works.

One of the greatest advertising reframes ever was done by Pepsi-Cola. For as long as anyone could remember, Coca-Cola was the preeminent cola drink. Its history and tradition and standing in the market were unchallenged. There was nothing Pepsi could do to beat Coke on its own turf. If you're up against a classic, you can't say, "We're more of a classic than they are." People just won't believe it.

Instead, Pepsi turned the game upside down; it reframed the perceptions people already had. When it started talking about the Pepsi Generation and issued its "Pepsi Challenge," it turned its weakness into strength. Pepsi said, "Sure the other guys have been king, but let's look at today. Do you want yesterday's product, or do you want today's?" The ads reframed Coke's traditional dominance into a weakness, as indication that it was the product of the past, not the future. And they reframed Pepsi's traditional second-fiddle status to the company's advantage.

What happened? Coke finally decided it had to play on Pepsi's turf. It came up with its oxymoronic "New" Coke, and the rest is marketing history. Now, we'll have to wait and see whether Coke's reframe of giving people both its old "Classic" Coke and its new "Pepsi" Coke will work. But the process was a classic example of reframing because the whole battle was over nothing but image. It was simply a question of whose frame would stick in people's brains. There's no inherent social content in a carbonated sugar beverage that rots your teeth. There is nothing inherently more contemporary about the taste of Pepsi versus the taste of Coke. But by changing the frame and defining the terms, Pepsi pulled off one of the great marketing coups in recent history.

Reframing was a major factor in the conclusion of General William C. Westmoreland's 120-million-dollar libel suit against CBS. Going into court, Westmoreland seemed to have considerable popular support for his point of view in the suit. A *TV Guide* cover story had labeled the conflict "Anatomy of a Smear." CBS began to realize its difficulty and finally hired a PR man, John Scanlon. His job was to reverse the tide of popular support for Westmoreland's point of view and get people to stop focusing on the tactics of the *60 Minutes* process and start paying attention to the charges against Westmoreland, charges that CBS was hoping to prove true. At last, Westmoreland dropped his suit in return for a simple apology, leaving CBS eternally grateful for Scanlon's reframing skills.

Think of politics. As marketing men and consultants have become more and more a part of the process, the battle to set the frame has become the dominant part of American politics. At times, it seems like the only part. After the Reagan-Mondale debates, reporters were besieged by operatives from both camps trying to put the best spin, the best frame, on every word that was said. The reason? It wasn't the content as much as the frame that mattered.

Reagan was responsible for one of the world's more artful reframes in the second presidential debate. In the first debate, his age became an issue for the first time in the campaign. Of course, that was a reframe, too. People already knew how old he was, didn't they? But his stumbling performance and the press coverage of it reframed his age from a simple fact to a potential liability. In the second debate, Mondale made comments that again implied Reagan's age was a liability. People waited for Reagan's rebuttal. In his best aw-shucks tone, he said, No, he didn't think age should be an issue in the campaign. He said he had no intention of making an issue of his opponent's youth and inexperience. In one sentence he completely reframed the question in a way that guaranteed it would no longer be a major factor in the race.

Many of us find it easier to reframe when communicating with others than when communicating with ourselves. If we're trying to sell someone our old car, we know we have to frame our presentation in a way that highlights what's good about the car and downplays what's bad. If your potential buyer has a different frame, your job is to change his perception. But few of us spend much time thinking about how to frame our communications with ourselves. Something happens to us. We form an internal representation of the experience. And we figure that's what we have to live with. Think how crazy that is. It's like turning on the ignition, starting up your car, and then seeing where it decides to go.

Instead, you need to learn to communicate with yourself with as much purpose and direction and persuasiveness as you would in a business presentation. You need to start framing and reframing experiences in a way that makes them work for you. One way is simply on the level of careful, conscious thought.

We all know people who've become gun shy after an unsuccessful romance. They get jilted or hurt, and they decide to back off from subsequent relationships. The fact is that the relationship brought them more joy than pain. That's why it was so difficult to give up. But blotting out the good memories and concentrating on the bad puts the worst-possible frame on an experience. The idea is to change the frame, see the joy, see the gain, see the growth. Then it's possible to move on from a positive rather than a negative frame and be empowered to create an even greater relationship in the future.

Take a minute and think of three situations in your life that are challenging you. How many different ways can you see each of the situations? How many frames can you put around them? What do you learn by seeing them differently? How does this free you to act differently?

I can already hear some of you saying, "That's not so easy to do. Sometimes I'm too depressed to do it." The heck you are. What's depression? It's a state. Remember earlier in the book when we discussed association/disassociation? A prerequisite to being able to reframe yourself is the ability to disassociate from the depressing experience and see it from a new perspective. Then you can change your internal representation and physiology. If you were in an unresourceful state, now you know how to change it. If you're putting something in a frame that doesn't do you any good, change the frame.

One way to reframe is by changing the meaning of an experience or behavior. Imagine a situation in which someone does something you don't like, and you think his behavior has a particular meaning. Let's consider a couple in which the husband expecially enjoys cooking, and it's important to him that his cooking is appreciated. His wife behaves quietly during the mean. The husband finds this very upsetting. If she's enjoying his meal, she should talk about it. If she's not talking, she must not be satisfied. What could you do to reframe his perception of his wife's behavior?

Remember, what was important to him was appreciation. A meaning reframe involves changing a perception to one that supports what's important to a person and does it in a way he had never considered before. We could suggest to the cook that perhaps his mate was enjoying the food so much that she didn't want to waste time talking when she could be eating. Action speaks louder than words, right?

Another possibility would be to get him to reframe the meaning of the behavior himself. We could ask, "Has there ever been a time you personally were quiet during a meal you were enjoying very much? What was going on for you?" His wife's behavior was only bothersome within the frame he put on it. In cases like this, it just takes a little flexibility to change the frame.

A second kind of reframe involves working with a behavior you don't like about yourself. Usually, you don't like it because you don't like what it says about you as a person or you don't like what it gets for you. The way to reframe it is to imagine another situation or context in which that behavior would be useful in getting you something you do want.

Suppose you are a salesman. You take great pains to know your product in every detail. But on the sales floor you tend to inundate your customers with so much information that they become overwhelmed, sometimes delaying their decision to buy. The question is, Where else would that behavior actually be quite effective? What about writing ad copy? Or technical writing on the product itself? Knowing a lot of information and being able to have ready access to it could even be useful in studying for a test or helping your kids with their homework. So, you see, it's not the behavior itself that's the problem, but where it's being employed. Can you think of examples in your own life? All human behaviors are useful in some context. Procrastination may seem useless, yet wouldn't it be nice to put off being angry or sad to another day—and then never get to it?

You can learn to do reframing exercises for images and experiences that bother you. For example, think of a person or experience that's preying on your mind. You come home after a lousy day at work, and all you can think of is the ridiculous project your supervisor gave you at the last minute. Instead of getting away from it, you take the frustration home with you. You're watching television with your kids, and all you're thinking about in this angry state is your "dumb" supervisor and his idiotic project.

Instead of letting your brain make you miserable for the weekend, you can learn to reframe the experience in a way that makes you feel better. Start by disassociating yourself from it. Take the image of your supervisor and put it in your hand. Put a pair of funny glasses with a big nose and mustache on him. Hear him talking in a funny, screechy cartoon voice. Feel him as being warm and cuddly, and hear him saying he needs your help on this project, could you please help? After you've concocted this, maybe you can appreciate that he's under stress, and maybe he forgot to tell you what he needed until the last minute. Maybe you can remember a time when you did the same thing with someone else. Ask yourself if this situation is such a big deal that you should allow it to ruin your weekend, if there's any reason to let it bother you when you're at home.

I'm not saying the problem isn't real. Maybe you need a new job, or maybe you need to communicate better in the job you're in. But if that's the case, you need to deal with the problem instead of being haunted by some lingering, negative specter in your mind that keeps you reacting and causes you to treat those closest to you in an unattractive way. Do this effectively a few times, and the next time you see your supervisor you may see him with glasses and a big nose and feel differently as he talks to you—thus creating new feedback to him and a new way for the two of you to interact, outside of the past stimulus/response dynamic you had set up with each other.

I've used these reframes in small ways for what some people consider to be major problems. Often, in complex situations, you may have to do a series of smaller reframes to gradually but thoroughly achieve the desired state.

In its broadest sense, reframing can be used to eliminate negative feelings about nearly anything. One of the most effective techniques is to picture yourself in a theater. See an experience that's troubling you as a movie up on the screen. First you might want to play it in fast forward, like a cartoon. You might want to put circus music on it, the sound of a calliope. Then you might want to play it backward, watching the image become more and more absurd. Try this technique with something that's bothering you. You'll find it soon loses its negative power.

The same technique can work with phobias, but you need to turn up the juice. Here's how. A phobia is often rooted at a deep kinesthetic level, so you need to provide more distance from it in order to do an effective reframe. Phobic reactions are so strong that people can react to the mere thought of something. The way to deal with such people is to disassociate them from their representations several times. We call this double disassociation. For example, if you have a phobia about something, try this exercise. Go back to a time when you felt totally empowered and alive. Go back to that state, and feel those strong, confident feelings. Now see yourself as protected by a radiant, protective bubble. Once you have that protection, go to your favorite mental movie theater. Sit down in a comfortable seat with a good view of the screen. Next, feel yourself float out of your body, up into the projection booth, all the time feeling your protective bubble around you. Look down and see yourself sitting in the audience looking up at the empty screen.

After you've done that, look up at the screen and see a still frame, black-and-white image of the phobia or some terrible experience that really used to bother you. You're looking down on yourself in the audience and watching yourself observe what's happening on the screen—you're doubly dissaociated from it. In that state, run the black-and-white image backward at an extremely fast pace so you see the thing that's been haunting you appear like a cheap home movie or an old slapstick comedy.

Notice your funny reactions to it as you watch yourself in the audience watching this movie on the screen.

Let's take it a step further. I want the part of you that's really resourceful, the part that's up in the booth, to float back down into where your body has been sitting, and then get up and walk to the front of the screen. You should be able to do that in a very strong, confident state. Then tell your earlier self that you've been watching over him or her and have come up with two or three ways that can help change that experience, two or three reframes of the meaning or the content that will help him or her to handle it differently, now and in the future—ways that the younger you could handle with your present-day, more mature perceptions. You don't need to have all that pain and fear. You're more resourceful now than when you were younger, and that old experience is just history, nothing more.

Help your younger self cope with something he or she couldn't handle earlier, then stride back to the seat and watch the movie change. Play the same scene in your head, but this time watch as your younger self handles the same situation with utter confidence. When you've done that, you should walk back to the screen and congratulate your younger self, give him or her a hug for breaking free of the phobia or trauma or fear. Then pull that younger you back inside of you, knowing he or she is more resourceful than ever before and an important part of your life. Do this with several other phobias you have. Then do the same thing for someone else.

This can be an incredibly powerful experience. I've been able to take people with terrible lifelong phobias and free them of their fears, many times in a matter of minutes. Why does this work? Because to go into a phobic state requires specific internal representations. If you change those representations, you will change the state that person creates when he thinks of that experience.

For some people, a number of these exercises involve a level of mental discipline and imaginative power they may not previously have accessed. As a result, several of the mental strategies I'm giving you may feel awkward at first. However, your brain can operate in these ways, and if you work carefully on these strategies, you'll feel more adept all the time.

One important thing to remember about reframing is that all human behaviors have a purpose in some context. If you smoke, you don't do it because you like to put carcinogens into your lungs. You do it because smoking makes you feel relaxed or more comfortable in certain social situations. You adopted this behavior to create some gain for yourself. So in some cases you may find it impossible to reframe the behavior without confronting the underlying need that the behavior fulfills. This is a problem that sometimes comes up when people try electroshock therapy to cure their smoking. Perhaps they might be shocked into something just as bad, like feeling anxious all the time or overeating. I'm not saying this approach is bad. I'm simply saying it's useful for us to discover the unconscious intent so that we can fill that need more elegantly.

All human behavior is adaptive in one way or another; it's designed to fill a need. It's no problem to make people hate smoking. But I also want to make sure that I create for them new behavioral choices that will fill their needs without negative side effects, such as those created by smoking. If smoking made them feel relaxed, confident, or centered, they need to come up with a more elegant behavior that will fulfill the same need.

Richard Bandler and John Grinder designed a six-step reframing process for changing any undesirable behavior you may have into desirable behavior, while maintaining the important benefits that the old behavior used to provide:

1. *Identify the pattern or behavior you wish to change.*
2. *Establish communication with the part of your unconscious mind that generates the behavior.* Go inside and ask the following question of yourself, remaining alertly passive to detect and report any changes in body sensations, visual images, or sounds that occur as a response to your questions. The question is, "Will the part of me that generates behavior X be willing to communicate with me in consciousness?"

Now ask that part, we'll call it part X, to intensify that signal when it wants to communicate yes, and to diminish it when it wants to communicate no. Now test the response by asking the part to communicate yes . . . and then no . . . so that you can distinguish between the two responses.

3. *Separate intention from behavior.* Thank the part for its willingness to cooperate with you. Now ask it if it would be willing to let you know what it's been trying to do for you by generating behavior X. As you ask that question, once again be alert to detect a yes or no response. Take note of what benefits this behavior has provided for you in the past and then thank that part of you for maintaining these important benefits for you.

4. *Creating alternative behaviors to satisfy intention.* Now go inside and contact the most creative part of you and ask it to generate three alternative behaviors that are just as good as or better than behavior X for satisfying the intention of the part we've been communicating with. Have your creative part signal you with a yes signal when it has generated the three new behaviors. . . . Now ask the creative part if it would be willing to reveal to you what the three new behaviors are.

5. *Have part X accept the new choices and the responsibility for generating them when needed.* Now ask part X if the three new behaviors are at least as effective as behavior X.

Now ask part X if it's willing to accept responsibility for generating the new behaviors in appropriate situations when its intention needs to be fulfilled.

6. *Make an ecological check.* Now go inside and ask if there are any parts that object to the negotiations that have just taken place or if all parts agree to support you. Then step into the future and imagine a situation that would have triggered the old behavior, and experience using one of your new choices and still achieving the benefits you desire. Step into another situation in the future that would have been a trigger to the undesirable behavior, and experience using another one of your new choices.

If you get a signal that other parts object to these new choices, you must start from the beginning, identify which part is objecting, what benefits it's been giving you in the past, and have it work with part X to generate new choices that would maintain the benefits it's always given you and also provide for you a new set of choices. It may sound a bit weird to talk about speaking to parts of yourself, but this is a basic hypnotic pattern that has been found quite useful by people like Drs. Erikson, Bandler, and Grinder.

If you found yourself consistently overeating, for example, you could do a swish pattern that would cause you to produce new kinds of behaviors, or you could identify this as a behavior that you would like to change. You could ask your unconscious to share with you the benefits of this pattern in the past. Maybe you'll discover that you used food to change your state when you felt alone. Or perhaps it helped you create a sense of security and got you to relax. Next you might create three new ways to give yourself the feeling of belonging and companionship or security and relaxation. Maybe you could join a health club, where the structure of events would make it easy for you to connect with people and feel the security of relaxing with friends and simultaneously becoming thinner, thereby gaining the further security of knowing you look good. Maybe you could meditate and create a feeling of unity with all the universe, and by that connection feel more secure and relaxed than you did when you overate.

Once you've come up with these alternatives, see if they feel congruent—that is, make sure all of you is willing to support your using these new choices in the future. If you feel congruent, these choices will produce behaviors that now support you in getting what you want, and you don't have to overeat to get it. Then step into the future and in your mind experience using these new choices effectively, noting the result you now produce. Thank your unconscious mind for these new choices, and enjoy your new behavior. You may even want to do a swish pattern, replacing the behavior you used to produce to the new behavior you desire, once you discover what would support your unconscious needs better than the old unwanted behavior did. You've given yourself new choices.

6-STEP REFRAME

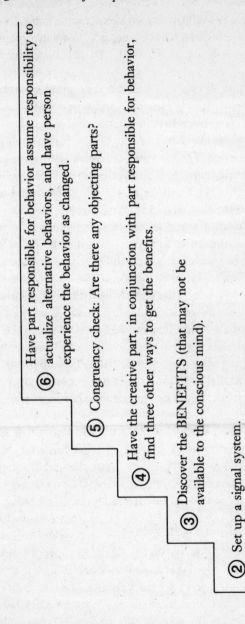

① Access the part of the person that has been responsible for the behavior.

② Set up a signal system.

③ Discover the BENEFITS (that may not be available to the conscious mind).

④ Have the creative part, in conjunction with part responsible for behavior, find three other ways to get the benefits.

⑤ Congruency check: Are there any objecting parts?

⑥ Have part responsible for behavior assume responsibility to actualize alternative behaviors, and have person experience the behavior as changed.

Almost any seemingly negative experience can be reframed into a positive. How often have you said, "Someday I'll probably look back and laugh at this." Why not look back and laugh at it now? It's all a matter of perspective.

It's important to note that you can reprogram someone's representation through swish patterns and other techniques, but if the person gets greater benefits from the older behavior than from the new choices he has developed, he will probably return to the old behavior. For example, if I work with a woman with an unexplainable numb foot and find out what she does in her head and physiology to create it, and she then learns to signal her body in a way that no longer creates numbness, her problem is now cleared up. But it may return when she goes home if she no longer gets the great secondary benefits she had when her foot was numb—such as her husband's doing the dishes, paying attention to her, massaging her feet, and so on. For the first couple of weeks or months, he's thrilled that she no longer has the problem. However, after a while, since she no longer has the problem, he not only expects her to start doing the dishes, but he doesn't massage her feet, and he seems to pay even less attention to her. Soon her problem flares back up mysteriously. She doesn't do this consciously. To her unconscious mind, the old behavior works much better in giving her what she wants— and wham, her foot's numb again.

In such a case, she must find other behaviors that will give her the same quality of experience with her husband. She must get more from the new behavior than she did from the past behavior. In one of my trainings, a woman who had been blind for eight years seemed unusually adept and centered. I later discovered that she was not blind at all. Yet she lived her life as if she were. Why? Well, she'd had an accident earlier in her life and developed poor eyesight. As she did, people around her gave her a tremendous amount of love and support, more than she had ever experienced before in her life. In addition, she began to discover that even doing average everyday things brought her great recognition when people thought she was blind. They treated her as special, so she maintained this be-

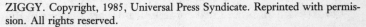

havior, even convincing herself of her blindness at times. She had not found a more powerful way to get people to automatically respond to her in a thoughtful and loving way. Even strangers would treat her as special. The behavior would change only if she developed something bigger to move away from or something that gave her more benefits than her present behavior offered.

So far we've been concentrating on the ways in which we can reframe negative perceptions into positive ones. But I don't want you to think of reframing as a therapy, as a way of going from situations you consider bad to ones you consider good. Reframing is really nothing more or less than a metaphor for potential and possibility. There are very few things in your life that can't be reframed into something better.

One of the most important frames to consider is possibilities.

We often fall into ruts. We might be getting comfortable results, but we could be getting spectacular results. So please do this exercise. Make a list of five things you're doing right now that you're pretty pleased with. They could be relationships that are going well, something at work, maybe something having to do with your children or your finances.

Now imagine them as even better. Spend a few minutes thinking about it. You'll probably surprise yourself by finding ways your life could be dramatically improved. Possibility reframing is something we can all do. All it takes is the mental flexibility to be alert for potential and the personal power to take action.

Let me add a final thought that applies to everything in this book. Reframing is another effective skill that you can pull out of your mental tool chest to produce greater results. Think of it in the broader sense as an ongoing process—of exploring assumptions and finding useful contexts for what you do well.

Leaders and all other great communicators are masters of the art of reframing. They know how to motivate and empower people by taking anything that happens and making it a model for possibility.

There's a famous story told about Tom Watson, the founder of IBM. One of his subordinates had made a horrendous mistake that had cost the company ten million dollars. He was called into Watson's office and said, "I suppose you want my resignation." Watson looked at him and said, "Are you kidding? We just spent ten million dollars educating you."

There's a valuable lesson in everything that happens. The best leaders are the ones who learn the lesson and put the most empowering frame on outside events. That works for politics, business, teaching, and your home life as well.

We all know people who are reverse reframers. No matter how bright the silver lining, they can always find a dark cloud. But for every disabling attitude, for every counterproductive behavior, there's an effective reframe. You don't like something?

Change it. You're behaving in a way that doesn't support you? Do something else. There's a way to not just produce effective behaviors, but make sure they're available when we need them. We'll learn how to retrigger any useful behavior the moment we desire it in the next chapter, when we look at ways of . . .

CHAPTER XVII

Anchoring
Yourself
to Success

"Do what you can, with what you have, where you are."

—*Theodore Roosevelt*

There are people—I'm one, you may be one, too—who get goose bumps every time they see an American flag. It's an odd reaction if you think about it analytically. After all, a flag is just a piece of cloth with a colorful, decorative pattern. There's nothing inherently magical about it. But of course that interpretation misses the whole point. Yes, it's just a piece of cloth. But at the same time, it has come to stand for all the virtues and characteristics of our nation. So when a person sees a flag, he also sees a powerful, resonant symbol of everything our nation stands for.

A flag, like countless other things in our environment, is an anchor, a sensory stimulus linked to a specific set of states. An anchor can be a word or a phrase or a touch or an object. It can be something we see, hear, feel, taste, or smell. Anchors have great power because they can instantly access powerful states.

That's what happens when you see the flag. You immediately experience the powerful emotions and sensations that represent how you feel about the nation as a whole because these feelings have been linked to or associated with this particular color and design of cloth.

Our world is full of anchors, some of them profound, some of them trivial. If I start to say to you, "Winston tastes good like a . . . " chances are you'll automatically say, "Cigarette should." If I ask you, "How do you spell relief?" most of you will spell it R-O-L-A-I-D-S. You may think all cigarettes taste awful. You probably know that relief is spelled R-E-L-I-E-F. But advertising has been so effective that it's anchored a response in you even though you don't believe it. The same sort of response occurs all the time. You can see people and instantly go into state—good or bad—depending on the feelings you have associated with them. You can hear a song and have an instantaneous change of state. All are the results of powerful anchors.

This section of the book ends with this chapter on anchoring for a very good reason. Anchoring is a way to give an experience permanence. We can change our internal representations or our physiology in a moment and create new results, and those changes require conscious thought. However, with anchoring you can create a consistent triggering mechanism that will automatically cause you to create the state you desire in any situation without your having to think about it. When you anchor something effectively enough, it will be there whenever you want it. You've learned any number of invaluable lessons and techniques so far in this book. Anchoring is the most effective technique I know for constructively channeling our powerful unconscious reactions so they're always at our disposal. Read over the quote with which this chapter begins. We all try to do the best with what we have. We all try to make the most of the resources at our disposal. Anchoring is a way to ensure that we always have access to our greatest resources. It's a way to make sure we always have what we need.

We all anchor regularly. In fact, it's impossible not to. All anchoring is a created association of thoughts, ideas, feelings, or states with a specific stimulus. Do you remember studying about Dr. Ivan Pavlov? Pavlov took hungry dogs and put meat where they could smell it and see it but not get to it. This meat became a powerful stimulus to the dogs' feelings of hunger. Soon they were salivating heavily. While they were in this intense state of salivation, Pavlov consistently rang a bell with a specific tone. Pretty soon he no longer needed the meat—he could just ring the bell and the dogs would salivate as if the meat itself were in front of them. He had created a neurological link between the sound of the bell and the state of hunger or salivation. From then on, all he had to do was ring the bell, and the dogs would literally go into a salivation state.

We, too, live in a stimulus/response world, where much of human behavior consists of unconscious programmed responses. For example, many people under stress immediately reach for a cigarette, alcohol, or in some cases something to snort. They don't think about it. They're just like Pavlov's dogs. In fact, many of these people would like to change their behavior. They feel their behavior is unconscious and uncontrollable. The key is to become conscious of the process so that if anchors do not support you, you can eliminate them and replace them with new stimulus/response linkages that automatically put you into states you desire.

So how do anchors get created? Whenever a person is in an intense state where the mind and body are strongly involved together and a specific stimulus is consistently and simultaneously provided at the peak of the state, the stimulus and the state become neurologically linked. Then, anytime the stimulus is provided, the intense state automatically results. We sing the national anthem, create certain feelings in our body, and look at the flag. We say the pledge of allegiance and see the flag. Pretty soon, merely looking at the flag automatically triggers these feelings.

Yet not all anchors are positive associations. Some anchors are unpleasant or worse. After you get a speeding ticket, you get a fleeting sinking feeling every time you pass the same corner on the highway. How do you feel when you see a red flashing

"CALL THE CAT, HARRY."

light in your rearview mirror? Does it instantly and automatically change your state?

One of the things that affects the power of an anchor is the intensity of the original state. Sometimes people have such an intense unpleasant experience—like fighting with their spouse or boss—that from then on, whenever they see the person's face, they immediately feel anger inside—and from that point on their relationship or job loses all its joy. If you have such negative anchors, this chapter will teach you how to replace them with positive anchors. You will not have to remind yourself; it will happen automatically.

Many anchors are pleasant. You associate a particular Beatles song with a wonderful summer, and for the rest of your life, whenever you hear the song, you'll think of that time. You finish off a perfect date by sharing an apple pie with chocolate ice cream, and from that point on it's your favorite dessert. You don't think about them any more than Pavlov's dogs did, but every day you have anchoring experiences that condition you to respond in a particular way.

Most of us are anchored utterly haphazardly. We're bombarded with messages from television, radio, and everyday life—some become anchors and others don't. A lot simply depends on chance. If you're in a powerful state—either good or bad—when you come in contact with a particular stimulus, chances are it will become anchored. Consistency of a stimulus is a powerful linkage or anchoring tool. If you hear something often enough (like advertising slogans), there's a good chance it will become anchored into your nervous system. The good news is that you can learn to control that anchoring process so you can install positive anchors and cast out negative ones.

Throughout history, successful leaders have known how to make use of the cultural anchors around them. When a politician is "wrapping himself in the flag," he's trying to make use of all the magic of that powerful anchor. He's trying to link himself to all the positive emotions that have been linked to the flag. At its best, that process can create a healthy common bond of patriotism and rapport. Think of how you feel when you watch a Fourth of July parade. Is it any wonder that no self-respecting candidate for office will miss showing up at a July Fourth parade? At its worst, anchoring can provide frightening displays of collective ugliness. Hitler had a genius for anchoring. He linked specific states of mind and emotion to the swastika, goosestepping troops, and mass rallies. He put people in intense states, and while he had them there, he consistently provided specific and unique stimuli until all he had to do later was offer those same stimuli—like raising his open hand in the gesture of heil—to call up all the emotion he had linked to them. He constantly used these tools to manipulate the emotions and thus the states and behaviors of a nation.

In our chapter on reframing, we noted that the same stimuli can have different meanings, depending on the frame put around them. Anchoring goes on in both positive and negative ways. Hitler linked positive, strong, proud emotions to Nazi symbols for party members. He also linked them to states of fear in his opponents. Did the swastika have the same meaning for a member of the Jewish community as it did for a stormtrooper? Obviously not. Yet the Jewish community took this experience in history and created a powerful positive anchor that helped them build a nation and protect it under what would seem like impossible odds. The auditory anchor of "never again" that many Jewish people use puts them in a state of total commitment to do whatever it takes to protect their sovereign rights.

Many political analysts believe it was a mistake on Jimmy Carter's part to try to demystify the office of the president of the United States. At the beginning of his term, at least, he cut down on the strongest anchors of the presidency—pomp and ceremony, things like playing "Hail to the Chief." The intent may have been admirable, although from a tactical point of view it was probably foolish. Leaders are most effective when they can make use of powerful anchors to mobilize support. Few presidents have ever wrapped themselves in the flag as assiduously as Ronald Reagan has. Whether or not you like his politics, it's hard not to marvel at his skill (or the skills of his advisers) at political symbolism.

Anchoring isn't restricted to the most profound emotions and experiences. Comedians are masters of anchoring. Good comedians know how to use a specific tonality, phrase, or physiology to get laughs instantly. How do they do it? They do something to get you to laugh, and while you're in that specific intense state they provide a specific and unique stimulus, like a certain smile or facial expression, or maybe a specific tone of voice. They do this consistently until the state of laughter is linked with their expression. Pretty soon they can just make the same facial expression, and you can't help laughing. Richard Pryor is a master at this. And Johnny Carson has the entire culture anchored. All he has to do is put on that tongue-in-cheek smirk, and even before he's finished a joke his audience starts to laugh. He's done it so many times before, they know what's coming and their minds trigger the same states. And what happens when Rodney Dangerfield says, "Take my wife"? There's nothing inherently funny in the words. But the phrase is anchored into a joke so well known that almost anyone can say those three words and get a laugh.

Let me give you an example of a time I was able to make maximum use of available anchors. John Grinder and I were negotiating with the United States Army to create a series of new training models to improve effectiveness in a variety of areas. The general in charge arranged for us to meet with the appropriate officers to work out times, prices, locations, and so on. We met with them in a big conference room, arranged in a horseshoe. At the head of the table was the chair reserved for the general. It was clear that even without him there, his chair was the most powerful anchor in the room. All of the officers treated it with the ultimate respect. It was where the decisions were made, where unquestioned commands were given. Both John and I made sure to walk over behind the general's chair, touching it and even eventually sitting in it. We did this until we had transferred to ourselves some of the responsiveness the officers had for the general and this symbol of him. When it was time for me to present the price I wanted, I stood next to the general's chair and told them in my most decisive, commanding voice and physiology what we wanted to be paid. Earlier we had dickered over the price, but this time no one even questioned it. Because we had made use of the anchor of the general's chair, we were able to negotiate a fair price without spending time bantering back and forth. The negotiations were as settled as if I'd ordered them. Most high-level negotiations make use of effective anchoring processes.

Anchoring is a tool used by many professional athletes. They may not call it that or even be aware of what they're doing, yet they are using the principle. Athletes who are known as clutch players are triggered, or anchored, by do-or-die situations to go into their most resourceful and effective states, from which they produce their most outstanding results. Some athletes do certain things to trigger themselves into state. Tennis players use a certain rhythm for bouncing the ball or a certain breathing pattern to put themselves in their best state before they serve.

I used anchoring and reframing in working with Michael O'Brien, the gold medal winner of the 1500 freestyle in the 1984 Olympics. I reframed his limiting beliefs, and I anchored his optimum states to the firing of the starter's gun (by having him recall the stimulus of the music he had used earlier in a successful match against his opponent) and to the black line he would focus on underwater as he swam. The results he produced in that peak state were the ones he desired most.

So let's review more specifically how you consciously create an anchor for yourself or others. Basically, there are two simple steps. First you must put yourself, or the person you're anchoring, into the specific state you wish to anchor. Then you must consistently provide a specific, unique stimulus as the person experiences the peak of that state. For example, when someone is laughing, he is in a specific congruent state—his whole body is involved at that moment. If you squeeze his ear with a specific and unique pressure and simultaneously make a certain sound several times, you can come back later, provide the stimulus (the squeeze and the sound), and the person will go back to laughing again.

Another way to create a confidence anchor for someone is to ask him to remember a time when he felt the state he wishes to have available on cue, then have him step back into that experience so that he is fully associated and can feel those feelings in his body. As he does this, you will begin to see changes in his physiology—facial expressions, posture, breathing. As you see these states nearing their peak, quickly provide a specific and unique stimulus several times.

You may enhance these anchors by helping the person get into a confident state more rapidly. For example, have him show you how he stands when he's feeling confident, and at the moment his posture changes, provides the stimulus. You then may ask him to show you how he breathes when he feels totally confident, and as he does, provide the same stimulus again. Then ask what he says to himself when he feels totally confident, and have him tell you in the tone of voice that he has when he's confident. As he does this, provide the exact same stimulus again

---

Intensity of the State
Timing (Peak of Experience)
Uniqueness of Stimulus
Replication of Stimulus

(for example, pressure on his shoulder in the same spot each time).

Once you believe you have an anchor, you need to test it. First get the person into a new or neutral state. The easiest way to do this is to get him to change his physiology or think of something completely different. Then, to test your anchor, simply provide the appropriate stimulus and observe. Is his physiology the same as it was when he was in state? If so, your anchor is effective. If not, you may have missed one of the four keys to successful anchoring:

1. *For an anchor to be effective, when you provide the stimulus you must have the person in a fully associated, congruent state, with his whole body fully involved.* I call this an intense state. The more intense, the easier it is to anchor, and the longer the anchor will last. If you anchor someone while part of him is thinking about one thing and another part about something else, the stimulus will become linked to several different signals and thus will not be as powerful. Also, as we discussed earlier, if a person is watching a time when he felt something and you anchor him in that state, then when you provide the stimulus in the future, it will be linked to seeing the picture rather than to having the whole body and mind associated.

2. *You must provide the stimulus at the peak of the experience.* If

you anchor too soon or too late, you won't capture the full intensity. You can discover the peak of the experience by watching the person go into the state and notice what he does when it begins to fade. Or you can get his help by asking him to tell you as he's nearing the peak and use that input to calibrate the key moment to provide your unique stimulus.

3. *You should choose a unique stimulus.* It's essential that the anchor gives a clear and unmistakable signal to the brain. If someone goes into a specific intense state and you try to link it with, say, a look you give that person all the time, it will probably not be a very effective anchor because it's not unique and it will be difficult for the brain to get a specific signal from it. A handshake, likewise, may not be effective because we shake hands all the time, though it could work if you shook hands in some unique way (such as a distinct pressure, location, and so forth). The best anchors combine several representational systems—visual, auditory, kinesthetic, and so forth—at one time to form a unique stimulus that the brain can more easily associate with a specific meaning. So anchoring a person with a touch and a certain tone of voice will usually be more effective than anchoring with just a touch.

4. *For an anchor to work, you must replicate it exactly.* If you put a person in a state and touch his shoulder blade in a specific spot with a specific pressure, you cannot retrigger that anchor later by touching him in a different place or with a different pressure.

If your anchoring procedure follows these four rules, it will be effective. One of the things I do in the firewalk is teach people how to produce anchors that mobilize their most resourceful, positive energies. I put them through a "conditioning" process, where they make a fist every time they summon up their most powerful energies. By the end of the evening, they can make a fist and immediately feel a powerful surge of productive energy.

Let's do a simple anchoring exercise now. Stand up and think of a time when you were totally confident, when you knew you could do whatever you wanted to do. Put your body in the same physiology it was in then. Stand the way you did when you were totally confident. At the peak of that feeling, make a fist and say, "Yes!" with a strength and certainty. Breathe the way you did when you were totally confident. Again make the same fist and say, "Yes!" in the same tonality. Now speak in the tone of a person with total confidence and control. As you do this, create the same fist and then say, "Yes!" in the same way.

If you can't remember a time, think how you would be if you did have such an experience. Put your body in the physiology it would be in if you did know how to feel totally confident and in control. Breathe the way you would if you felt total confidence. I want you to actually do this, like every other exercise in this book. Just reading about it won't help you. Doing it will work wonders.

Now as you stand there in a state of total confidence, at the height of that experience, gently make a fist and say, "Yes!" in a powerful tone of voice. Be aware of the power at your disposal, of the remarkable physical and mental resources you have, and feel the full surge of that power and centeredness. Start over and do this again and again, five or six times, each time feeling stronger, creating an association in your neurology between this state and the act of making a fist and saying, "Yes!" Then change your state, change your physiology. Now make your fist and say, "Yes!" in the same way as you did when you anchored, and notice how you feel. Do that several times over the next few days. Get yourself into the most confident, powerful state you're aware of, and at the peak of those states make a fist in a unique way.

Before too long, you'll find that by making a fist, you can bring forward that state at will, instantaneously. It may not happen after one or two times, but it won't take long for you to do this consistently. You can anchor yourself with only one or two repetitions if the state is intense enough and your stimulus is unique enough.

Once you've anchored yourself in this way, you should use it the next time you're in a situation you find difficult. You can make that fist and feel totally resourceful. Anchoring has such

HOW TO ANCHOR

1. Clarify the specific outcome you desire to use an anchor for and the specific state that will have the greatest effect in supporting the achievement of that outcome for yourself and/or others.

2. Calibrate baseline experience.

3. Elicit and shape that individual into the desired state through the use of your verbal and nonverbal communication patterns.

4. Use your sensory acuity to determine when the person is at the peak of the state and at that exact moment provide the stimulus (anchor).

5. Test anchor by:
   a. changing physiology to break state.
   b. triggering stimulus (anchor), and note if response is the desired state.

power because it aligns your neurology in an instant. Traditional positive thinking requires you to stop and think. Even getting yourself into a powerful physiology takes some time and conscious effort. Anchoring works in an instant to summon up your most powerful resources.

It's important for you to know that anchors can be made most powerful by being "stacked"—one piled on top of another—adding many of the same or very similar resourceful experiences together on a cumulative basis. For instance, I get into one of my most powerful and centered states by going into a physiology and stance that's something like that of a karate master. In that state, I've done hundreds of firewalks, I've done free-fall sky-dives, I've overcome remarkable challenges of all kinds. In each of these situations when I got myself most resourceful, at the

peak of the experience I made a unique fist. So now, when I
make the same fist, all those powerful feelings and physiologies
are simultaneously triggered within my nervous system. It's a
greater feeling than any drug could ever hope to create. I get
the experience of skydiving, night-diving in Hawaii, sleeping in
the great pyramids, swimming with dolphins, firewalking,
breaking through limitations, and winning a sports competition—all at once. So the more often I get into that state and
attach new, powerful, positive experiences to it, the more power
and success is anchored to it. It's another example of the success
cycle. Success breeds success. Power and resourcefulness breed
more power and resourcefulness.

I have a challenge for you: Go out and anchor three different
people in positive states. Have them remember a time when
they were feeling exuberant. Make sure that they are reexperiencing it fully, and anchor them several times in the same state.
Then engage them in conversation and test the anchor while
they are distracted. Do they return to the same state? If not,
check the four key points and anchor again.

If your anchor fails to trigger the state you desire, you've
missed one of the four points. Maybe you or the other person
weren't in a specific and fully associated state. Maybe you applied the anchor at the wrong time, after the peak of the state
had passed. Maybe the stimulus wasn't distinctive enough, or
you didn't replicate it perfectly when you tried to bring back
the anchored experience. In all these cases, you simply need the
sensory acuity to make sure the anchoring is being done correctly
and, when anchoring again, to make the appropriate changes in
your approach until you produce an anchor that works.

Here's another task: Select three to five states or feelings that
you would like to have at your fingertips, then anchor them to
a specific part of yourself so that you have easy access to them.
Let's say you're the kind of person who has a difficult time
making decisions, but you'd like to change. You want to feel
more decisive. To anchor the feeling of being able to make a
decision quickly, effectively, and easily, you might select the
knuckle of your pointer finger. Next, think of a time in your

life when you felt totally decisive, step into that situation in your mind, and fully associate to it so you feel the same way you did then. Begin to experience yourself making that great decision from your past. At the peak of the experience, while you feel most decisive, squeeze your knuckle and make a sound in your mind—like the word "yes." Now think of another such experience, and at the peak of that decision-making process create the same pressure and the same sound. Do this five or six times to stack a series of powerful anchors. Now think of a decision you need to make—think of all the facts you need to know. Then reach down and fire off the anchor—and you should be able to make a decision quickly and easily now. You can use another finger to anchor feelings of relaxation, if you need to. I anchored creativity feelings to a knuckle. I could take myself in a matter of moments from feeling stuck to feeling creative. Take the time to select five states and install them, and then have fun using them to direct your nervous system with pinpoint accuracy and speed. Please do this now.

Anchoring is often most effective when the person who has been anchored doesn't know what's happened. In his book *Keeping Faith*, Jimmy Carter gives an exceptional example of anchoring. During arms control talks, Leonid Brezhnev startled him by placing his hand on Carter's shoulder and saying in perfect English, "Jimmy, if we do not succeed, God will not forgive us." Years later, when interviewed on TV, Carter described Brezhnev as "a man of peace" and told this story. As he spoke, Carter actually reached up and touched his shoulder and said, "I can still feel his hand on my shoulder now." Carter remembers the experience so vividly because Brezhnev startled him by using perfect English and speaking about God. Being deeply religious, Carter obviously had intense feelings about what Brezhnev said, and the key moment was when Brezhnev touched him. The intensity of Carter's emotion and the importance of the issue virtually guarantee he will remember that experience for the rest of his life.

Anchoring can be remarkably successful in overcoming fears and changing behaviors. Let me give you an anchoring example

WAYS TO CALIBRATE
(IDENTIFY) STATE CHANGE

Note Changes in:

Breathing

location
pauses
rate
volume

Eye Movement

Lower Lip Size

Posture

Muscle Tonus

Pupil Dilation

Skin Color / Reflection

Voice

predicates
tempo
timbre
tone
volume

I use in my seminars. I ask someone, man or woman, who has difficulty dealing with the opposite sex to come to the front of the room. Recently, it was a young man who somewhat timidly volunteered. When I asked him how he felt about talking to a strange woman or asking a strange woman out, I could see an immediate physical reaction. His posture slumped, his eyes went down, his voice got shaky. "I'm not really comfortable doing that," he said. But he didn't really need to say anything. His physiology had already told me what I needed to know. I broke his state by asking him if he could remember a time when he felt very confident and proud and secure, a time when he knew he would succeed. He nodded, and I guided him into that state. I had him stand that way, breathe that way, to feel as confident in every way as he did then. I told him to think about what someone had said to him at that time when he felt confident and proud, and to remember the things he said to himself while he was in that state. At the peak of his experience, I touched him on the shoulder.

Then I took him through the exact same experience again several times. Each time I made sure he felt and heard the exact same things. At the peak of each experience, I did the same anchoring touch. Remember, successful anchoring depends on precise repetition, so I was careful to touch him in the same way and put him in exactly the same state every time.

By this point I had the reaction pretty well anchored. So I needed to test it. I broke his state and asked him again how he felt about women. Immediately he started to fall back into that depressed physiology. His shoulders went down, his breathing stopped. When I touched his shoulder in the spot I had set as an anchor, his body automatically began to shift back into that resourceful physiology. Through anchoring, it's amazing to watch how quickly someone's state can change from despair or fright to confidence.

At this point in the process, a person can touch his shoulder (or whatever spot he's set as an anchor) and trigger his desired state whenever he wants to. Yet we can take things a step further. We can transfer this positive state to the very stimuli that used to create feelings of unresourcefulness, so that those same stimuli will now create feelings of resourcefulness! Here's how. I asked the young man to pick an attractive woman from the audience, someone he would normally never dream of approaching. He hesitated for a moment until I touched his shoulder. The minute I did, his body posture changed and he picked an attractive woman. I asked her to come to the front of the room. Then I told her that this guy was going to try to get a date with her, and that she was to reject him completely.

I touched his shoulder, and he went into his resourceful physiology, his eyes up, his breathing deep, his shoulders back. He walked toward her and said, "Hi, how's it going?"

She snapped, "Leave me alone." It didn't faze him. Before, even looking at a woman caused his whole physiology to go haywire. Now he just smiled. I continued to hold his shoulder, and he continued to pursue her. The more verbal abuse she dished out, the more he stayed in his power state. He continued to feel resourceful and confident even after I took my hand from his shoulder. I had created a new neurological link that now caused him to become more resourceful when he saw a beautiful woman or when he encountered rejection. In this case, the woman finally said, "Can't you leave me alone?" and he said to her in a deep voice. "Don't you know power when you see it?" The whole audience exploded in laughter.

Now he was in a very powerful state by himself, and the stimulus that kept him there was a beautiful woman and/or her rejection—the same stimulus that made him feel terrified before. In short, I had taken an anchor and transferred it. By holding him in a powerful state while she rejected him, his brain began to associate the woman's rejection with his calm, confident state. The more she rejected him, the more relaxed, confident, and calm he became. It's quite remarkable to see the transformation that occurs in a matter of moments.

The logical question is, "Well, that's great in a seminar. Now what will happen in the real world?" The same stimulus/response loop is set up. In fact, we have the people we work with go out that evening and meet other people—and the results are amazing. Because the fear is gone, they begin to develop relationships with people they never would have approached in the past. It's really not that amazing if you think about it. After all, you had to learn how to respond to rejection as you grew up. There were plenty of models. Now you simply have a new set of neurological responses to choose from. One man who attended our seminar over two years ago and who was totally afraid of women is now a singer with an all-female entourage and loving it. I use some variation of this situation in every "Mind Revolution" seminar I conduct, and in each case the change in the person is remarkable. I use variations of this anchoring technique to alter phobic responses.

> *"If you do what you've always done, you'll get what you've always gotten."*
>
> —*Anonymous*

It's crucial to be aware of anchoring because it is always going on around us. If you're aware when it's going on, you can deal with it and change it. If you're not aware of it, you'll be mystified at the states that come and go seemingly without reason. I'll give you a common example. Let's say there's been a death in a person's family. He's in a state of deep grief. At the funeral, a number of people come over and touch him sympathetically on the upper part of his left arm, offering condolences. If enough people touch him in the same way, and he remains in a depressed state while they do, that kind of touch in that location can, and many times does, get anchored to his depressed state. Then, several months later, when someone touches him there with the same kind of pressure in a completely different context, it can set off the same feeling of grief, and he won't even know why he's feeling that way.

Have you ever had an experience like this, when all of a sudden you're depressed and you don't even know why? Chances are you have. Maybe you didn't even notice the song playing low in the background—a song you'd linked to someone you used to love a lot who is no longer in your life. Or maybe it was a certain look somebody gave you. Remember, anchors work without our conscious awareness.

Let me give you a few techniques for handling negative anchors. One is to fire off opposing anchors at the same time. Let's take that anchored feeling of grief triggered at the funeral. If it's anchored on the upper part of your left arm, one way to deal with it is to anchor on opposite feeling—your most powerful, resourceful feelings—in the same place on your right arm. If you trigger both anchors at the same time, you'll find something remarkable happens. The brain connects the two in your nervous system; then, any time either anchor is touched, it has a choice of two responses. And the brain will almost always choose the more positive response. Either it will put you in the positive state, or you'll go into a neutral state (in which both anchors have canceled each other out).

Anchoring is critical if you wish to develop a long-lasting, intimate relationship. For example, my wife, Becky, and I travel together a lot, sharing these ideas with people all over the country. We consistently go into powerful positive states, and often we are looking at or touching each other during these peak experiences. As a result, our relationship is filled with positive anchors—whenever we look at each other's faces, all those powerful, loving, happy moments are triggered. By contrast, when a relationship gets to the point where the two partners can't stand each other, negative anchors are many times the reason. There's a period in many relationships when a couple may have more negative than positive experiences associated to each other. If they are seeing each other consistently while in those states, the feelings get linked; sometimes just looking at each other makes them want to be apart. This especially happens if a couple begins to fight a lot, and if, during those angry states, each makes statements that are designed to hurt or anger the other. (Remember to use pattern interrupts!) These intense states get linked to the other person's face. After a while, each of them wants to be with someone else, maybe someone new, someone who represents only associated positive experiences.

Becky and I had an experience like this when we checked

into a hotel, late one evening. There was no bellman or valet out front, so we asked the man at the front desk to have the valet park the car and ask the bellman to bring up our bags. He said that was no problem, so we went up to our room and began to relax. After an hour went by and our bags had still not arrived, we called downstairs. To make a long story short, everything we owned had been stolen—our credit cards, passports, and a large cashier's check, which I had already countersigned. We had packed for a two-week trip. You can imagine what kind of state I went into. While I was in this angry, upset state, I kept looking at Becky, and she was also mad. After about fifteen minutes, I realized that being upset was not going to change anything, and since I believe everything happens for a reason, there had to be some benefit here. So I changed my state and I was feeling fine again. But about ten minutes later I looked at Becky, and as I did, I started feeling angry about things she hadn't done that day. I certainly wasn't feeling attracted to her. Then I stopped and asked myself, What's going on here? I realized I had linked all my negative feelings about losing our things to Becky, even though she didn't have a thing to do with it. Looking at her made me feel lousy. When I told her what I was experiencing, it turned out she was experiencing similar feelings about me. So what did we do? We simply collapsed the anchors. We started doing some exciting positive things with each other, things that within ten minutes put us both in a great state while we looked at each other's faces.

Virginia Satir, the world-famous marriage and family counselor, uses anchoring in her work all the time. Her results are outstanding. In modeling her, Bandler and Grinder noted the difference between her style and that of the traditional family therapist. When a couple comes in for therapy, many therapists believe that the underlying problem is the suppressed emotion and anger that the couple have for each other, and that it will help them to tell each other exactly how they feel about each other, all the things they're angry about, and so on. You can imagine what happens many times when they begin to tell each other all the things they're angry about. If the therapist encourages them to deliver the message of anger with force and vigor, they create even stronger negative anchors tied just to the sight of each other's faces.

I can certainly see that expressing these feelings may help if a person has held them inside for a long time. And while I believe that telling the truth in a relationship is necessary for success, I question the effects of the negative anchors this process can create. We've all been in arguments where we began to say things we really didn't mean, and the more we said, the more it escalated. So when does a person know what his "real" feelings are? There are quite a few disadvantages to putting yourself into a negative state before communicating your feelings to a loved one. Instead of having them yell at each other, Virginia Satir has her patients look at each other as they did when they first fell in love. She asks them to speak to each other as they spoke when they first fell in love. And she continues throughout the session to stack positive anchors so that seeing each other's faces now causes them to feel great about each other. From this state they can resolve their problems through clear communication, without harming the other person's feelings. In fact, they treat each other with so much caring and sensitivity that it sets up a new pattern, a new way to resolve problems in the future.

Let me give you another powerful tool for dealing with negative anchors. First let's create a positive and powerful resource anchor. It's always best to start with the positive rather than the negative, so if the negative becomes difficult to deal with, you have a tool to help yourself get out of that state quickly and easily.

I want you to think of the most powerful positive experience you've ever had in your life. Place that experience and its feelings in your right hand. Imagine doing this, and feel what it's like to have it in your right hand. Think of a time when you felt totally proud of something you did, and place that experience and feeling in your right hand as well. Now think of a time when you felt powerful, positive, loving feelings, and put them into your right hand as well, experiencing how they feel there. Remember a time when you laughed hysterically, maybe a time when you had the giggles. Take that experience and put it into your right hand as well, and notice how it feels with all those loving, resourceful, positive powerful feelings. Now notice what color these powerful feelings have come together to create in your right hand. Just note what color first comes to mind. Notice what shape they have come together to form. If you were to give them sound, what would they all sound like? What is the texture of all these feelings together in your hand? If they were all to come together to say one powerful positive statement to you, what would it be? Enjoy all these feelings, and then close your right hand and just let them remain there.

Now open your left hand, and in it place a negative, frustrating, depressing, or angry experience, something that is or has been bothering you. Maybe something you're afraid of, something that worries you. Place it in your left hand. There is no need to feel it inside. Make sure you disassociate from it— it's just over there in your left hand. Now I want you to become aware of its submodalities. What color does this negative situation create in your left hand? If you don't see a color or have a feeling right away, act as if you did. What color would it be if it did have one? Run through the other submodalities. What shape is it? Does it feel light or heavy? What's the texture of it? What sound does it make? If it were to say one sentence to you, what would it say? What sound does it make? What texture is it?

Now we're going to do what's called collapsing anchors. You can play with this in whatever way feels natural for you. One approach would be to take the color in your positive right hand, make believe it's a liquid, and pour it into your left hand at a very fast pace, making humorous noises and having fun as you do. Do it until the negative anchor in your left hand is the color of the positive experience in the right.

Next take the sound that your left hand was making and drop it into your right hand. Notice what your right hand does to it. Now take the feelings of your right hand and pour them into your left, noticing what they do to your left hand the minute they enter it. Bring your hands together in a clap, continuing to hold them there for a few moments until they feel balanced. Now the color in your right hand and left should be the same— the feelings should be similar.

When you're through, see how you feel about the experience in your left hand. Chances are you'll have stripped it of all its power to bother you. If you haven't, try the exercise again. Do it with different submodalities and a more active sense of play. After one or two times, almost anyone can utterly obliterate the power of something that used to be a strong negative anchor. You should now either feel good at this point or at least have neutral feelings about the experience.

You can do this same process if you're upset with someone and want to change how you feel about him. You can imagine the face of someone you really like in your right hand and the face of someone you don't like very much in your left. Begin by looking at the person you don't like, then at the person you do like, the person you don't like, the person you do. Do this faster and faster, no longer labeling which you like or do not like. Bring your hands together, breathe, wait a moment. Now think about the person you didn't like. You should now like him or at least feel okay about him. The beauty of this exercise is it can be done in a matter of moments, and you can change how you feel about almost anything! I did this three-minute process in a seminar recently with a whole group. One woman in the group put in her right hand someone she really liked, and in her left hand she put the face of her father, to whom she had not spoken in almost ten years. This way, she was able to neutralize her negative feelings about her father. She called him that night and spoke to him till four in the morning, and they have now redeveloped their relationship.

It's critical that we realize the power of our actions in anchoring kids. For example, my son Joshua went to school one day, and a group of concerned individuals delivered a presentation to the children about not accepting rides from strangers— an admirable and important message. I appreciated my son's being reinforced about it. The problem came in the way the message was delivered. The group showed a set of slides, much like the gruesome ones shown adults who go to traffic school. They showed posters of missing children. They even showed the bodies of young children being picked out of ditches. Kids, they said, who accept rides from strangers can end up like this. Obviously this was a major moving-away-from strategy for motivation.

The results, however, were quite destructive, at least for my son, and I might guess for other kids. What they did was the equivalent of installing a phobia. My son now had these big, bright, gory pictures of being murdered, which he associated with walking home. That day he refused to walk home and had to be picked up from school. For the next two or three days he would wake up at night with nightmares, and he refused to walk to school with his sister. Fortunately, I understand the principles of what creates and affects human behavior. I had been out of town, and when I finally found out about the situation, I did a series of collapse anchors and a phobia cure on the phone. The next day he walked to school by himself, confidently, strongly, and resourcefully. He was not going to be foolhardy—he knew what to avoid and what to do to take care of himself. Yet now he was empowered to live his life the way he wanted to, rather than living in fear.

The people who gave the presentation obviously had nothing but the best of intentions. However, sincerity doesn't guarantee that damage won't result from a lack of understanding of the effects of anchoring. Pay attention to the effect you're having on people—especially our little ones!

Let's do one last exercise. Put yourself in that powerful, resourceful state and pick the color that's most resourceful for you. Do the same thing with a shape and a sound and a feeling that you would associate with your most powerful, resourceful state. Then think of a phrase you would say when you were feeling happier, more centered, and stronger than you've ever felt before. Next, think of an unpleasant experience, a person who's a negative anchor, something you're afraid of. In your mind, put that positive shape around the negative experience. Do it with the utter belief that you can capture the negative feeling within it. Then take your resourceful color and physically blow it all over the negative anchor, with such force that the anchor just dissolves. Hear the sound and feel the feeling that occurs when you're totally resourceful. Finally say the thing you would say in your most powerful state. As the negative anchor dissolves into a mist of your favorite color, say the thing that accentuates your power. How do you feel about the negative situation now? Chances are you'll find it hard to imagine that it bothered you so much before. Do this with three other experiences, and then do it with someone else.

If you've just been reading along, these will come across as odd, even silly exercises. But if you do them, you'll be able to see the incredible power they have. This is the key ingredient of success: *the ability to eliminate from your own environment triggers that tend to put you in negative or unresourceful states, while installing positive ones in yourself and in others*. One way to do this is to make a chart of the major anchors—positive and negative—in your life. Note whether they're primarily triggered by visual, auditory, or kinesthetic stimuli. Once you know what your anchors are, you should go about collapsing the negative ones and making best use of the positive ones.

Think of the good you can do as you learn how to anchor those positive states effectively, not just in yourself but in others. Suppose you talked to your associates, got them in a motivated, upbeat frame of mind, and anchored it with a touch or expression or tone of voice that you could produce in the future? After a while, by anchoring those positive mental states several times, you could elicit that kind of intense motivation at any time. Their work would be more rewarding, the company would be more profitable, and everyone would be much happier. Think of the power you could have in your own life if you could take the things that used to bother you and have them make you feel great or resourceful enough to change them. You have the power to do it.

Let me leave you with a final thought, not just on anchoring, but on all the techniques you've learned thus far. There's an incredible synergy, a processional sense, that comes from mastering any of these skills. Just as a rock thrown in a quiet pond sets off a pattern of ripples, success with any of these skills breeds more and more success. You should already have a strong and clear sense of how powerful these skills are. My hope is that you will use them, not just today, but on an ongoing basis in your life. Just as the stacked anchors in my karate stance get more powerful every time I use them, you will increase your own personal power with each skill you learn, master, and use.

There is a filter to human experience that affects how we feel about everything we do or do not do in our lives. These filters affect anchoring and everything else we've discussed in this book. I'm talking about . . .

Leadership: The Challenge of Excellence

CHAPTER XVIII

Value Hierarchies: The Ultimate Judgment of Success

"A musician must make music, an artist must paint,

a poet must write, if he is to be ultimately

at peace with himself."

—Abraham Maslow

Every complex system, whether it's a factory tool or a computer or a human being, has to be congruent. Its parts have to work together; every action has to support every other action if it's to work at a peak level. If the parts of a machine try to go in two different directions at once, the machine will be out of sync and could eventually break down.

Human beings are exactly the same. We can learn to produce the most effective behaviors, but if those behaviors don't support our deepest needs and desires, if those behaviors infringe upon other things that are important to us, then we have internal conflict, and we lack the congruency that is necessary for success on a large scale. If a person is getting one thing, but vaguely wanting something else, he won't be totally happy or fulfilled. Or if a person achieves a goal but, in order to do so, violates his own belief about what is right or wrong, then turmoil results.

In order to truly change, grow, and prosper, we need to become consciously aware of the rules we have for ourselves and others, of how we really measure or judge success or failure. Otherwise we can have everything and still feel like nothing. This is the power of the final and critical element called values.

What are values? Simply, they are your own private, personal, and individual beliefs about what is most important to you. Your values are your belief systems about right, wrong, good, and bad. Maslow talks about artists, but the point is universal. Our values are the things we all fundamentally need to move toward. If we don't, we won't feel whole and fulfilled. That feeling of congruity, or personal wholeness and unity, comes from the sense that we are fulfilling our values by our present behavior. They even determine what you will move away from. They govern your entire life-style. They determine how you will respond to any given experience in life. They are much like the executive level in a computer. You can put in any program you like, but whether the computer accepts the program, whether it uses it or not, all depends on how the executive level was programmed by the factory. Values are like the executive level of judgment in the human brain.

From what you wear and what you drive to where you live, whom you marry (if you marry), or how you raise your children, from what causes you support to what you choose to do for a living, the impact of your values is endless. They are the base that defines our responses to any given situation in life. They are the ultimate key to understanding and predicting your own behaviors as well as the behaviors of others—the master key to unleashing the magic within.

So where do they come from, these powerful instructions as to right and wrong, good and bad, what to do and what not to do? Since values are specific, highly emotional, connected beliefs, they come from some of the same sources we discussed earlier in the chapter on belief. Your environment plays a role, starting when you are a baby. Your father and, especially in traditional families, mother play the biggest role in programming most of your original values. They constantly expressed their values in telling you what they did or did not want you to do, say, and believe. If you accepted their values, you were rewarded; you were a good boy or girl. If you rejected them, you were in trouble; you were a bad kid. In some families, if you continued to reject your parents' values, you were punished.

In fact, most of your values have been programmed through this punishment-reward technique. As you got older, your peer groups were another source of values. When you first encountered other kids in the street, they may have had values different from yours. You blended your values with theirs, or you may have altered your own, because if you didn't, they might beat you up or worse—not play with you! Throughout your life, you've constantly been creating new peer groups and accepting new values or blending or installing your own in others. Also, throughout your life, you've had heroes or maybe antiheroes. And because you admire their accomplishments, you try to emulate who you think they are. Many kids originally got into drugs because their heroes, whose music they loved, seemed to value drugs. Fortunately, today, many of these heroes—realizing their responsibility and opportunity as public figures to shape the values of large numbers of people—are now making it clear that they do not use or support the use of drugs. Many artists are making it clear that they stand for positive change in the world. This is shaping a lot of people's values. Understanding the power of the media to raise money to feed starving people, Bob Geldoff (of Live Aid and Band Aid fame) has tapped into the values of other powerful stars. Through their efforts and example, they have helped to strengthen the value of giving and compassion for others. Many people who did not hold this value as most important in their lives changed their behaviors when they saw their heroes—Bruce Springsteen, Michael Jackson, Kenny Rogers, Bob Dylan, Stevie Wonder, Diana Ross, Lionel Richie, and others—telling them directly and daily through their music and videos that people are dying and we've got to do something! In the next chapter, we'll look closer at trend creation. For now, just realize the power that the media have in directing and creating values and behavior.

Value formation doesn't end with heroes. It also happens at work, where the same punishment-reward system goes on. To work for someone and rise in the company, you adopt some of their values. If you don't share your boss' values, promotions may be impossible. And if you don't share the company's values to begin with, you will be unhappy. Teachers in our school system are constantly expressing their values, and often unconsciously using the same punishment-reward system to ensure their adoption.

Our values also change when we change goals or self-image. If you set a goal to be number one in the company, when you reach it you will be earning more money and expecting different things from others. Your values of how hard you will work from now on may also change. What you regard as a nice car will be quite different. Even the people you spend your time with may also change to match your "new" self-image. Instead of going to get a beer with the boys, you may be sipping a Perrier with the other three people in your office who are planning the expansion.

What you drive, where you go, who your friends are, what you do, all reflect your self-identification. They may involve what industrial psychologist Dr. Robert McMurray has called inverted ego symbols, which also demonstrate your values. For example, the fact that someone drives an inexpensive car does not mean he does not think highly of himself or that gas mileage is a major value. Instead, he may want to show that he is above the main stream of humanity by adopting incongruous symbols. A highly educated scientist or entrepreneur who has a very substantial income may want to prove to himself and others how different he is by driving a cheap, beat-up economy car. The multimillionaire who lives in a shack may value not wasting space, or he may want to demonstrate his unique values to himself and others.

So I think you can see just how important it is that we discover what our values are. The challenge for most people is that many of these values are unconscious. Often people don't know why they do certain things—they just feel they have to do them.

People feel very uncomfortable and suspicious of individuals who have values very different from their own. Much of the conflict that people have in life results from conflicting values. Just as this is true on a local scale, so it is on an international scale. Almost every war is a war over values. Look at the Middle East, Korea, Vietnam, and so on. And what happens when one country conquers another? The conquerors begin to convert the culture to their own values.

Not only do different countries have different values and different people have different values, but each individual thinks some values are more important than others. Almost all of us have a bottom line—things that are more important to us above anything else. For some people it's honesty; for others it's friendship. Some people may lie to protect a friend, even though honesty is important to them. How can they do this? Because friendship is higher on their ladder of importance (hierarchy of values) than honesty in this context. You may place a high personal value on business success, but also on having a close family life. So conflict occurs when you promise to be with your family one evening and then a business opportunity arises. What you choose to do depends on what you place as your highest value at the time. So rather than saying it is bad to spend time on business and not your family or vice versa, just discover what your values truly are. Then for the first time in your life you'll understand why you do certain things, or why other people do what they do. Values are one of the most important tools for discovering how a person works.

To deal effectively with people, we need to know what's most important to them, specifically what their hierarchy of values is. A person may have great difficulty understanding other people's basic behaviors or motivations unless he understands the relative importance of values. Once he does, he can virtually predict how they will respond to any specific set of circumstances. Once you know your own value hierarchy, you can be empowered to resolve any relationship or any internal representation that's causing you conflict.

There's no real success except in keeping with your basic

values. Sometimes it's a matter of learning how to mediate between existing values that are in conflict. If a person is having trouble in a high-paying job and one of his main values is that money is evil, it is not enough to concentrate on the job. The problem is at the higher level of conflicting values. If a person can't concentrate at work because his highest value is family and he's spending all his time on the job, you have to address the inner conflict and the feeling of incongruity it produces. Reframing and finding the intent does this to a great degree. You can have a billion dollars, but if your life conflicts with your values, you won't be happy. We see this all the time. People with wealth and power lead impoverished lives. On the other hand, you can be poor as a church mouse financially, but if the life you lead is in accordance with your values, you will feel fulfilled.

It's not a matter of which values are right or wrong. I'm not going to impose my values on you. It's important to learn what your values are so you will be able to direct, motivate, and support yourself at the deepest level. We all have a supreme value, the one thing we most desire from any situation, whether it's a relationship or a job. It may be freedom, it may be love, it may be excitement, or it may be security. You probably read that list and said to yourself, "I want all those things." Most of us do. But we put a relative value on them all. What one person wants most from a friendship is ecstasy; another, love; a third, honest communication; a fourth, a sense of security. Most people are totally unaware of their hierarchies or those of their loved ones. They have a vague sense of wanting love, or challenge, or ecstasy, but they don't have a sense of how these pieces fit together. These distinctions are absolutely critical. They determine whether or not a person's ultimate needs will be met. You can't fill someone else's needs if you don't know what they are. You can't help someone do the same for you, and you can't deal with your own conflicting values, until you understand the hierarchies in which they are interacting. The first key to understanding is to elicit them.

How do you discover your own or someone else's hierarchy

of values? First, you need to place a frame around the values you are looking for. That is, you need to elicit them in a specific context. They are compartmentalized. We often have different values for work, relationships, or family. You must ask, "What's most important to you about a personal relationship?" The person might answer, "The feelings of support." Then you might ask, "What's important about support?" He might respond, "It shows that someone loves me." You might ask, "What's most important about someone loving you?" He might answer, "It creates feelings of joy for me." By continuing to ask over and over again, "What's most important?" you begin to develop a list of values.

Then, to have a clear understanding of someone's hierarchy of values, all you need to do is take this list of words and compare them. Ask, "Which is more important to you? Being supported or feeling joy?" If the answer is, "Feeling joy," then obviously it is higher in the hierarchy of values. Next you would ask, "What is more important to you, feeling joy or being loved?" If the answer is, "Feeling joy," then of those three values, joy is number one. You then ask, "What is more important to you? Feeling loved or being supported?" The person may look quizzically at you and respond, "Well, they're both important." You reply, "Yes, but which is more important, that someone loves you or that someone supports you?" He may say, "Well, it's more important that someone loves me." So now you know the second-highest value behind joy would be love, and the third would be support. You can do this with any size of a list to understand what's most important to a person and the relative weight of other values. The person in this example can still feel strongly about a relationship, even if he doesn't feel supported. Another person, however, may put support over love (which you may be surprised to find many people do). That person won't believe someone loves him unless she supports him, and it won't be enough for him to feel loved if he doesn't feel supported.

People have certain values that when violated cause them to leave a relationship. For example, if support is number one on a person's value list, but he doesn't feel supported, he may end the relationship. Someone else who ranks support as third or fourth or fifth, and love as first, won't leave the relationship no matter what happens—as long as he feels loved.

I'm sure you could come up with several things that matter to you in an intimate relationship. I've listed some important ones below.

Personal Value List

_____ Love
_____ Ecstasy
_____ Mutual communication
_____ Respect
_____ Fun
_____ Growth
_____ Support
_____ Challenge
_____ Creativity
_____ Beauty
_____ Attraction
_____ Spiritual unity
_____ Freedom
_____ Honesty

These are by no means all the important values there are. You may find many other values more important than the ones listed here. If you can think of some, jot them down now.

Now rank these values in order of importance, with number one as the most important and number fourteen as the least important.

Did you find this difficult? If you don't form a hierarchy systematically, ranking can become a bit tiresome and confusing as a list gets larger.* So let's compare values with one another to determine which are more important than the others. Let's

* A computer program that discovers metaprograms and value hierarchies is available through Robbins Research.

start with the first two on the list: Which is more important to you, love or ecstasy? If the answer is love, is it more important than mutual communication? You need to go completely through the list and see if anything is more important than the value you begin with. If not, it's at the top of the hierarchy. Now, go to the next word on the list. What means more to you, ecstasy or mutual communication? If the answer is ecstasy, continue down the list, comparing it to the next word. If at any time another choice is preferable to the beginning choice (in this case, ecstasy) start making the comparisons to that value.

For example, if mutual communication is valued more than ecstasy, you would then continue by asking, "What's more important, mutual communication or respect?" If it's still mutual communication, then ask, "Mutual communication or fun?" If no value is deemed more important than mutual communication, it's second in the hierarchy. If another value is deemed more important, you would compare the remaining values with it until you complete the list.

For example, if you compared mutual communication to all the words in this example and came to the last value on the list, honesty, and it (honesty) turned out to be more important than mutual communication, then you don't have to compare honesty to creativity since creativity is not as important as mutual communication. Thus, we know that since honesty is more important than mutual communication, it will also be higher than creativity or any other word on the list already below mutual communication. To complete the hierarchy, repeat this process all the way through the list.

As you'll see, ranking is not always an easy process. Some of these are very fine distinctions that we're not used to making. If a decision isn't clear, make the distinctions more specific. You might ask, "Which is more important, ecstasy or growth?" A person may respond, "Well, if I'm growing, I have ecstasy." Then you need to ask, "What does ecstasy mean to you? What does growth mean to you?" If the answer is, "Ecstasy means feeling a total sense of personal joy, and growth means overcoming obstacles," then you can ask, "Which is more important, overcoming obstacles or feeling a total sense of joy?" This will make the decision easier.

If the distinctions are still not clear, ask what would happen if you took away one value. "If you could never be ecstatic but you could grow, would that be your choice, or if you could never grow but you could be ecstatic, which one would you want more?" This will usually provide the information needed to distinguish which value is more important.

Putting together one of your own value hierarchies is one of the most valuable exercises you can do in this book. Take the time now to decide what you desire from a relationship. You should do the same thing with your partner if you're in a relationship now. The two of you will develop a new awareness of each other's deepest needs. Make a list of all the things that are most important to you in a relationship—for example, attraction, joy, excitement, and respect. To expand this list, you might ask, "What's important about respect?" And your partner might say, "That's the most important thing in a relationship." So you already have the number-one value. Or your partner may say, "When I feel respected, I feel unified with another person." So you have another word, "unity." You might ask, "What's important about unity?" And your partner may say, "If I feel unity with another person, I feel loved by him." You might then ask, "What's important about love?" Continue in this way to develop a list of words until you are satisfied that you have most of the major values that are important to you in a relationship. Now, create a hierarchy of importance by using the technique described above. Systematically compare each of the values until you have a clear hierarchy that feels right to you.

After you've created a hierarchy of values for your personal relationships, do the same thing with your work environment. Create the context of work and ask, "What's important to me about working?" You might say creativity. The next obvious question would be, "What's important about creativity?" You may answer, "When I'm creative I feel like I'm growing." "What's important about growing?" Continue from there. If you're a parent, I suggest you do the same thing with your kids. By finding out the things that truly motivate them, you'll come up with uniquely effective tools for more effective parenting.

What have you discovered? How do you feel about the list you've created. Is it accurate in your estimation? If not, make additional comparisons until it feels right. Many people are surprised to discover their highest values. However, by becoming consciously aware of their value hierarchy, they do come to understand why they do what they do. In personal relationships, or at work, now that you know what your values are, you can express what's most important to you, and by knowing that, you can begin to direct your energies to achieve it.

Putting a hierarchy together is not enough. As we'll see later, people mean very different things by the same word when talking about values. Now that you've become conscious of your hierarchy, take the time to ask what it means.

If the primary value in a relationship is love, you might ask, "What makes you feel loved?" or, "What causes you to love someone?" or, "How do you know when you're not loved?" You should do this with as much precision as possible for at least the first four items on your hierarchy. The single word "love" probably means dozens of things to you, and it's worthwhile to discover what they are. This is not an easy process, but if you do it carefully, you'll know more about yourself, what you truly desire, and what evidence you use to know whether your desires are being fulfilled.

Of course, you can't go through life doing full-scale value elicitations for everyone you know. How precise and specific you want to be will depend entirely on your outcome. If it is to have a relationship that will last forever with a spouse or a child, you'll want to know everything you possibly can about how that person's brain works. If you're a coach trying to motivate a player or a businessman trying to evaluate a possible client, you still would want to know the person's values, but not nearly in as much depth. You're just looking for the big, overriding chunks. Remember, in any relationship—whether it's as intense as it is between a father and son or as casual as it is between two salespeople sharing the same phone—you have a contract, whether you verbalize it or not. You both expect certain things from each other. You both judge each other's actions and words, at least unconsciously, by your values. You might as well get clear on what those values are and create agreement so that you know in advance how your behaviors will affect you both and what your true needs are.

You can elicit these overriding values in casual conversation. One simple but invaluable technique is to listen carefully to the words people use. People tend to use over and over key words that denote the values at the top of their hierarchy. Two people may share an ecstatic experience together. One may rave about it, saying how much it got his creativity going. Another may be just as enthused, and she'll say how intense the shared feelings of community were. Chances are they're giving you strong clues about their highest values and about what you should understand if you want to motivate or excite them.

Value elicitations are important in both business and personal life. There's an ultimate value everyone looks for in work. It will make a person take a job, and if not fulfilled—or if violated—it will make him leave it. For some people, it may be money. If you pay them enough, you'll keep them. But for many others, it's something else. It might be creativity or challenge or a sense of family.

It's crucial for managers to know the supreme value of their employees. To elicit it, the first thing to ask is, "What would it take to cause you to join an organization?" Let's say the employee answers, "A creative environment." You develop a list of what is important about that by asking, "What else would it take?" Then you would want to know, even if all those existed, what would cause him to leave. Suppose the answer is, "A lack of trust." You would keep on probing from there: "Even if there were a lack of trust, what would make you stay?" Some people might say that they would never stay in an organization with a lack of trust. If so, that's their ultimate value—the thing they must have to stay at a job. Someone else might say he would stay, even if there was no trust, if he had a chance to rise through the organization. Keep probing and questioning until you've found the things the person has to have to stay happy, and then you'll know in advance what would make him leave. The value words people use are like superanchors—they have strong emotional associations. To be even more effective, be clear: "How would you know when you have that?" "How do you know when you don't have that?" Also, it's critically important to note a person's evidence procedure to determine how your concept of trust differs from his. He may believe there is trust only if he's never questioned in his decisions. He may believe there is a lack of trust if his job responsibility is changed without a clear explanation to him. It is invaluable for a manager to understand these values and be able to anticipate in advance when dealing with people in any given situation.

There are some managers who figure they're being good motivators if they're good on their own terms. They think, I pay this guy good money, so I expect such and such in return. Well, that's true to an extent. But various people value different things. For some, the most important thing is to work with people they care about. When those people start drifting off, the job loses its luster. Some value a sense of creativity and excitement. Some value other things. If you want to manage well, you need to know an employee's supreme values and how to fulfill them. If you don't provide those, you'll lose him, or at least never have him working at peak performance and enjoying his job.

Does all this take more time and sensitivity? Sure. But if you value the people you work with, it's worth it—for your sake and for theirs. Remember that values have enormous emotional power. If you just manage from your values and assume you're being fair from your point of view, you'll probably spend a lot of time feeling bitter and betrayed. If you can bridge the values gap, you'll probably have happier associates, friends, and family members—and you'll feel happier yourself. It's not essential in life to have the same values as someone else. But it is essential to be able to align yourself with other people, to realize what their values are, and to support them and work with them.

Values are the most powerful motivating tool we have. If you want to change a bad habit, the change can be made very rapidly if you will link the successful maintenance of that change with high values. I know of one woman who placed an extremely high value on pride and respect. So what she did was write a note to the five people she respects most in the world, saying that she would never smoke again, that she had more respect for her own personal body and for others than to ever allow it to happen again. After she sent her letters out, she quit. There were many times when she said she would have given anything for a cigarette, but her pride would never let her go back. It was a value more important than the feeling of puffing on a cigarette. Today she is a healthy non-smoker. Values properly used have the greatest power in changing our behavior!

Let me share with you a recent experience I had. I was working with a college football team that had three quarterbacks. All had very different values. I elicited their values simply by asking each man what was important about playing football—what it gave him. One said football was a way to make his family proud and to glorify God and Jesus Christ our Savior. The second said football was important as an expression of power, that breaking through limitations, winning, and overpowering others were the ultimate values for him. The third was a young man from the ghetto who wasn't able to find any particular value at all in football. When I asked, "What's important about playing football?" he said he didn't know. It turned out that he was mostly moving away from things, like poverty and a bad home life, and he didn't have any clear sense of what football meant to him.

Obviously, you would motivate these three in very different ways. If you tried to motivate the first one (whose values were making Jesus and his family proud) by pumping him up about the importance of crushing his opponents and grinding them into the dirt, it would probably cause inner conflict because he sees a positive, not a violent, negative, value in the game. If you gave the second one a fervent talk about glorifying God and making his family proud, he wouldn't be motivated because that's not the major reason he's playing the game.

It turned out the third quarterback had the most talent, but he was making less use of it than the other two. The coaches were having a rough time motivating him because he had no clear values—nothing clear to move toward or away from. In this case, they had to find some value he had in another context—like pride—and transfer it to the context of football. Eventually, although he had already injured himself before the first game, he at least became motivated to support the team, and the coaches had a way to motivate him in the future when his body healed.

Values work in a way that's as complex and delicate as anything we've talked about in this book. Remember that when we use words, we're using a map—and the map is not the territory. If I tell you that I'm hungry or that I want to take a ride in a car, you're still working from a map. Hungry might mean ready for a big meal or wanting a small snack. Your idea of a car could be a Honda or a limousine. But the map comes pretty close. Your complex equivalence is close enough to mine that we don't have too much trouble communicating. Values present us with the most subtle maps of all. So when I tell you what my values are, you're working from a map of a map. Your map, your complex equivalence of the value, may be very different from mine. If you and I both say that freedom is our highest value, that would create rapport and agreement between us because we want the same thing, we're motivated in the same direction. But it's not that simple. Freedom for me may mean being able to do whatever I want, whenever I want, wherever I want, with whomever I want, as much as I want. Freedom for you may mean having someone take care of you all the time, being free from hassles by living in a structured environment. Freedom for someone else might be a political construct, the discipline needed to maintain a particular political system.

> *"If a man hasn't discovered something that he will die for,*
> *he isn't fit to live."*
>
> —*Martin Luther King, Jr.*

Because values have such primacy, they carry an incredible

emotional charge. There's no closer way to bond people than to align them through their highest values. That's why a committed force fighting for its country will almost always defeat a group of mercenaries. There's no more traumatic way to drive people apart than to create behaviors that put their highest values in conflict. The things that matter most to us, whether it's a sense of patriotism or a love of family, are all reflections of values. So by constructing precise hierarchies, you develop something you've never had before—the most useful map possible of what someone else needs and what he'll respond to.

We see the explosive power and delicate nuance of values all the time in relationships. A person may feel betrayed by a failed romance. "He told me he loved me," she says. "What a joke." For one person, love may be a commitment that lasts forever. For another, it may be a brief but intense union. This person may have been a cad, or he may just have been a person with a different complex equivalence of what love is.

So it's absolutely crucial that you construct a map that's as accurate as possible, that you determine what the other person's map really is. You need to know not just the word they're using, but what it means. The way to do that is to ask with as much flexibility and persistence as you need to construct a precise complex equivalence of what their value hierarchy is.

Very often, ideas of values vary so much that two people who profess common values may have nothing in common, and two people who profess very different values may find they really want the same thing. For one person, fun may mean using drugs, staying up all night at parties, and dancing until dawn. For another person, fun might mean climbing mountains or shooting rapids—anything that's new, exciting, or challenging. The only thing their values have in common is the word they use for it. A third person may say his most important value is challenge. To him that might also mean climbing mountains and shooting rapids. Ask him about fun, and he might dismiss it as frivolous and unimportant. But he may mean precisely the same thing by challenge as the second person did by fun.

Common values form the basis for the ultimate rapport. If

two people have values that are totally linked, their relationship can last forever. If their values are totally different, there's little chance for a lasting, harmonious relationship. Few relationships may be classified in either of those extreme categories. As a result, you have to do two things. First, find the values you have in common so that you can use them to help bridge the others that are not alike. (Isn't that what Reagan and Gorbachev tried to do in their summit meetings? Maintain the values both countries have in common that would support their relationship—like survival?) Second, seek to support and fulfill the other person's most important values as much as you can. This is the basis of a powerful, supportive, and lasting relationship, whether it be business, personal, or family.

Values are the overriding factor that causes congruence or incongruence, causes people to be motivated or not. If you know their values, you have the final key. If you don't, you may create a powerful behavior that doesn't last or doesn't produce its desired end. If it's in conflict with a person's values, it will act like a circuit breaker to override them. Values are like the court of last resort. They decide which behaviors work and which don't, which produce desired states and which produce incongruity.

Just as people have different ideas of what values mean, they have different ways of determining if their values are being fulfilled.

On a personal level, eliciting an evidence procedure is one of the most valuable things you can do to set goals for yourself. Here's a worthwhile exercise: Take five values that are important to you and figure out your evidence procedure. What has to happen for you to know that your values are being met or fulfilled? Answer it now on another piece of paper. Evaluate whether your evidence procedure helps you or holds you back.

You can control and change your own evidence procedures. The ones we come up with are just mental constructs, nothing more. They should serve us instead of holding us back.

Values change. Sometimes they change radically, but usually they change on an unconscious level. Many of us have evidence procedures that are either self-defeating or outdated. When you were in high school, you might have needed multiple romantic involvements to feel attractive. As an adult, you might want to develop more elegant strategies. If you value personal attractiveness, but you only feel attractive if your looks rival those of Cheryl Tiegs or Robert Redford, you might be guaranteeing yourself frustration. We all know of people who were fixated on an outcome, something that symbolized some ultimate value for them. And then, when they reached it, they found it didn't have meaning at all. Their values had changed, but the evidence procedure had taken on a life of its own. Sometimes people have an evidence procedure that's not attached to any values at all. They know what they want, but they don't know why. So when they get it, it turns out to be a mirage, something the culture sold them on but they didn't really desire. The incongruity between values and behaviors is one of the great themes in literature and films ranging from *Citizen Kane* to *The Great Gatsby*. You need to develop an ongoing sense of your values and how they're changing. So just as you need to regularly reassess the outcomes and goals you charted in chapter 11, you should regularly review the values that most motivate you.

Another way to review evidence procedures is to note whether they are accessible at a level that is attainable within a reasonable period of time. Take two high school graduates starting out in life. For one kid, success may mean a stable family, a job that pays $40,000 a year, a $100,000 home, and being physically fit. For another it may mean a great family, a $240,000-a-year income, a $2 million home, the body of a triathlete, lots of friends, a professional football team, and a chauffeured Rolls-Royce. Having lofty goals is fine if they work for you. I certainly set large goals for myself, and as a result of creating those internal representations, I was able to create the behaviors that supported them.

But just as goals and values change, evidence procedures do, too. People are happier if they also find intermediate goals to shoot for. These provide feedback that you are succeeding, that you can achieve your dreams. Some people might be totally motivated by the goal of a triathlete's body, the $2 million house, football team, and a Rolls-Royce. Others might first view success as running a 10K race effectively or working out consistently or changing dietary habits or having a beautiful $100,000 home or a loving relationship or family. After creating this outcome, they can set new ones. They could still reach for the more opulent vision, but they might get more satisfaction after achieving the earlier goal.

Another aspect of evidence procedures is specificity. If you place a value on romance, you might say your evidence procedure is to have a good relationship with an attractive and loving woman. That's a reasonable outcome worth pursuing. You may even have a good picture of the looks and personality traits you most want. That's fine, too. Another may have as an evidence procedure a tempestuous romance with a blond, blue-eyed Playboy bunny with a forty-two-inch bust, a Fifth Avenue condo in Manhattan, and a six-figure income. Only those exact submodalities will satisfy him. There's nothing wrong with having a target, but there is a great deal of potential for frustration if you link your values to a picture that's too specific. You're ruling out 99 percent of the people, things, or experiences that could satisfy you. That doesn't mean you can't create such results in your life—you can. However, with more flexibility in your evidence procedure, you will more easily fulfill your true desire or values.

There's a common thread here: the importance of flexibility. Remember that in any context, the system with the most flexibility, with the most choices, will be the most effective. It's absolutely crucial to remember that values have primacy for us, but we represent their primacy by the evidence procedures we adopt. You can choose a map of the world that's so circumscribed it almost guarantees frustration. Many of us do that. We say success is precisely this and a good relationship is precisely another thing. But taking all the flexibility out of the system is one of the surest ways to guarantee frustration.

The most wrenching questions people must grapple with usually involve their values. Sometimes two different values, like freedom and love, pull us in opposite directions. Freedom may mean the ability to do whatever you want at any time. Love may mean a commitment to one single person. Most of us have felt that conflict. When we do, it's not pleasant. However, it's critically important to know what our highest values are so that we choose behaviors that support them. If we don't, we will pay the emotional price later for not supporting what we believe is most important in our lives. Behaviors tied to the values higher on the hierarchy will supersede behaviors tied to lower-ranked values.

There's nothing so dismaying as having strong values pulling you in opposite directions. This creates a tremendous sense of incongruity. If the incongruity lasts long enough, it can destroy a relationship. You can act on one—for example, exercise your freedom—in a way that ruins the other. You can try to adapt—that is, stifle your urges toward freedom—in such a way that you become frustrated and destructive in the relationship. Or, since few of us really confront and understand our values, we might just experience a general sense of frustration and unease; soon we'll begin to filter all our experiences in life through these negative emotions until they become part of us, feelings of dissatisfaction that we may try to alleviate by overeating, smoking, and so on.

If you don't understand how values work, it's hard to come up with any sort of an elegant compromise. But if you do, you don't need to undermine either the relationship or your sense of freedom. You can change the evidence procedure. When you were a high school kid, maybe freedom meant trying to imitate Warren Beatty's sex life. But perhaps a loving relationship provides the comfort, the resources, and the joy that embody more real freedom than the ability to jump into bed with any person you meet at a bar. That's essentially the process of reframing an experience in a way that creates congruity.

Sometimes the incongruity comes not from the values themselves, but from the evidence procedures for different values. Success and spirituality don't have to produce incongruity. You can be a great success and still have a rich spiritual life. But what if your evidence procedure for success is having a great big mansion, and your evidence procedure for spirituality is living a simple, austere life? You'll have to either redefine your evidence procedures or reframe your perception. Otherwise, you could be dooming yourself to a life of inner conflicts. It may be useful to remember the belief system W. Mitchell has used to support himself in having a rich and happy life in spite of what would seem to be limiting circumstances: There is no absolute relationship between any two factors. That is, for him, being paralyzed does not mean you have to be unhappy. Having lots of money does not mean you're not spiritual, and living an austere life does not necessarily mean you are spiritual.

NLP provides tools for changing the structure of most experiences so they can create congruence. I once worked with a man who had a not uncommon problem. He had a loving relationship with a woman. But he also put a high value on being sexually attractive and interacting with other women. When he'd elicit sexual signals from an attractive woman, he'd begin to feel guilty because of the value he put on his relationship.

When he met an attractive woman, his syntax for attraction worked this way. He'd see such a woman (Ve) and he'd say something to himself (Aid): "This woman is gorgeous, and she wants me." This would lead to a feeling or desire to follow through (Ki), and sometimes desire became reality and he took action (Ke). But both the desire and any romantic adventures that ensued resulted in severe conflicts with his need for a strong, one-on-one relationship, which was a deep desire for him.

I taught him to add a new piece to his strategy, which had been Ve-Aid-Ki-Ke. I set it up so that after he saw a woman (Ve) and said to himself, "This is a beautiful woman, and she wants me" (Aid), I added another auditory internal phrase: "And I love the woman I'm with." Then I had him picture the woman he was involved with smiling at him and looking at him in a totally loving way (Vi), which created for him a new kinesthetic internal feeling, one that made him feel like loving the woman he was with. I had him install the strategy by repetition. I had him simply see a woman he'd be attracted to, say to himself,

"This is a beautiful woman and she wants me," immediately say the new auditory internal, "And I love the woman I'm with," in a loving tone of voice, and then picture his partner smiling at him in a loving way. I had him do this time after time after time until I was installed, just like a swish pattern, so that whenever an attractive woman walked by, it would immediately cause him to go through this new pattern.

This strategy allows him to have it all. His old strategy was pulling him in two directions at once, putting great strain on his relationship. Just stifling the urge to feel attractive would have made him frustrated and conflicted. The new strategy allows him to get the positive feelings of attraction he needs, while taking away the conflict that was undermining his relationship. Now the more he sees attractive women, the more he feels like loving the woman he's with.

The ultimate way to use values is to integrate them with metaprograms in order to motivate and understand ourselves and others. Values are the ultimate filter. Metaprograms are the operative patterns that guide most of our perceptions and thus our behaviors. If you know how to use the two together, you can develop the most precise motivational patterns.

I once worked with a young man who was so irresponsible he drove his parents crazy. His problem was that he lived completely in the moment, without any consideration for the consequences. If some things came along that kept him out all night, he didn't mean to be irresponsible. But he responded to the things that were directly in front of him (the things he was moving toward) rather than to the consequences of his actions (things he should move away from).

When I met this young man and talked with him, I elicited his metaprograms. I learned he moved toward things and acted from necessity. Then I began to elicit his values. It turned out his three highest values were security, happiness, and trust. Those were the main things he needed in life.

So I established rapport by matching and mirroring him. Then, in a totally congruent way, I began to explain how his behaviors were undermining all the things he placed the highest value on. He had just come home after being away for two full days without permission from or communication with his desperately upset parents. I told him that they were losing all patience and that his behavior was going to undermine all the security, happiness, and trust the family was providing for him. If he kept it up, he was going to be in a place with no security, no happiness, and no trust. That could be jail. It could be reform school. But if he wasn't responsible enough to live at home, his parents would have to send him someplace where someone else would be responsible for him.

So I gave him something to move away from, something that was the antithesis of his values. (Most people, even if they normally move toward, will move away from losing a key value.) Next I gave him the upbeat alternative, something to move toward. I gave him specific tasks that would serve as an evidence procedure for his parents to use to determine their ability to continue supporting the values of security, happiness, and trust that were so important to him. He was to be at home every night by ten P.M. He was to have a job within seven days. He was to do his duties at home every day. I told him that we would review his progress in sixty days, and if he kept his agreements, his parents' trust level would expand—and so would their support of his personal happiness and security. I made it clear to him that these were necessities, things he had to move toward right now. If he broke his agreement once, it would be viewed as a learning experience. If he broke his agreement twice, it would earn him a warning. If he broke his agreement a third time, he'd be gone.

What I did was give him things to move toward right away in order to maintain and increase his enjoyment of the things he valued. In the past, he just hadn't had the right things to move toward that supported his relationship with his parents. I also made it clear that these changes were totally necessary and gave him a very specific evidence procedure to follow. When last heard from, he was still behaving like a model kid. His values and metaprograms together provided the ultimate motivating tools. I had given him a way to create for himself the security, happiness, and trust he needed.

> *"He who knows much about others may be learned, but he who understands himself is more intelligent. He who controls others may be powerful, but he who has mastered himself is mightier still."*
>
> —Lao-Tsu, *Tao Teh King*

I think you can see just how explosive values are and how valuable they can be as tools for change. In the past, your values have operated almost entirely at the subconscious level. Now, you have the ability to both understand and manipulate them for positive change. There was a time when we didn't know what an atom was, so we were unable to make use of its awesome power. Learning about values has much the same effect on us. By bringing them to consciousness, we can produce results we never could before. We can play with buttons that we didn't know existed before. Remember, values are belief systems that have global effects. So by making changes in values—either in eliminating conflicts or enhancing the power of empowering values—we can make profound changes in our entire life.

Instead of feeling uneasy about value conflicts we barely understood in the past, we can understand what's going on within us, or between us and others, and begin to generate new results. We do this in many ways. We can reframe the experience so that it's most effective. We can change our evidence procedures by manipulating their submodalities, as we've done throughout this book. When values conflict, the real conflict is often between one of many evidence procedures. We can turn down the picture and the sound in such a way as to make the conflict unnoticeable. In some cases, we can even change the values themselves. If you have a value you wish were higher on your hierarchy, you can change its submodalities so it's more like those at the top of the hierarchy. In most cases, it's much easier and more effective to deal with submodalities, but I think you can see just how powerful these techniques can be. In this way, you can change the level of importance of values by changing the way you represent them to your brain.

For example, there was a man I was counseling whose number-one value was usefulness. Love was number nine on his ladder. As you can imagine, with this kind of a value hierarchy he did many things that did not build tremendous amounts of rapport with other human beings. I found out that he represented his number-one value, usefulness, as a big picture, moved to the right, very bright, with a certain tone associated with it. After comparing it with how he represented a much lower-ranked value, love (a much smaller picture in black and white with a different position, lower, darker, dimmer, defocused), all I needed to do was make the submodalities of the lower-ranked value exactly like those of the higher-ranked value and make the submodalities of the higher-ranked value just like those of the lower-ranked value, then create a swish pattern to keep them there. By doing this, we changed the way he felt about his values; we changed his hierarchy. Love became his number-one value. This radically altered the way he perceived the world, what was most important to him, and thus the kind of actions he created on a consistent basis.

Changing someone's value hierarchy can have huge implications that may not be immediately apparent. It's usually best to start by discovering a person's evidence procedure and changing his perception of whether he's achieving his values before actually changing the ladder of importance.

I think you can see how this would be valuable in a personal relationship. Suppose a person's number-one value is attraction, number two is honest communication, number three is creativity, and number four is respect. There are two approaches to creating a feeling of satisfaction within this same relationship. One would be to make respect the number-one value and make attraction number four. Thereby, you could take an individual who is no longer attracted to his partner and make that feeling less important than his respect for her. As long as he felt he respected her, he would feel his highest need was being fulfilled. A simpler and less radical approach would be to determine his evidence procedure for finding someone attractive. What does he have to see, hear, feel? Then, either change that attraction strategy or have him share with his partner what he needs to have that value fulfilled.

Most of us have some values that conflict. We want to go out and produce great results in the world, and we want to relax on the beach; we want to spend time with our families, and we want to work hard enough to be a success at our jobs. We want security and we want excitement. Some value conflict is inevitable; it lends a certain richness and texture to life. The problem comes when fundamental values pull us in different directions. After reading this chapter, look at your value hierarchy and evidence procedures to see where the conflicts are. Seeing them clearly is the first step to resolving them.

Values have primacy for societies as well as for individuals. The history of the United States over the past twenty years is a wrenching study in the importance and variability of values. What was the upheaval of the sixties but a cataclysmic example of values in conflict? Suddenly, a huge and vocal segment of society was professing values that clashed radically with those of society as a whole. Many of our country's most cherished values—patriotism, family, marriage, the work ethic—were suddenly being questioned. The result was a period of societal incongruity and turmoil.

There are two main differences between now and then. One is that most of the kids of the sixties have found new and more positive ways to express their values. In the sixties, a person may have felt that freedom meant using drugs and growing long hair. Now, in the eighties, the same person may feel that owning a business and being in control of his life is the most effective way to achieve the same result. The other difference is that our values have changed. When you look at the evolution of American values over the last twenty-five years, you don't really see the victory of one set of values over another. Instead, you see that a different set of values has evolved. In some ways, we've gone back to some traditional values about patriotism or family life. In others, we've adopted many of the values of the sixties.

We're more tolerant, we have different values about the rights of women and minorities, about the nature of productive and satisfying work.

There's a helpful lesson for all of us in what's evolved. Values change, and people change. The only people who don't change are those who don't breathe. So the important thing is to be aware of that flux and to move with it. Remember the example of the people who are stuck on one outcome, only to find it no longer fits their values? A lot of us find ourselves in that situation at different times. The way around it is to attentively and actively recognize our values and the evidence procedures we've constructed for them.

We all have to live with some degree of incongruity. That's part of the ambiguity of being human. Just as societies go through periods of flux like the sixties, people do, too. But if we know what's happening, we're better able to cope with it and to change what we can. If we feel the incongruity and don't understand it, we'll often take inappropriate kinds of action. We'll start smoking, or drinking, or whatever we do to handle frustration we don't understand. So the first step toward dealing with value conflicts is to understand them. The Ultimate Success Formula holds true for values as well as for anything else. You need to know what you want—your primary values and your value hierarchy. You need to take action. You need to develop the sensory acuity to know what you're getting. And you need to develop the flexibility to change. If your present behaviors don't match your values, you need to modify your behaviors to resolve the conflict.

There's a final point worth considering. Remember, we're all modeling all the time. Our kids, our employees, and our business associates are always modeling us in different ways. If we want to be effective models, there's nothing more important than to effect strong values and congruent behavior. Modeling behaviors is important, but values override almost everything else. If you stand for commitment as your life reflects unhappiness and confusion, those who see you as a model will link up the idea of commitment with confused unhappiness. If you stand for commitment as your life reflects excitement and joy, you're providing a congruent model that links up commitment and joy.

Think of the people who have affected you most in your life. Chances are they've provided the most effective, congruent models. They're the people whose values and behaviors provided the most vibrant, compelling model of success. The most important motivating forces in history, religious books like the Bible, are about nothing so much as values. The stories they tell, the situations they describe, are models that have enriched the lives of most people on the planet by giving those values great power.

Discovering someone's values is simply a matter of finding out what is most important to him or her. In knowing that, you can more effectively know not just their needs but your own. In the next chapter, we are going to look at the five things every successful person has to confront and deal with in order to use and apply all we've talked about in this book. I call them the . . .

CHAPTER XIX

The Five Keys to Wealth and Happiness

"Man is not the creature of circumstances.

Circumstances are the creatures of men."

—Benjamin Disraeli

You now have the resources to take absolute charge of your life. You have the ability to form the internal representations and produce the states that lead to success and power. But having the ability isn't always the same as using it. There are certain experiences that time and again put people in unresourceful states. There are bends in the road, rapids in the river, that snare people time and time again. There are experiences that consistently prevent people from being all they can be. In this chapter, I want to give you a map showing where the perils are and what you need to know to overcome them.

I call these the five keys to wealth and happiness. If you're going to use all the abilities you now have, if you're going to be all you can be, you're going to have to understand these keys. Every person who is successful has to, sooner or later. If you

371

do, if you can handle them consistently, your life will be an indomitable success.

Not long ago I was in Boston. After a seminar one night, I took a midnight stroll around Copley Square. I was taking in the buildings, which range from modern skyscrapers to structures as old as America, when I noticed a man wobbling back and forth, coming my way. He looked as though he'd been sleeping in the street for weeks. He smelled of alcohol and looked as if he hadn't shaved for months.

I figured he would come up and beg for money. Well, as you think, so you attract. He approached and asked, "Mister, could you loan me a quarter?" First I asked myself if I wanted to reward his behavior. Then I told myself I didn't want him to suffer. Either way, a quarter was not going to make much difference. So I figured the least I could do was try to teach him a lesson. "A quarter? That's what you want, a quarter?" And he said, "Just a quarter." So I reached in my pocket, pulled out a quarter, and said, "Life will pay any price you ask of it." The guy looked stunned, and then he staggered away.

As I watched him go, I thought about the differences between those who succeed and those who fail. I thought, What's the difference between him and me? Why is my life such a joy that I can do whatever I want, whenever I want, wherever I want, with whomever I want, as much as I want? He's maybe sixty years old and living in the street, begging for quarters. Did God come down and say, "Robbins, you've been good. You get to live your dream life"? It's not likely. Did someone give me superior resources or advantages? I don't think so. I was once in a state almost as bad as his, although I didn't drink as much alcohol or sleep in the street.

I think part of the difference is the answer I gave him—that life will pay you whatever you ask of it. Ask for a quarter, and that's what you'll get. Ask for resounding joy and success, you'll get that, too. Everything I've studied convinces me that if you learn to manage your states and manage your behaviors, you can change anything. You can learn what to ask of life, and you can be sure to get it. Over the following months, I met more street people and asked them about their lives and how they got there. I began to find we had similar challenges in common. The difference was how we handled them.

> *"Whatever kind of word thou speakest, the like shalt thou hear."*
>
> —*Greek Proverb*

Let me share with you five things to use as road signs to success. There's nothing profound or abstruse about them. But they're absolutely crucial. If you master them, there's no limit to what you can do. If you don't use them, you've already placed the limits on how high you can go. Affirmation and positive thinking are a start, but they're not the full answer. Affirmation without discipline is the beginning of delusion. Affirmation with discipline creates miracles.

Here's the first key to the creation of wealth and happiness. *You must learn how to handle frustration.* If you want to become all you can become, do all you can do, hear all you can hear, see all you can see, you've got to learn how to handle frustration. Frustration can kill dreams. It happens all the time. Frustration can change a positive attitude into a negative one, an empowering state into a crippling one. The worst thing a negative attitude does is wipe out self-discipline. And when that discipline is gone, the results you desire are gone.

So to ensure long-term success, you must learn how to discipline your frustration. Let me tell you something. The key to success is massive frustration. Look at almost any great success, and you'll find there's been massive frustration along the way. Anybody who tells you otherwise doesn't know anything about achieving. There are two kinds of people—those who've handled frustration and those who wish they had.

There's a little company called Federal Express. A guy named Fred Smith started the company, and he built a multimillion-dollar business out of mounds of frustration. When he started the company, after financing it with every dime he had, he hoped to deliver approximately 150 packages. Instead, he delivered sixteen, five of which the business sent to the home of one of its employees. Things got worse from there. Periodically, employees cashed their payroll checks at convenience stores because funds weren't available to cover the checks. Many times their planes were in the process of being repossessed, and sometimes they had to bring in a certain amount in sales during a day to keep operating. Federal Express is now a billion-dollar company. The only reason it's still there is that Fred Smith was able to handle frustration upon frustration.

People get paid very well to handle frustration. If you're broke, it's probably because you're not handling very much frustration. You say, "Well, I'm broke, and that's why I'm frustrated." You've got it backward. If you handled more frustration, you would be rich. A major difference between people who are financially secure and people who are not is how they handle frustration. I'm not callous enough to suggest that poverty doesn't have huge frustrations. I'm saying the way not to be poor is to take on more and more frustration until you succeed. People say, "Well, people with money don't have any problems." If they take on enough, they probably have more problems. They just know how to deal with them, to come up with new strategies, new alternatives. Remember, being rich is not just a matter of having money. A superb relationship provides problems and challenges. If you don't want problems, you shouldn't have a relationship at all. There's great frustration on the road to any great success—in a business, in a relationship, in a life.

The greatest gift that *Optimum Performance Technologies*® provide us is that they teach us how to handle frustration in an effective way. You can take things that used to make you frustrated and program them so they make you excited. Tools like NLP are not just positive thinking. The problem with positive thinking is that you have to think about it—and by that time, it's often too late to do what you want to do.

What NLP offers is a way to turn stress into opportunity. You already know how to take the images that once depressed you and make them wither and disappear or change them to the images that bring you ecstasy. It's not hard to do. You already know how.

Here's a two-step formula for handling stress. Step 1: Don't sweat the small stuff. Step 2: Remember, it's all small stuff.

All successful people learn that success is buried on the other side of frustration. Unfortunately, some people don't get to the other side. People who fail to achieve their goals usually get stopped by frustration. They allow frustration to keep them from taking the necessary actions that would support them in achieving their desire. You get through this road-block by plowing through frustration, taking each setback as feedback you can learn from, and pushing ahead. I doubt you'll find many successful people who have not experienced this.

Here's the second key. *You must learn how to handle rejection.* When I repeat that in a seminar, I can feel the physiology in the room change. Is there anything in the human language with more sting than the tiny word "no"? If you're in sales, what's the difference between making $100,000 and making $25,000? The main difference is learning how to handle rejection so that this fear no longer stops you from taking action. The best salesmen are those who are rejected the most. They're the ones who can take any "no" and use it as a prod to go onto the next "yes."

The biggest challenge for people in our culture is that they can't handle the word "no." Remember the question I asked earlier? What would you do if you knew you could not fail? Think about it now. If you knew you couldn't fail, would that change your behavior? Would that allow you to do exactly what you want to do? So what's keeping you from doing it? It's that tiny word "no." To succeed, you must learn how to cope with rejection, learn how to strip that rejection of all its power.

I once worked with a high jumper. He had been an Olympic athlete but had reached the point where he no longer could jump his hat size. I immediately saw what his problem was when I watched him jump. Sure enough, he hit the bar and started going through all sorts of emotional gyrations. He turned each failure into a big event. I called him over and told him that if he wanted to work with me, he would never do that again. He was storing the whole thing as failure. He was sending a message to his brain that reinforced the image of failure, so it was there the next time he jumped. Each time he jumped, his brain was more concerned with failing than with being in the resourceful state that brings succcess.

I told him if he hit the bar again, he should tell himself, Aha! Another distinction, not, @#&*@!%$*!!! Another failure. He should put himself back into a resourceful state and go for it again. Within three jumps he was performing better than he had in two years. It doesn't take a lot to change. The difference between seven feet and six feet four inches is only 10 percent. It's not a big difference in height, but it's a big difference in performance. In the same way, small changes can make a big change in the quality of your life.

Ever hear of a guy named Rambo? Sylvester Stallone? Did he just show up at the door of some agent or studio and hear, "Hey, we like your body. We're going to put you in a movie"? Not exactly. Sylvester Stallone became a success because he was able to withstand rejection after rejection. When he started out, he was rejected more than a thousand times. He went to every agent he could find in New York, and everyone said no. But he kept pushing, kept trying, and finally he made a movie called *Rocky*. He could hear the word "no" a thousand times and then go knock on door 1,001.

How many "no's" can you take? How many times have you wanted to go up and talk to someone you found attractive, then decided not to do it because you didn't want to hear the word "no"? How many of you decided not to try for a job or make a sales call or audition for a part because you didn't want to be rejected? Think about how crazy that is. Think how you're creating limits just because of your fear of that little two-letter word. The word itself has no power. It can't cut your skin or sap your strength. Its power comes from the way you represent it to yourself. Its power comes from the limits it makes you create. And what do limited thoughts create? Limited lives.

So when you learn to run your brain, you can learn to handle rejection. You can even anchor yourself so the word "no" turns you on. You can take any rejection and turn it into an opportunity. If you're in telephone sales, you can anchor yourself so that simply reaching for the phone puts you in ecstasy rather than raising the fear of rejection. Remember, success is buried on the other side of rejection.

There are no real successes without rejection. The more rejection you get, the better you are, the more you've learned, the closer you are to your outcome. The next time somebody rejects you, you might give him a hug. That'll change his physiology. Turn "no's" into hugs. If you can handle rejection, you'll learn to get everything you want.

Here's the third key to wealth and happiness. *You must learn to handle financial pressure.* The only way not to have financial pressure is not to have any finances. There are many kinds of financial pressure, and they've destroyed many people. They can create greed, envy, deceit, or paranoia. They can rob you of your sensitivity or rob you of your friends. Now remember, I said they can, not that they will. Handling financial pressure means knowing how to get and knowing how to give, knowing how to earn and knowing how to save.

When I first started to make money, I started to catch hell for it. My friends disowned me. They said, "You're into money. What's your problem?" I said, "I'm not into money. I just have some." They wouldn't see it that way. People somehow suddenly perceived me as a different person because I had a different financial status. Some were very resentful. So that's one kind of financial pressure. Not having enough money is another kind of financial pressure. You probably feel that pressure every day. Most people do. But whether you have a lot or a little, you deal with financial pressure.

Remember that all of our actions in life are guided by our philosophies, our guiding internal representations about how to act. They give us the models of how to behave. George S. Clason provided a great model for learning to handle financial pressure in *The Richest Man in Babylon*. Have you read it? If so, read it again. If not, run out and get it now. It's a book that can make you totally wealthy, happy, and excited. To me, the most im-

portant thing the book teaches is to take 10 percent of all you
earn up front and give it away. That's right. Why? One reason
is that you should put back what you take out. Another is that
it creates value for you and for others. Most important, it says
to the world and to your own subconscious that there is more
than enough. And that's a very powerful belief to nurture. If
there's more than enough, it means you can have what you want
and others can, too. And when you hold that thought, you make
it come true.

When do you start to give the 10 percent away? When you're
rich and famous? No. You should do it when you're starting
out. Because what you give away becomes like your seed corn.
You've got to invest it, not eat it, and the best way to invest it
is to give it away so that it produces value for others. You won't
have trouble finding the ways. There is need all around us. One
of the most valuable things about doing this is how this makes
you feel about yourself. When you're the kind of person who
tries to find and fill other people's needs, it makes you feel differently about who you are. And from those kinds of feelings
or states, you live your life in an attitude of gratitude.

I had the good fortune the other day to return to my high
school in Glendora, California. I'm doing a program for teachers, and I wanted to acknowledge the teachers who have affected
my life. When I arrived, I realized that a speech program that
taught me how to express myself had been cut for lack of funding
and because people didn't think it was important enough. So I
funded the program. I gave back a portion of what had been
given to me. I didn't do it because I'm a swell guy. I did it
because I owe it. And isn't it nice to know that when you owe
something, you can pay it back? That's the real reason to have
money. We all have positive debts. The best reason to have
money is to be able to pay them back.

When I was a kid, our parents worked extremely hard to take
good care of us. For various reasons we found ourselves in extremely tight financial situations. I remember one Thanksgiving
when we had no money. Things were looking dim until someone
arrived at the front door with a box full of canned goods and a

turkey. The man who delivered it said it was from someone who knew we would not ask for anything and loved us and wanted us to have a great Thanksgiving. I never forgot that day. So every Thanksgiving, I do what someone did for me that day: I go out and buy about a week's worth of food and deliver it to a family in need. I deliver the food as the worker or delivery boy, never as the person actually providing the gift. I always leave a note that says, "This is from someone who cares about you and hopes someday you will take good-enough care of yourself that you'll go out and return the favor for someone else in need."

It's becoming one of the highlights of my year. Seeing people's faces when they know someone cares—making a difference—that's what life is all about. One year I wanted to give away turkeys in Harlem, but we didn't have a van, or even a car, and everything was closed. My staff said, "Let's forget it this year," and I said, "No, I'm going to do it." They asked, "How are you going to do it? You don't even have a van to make deliveries from." I said there were plenty of vans on the street; we just needed to find one that would take us. I started to flag down vans, not a practice I would recommend in New York. Many drivers there think they're on a search-and-destroy mission, and the fact that it was Thanksgiving didn't change anything.

So I went to a stoplight and started knocking on van windows, telling people I'd give them $100 if they'd take us to Harlem. When that didn't work too well, either, I changed my message a little. I told people I wanted to take an hour and a half of their time to deliver food to needy people in an "impoverished area" of the city. That got us a little closer.

I had already decided that I wanted to go in a van that was long enough and big enough to make a large delivery. Sure enough, this beautiful van, fire-mist burgundy, pulled up, and it was extra long, with an extension on the back. I said, "That's it." One of my people ran across the street and caught it at the light, knocked on the window, and offered the driver $100 if he'd drive us where we wanted. The driver said, "Look, you

don't have to pay me. I'll be happy to take you." This was the
tenth person we'd tried. Then he reached over, picked up his
hat, and put it on. It said Salvation Army. He said his name
was Captain John Rondon, and he wanted to make sure we
brought food to people who were really needy.

So instead of just delivering food to Harlem, we also went
to the South Bronx, which is one of the most blighted landscapes
in the country. We drove past the vacant lots and the bombed–
out buildings to a grocery in the South Bronx. There we bought
food and delivered it to the squatters, urban refugees, street
people, and families struggling to make a decent life.

I don't know how much we changed those people's lives, but
according to Captain Rondon, it changed their belief about people caring. No amount of money can buy what you get when
you give of yourself. No amount of financial planning could do
more for you than if you give 10 percent away. It teaches you
what money can do, and it teaches you what money can't do.
And those are two of the most valuable lessons you can learn.
I used to think the best way to help poor people was to be one
of them. I found out the opposite may be true. The best way
to help poor people is to be a model of other possibilities, to let
them know there is another set of choices available, and to assist
them in developing the resources to become self-sufficient.

After you give away 10 percent of your income, take another
10 percent to reduce your debts and a third 10 percent to build
up capital to invest. You need to live on 70 percent of what you
have. We live in a capitalistic society in which most human
beings are not capitalists. As a result, they don't have the life–
style they desire. Why live in a capitalistic society, surrounded
by opportunity, and not take advantage of the very system our
forefathers fought to create? Learn to take your money and use
it as capital. If you are spending it, you'll never build up any
capital. You'll never have the resources you need. It's been said
that in California the average income is now $25,000 a year.
The average outgo is $30,000. The difference is called financial
pressure. You don't want to join that crowd.

The bottom line is that money is like everything else. You

can make it work for you, or you can let it work against you. You should be able to deal with money as with anything else in your mind, with the same purpose and elegance. Learn to earn, to save, and to give. If you can do that, you'll learn to handle the financial pressure, and the money will never again be a stimulus to putting you in a negative state that causes you to be unhappy or treat others around you in a less–than–resourceful way.

When you master the first three keys, you will begin to experience your life as hugely successful. If you can handle frustration, rejection, and financial pressure, there's no limit to what you can do. Ever see Tina Turner perform? She is someone who has handled massive amounts of all three. After becoming a star, she lost her marriage, lost her money, and spent eight years in a show business purgatory of hotel lounges and cheap clubs. She couldn't get people to return her phone calls, much less offer her a recording contract. But she kept plugging, kept tuning out the "no's," kept working to pay off debts and put her financial house in order. Finally she came all the way back to the top of the entertainment world.

So you can do anything. And that's where number four butts in. *You must learn how to handle complacency*. You've seen people in your life, or celebrities or athletes, who reach a level of success and then stop. They start to get comfortable, and they lose what got them there in the first place.

> *"That which is achieved the most, still has the whole if its future yet to be achieved."*
> —*Lao-Tsu, Tao Teh King*

Comfort can be one of the most disastrous emotions a body could have. What happens when a person gets too comfortable? He stops growing, stops working, stops creating added value. You don't want to get too comfortable. If you feel really comfortable, chances are you've stopped growing. What did Bob Dylan say? "He who's not busy being born is busy dying." You're either climbing or your sliding. Ray Kroc, the founder of McDonald's, was once asked if he were to give one piece of advice to someone to guarantee a long life of success, what would it be? He said to simply remember this: When you're green you grow; when you ripen, you rot. As long as you remain green, you grow. You can take any experience and make it an opportunity for growth, or you can take it and make it an invitation to decay. You can see retirement as the beginning of a richer life, or you can see it as the end of your working life. You can see success as a springboard to greater things, or you can see it as a resting place. And if it's a resting place, chances are you won't keep it for long.

One kind of complacency comes from comparison. I use to think I was doing well because I was doing well compared with people I knew. That's one of the biggest mistakes you can make. Maybe it just means your friends aren't doing very well. *Learn to judge yourself by your goals instead of by what your peers seem to be doing*. Why? Because you can always find people to justify what you're doing.

Didn't you do that as a kid? Didn't you say, "Johnny did this, why can't I?" Your mother probably said, "Well, I don't care what Johnny does," and she was right. You shouldn't care what Johnny or Mary or the Joneses do. Care about what you're capable of. Care about what you create and what you want to do. Work from a set of dynamic, evolving, enabling goals that will help you do what you want, not what someone else has done. There will always be someone who has more than you. There will always be someone who has less. None of that matters. You need to judge yourself by your goals and nothing else.

> *"Little things affect little minds."*
>
> —*Benjamin Disraeli*

Here's another way to avoid complacency. Stay away from coffeepot seminars. You know what I'm talking about. The sessions where everyone else's work habits, sex life, financial status, and everything else become fair game. "Coffeepot seminars" are like suicide. They poison your brain by getting you to focus your attention on what other people are doing in their private lives instead of what you can be doing to enhance your experience of life. It's easy to get caught up in these "seminars," but just remember that people who do are merely trying to distract themselves from the boredom created by their inability to produce the results they desire in their own life.

There's a phrase that Rolling Thunder, the Indian wise man, used often, and that was, "Speak with good purpose only." Remember, what we put out comes back to us. So my challenge to you is to stay away from the garbage of life. *Don't major in minor things*. If you want to be complacent and mediocre, spend your time gossiping about who is sleeping with whom. If you want to make a difference, make sure you challenge yourself, test yourself, make your life special.

Here's the last key. *Always give more than you expect to receive*. This may be the most important key of all because it virtually guarantees true happiness.

I remember driving home from a meeting one night, almost asleep. The speed bumps kept jolting me into consciousness. And in this half-awake state, I was trying to figure out what gave life meaning. All of a sudden, a little voice in my head said, "The secret to living is giving."

If you want to make your life work, you have to start with how to give. Most people start their life thinking about nothing but how to receive. Receiving is not a problem. Receiving is like the ocean. But you've got to make sure you are giving so you can start the process in motion. The problem in life is people want things first. A couple will come to me, and the man will say his wife doesn't treat him well. And the woman will say that's because he's not very affectionate. So they're each waiting for the other to make the first move, provide the first proof.

What kind of a relationship is that? How long is it going to last? The key to any relationship is that you have to give first and then keep giving. Don't stop and wait to receive. When you start keeping score, the game's over. You're standing there saying, "I gave, now it's her turn," and the game is over. She's gone. You can take your score to the next spinning planet because the scoreboard doesn't work that way here. You've got to be willing to plant the seed and then nurture its growth.

What would happen if you went to the soil and said, "Give me some fruit. Give me some plants"? The soil would probably respond, "Excuse me, sir, but you're a little confused. You must be new here. That's not the way the game is played." Then it would explain that you plant the seed. You take care of it. You water it and till the soil. You fertilize it. You protect it and nurture it. Then, if you do it well, you will get your plant or your fruit sometime later. You could ask of the soil forever, but it wouldn't change things. You have to keep giving, keep nurturing, for the soil to bear fruit—and life's exactly the same way.

You can make a lot of money. You can lord over kingdoms or run huge businesses or control vast terrain. But if you're just doing for yourself, you're not really a success. You don't really have power. You don't have real wealth. If you make it to the top of "success mountain" by yourself, you'll probably jump off.

You want to know the biggest illusion about success? That it's like a pinnacle to be climbed, a thing to be possessed, or a static result to be achieved. If you want to succeed, if you want to achieve all your outcomes, you have to think of success as a process, a way of life, a habit of mind, a strategy for life. That's what this chapter has been about. You must know what you have, and you must know the perils in your way. You must have the ability to use your power in a responsible and loving way if you are to experience true wealth and happiness. If you can handle these five things, you'll be able to use all the skills and powers taught in this book to do wondrous things.

Now let's take a look at how change works on a larger level, the level of groups and communities and nations.

CHAPTER XX

Trend Creation: The Power of Persuasion

"We are not going to be able to operate our Spaceship Earth successfully nor for much longer unless we see it as a whole spaceship and our fate as common. It has to be everybody or nobody."

—*Buckminster Fuller*

So far we've dealt mostly with individual change, the ways people can grow and become empowered. But one of the unmistakable aspects of the modern world is the amount of change that happens on a mass level. The idea of a global village has long since become a cliché, but it's still true. Never before in the history of the world have there been so many powerful mechanisms for massive, lasting group persuasion. That can mean more people buying Cokes, wearing Levi's jeans, and listening to rock-and-roll bands. It can also mean massive, positive shifts in attitudes around the world. It all depends on who's doing the persuading and why. In this chapter, we're going to look at the changes that happen on a mass scale, see how they happen, and examine what they mean. Then we're going to look at how you can become a persuader and what you can do with your abilities.

We think of our world today as being awash in stimuli, but that's not what realy differentiates it from earlier times. An Indian walking through the woods was constantly confronted with sights and sounds and smells that could mean the difference between life and death, between eating and starving. There was no shortage of stimuli in his world.

The biggest difference today is in the intent and reach of the stimuli. The Indian in the forest had to interpret the meaning of the random stimuli. In contrast, our world is full of stimuli that are consciously directed to get us to do something. It might be a plea to buy a car or a mandate to vote for a candidate. It might be an appeal to save starving children or a pitch to get us to buy more cake and cookies. It might be an attempt to make us feel good about having something or a message to make us feel bad that we don't have something else. But the main thing that characterizes the modern world is the persistence of persuasion. We're constantly surrounded by people with the means and the technology and the know-how to persuade us to do something. And that persuasion has global reach. The same image that's being pounded into us can be pounded into most of the world at the exact same instant.

Let's consider the habit of smoking cigarettes. People in earlier times could have pleaded ignorance. But today we know that cigarettes are harmful to our health. They contribute to everything from cancer to heart disease. There's even a large amount of powerful public sentiment—expressed through local antismoking drives or referenda—that makes smokers feel they're doing something bad. People have every reason in the world not to smoke. Yet the tobacco industry continues to profit, and millions of people continue to smoke cigarettes, with more starting all the time. Why is that?

People may learn to enjoy the experience of smoking, but is that what got them started? They had to be taught how to use a cigarette as a trigger to create pleasure; it was not a natural response. What happened when they first smoked? They hated it. They coughed and gagged and felt nauseated. Their body said, "This stuff is terrible. Get it away from me." In most cases, if your own physical evidence tells you something is bad, you would expect to listen. So why don't people do that with smoking? Why do they continue to smoke until the body gives in and finally becomes addicted?

They do it because they've been reframed as to what smoking means, and then that new representation and state have been anchored into place. Someone with a great deal of knowledge about persuasion has spent millions and millions of dollars to convince the public that smoking is something desirable. Through skillful advertising, clever images and sounds were used to put us in positive-feeling states; then those desired states were associated with or linked to a product called cigarettes. Through massive repetition, the idea of smoking has been linked with various desirable states. There's no inherent value or social content to a piece of paper wrapped around tiny tobacco leaves. But we've been persuaded that smoking is sexy, or suave, or adult, or macho. Want to be like the Marlboro man? Smoke a cigarette. Want to show that you've come a long way, Baby? Smoke a cigarette. You've come a long way all right—if you've been smoking, you've probably come a long way closer to the possibility of lung cancer.

How crazy is this? What in the world does putting carcinogens into your lungs have to do with any desirable state? But advertisers do on a mass scale exactly what we've talked about in this book. They put out images that put you in a receptive, elevated state—and at the peak of the experience, they anchor you with their message. Then they repeat it on television, in magazines, or on the radio so that the anchor gets constantly reinforced and triggered.

Why does Coke pay Bill Cosby or Pepsi pay Michael Jackson to sell its products? Why do politicians wrap themselves in the flag? Why is Miller brewed the American way? Why do we love hot dogs, baseball, apple pie, and Chevrolet? These people and symbols are already powerful anchors in the culture, and the advertisers are simply transferring the feeling we have for these people or symbols to their products. They use them as ways to make us receptive to their products. Why did the Reagan TV campaign ads play off the ominous symbol of the bear in the woods? The bear, symbolizing Russia, was a powerful negative anchor that reinforced the image of the need for strong leadership, something Reagan proposed he would continue to provide. Haven't you seen bears in the woods and felt they were cuddly? Why did this ad affect people in such an ominous way? Because of the setting—the lighting and the words and music used.

You can break down any effective ad or political campaign and find it follows the precise framework we've set up in this book. First it uses visual and auditory stimuli to put you in the state the promoters desire. Then it anchors your state to a product or action they wish you to take. This, of course, is done time and time again until your nervous system effectively links the state with the product or desired behavior. If it's a good ad, it will use images and sounds that attract and affect all three major representational systems: visual, auditory, and kinesthetic. TV is such a persuasive medium because it can make the best use of all three: it can give you pretty pictures, it can include a catchy song or jingle, and it can provide a message with emotional punch. Think of the most effective ads done for a soft drink like Coke or a beer like Miller or a fast-food restaurant like McDonald's. Think of the "Reach Out and Touch Someone" ads for the phone company. What they all have in common is a strong V-A-K mix that offers a hook for everyone.

Of course, there are some ads that are effective in producing the opposite image—they break the state in as stark a manner as possible. Think of antismoking ads. Have you ever seen the one showing a fetus smoking a cigarette in its mother's womb? Or Brooke Shields looking dopey with cigarettes coming out of her ears? Those ads are most effective when they function as pattern interrupts, when they destroy the aura of glamour someone else has tried to create around an unhealthful product.

In a world full of persuaders, you can be one, too, or you can be someone who gets persuaded. You can direct your life or be directed. This book has really been about persuasion. It's shown you how to develop the personal power that can put you in control so you can do the persuading, whether as a role model for your kids or as a powerful force at work. The people in power are the persuaders. The people without power simply act on the images and commands that are directed their way.

Power today is the ability to communicate and the ability to persuade. If you're a persuader with no legs, you'll persuade someone to carry you. If you have no money, you'll persuade someone to lend you some. Persuasion may be the ultimate skill for creating change. After all, if you're a persuader who's alone in the world and doesn't want to be, you'll find a friend or a lover. If you're a persuader with a good product to sell, you'll find someone who'll buy it. You can have an idea or a product that can change the world, but without the power to persuade, you have nothing. Communicating what you have to offer is what life is all about. It's the msot important skill you can develop.

Let me give you an example of how powerful this technology is and how much you can do once you master the techniques NLP offers. When I created my first twelve-day Neuro-Linguistic Professionals training, I decided to come up with an exercise that would really make people use what they had learned. So here's what I did. I got everyone in the course together at eleven-thirty at night and told them to give me their keys, their cash, their credit cards, their wallets—everything but the clothes on their backs.

I told them I wanted to prove that to succeed they didn't need anything but their own personal power and persuasive abilities. I said they had the skills to find and fill people's needs, and they didn't need money, status, a vehicle, or anything else the culture teaches us we need to make our lives the way we want them.

We were meeting in Carefree, Arizona. The first challenge was to find a way to get to Phoenix, about an hour away by car. I told them to take excellent care of themselves, to use their skill to arrive healthfully in Phoenix, find a nice place to stay, eat well, and use their persuasion skills in any other ways that seemed effective and empowering, both for themselves and for others.

The results were amazing. Many of them were able to get bank loans of from $100 to $500 simply on the force of their personal power and congruence. Remember, they had no identification whatsoever, and they were in a city they'd never been in before. One woman went to a large department store and, without any identification at all, got credit cards she used on the spot. Of the 120 people who went out, about 80 percent were able to get a job, and 7 people got three or more jobs in that one day. One woman wanted to work at the zoo. She was told the zoo had a six-month waiting list just for volunteers. But she developed so much rapport that she was allowed to come in and work with the animals. She even treated a sick parrot by using NLP skills to stimulate its nervous system. The zoo trainer was so impressed that she ended up doing a miniseminar on how to use these tools to positively affect animals. One guy, who loved children and always wanted to speak to a large group of them, went to a school and said, "I'm the speaker for the assembly. When do I start?" The people said, "What assembly?" He said, "You know, the assembly scheduled for today. I've come a long way. I can wait for up to an hour, but we've got to get started soon." No one was quite sure who he was, but he seemed so sure and congruent, they decided there had to be an assembly. So they got the kids together, and he talked for an hour and a half on how kids could make their lives better. The kids and teachers loved it.

Another woman walked into a bookstore and started autographing a book by TV evangelist Terry Cole-Whittaker. She didn't look anything like Terry Cole-Whittaker, whose picture was on the cover. But she modeled Terry Cole's walk and facial expressions and laugh so well that the store manager—after being upset with this stranger writing in his books—did a double-take and said, "I'm so sorry, Ms. Cole-Whittaker. It's an honor to have you here." A couple of other people asked for autographs and bought books while she was there. That day, a number of resourceful individuals cleared up people's phobias and other assorted emotional problems. The point of this exercise was to show these people that they needed nothing more than their own resourceful behaviors and skills to find their way around—without all the usual support systems (such as transportation, money, reputation, contacts, credit, and so on)—and the majority of them had one of the most powerful and enjoyable days of their lives. They all made great friends and helped hundreds of people.

In the first chapter, we talked about how people have different feelings about power. Some think it's somehow unseemly; it means having undue control over others. Let me tell you, in the modern world, persuasion isn't a choice. It's an ever-present fact of life. Someone is always doing the persuading. People are spending millions and millions of dollars to get their messages out with ultimate power and skill. So either you do the persuading, or someone else does. The difference in our chidren's behavior may be the difference between who is a greater persuader—you and I or the drug pusher. If you want to have control of your life, if you want to be the most elegant, effective model for those you care about, you've got to learn how to be a persuader. If you abdicate responsibility, there are plenty of others ready to fill the void.

By now, you know what these communication skills can mean to you. Now we need to consider what these skills can mean to all of us together. We live in the most remarkable era in human history, a time when changes that once took decades can now take days, when voyages that once took months can now be made in hours. Many of those changes are good. We live longer, in better comfort, and with more stimulation and freedom than ever before.

Some of the changes, however, can also be terrifying. For the first time in history, we know we have the ability to destroy the entire planet, either through horrifying explosions or a long, slow death from polluting and poisoning the planet and ourselves. It's not something most of us want to talk about; it is something our minds move away from, not toward. But these situations are a fact of life. The good news is that while God or human intelligence or pure dumb chance, or whatever force or combinations of force you believe affect where we are today, has created these terrifying problems, it has also created the means to change them. I believe all the world problems are factors, but I also believe in a source much larger than my present understanding. To say that there is no source of intelligence that we may call God is like saying *Webster's Dictionary* is the result of an explosion in a print factory and everything came together perfectly and in balance.

One day when I started thinking of all the "problems" of the world, I got very excited because I noticed a common relationship to them all. All human problems are behavioral problems! I hope you're using your precision model right now and are asking, "All?" Well, let me put it this way: If the source of the problem is not human behavior, there is usually a behavioral solution. For example, crime is not the problem—it's people's behavior that creates this thing we call crime.

Many times we take sets of actions and turn them into nouns as if they were objects, when actually they are processes. As long as we represent human problems as if they were things, I believe we disempower ourselves by turning them into something big and beyond our control. Nuclear power or nuclear waste is not the problem. How humans use the atom can be a problem if it's not handled effectively. If we as a country decide these tools are not the most effective or healthful approaches to energy development and consumption, we can change our behavior. Nuclear war is not a problem in and of itself. The way human beings behave is what creates or prevents war. Famine is not the problem in Africa. Human behavior is the problem. Destroying each other's land does not support the creation of a larger food supply. If food shipped in from other humans all over the world is rotting on the docks because humans can't cooperate, that's a behavioral problem. In contrast, the Israelis have done okay in the middle of the desert.

So if we can agree, as a useful generalization, that human behavior is the source of human problems or that new human behaviors can solve most other problems that arise, then we can become quite excited because we will understand that these behaviors are the results of the states human beings are in and are their models of how to respond when they are in these states.

We also know that the states from which behavior springs are the result of their internal representations. We know, for example, that people have linked the process of smoking to a particular state. They don't smoke every minute of every day, only when they're in a smoking state. People don't overeat every minute of every day, only when they are in a state they have linked to overeating. If you effectively change those associations or the linked response, you can effectively change people's behavior.

We are now living in an age where the technology needed to communicate messages to almost the entire world is already in place and being used. The technology is the media—radio, television, movies, and print.

The movies we see in New York and Los Angeles today are seen in Paris and London tomorrow, Beirut and Managua the day after that, and around the whole world a few days later. So if those movies or books or television shows or other forms of media change people's internal representations and states for the better, they can change the world for the better, too. We've seen how effective the media can be for selling products and spreading culture. We're just now learning how effective they can be in changing the world for the better. Think of the Live Aid concerts. If they weren't an awesome display of the positive power of communication technology, I don't know what is.

Therefore, the means to change massive numbers of people's internal representations, and thus massive numbers of people's states, and thus massive numbers of people's behaviors, is available to us now. By effectively using our understanding of the triggers to human behavior and the present-day technology for communicating these new representations to the masses, we can change the future of our world.

The documentary film *Scared Straight* is a great example of how we can change people's internal representations and thereby change their behaviors by using the resources of the media. It's a documentary of a program in which kids who are producing destructive or delinquent behavior are brought to a prison, where inmate volunteers proceed to change the kids' internal representations of what crime and imprisonment really mean. These kids were interviewed in advance. Most were real tough and said that going to prison wouldn't be a very big deal. Their internal representations and states were effectively changed when a mass murderer began to tell them what life in prison was really like, relating the details with an intensity that would change anyone's physiology! *Scared Straight* is must viewing. Follow-up on the program found it incredibly effective in changing the behaviors of these kids. Television was then able to carry that same experience to huge numbers of kids (and adults), simultaneously changing many people's thoughts and behaviors.

We can change massive numbers of human behaviors if we can make effective representations that appeal to people in all the primary representational systems and if we frame things in ways that appeal to all the major metaprograms. When we change the behaviors of the masses, we change the course of history.

For example, what was the feeling of most young men in America when asked, "How would you feel about going over to fight during World War One?" Pretty positive, wasn't it. Why? The representations of most young men about war were created by songs like "Over There" and by Uncle Sam posters everywhere saying, "I want you." The young man of the WWI era probably pictured himself as a savior of democracy and free peoples everywhere. Those kinds of external stimuli represented war in a way that put him in a positive state of desire to go and fight. He volunteered. By contrast, what happened when the Vietnam War hit? What was the feeling of most young men about going and fighting "over there"? Quite different, wasn't it. Why? Because there was a different set of external stimuli being offered to huge numbers of individuals every night through this new technology called the evening news. It changed their internal representations on a daily basis. People began to represent war as something quite different from what it had been. It was no longer "over there"—it was now in our living room at dinnertime as we watched in vivid detail. It was not big parades or rescuing democracy. Rather it was watching some eighteen-year-old kid, just like your own or your neighbor's, getting his face blown off and dying in a faraway jungle. As a result, more and more people developed a new internal representation of what this war meant, and consequently their behaviors changed. I'm not saying the war was bad or good; I'm simply pointing out that as people's internal representations were changed, so was their behavior, and the media created the vehicle for that change.

Our feelings and behaviors are even now being changed some in ways we may not have noticed before. For example, how do you feel about extraterrestrials? Think of movies like *E.T.* or *Starman* or *Cocoon* or *Close Encounters of the Third Kind*. We used to think of aliens as horrible gooey monsters who would come and eat your face off, swallow your home, and spit out your mother. Now we think of them as beings who hide in a boy's closet and ride bikes with your children till they have to go home—or as guys who loan your grandpa their swimming pool to cool off on hot days. If you were an alien who wanted people to respond to you in a positive way, would you want them to meet you after they saw *Invasion of the Body Snatchers* or after they watched a few Steven Spielberg movies? If I were an alien, before I came to a planet like this, I'd get someone to make lots of movies about what a great guy I am, so people would greet me enthusiastically with open arms. I'd get myself a great PR agent to change the masses' internal representation of who I am and what I'm like. Maybe Steven Spielberg is from a different planet after all.

How does a movie like *Rambo* make you feel about war? It makes killing and napalming seem like great, merry, furious fun, doesn't it? Does that make us more or less receptive to the idea of fighting in a war? Obviously one movie would have difficulty in changing the behaviors of a country. It's also important to note that Sylvester Stallone is not trying to promote killing people. Quite the contrary—his movies are all about overcoming great limitation through hard work and discipline. They are models of the possibility of winning in spite of great odds. However, it's important for us to observe the effect of the mass culture we impact consistently. It's important for us to be conscious of what we're placing in our minds and make sure it is supporting our desired outcomes.

What would happen if you changed an entire world's internal representation of war? What if the same power and technology that could get massive numbers of individuals to fight could be used effectively to bridge value differences and represent the unity of all peoples? Does the technology exist? I believe it does. Don't get me wrong—I'm not suggesting that this is easy, that all we have to do is make a few films, show them to everyone, and the world will change. What I am suggesting is that the mechanisms for change are as available as the tools for destruction. I am suggesting that we become more conscious of what we see, hear, and experience on a consistent basis and that we pay attention to how we represent these experiences to ourselves individually and collectively. If we are to create the results we want within our families, communities, countries, and world, we must become much more conscious.

What we consistently represent on a mass scale tends to become internalized in mass numbers of people. These representations affect the future behaviors of a culture and a world. Thus, if we want to create a world that works, we might want to consistently review and plan what we can do to create representations that empower us on a unified global scale.

You can live your life one of two ways. You can be like Pavlov's dogs, responding to all the trends and messages that are sent your way. You can be romanced by war, lured by junk food, or captivated by every trend that pours through the tubes. Someone once described advertising as "the science of arresting the human intelligence long enough to get money from it." Some of us live in a world of perpetually arrested intelligence.

The alternative is to try something more elegant. You can learn to use your brain so that you choose the behaviors and internal representations that will make you a better person and this a better world. You can become aware of when you're being programmed and manipulated. You can determine when your behaviors and the models beamed out at you reflect your real values and when they don't. And then you can act on the things that have real value as you tune out the ones that don't.

We live in a world where there seems to be a new trend every month. If you're a persuader, you become a trend creator rather than someone who just reacts to the multitude of messages. The direction in which things are going is as important as what is happening. Directions cause destinations. So it's important to discover the direction of the stream, not wait until you get to the edge of Niagara Falls and find out you're in a small boat with no oars. The job of a persuader is to lead the way, map the terrain, and find the paths that lead to better outcomes.

Trends are created by individuals; for example, the national holiday of Thanksgiving was created, not by a political officer, but by a woman who had a strong desire to unite our country. Her name was Sarah Joseph Hale, and she succeeded in a task that had frustrated others for over 250 years.

Many people have a false notion that the Thanksgiving holiday has been an American tradition since the Pilgrims first "gave thanks" in October of 1621, but this is not true. For 155 years after that, there was no regular or unified Thanksgiving celebration held in the Colonies. The War of Independence brought forth a victory that was celebrated by the entire country for the first time. And still the tradition was not upheld. The third Thanksgiving was held after the successful drafting of the Constitution, when President George Washington proclaimed November 26, 1789, a day of national thanksgiving. However, this, too, failed to become a recurring event.

Then, in 1827, along came Sarah Joseph Hale, a woman with enough commitment and persistence to make it all happen. The mother of five children, she chose to support herself and family by becoming a professional writer at a time in our history when few women were known to be successful in this profession. As the editor of a ladies' magazine, she helped to make it a major national periodical with a circulation of 150,000. She was known for her editorial campaigns on behalf of women's colleges, free public playgrounds, and day nurseries. And she wrote the nursery rhyme "Mary Had a Little Lamb." However, the most important cause in her life was to create a permanent national Thanksgiving Day. She used her magazine as a major tool to influence those who could institute such a trend for the nation. For almost thirty-six years she campaigned for this dream by constantly writing personal letters to presidents and governors. In her magazine, she annually published tempting Thanksgiving menus, featured stories and poetry that focused on Thanksgiving themes, and she wrote editorial after editorial in support of an annual Thanksgiving Day.

Finally, the Civil War provided Hale with an opportunity to express her point in a way that would capture the nation. She wrote, "Would it not be a great advantage socially, nationally, and religiously to have the day of our American Thanksgiving positively settled?" In October 1863, she editorialized, "Putting aside the sectional feelings and local incidents that might be urged by any single state or isolated territory that desired to choose its own time, would it not be more noble, more truly American, to become national in unity when we offer to God our tribute of joy and gratitude for the blessings of the year?" She wrote a letter to Secretary of State William Seward, who then showed it to President Abraham Lincoln, who felt the concept of a national unity was precisely right. Four days later, the president issued a proclamation setting the last Thursday in November 1863 as a national Thanksgiving Day. The rest is history. All because a woman with persistence and persuasive ability effectively used the existing media.*

Let me offer you two possible models for effective trend creation. I try to make a positive difference through education. If we want to have a positive effect on the future, we must give the next generation the most effective tools available for creating their world the way they want it. Our organization attempts to

---

* Information provided by Marshall Berges from the *Los Angeles Times*.

do this through our Unlimited Excellence Camps. In these camps, we teach kids to use the specific tools for running their own brains, to direct their own behaviors and thus the results they create in their lives. They learn to develop deep levels of rapport with people from all backgrounds, to model effective people, to break through limitations, and to reframe their perceptions of what is possible for them. At the end of the course, the majority of the kids tell me it was the most powerful learning experience they've ever had. It's one of the most enjoyable and rewarding programs I have had the privilege to conduct.

However, I'm just one person, and our associates can reach out to only so many kids. So we developed a training program to provide teachers with NLP and other *Optimum Performance Technology*® skills. That was a great step in the direction of affecting more kids, though not on a large-enough scale to truly create a new trend in education. Now we are in the first stages of conceptualization for another project, which we call the Challenge Foundation. One of the challenges many kids face—particularly those in disadvantaged areas—is that they don't have access to powerful and positive role models. The idea for the Challenge Foundation is to put together a library of interactive video presentations featuring the most powerful, positive role models in our culture: contemporary people like Supreme Court justices, entertainers, and businessmen as well as powerful figures who are no longer alive, like John F. Kennedy, Martin Luther King, Jr., or Mahatma Gandhi. This will give kids powerful experiences to emulate. You can hear about a Martin Luther King, Jr., from a teacher, and you can read King's words, but that's only part of the experience. What if you could spend thirty minutes and have him personally tell you his philosophies and beliefs? And what if in the last five minutes he challenged you to do something with your life? I would like kids to be able to model not just words, but tonality, physiology, and the total presence of these master persuaders. Many kids studying the Constitution, for example, have no idea how it relates to life today. What if we had a video of the chief justice of the Supreme Court telling students why he dedicates every day of his life to upholding this document and how it affects them today? What if at the end of this he gave these young people a challenge? Could you imagine what would happen if massive numbers of kids across the country could have regular and consistent access to this kind of positive input and challenge? Such a program could change the future. If you have input about such a system, I invite your letters and comments.

Another example of how to use influence to create positive new trends is the work of a man named Amory Lovins, director of research at the Rocky Mountain Institute in Snowmass, Colorado. Lovins has been involved in alternative energy projects for several years. Today, many people believe that nuclear power is too costly, too ineffective, and too dangerous to be used. Yet the antinuclear movement has made little headway—because it's just that. It's *anti*nuclear. Many people who move toward solutions wonder what the movement is *for*. Sometimes it's hard to tell. But Lovins has been able to have enormous success with energy companies by being a skillful persuader rather than a mere protester. Instead of attacking nuclear power companies, Lovins is providing alternatives that are more profitable because they do not require huge plants with costs that can run billions over budget.

Lovins likes to practice what he calls "aikido politics." It uses the same principle as the agreement frame to direct behavior in a way that minimizes conflict. In one case, he was asked to testify at a rate hearing for a utility that was planning a massive new nuclear plant. Construction hadn't begun, but the plant had already cost $300 million. He began by saying he wasn't there to testify for or against the plant. He said it was in everyone's best interest—the utility's and the customers'—to have a utility that operated on a sound fiscal footing. Then he went on to explain how much money could be saved by conservation and how much energy would cost if the hugely expensive new plant was built. In conservative financial terms, he discussed what that would mean to the company. It was a low-key presentation. There was no effort to rail against the plant or nuclear power.

After he was through, he got a call from the utility's vice-president of finance. When the two got together, the official talked about the effect the plant could have on the company's finances. He said the plant, if built, could cause the company to omit its dividend, a disaster for the company's stock. Finally, the official said that if the interveners wanted, the company would be willing to walk away from the plant, taking the 300-million-dollar loss. If Lovins had begun in an adversarial manner, the company would have dug in its heels in a way that would have satisfied no one. But by finding common ground, by trying to create a viable alternative, they were able to reach an agreement that benefited both sides. A new tend is beginning to occur as a result of Lovins's work. Other electrical companies have now contracted him as a consultant to limit nuclear dependency and simultaneously increase profit.

Another case involved farmers in the San Luis Valley in Colorado and New Mexico. Farmers there had traditionally gathered firewood as their main energy source. But the landowners fenced off the area where they had gathered wood. These were very poor people, but a few leaders managed to persuade the farmers that the situation was not a setback but an opportunity. They began one of the most successful solar projects in the world as a result, and they gained a sense of collective power and goodwill they'd never had before.

Lovins cites a similar case in Osage, Iowa, where the small local utility cooperative decided it was not using its power efficiently. The result was a push for weatherizing houses and conserving fuel, a drive so successful that the utility was able to retire its debt. It had three rate cuts in two years, and customers in a town of 3,800 people saved $1.6 million a year in fuel costs.

Two things happened in both these cases. People were able to benefit one another by finding a win-win frame that helped them all. And they were able to develop a new sense of authority and security by learning to take action to achieve a desired outcome. The secondary gains in goodwill and community spirit that came from working together and taking action were as important as the money saved. These are the kinds of positive trends that can be created by a few committed persuaders.

There's a saying in the computer world, "GIGO: Garbage In—Garbage Out." It means that the quality you get out of a system depends entirely on what you put into it. If you put in bad, faulty, or incomplete information, you'll get the same kind of results. Many people in our culture today give little or no conscious thought to the quality of information and experience being input daily. According to the latest statistics, the average American watches television seven hours a day. *U.S. News & World Report* states that young adults between grades nine and twelve will see an average of 18,000 murders. They will watch 22,000 hours of television—more than twice the time spent in class during twelve years of schooling. It's critical we look at what we are feeding our minds if we expect them to grow and nurture our ability to fully experience and enjoy this thing we call life. We work like a computer. If we form internal representations that tell us blowing away villages with a machine gun is neat or that unhealthy junk food is what successful people eat, those representations will govern our behavior.

We have more power now than ever before to shape the inner perceptions that govern behavior. There's no guarantee we'll shape them for the better. But the potential is there, and we should start doing something about it. The most important issues we face as a nation and as a planet deal with the kinds of images and mass representations we produce.

Trend creation is what leadership is about, and it's the real message of this book. You now know how to run your brain to process information in the most empowering fashion. You know how to turn down the sound and turn off the brightness of the junk communication, and you know how to resolve conflicts within your own values. But if you really want to make a difference, you also need to know how to be a leader, how to take these persuasion skills and make the world a better place. That means being a more positive, more skillful model for your kids, for your employees, for your business associates, for your world. You can do this on the level of one-on-one persuasion, and you can do it on the level of mass persuasion. Instead of being in-fluenced by images of Rambo deliriously blowing away other human beings, you might want to dedicate your life to com-municating the empowering messages that can be the difference in making this world the way you want it to be.

Remember, the world is governed by the persuaders. Every-thing you've learned in this book and everything you see around you tells you that's so. If you can externalize on a mass scale your internal representations about human behavior, about what is elegant, what is effective, what is positive, you can change the future direction of your children, your community, your country, your world. We have the technology to change it right here. I suggest we make use of it.

That's ultimately what this book is about. Sure, it's about maximizing your personal power, learning how to be effective and successful in what you try to do. But there's no value to being a sovereign of a dying planet. Everything we've talked about—the importance of agreement frames, the nature of rap-port, the modeling of excellence, the syntax of success, and all the rest—works best when it's used in a positive way that breeds success for others as well as for ourselves.

Ultimate power is synergistic. It comes from people working together, not working apart. We now have the technology to change people's perceptions almost in an instant. It's time to use it in a positive way for the betterment of us all. Thomas Wolfe once wrote, "There is nothing in the world that will take the chip off one's shoulder like a feeling of success." That's the real challenge of excellence—using these skills on a broad level to empower ourselves and others in ways that are truly positive, in ways that generate massive, joyous, communal success.

The time to start using them is now.

CHAPTER XXI

Living Excellence: The Human Challenge

"Man is not the sum of what he has but the totality of what he does not yet have, of what he might have."

—*Jean Paul Sartre*

We have come a long way together. How much farther you'll go will be your decision. This book has given you tools and skills and ideas that can change your life. But what you'll do with them is totally up to you. When you put this book down, you can feel you've learned a little something and go on as you used to. Or you can make a concerted effort to take control of your life and your brain. You can create the powerful beliefs and states that will produce miracles for you and the people you care about. But it will happen only if you make it happen.

Let's review the main things you've learned. You know now that the most powerful tool on the planet is the biocomputer between your two ears. Properly run, your brain can make your life greater than any dream you've ever had before. You've learned the Ultimate Success Formula: Know your outcome, take action, develop the sensory acuity to know what you're getting, and change your behavior until you get what you want. You've learned that we live in an age where fabulous success is available to all of us, but that those who achieve it are those who take action. Knowledge is important, but it's not enough. Plenty of people had the same information as a Steve Jobs or a Ted Turner. But the ones who took action created fabulous success and changed the world.

You've learned about the importance of modeling. You can learn by experience, by trial and error—or you can speed up the process immeasurably by learning how to model. Every result produced by an individual was created by some specific set of actions in some specific syntax. You can greatly decrease the time it takes to master something by modeling the internal actions (mental) and external actions (physical) of people who produce outstanding results. In a few hours or a few days or few years, depending on the type of task, you can learn what took them months or years to discover.

You've learned that the quality of your life is the quality of your communication. Communication takes two forms. The first is your communication with yourself. The meaning of any event is the meaning you give it. You can send your brain powerful, positive, empowering signals that will make everything work for you, or you can send your brain signals about what you can't do. People of excellence can take any situation and make it work for them—people like W. Mitchell, Julio Iglesias, Commander Jerry Coffey, who can take terrible tragedy and turn it into triumph. We can't go back in time. We can't change what actually happened. But we can control our representations so they'll give us something positive for the future. The second form of communication is with others. The people who've changed our world have been master communicators. You can use everything in this book to discover what people want so you can become an effective, masterful, elegant communicator.

You've learned about the awesome power of belief. Positive beliefs can make you a master. Negative beliefs can make you a loser. And you've learned that you can change your beliefs to make them work for you. You've learned about the power of state and the power of physiology. You've learned the syntax and strategies that people use, and you've learned how to establish rapport with anyone you meet. You've learned powerful techniques for reframing and anchoring. You've learned how to communicate with precision and skill, how to avoid the fluff language that kills communication, and how to use the precision model to get others to communicate effectively with you. You've learned about handling the five roadblocks in the way of success. And you've learned about the metaprograms and values that serve as the organizing principles for personal behavior.

I don't expect you to find yourself utterly transformed when you put down this book. Some things we've discussed will come easier to you than others. But life has a processional effect. Changes lead to more changes. Growth leads to more growth. By starting to make changes, by growing in bits and pieces, you can slowly but steadily change your life. Like the rock thrown into the still pond, you create ripples that grow larger in the future. It's often the littlest thing, viewed over time, that makes the biggest difference.

Think of two arrows pointing in the same general direction. If you make a tiny change in the direction of one of them, if you push it three or four degrees in a different direction, the change will probably be imperceptible at first. But if you follow that path for yards and then for miles, the difference will become greater and greater—until there's no relation at all between the first path and the second.

That's what this book can do for you. It won't change you overnight (unless you go to work on yourself tonight!). But if you learn to run your brain, if you understand and make use of things like syntax, submodalities, values, and metaprograms, the differences over six weeks and six months and six years will change your life. Some things in this book, like modeling, you already do in some form. Others are new. Just remember, everything in life is cumulative. If you use one of the principles in this book today, you've taken a step. You've set a cause in motion, and every cause creates an effect or result, and every result piles on the last one to take us in a direction. Every direction carries with it an ultimate destination.

> *"There are two things to aim at in life: first, to get what you want; and, after that, to enjoy it."*
>
> —*Logan Pearsall Smith*

Here's a final question to consider. In what direction are you presently going? If you follow your current direction, where will you be in five years or ten years? And is that where you want to go? Be honest with yourself. John Naisbitt once said that the best way to predict the future is to get a clear idea of what's happening now. You need to do the same thing in your life. So when you finish this book, sit down and think about the direction you're going in, and whether it's where you really want to go. If it's not, I suggest you change. If this book has taught you anything, it's the possibility of creating positive change with almost lightning speed—on both a personal and a global level. Ultimate power means the ability to change, to adapt, to grow, to evolve. Unlimited power doesn't mean you always succeed or that you never fail. Unlimited power just means you learn from every human experience and make every experience work for you in some way. It is unlimited power to change your perceptions, to change your actions, and to change the results you're creating. It's your unlimited power to care and to love that can make the biggest difference in the quality of your life.

I'd like to suggest another way to change your life and ensure continued success. Find a team you want to play on. Remember, we've talked about power in terms of what people can do together. Ultimate power is the power of people working together, not pulling apart. That might mean your family, or it might mean good friends. It could be trusted business partners or people you work with and care about. But you work harder and better if you're working for others as well as for yourself. You give more, and you get more.

If you ask people about their richest experiences in life, they'll

408   *Unlimited Power*

usually come up with something they did as part of a team. Sometimes it's literally that, a sports team they'll remember forever. Sometimes it's a business team that did something memorable. Sometimes the team is your family or your spouse. Being on a team makes you stretch, it makes you grow. Other people can nurture and challenge you in ways you can't yourself. People will do things for others they won't do for themselves. And they'll get things from others that will make it worthwhile.

If you're alive, you're on some team. It can be your family, your relationship, your business, your city, your country, your world. You can sit on the bench and watch, or you can get up and play. My advice to you is to be a player. Join the hunt. Share your world. Because the more you give, the more you get; the more you use the skills in this book for yourself and for others, the more they'll bring back to you.

And make sure you're on the team that challenges you. It's easy for things to get off track. It's easy to know what to do and still not to do it. That just seems to be the way life is. The normal pull of life is gravity, and that's downward. All of us have our off days. All of us have times when we don't use what we know. But if we surround ourselves with people who are successful, who are forward-moving, who are positive, who are focused on producing results, who support us, it will challenge us to be more and do more and share more. If you can surround yourself with people who will never let you settle for less than you can be, you have the greatest gift that anyone can hope for. Association is a powerful tool. Make sure the people you surround yourself with make you a better person by your association with them.

Once you have a commitment to a team, the challenge of excellence is to become a leader. That can mean being the president of a Fortune 500 company, or it can mean being the best teacher you can be. It can mean being a better entrepreneur or a better parent. True leaders have a knowledge of the power of procession, a sense that great changes come from many small things. They realize that everything they say and do has an enormous power to empower and embolden others.

That happened in my life. When I was in high school, I had a speech teacher who asked me to stay after class one day. I wondered what I had done wrong. He said, "Mr. Robbins, I think you have the makings of an incredible speaker, and I want to invite you to speak in competition next week with the squad from our school." I didn't think I was anything special as a speaker, but he was so strong and congruent, I believed him. His message changed my life. It led me to my profession as a communicator. He did a small thing, but he changed my life forever.

The challenge of leadership is to have enough power and vision to be able to project in advance what outcome will result from your actions, large and small. The communication skills in this book offer critical ways to make those distinctions. Our culture needs more models of success, more symbols of excellence. My life has been graced by teachers and mentors who gave me things of immeasurable value. My goal in life is to give some of them back. That's what I hope this book has helped you do, and it's what I try to do in my work.

My first mentor was a man named Jim Rohn. He taught me that happiness and success in life are not the result of what we have, but rather of how we live. What we do with the things we have makes the biggest difference in the quality of life. He taught me that even the smallest things could make big differences in life. For instance, he told me to always be a two-quarter person. He gave the example of a shoeshine. Let's say the shoeshine man is doing a great job. He's whistling and snapping his shoeshine rag. He's giving you great value. Jim said when you dip into your pocket to tip him, and you're not sure whether to give him one quarter or two, always go for the higher number. You do it not just for him, but for yourself as well. If you just give him one quarter, later in the day you'll look down and see your shoes and think, I only gave him one quarter. How could I be so cheap when he did such a great job? If you give him two, it will affect the way you feel about yourself for the better. What if you made it a principle that every time you passed someone taking a collection for anything, you always put some money in the collection plate? What if you made an automatic commitment always to buy from a Boy Scout, Girl Scout, or whomever? What if you made it a point to call friends, every now and then, just to say, "I'm not calling for any special reason, I just wanted you to know I love you. I don't want to interrupt you—I just want to communicate that to you"? What if you made it a point to send little thank-you notes to people who have done things for you? What if you spent conscious time and effort figuring new and unique ways to get more joy out of life by adding value to other people's lives? That's what life-style is all about. We all have the time; the question of the quality of life is answered by how we spend it. Do we fall into a pattern, or do we continuously work at making it unique and special? It seems like a little thing, but the effect that all these little things have on how you feel about who you are as a person is very powerful. They affect your internal representations of who you are and thus the quality of your states and life. I've kept that two-quarter commitment with myself and reaped the rewards it provides. I offer it for your perusal. I believe it's a philosophy that can enrich your life immensely if you're not already practicing it.

> *"The chemist who can extract from his heart's elements compassion, respect, longing, patience, regret, surprise, and forgiveness and compound them into one can create that atom which is called love."*
>
> —*Kahlil Gibran*

My last comment is to challenge you to share this information with others—for two reasons, really. First, we all teach what we most need to learn. By sharing an idea with others, we get to hear it again and remind ourselves of what we value and believe is important in life. The other reason is there is incredible, almost unexplainable, richness and joy that comes from helping another person make a truly important and positive change in his life.

I had an experience last year at one of our children's programs that I will never forget. The camps are twelve-day programs during which we teach children a lot of what is discussed in this book and give them experiences that change their competency, their learning skills, and their confidence as fully alive human beings. During the summer of 1984, we ended the camp with a ceremony in which all the kids got gold medals like the ones in the Olympics. On the medals it said, "You can do magic." We didn't finish until about two in the morning, and it was a very joyous emotional event.

I got back to my room feeling bone-tired, knowing I had to be up at six A.M. in order to catch a plane to my next event but also feeling the way you do when you know you've really made a day count. So I was ready to get to sleep around 3 A.M. when I heard a knock at my door. I thought, Who in the world can that be?

I opened the door to find a young boy there. He said, "Mr. Robbins, I need your help." I started to ask him if he could call me in San Diego the following week, when I heard this sound behind him, and there was a little girl crying her eyes out.

I asked what the matter was, and the boy told me she didn't want to go home. I said to bring her in, and I'd anchor her, and she'd feel better and go home. He said that wasn't the problem. He said she didn't want to go home because her brother, who lived with her, had been sexually abusing her for the last seven years.

So I brought them both in, and using the tools we've talked about in this book, I changed her internal representation of those negative past experiences so that they no longer created any pain. Then I anchored her into her most resourceful and powerful states and linked them with her now altered internal representations so that the very thought or sight of her brother would immediately put her in a state of being in charge. After this session, she decided to call her brother. She got on the phone in a totally resourceful state and woke him up. "Brother!" she said in a tone he'd probably never heard before in his life. "I just want you to know that I'm coming home, and you best not even look at me in a way that makes me even think you're thinking of the things you used to do. Because if you do, you'll go to jail for the rest of your life and be totally embarrassed. You will absolutely pay the price. I love you as my brother, but I will never accept those behaviors again. If I even think you're moving toward them, it's over for you. Bear in mind that I am serious. And I love you. Good-bye." He got the message.

She hung up the phone, feeling totally strong and in charge for the first time in her life. She hugged her little boyfriend, and together they cried in relief. The night I worked with them, they both gave me the most incredible hugs I'd ever had. The young man said he didn't know how he could repay me. I told him that seeing the changes in her was the greatest thanks I could receive. He said, "No, I've got to pay you in some way." Then he said, "I know something that means a lot to me." He reached up and slowly took off his gold medal, and he put it on me. They kissed me and left, saying they would never forget me. I walked upstairs after they left and got into bed. My wife, Becky, who had been listening to the whole thing, was crying, and so was I. She said, "You're incredible. That child's life will never be the same." I said, "Thanks, honey, but anybody with the skills could have helped her." She said, "Yeah, Tony, anybody could have, but you did."

> *"If you could only love enough, you could be the most*
> *powerful person in the world."*
>
> —*Emmett Fox*

So that's the ultimate message of this book. Be a doer. Take charge. Take action. Use what you've learned here, and use it now. Don't just do it for you—do it for others as well. The gifts from such actions are greater than can be imagined. There are a lot of talkers in the world. There are a lot of people who know what's right and what's powerful, yet still aren't producing the results they desire. It's not enough to talk the talk. You've got to walk the talk. That's what unlimited power is all about. Unlimited power to get yourself to do the necessary things to produce excellence. Julius Erving of the Philadelphia 76ers has a philosophy of life that I think sums up the philosophy of a "walker." It's worthy of modeling. He says: "I demand more from myself than anybody else could ever expect." That's why he's the best.

There were two great orators of antiquity. One was Cicero, the other Demosthenes. When Cicero was done speaking, people always gave him a standing ovation and cheered, "What a great speech!" When Demosthenes was done, people said, "Let us march," and they did. That's the difference between presentation and persuasion. I hope to be classified in the latter category. If you just read this book and think, Wow, that was a great book; it has lots of neat tools, and don't use anything in it, we've wasted our time together. However, if you start right now and go back through this book and use it as a handbook for running your mind and body, as a guide to changing anything you want to change, then you may have begun a life journey that will make even the greatest dreams of your past seem almost trivial. I know that's what happened to me when I began to apply these principles daily.

I challenge you to make your life a masterpiece. I challenge you to join the ranks of those people who live what they teach, who walk their talk. They are the models of excellence the rest of the world marvels about. Join this unique team of people known as the few who do versus the many who wish—result-oriented people who produce their life exactly as they desire it. My life is inspired by the stories of people who use their resources to create new success and achievement for themselves and others. Someday maybe I'll get to tell your story. If this book helps you move in that direction, I'll consider myself very lucky indeed.

In the meantime, I thank you for your commitment to learning and growing and developing yourself and for allowing me to share with you some of the principles that have made a difference in my life. May your hunt for human excellence be fruitful and never-ending. May you dedicate yourself, not only to strive for the goals you have set, but to meet them and set even more; not only to hold to the dreams you have had, but to dream greater dreams than before; not only to enjoy this land and its wealth, but to make it a better place to live; and not only to take what you can from this life, but to love and give generously.

I leave you with a simple Irish blessing. . . . May the road rise to meet you. May the wind be always at your back. May the sun shine warm on your face, the rains fall soft upon your fields, and, until we meet again . . . may God hold you softly in the palm of His hand.* Good-bye and God bless.

---

* Irish blessing, copyright 1967 Bollind, Inc., Boulder, CO 80302

GLOSSARY

Accessing Cues—Behaviors that affect our neural processing in such a way that we can access one representational system more strongly than others. For instance, slowing your breathing rate and the tempo of your voice can direct you to access in a kinesthetic mode, tilting your head as though you're holding a telephone can direct you in an auditory mode, and so on.

Anchoring—The process by which any representation (internal or external) gets connected to and triggers a subsequent string of representation and responses. Anchors can be naturally occurring or set up deliberately. An example of an anchor for a particular set of responses is what happens when you think of the way a special, much loved person says your name.

Behavior—Activity humans engage in. Includes "large" behavior, like gestures or throwing a ball, and "small" behavior (maybe less easily observed), like thinking, eye movements, breathing changes, and so forth.

Calibration—The ability to notice and measure changes with respect to a standard. Calibrating depends on refined sensory acuity. You probably have a good idea of when a loved one is feeling a little unsure or very happy. This is because you have calibrated what their philosophy means.

Communication—The process of conveying information by language, signs, symbols, and behavior. It can be directionalized, which is to say that the place you end a conversation is different from where it began, as in negotiation, therapy, sales. It moves toward an outcome.

Congruity/Incongruity—A situation in which the message a person communicates is the same or similar in all output channels—that is, the words of the message convey the same meaning as the tone of voice, and the gestures convey the same meaning as the previous two. All output channels are being aligned. Incongruency exhibits conflicting messages between output channels. Example: saying, "Yes, I'm sure!" in a soft, querulous voice.

Deletion—What was there in your original experience that has been left out of your internal representation. This is one of the cognitive processes that keep us from being overwhelmed by incoming sensory data. There are things we leave out, however, that would be much more useful for us to include.

Distortion—The process by which things are inaccurately included in a person's internal representation in some way that limits him. It could be "blown out of proportion," "twisted a bit," and the like. It allows us to shift our sensory data.

Ecology—A concern for the totality or pattern of relationships between a being and its environment. In NLP we also use the term in reference to internal ecology—the pattern of values, strategies, and behaviors a person embodies in relationship to himself.

Elicitation—Information gathering, by direct observation of a person's accessing cues, gestures, and so on, and by well-formed questions to determine the structure of their internal experience.

Eye-Scanning Patterns—A particular set of accessing cues that have to do with how the eyes move and the sequence of positions they go to. Knowing which internal process each position correlates to is the precursor to understanding and eliciting strategies.

Generalization—The cognitive process by which parts of a person's internal experience get separated from the original experience and become a class of their own. In many cases this is useful. For example, a child has an experience of touching a stove top and getting slightly burned. He may generalize to "Burners are hot" or "Don't touch stoves when they're on." In other cases it can limit a person's model of the world in nonuseful ways.

Internal Representation—The configuration of information you create and store in your mind in the form of pictures, sounds, feelings, smells, and tastes. To "recall" what the house you grew up in looked like, unless you are actually there, you remember an internal representation.

Matching—Adopting parts of another person's behavior—such as particular gestures, facial expressions, forms of speech, tone of voice, and so on. Done subtly, it helps create a feeling of rapport between people.

Mirroring—Adopting other people's behaviors as though you were a "mirror image." If you were facing someone who had his left hand on his cheek, you would put your right hand on your cheek in the same way.

Model—A description of how something works (but not of possible reasons for how it can work). When we say "someone's model of the world," we mean the composite of his beliefs, internal process, and behavior that allows him to work a certain way. A model is a way of organizing experience.

Modeling—The process of discovering the sequence of internal representations and behaviors that allows someone to accomplish a task. Once the components of the strategy, language beliefs, and behavior have been detailed, the skill can be much more easily learned by another.

Pacing—Gaining and maintaining rapport for some period of time while interacting with another. You can pace beliefs and ideas as well as behaviors.

Rapport—The phenomenon of people trading and/or sharing particular behaviors. It happens naturally and unconsciously as people spend time together. It can be done consciously, by mirroring and matching, to enhance communication.

Representational Systems—How we code sensory information in our mind. These include the visual system, auditory system, kinesthetic system, olfaction, and gustation. They enable us to take in and store information, sort it, and use it. The distinctions we make as human beings (internally and externally) come to us through these sytems.

Sensory Acuity—The process of refining our ability to make distinctions among the visual, auditory, kinesthetic, olfactory, and gustatory systems. This gives us fuller, richer sensory experiences and the ability to create detailed, sensory-based descriptions from our interaction with the external world.

Sensory-Based Description—Using words that convey information that is directly observable, yerifiable, by your five senses. It is the difference between "Her lips are pulled taut, some parts of her teeth are showing, the edges of her mouth are higher than the main line of her mouth" and "She's happy."

Sensory-Based Experience—An experience that is processed on the level of what can be seen, heard, felt, smelled, and/or tasted.

State—The sum total of all neurological processes within an individual at any one moment in time. The state one is in will filter or affect the final result of our interpretation of any experience we have at that moment.

Strategy—An anchored sequence of representations used to guide our behaviors. A strategy usually includes each of the sensory representational systems (visual, auditory, kinesthetic) in some order. We can discover them in ourselves and in others by listening to the words we choose, observing eye-scanning patterns, and asking about the form and sequence of internal representations.

Submodalities—The subclassifications of external experience: a picture has brightness, distance, depth. Sounds have volume, location, tone, and so forth.

Syntax—A connected or orderly system; the sequence in which events, internal and external, can be put together. In language it refers to the order in which words occur to form grammatical sentences.

ROBBINS RESEARCH INSTITUTE

Every human is an invaluable, irreplaceable resource. Our purpose is to empower every individual to recognize unlimited choice in any action undertaken. Through exercising choice we can each attain the physical, mental, financial, and spiritual wealth available to every human being. And we can eliminate the needless pain that derives from ineffective beliefs, strategy, or physiology.

We are committed to finding excellence, understanding the steps to produce it, and making those steps publicly known. Although none of us may exactly duplicate the achievements of this world's greatest individuals, each of us can duplicate their excellence. We can each strive to make every moment better than the last, and we can seek more effective tools to use in the shaping of our personal, social, political, and corporate environments.

Neuro-Linguistic Programming is an incredibly powerful tool, and RRI is committed to bringing it, along with the other *Optimum Performance Technologies*© we've researched, to our world community. We recognize that all change occurs through individuals, and we are committed to improving the world by teaching its citizens to improve themselves. Through the forming of each link, the mightiest chain is forged.

RRI conducts personal and professional seminars that cover topics ranging from basic communication in the business environment to effective sales, from treating phobias to improving love relationships. We also conduct research on how to produce excellence in both the private and corporate realms. Everyone in your organization can produce in the same way as your most treasured employee. For a list of available services write to:

Anthony Robbins
Robbins Research Institute, Inc
Torrey Pines Business and Research Park
3366 North Torrey Pines Court, Suite #100
La Jolla, CA 92037

Corporate Seminars ★ Modeling Projects
Videotapes with Individual and Corporate Training Programs
Research Newsletter ★ Health Seminars